Matters of Life and Death

Matters of Life and Death

Calm Answers to Tough Questions about Abortion and Euthanasia

Francis J. Beckwith
and
Norman L. Geisler

Including the Complete Texts of
Roe v. *Wade*
Doe v. *Bolton*
Webster v. *Reproductive Health Services*
and
Cruzan v. *Harmon*

BAKER BOOK HOUSE
Grand Rapids, Michigan 49516

Library of Congress Cataloging-in-Publication Data
Beckwith, Francis. (1960–   )
    Matters of life and death: calm answers to tough questions about abortion and
    euthanasia / Francis J. Beckwith and Norman L. Geisler.
        p.   cm.
    Includes bibliographical references and index.
    ISBN: 0-8010-1001-2
    1. Abortion—Miscellanea. 2. Euthanasia—Miscellanea.
    I. Geisler, Norman L.   II. Title
    HQ767.B43 1991
    363.4'6—dc20   91–629
                                                                    CIP

Printed in the United States of America

Contents

Preface   9
Acknowledgments   11

Part One: Abortion

1   Medical Questions   15
2   Legal Questions   39
3   Moral Questions   77
4   Social Questions   97

Part Two: Euthanasia

5   Questions about Infanticide   131
6   Questions about Adult Euthanasia   141
7   Conclusion: Social Activism   165

Notes   189

Appendices

1   *Roe* v. *Wade* (1973)   205
2   *Doe* v. *Bolton* (1973)   240
3   *Webster* v. *Reproductive Health Services* (1989)   265
4   *Cruzan* v. *Harmon* (1990)   314
5   A Living Will (Sample)   372
6   *The Beginning of Individual Life*   375

Bibliography   381
Index   387

Dedication

To my parents, Elizabeth and Harold "Pat" Beckwith, and their first grandchild, Dean James Beckwith (b. January 19, 1991), for they have taught me well of the value of life: my parents by doing and Dean by being.

Francis J. Beckwith

To my wonderful grandchildren who would never have had the opportunity to enjoy life had their parents aborted them.

Norman L. Geisler

Preface

The book is divided into two main parts. Part one deals with abortion and part two with infanticide and euthanasia. The first chapter deals with medical questions about abortion. The second chapter is concerned with legal questions. In chapter 3 we will answer moral and philosophical questions asked by both professional ethicists and ordinary people. Social questions of abortion will be answered in chapter 4. Chapter 5 concerns the topic of infanticide and chapter 6 the topic of euthanasia. Our concluding chapter deals with questions about social activism and civil disobedience. The book also has six appendices. The first four deal with crucial Supreme Court decisions on abortion and euthanasia. The fifth is a sample of a living will, and the last deals with the question of when individual human life begins.

The authors of this book are prolife, but we have attempted to be as objective and factual as possible in presenting the questions and answers. Nor have we evaded any of the tough questions. We have simply asked what people are asking and tried to answer in a factual and ethical manner. In this way it is our hope that the reader will be better informed and better prepared to face these issues, since they are matters of life and death.

Acknowledgments

We gratefully acknowledge the able assistance of Sharon Coomer, Thomas Howe, Terri Hayden, Paul Krisak, and Renee Willard in preparation of this manuscript. Their skills in researching, editing, typing, and preparing the indexes greatly improved the final product. Special thanks also to Mark Wiegand, J. P. Moreland, and Bob and Gretchen Passantino for their helpful suggestions, ideas, and comments, as well as enlightening discussions.

Part One

Abortion

Medical Questions

The Beginning of Human Life

Is a male sperm a human being?

No. A male sperm has only twenty-three chromosomes, whereas a human being has forty-six chromosomes. There are only two things a male sperm can do: die or fertilize a female ovum. If it fertilizes the ovum, by combining its twenty-three male chromosomes with the twenty-three female chromosomes, then and only then does this constitute a human life. At the moment of fertilization the sperm ceases to exist as an individual entity.

Is a female ovum a human being?

No. Like the male sperm, it, too, can do only two things: die or become fertilized. Only after it is fertilized do we have another human life. And, like the male sperm, the female ovum ceases to exist as an individual entity at the moment of fertilization.

Is any human cell a human being?

No. A human cell is part of a human body, but a fertilized ovum (human zygote) has its own body. Furthermore, a cell can die while the body of which it was a part lives on. Not so with a human zygote or embryo. Also, individual cells only produce their own kind of cell, not a whole human being.

Does human life begin at conception (fertilization)?

Yes. This is the point in the process when we first have a separate, individual life with all human genetic characteristics present. Since the conceptus has its own individual genetic code, it is not part of either the father's or mother's body. As we just noted, neither a sperm nor an ovum has all human genetic characteristics. And at no time after conception (fertilization) are any new genetic characteristics added. What takes place after conception is the growth and development of a particular human individual. The process this individual undergoes continues into infancy, childhood, adolescence, and adulthood. Thus, fertilization is the point at which a new human life begins.

What do scientific experts say about when life begins?

It is a scientific fact that life begins at conception. On this point scientific experts agree. World famous geneticist, Dr. Jerome LeJeune, declared: "But now we can say, unequivocally, that the question of when life begins is no longer a question of theological or philosophical dispute. It is an established scientific fact. . . . All life, including human life, begins at the moment of conception."[1]

It is interesting to note that the more sophisticated defenders of abortion rights do not deny the humanness of the unborn. They fully agree with LeJeune's scientific observation. But they argue philosophically that at this stage in its human development the unborn being is not worth protecting if its existence conflicts with the liberty of its mother. Some put forth this view by claiming that although the unborn is human it is not yet fully a person.

Prochoice ethicists Peter Singer and Helga Kuhse write:

> The pro-life groups are right about one thing: the location of the baby inside or outside the womb cannot make such a crucial moral difference. We cannot coherently hold that it is all right to kill a fetus a week before birth, but as soon as the baby is born everything must be done to keep it alive. The solution, however, is not to accept the pro-life view that the fetus is a human being with the same moral status as yours or mine. The solution is the very opposite: to abandon the idea that all human life is of equal worth.[2]

We will deal with the argument for this position in chapter 3 when we discuss many of the philosophical and moral questions about abortion.

Is a fertilized ovum a genetic blueprint?

No, it is not a "blueprint"; it is a tiny living, human "house." Describing it as a mere blueprint neglects the fact that a conceptus (a fertilized ovum) is a living human being with its own genetic structure. Furthermore, a blueprint is merely an instruction sheet that can be thrown away after the house is built. It never becomes the house. The conceptus, however, is a miniature "house" that will grow into a bigger house in time.

At what stage is sex determined?

Sex is determined at the moment of conception. All human genetic characteristics are determined at the moment of conception, including the unborn's gender. Hence, if we knew the sex of the conceptus we would be proper to refer to it not as it but rather as he or she.

Is the conceptus human before twinning?

Yes. Life begins at conception, and the potential for identical twins is present from the moment of conception. Thus it follows that human life is present from the very conception of identical twins. Furthermore, the zygote is genetically distinct from its parents, even before twinning occurs. Hence, it is a distinct human being(s) even before it twins.

Some people argue that because a conceptus may divide into two or more individuals some time after conception, the prolife advocate is wrong in arguing that individual human life begins at the moment of conception. However, when one carefully examines the nature of conception and twinning, it becomes apparent that the division of a conceptus does not mean that the original conceptus was not fully human. The following will help clarify what we mean.

Scientific opinion is not agreed on twinning. Twinning may be a nonsexual form of "parenting" or parthenogenesis. We know this occurs in certain plants or animals. Or, twinning may be a case of the existing human being dying to give life to two new and identical human beings like himself or herself. Or, since not all human zygotes are capable of twinning, a zygote capable of twinning may indicate a basic duality already there before the split. So, the two individual lives may be said to be present from the beginning, at least in some incipient form.

In any case, they were human before and after splitting. The fact that an identical clone splits off from the "parent" (as is possible in some animals) does not prove that either the "parent" or the "child" was not human.

How can two humans become one?

In addition to the phenomenon of twinning is the phenomenon of recombination. This occurs when a conceptus twins and then recombines as one. Some persons argue that prior to recombination there is no individual human existence. But if we view recombination in the same way we view twinning, there is really no inconsistency in affirming the individuality of each conceptus and the individuality of the conceptus resulting from recombination. First, each conceptus was genetically an individual human prior to the recombination. The fact that an identical clone recombines with a "parent" does not prove that either the "parent" or the "child" was not human.

Second, as bioethicist Andrew Varga points out, since "it has been observed that life at an early stage of development sometimes reproduces by asexual fission[,] . . . recombination, too, could be understood as one of the original beings continuing its development and existence while the other ceases to exist." In the cases of both twinning and recombination, "one definite cause and source of the activities and development of a human individual is there from the beginning."[3]

Philosopher Robert Wennberg provides a useful analogy to help us understand why the argument from the phenomena of twinning and recombination is not decisive in overturning the prolife view that life begins at conception.

> Imagine that we lived in a world in which a certain small percentage of teenagers replicated themselves by some mysterious natural means, splitting in two upon reaching their sixteenth birthday. We would not in the least be inclined to conclude that no human being could therefore be considered a person prior to becoming sixteen years of age; nor would we conclude that life could be taken with greater impunity prior to replication than afterward. The real oddity—to press the parallel—would be two teenagers becoming one. However, in all of this we still would not judge the individual's claim to life to be undermined in any way. We might puzzle over questions of personal identity . . . , but we would not allow these strange replications and fusions to influence our thinking about an individual's right to life. Nor therefore does it seem that such considerations are relevant to determining the point at which an individual might assume a right to life in utero.[4]

Do clones prove that life does not begin at conception?

First of all, no human clones have been produced, so the question is merely hypothetical, not actual; an actual human clone may never occur. Furthermore, if human clones are ever produced, they will be human. A carbon copy of a human is human. They will be just as human as both pairs of identical twins.

Finally, if clones are produced, they will disprove the proabortion claim that life begins at birth, because when an individual is cloned, his clone's genetically separate existence begins at conception. From that point onward the clone merely grows and develops from embryo to fetus to infant to child to adolescent and onward into adulthood. Clones will support the claim that an individual human life exists when all the human genetic information exists in a separate individual.

Does birth change the human status of an individual?

No. Birth just changes one's location, not human status. Birth is a change in the method of feeding but not in one's humanity. Birth no more changes a human being's status as such than does moving across the street. Birth is only a change in address, not in the addressee. It is only an accidental change, not a substantial change.

Is an unborn entity a potential human life?

No. The unborn is not a potential human; it is a realized human with great potential. As we have seen, a conceptus is already genetically 100 percent human. What it gains after conception is growth, not life. It already has human life.

As we noted earlier, some have admitted the biological humanness of the unborn, but have philosophically denied its status as protectable human life. They often argue that the unborn is human, but is only potentially a person. In chapter 3 we will answer the questions surrounding the arguments used to defend this position.

Isn't an embryo like an acorn, which is only a potential oak tree?

No. An embryo is to an adult what an acorn is to an oak tree. An acorn is the tiny oak tree living in a dormant state inside the shell. Likewise, a human embryo is a tiny human being living inside his or her mother's womb, although the embryo is not dormant since he or she is always in the process of growing. The acorn analogy is misused when it is wrongly assumed that an acorn is only a potential oak tree.[5]

It can be argued that there really is no analogy between a human being and an oak tree, since a human being is a mammal while an oak tree is a plant. A good analogy would compare a human being to another mammal. But this hurts the proabortion position, because unborn mammals, such as dogs and cats, are developing, growing, and living organisms of the same species as their parents, just as are unborn human beings. That is, an unborn canine is still a canine and an unborn human is still a human.

What do test-tube babies reveal about life's beginning?

Test-tube babies (really conceptions) reveal that a conceptus is a tiny human being independent from its mother's body. Otherwise, it could not be conceived outside of her womb in the petri dish. That is, an embryo is no more an extension of his or her mother's womb than a conceptus is an extension of the petri dish. He or she is no more a part of the mother's body than a nursing baby is part of the mother's breast.

The Development of Human Life[6]

When are all of the genetic characteristics present?

All human genetic characteristics are present from the very moment of conception (fertilization). No new genetic information is added to the individual from this moment to death. All that individual needs, as do the rest of us, is food, water, air, and an environment conducive to survival.

When do arms, legs, and head begin to develop?

The arms, legs, and head buds begin to appear during the first month after conception. In most cases they are already forming before the mother knows she is pregnant.

When does the heart muscle begin to pulsate?

The heart muscle begins to pulsate before the embryo is a month old. Again, the mother has not yet missed her first period when the heart muscle is pulsating.

At what stage can the unborn feel pain?

By the end of the second month of development in the womb the embryonic lips become sensitive to touch. Between eight and thirteen weeks after conception the nervous system develops. By this time the tiny human being can feel organic pain. Psychological (subjective) pain is not possible to measure in a scientific way, but physical pain is definitely possible.[7] Many abortions occur after this period and can, therefore, be felt by the unborn baby.

According to a booklet coauthored by Vincent J. Collins, M.D., professor of Anesthesiology at Northwestern University and the University of Illinois as well as the author of *Principles of Anesthesiology,* one of the leading medical texts on the control of pain: "Certain neurological structures are necessary to pain sensation: pain receptive nerve cells, neural pathways, and the thalamus [two egg-shaped masses of nerve tissue located deep within the brain at the top of the brain-stem]." Since these requisite neurological structures are completely in place at 13-1/2 weeks and because they are functioning at that time, "as evidenced by the aversive response of the human fetus, it may be concluded with reasonable medical certainty that the fetus can sense pain at least by 13-1/2 weeks." However, it should not be ignored that since "the neurological structures are at least partially in place between 8 and 13-1/2 weeks, it seems probable that some pain can also be felt during this time of gestation."[8]

When can brain waves first be detected?

Brain waves can be detected between forty and forty-two days after conception. The absence of brain waves is considered a sign of death in most states. This is because the absence of such brain waves after the brain waves have come into existence indicates that the individual no longer has any potency to function as a human being, since there is no known way by which to "reactivate" the brain. But if there were, "brain death" would no longer be an adequate criterion of death. On the other hand, an unborn entity which has not reached the point in its development at which brain waves can be detected still has the potency to have brain waves. Hence, there is no analogy between the deceased adult who has no potency for brain waves and the living unborn entity who does have such potency. In any event, the fact remains that a large number of abortions in the United States are performed after brain waves can be detected. This is a serious problem for those prochoice moderates who use the brain wave criterion to distinguish person from nonperson and seek to restrict almost all abortions after the time at which brain waves can be detected.[9]

Does the unborn entity have its own blood type?

Yes, the unborn entity has his or her own blood type, which is often different from that of the mother. This is another proof that the unborn is not an extension of the mother's body. If it were, it would always have the same blood type.

When are all the bodily systems functioning?

All bodily systems are present and functioning by the end of the second month. The baby's heart is pumping, its blood is flowing in its veins, and its lungs are working. At this point many mothers may not be sure they are pregnant, yet it is legal in all fifty states and the District of Columbia to abort this unborn entity for any reason its mother deems fit, as long as it's done by a licensed physician.

Can the unborn swim in the womb?

Yes. These tiny little humans are excellent swimmers. "Windows" on the womb, such as ultrasound, make it possible to witness their beauty as they move gracefully through the amniotic fluid.

Do fetuses suck their thumbs?

Yes, many fetuses do suck their thumbs in the womb. Some are even born sucking their thumbs. Thumb sucking often begins in the third month after conception. With a head start like this, no wonder it is a habit hard to break!

Can unborn offspring hear their mothers' voices?

Yes, babies can hear the mother's voice in the womb and become accustomed to it before they are born. This may account, in part, for the fact that they often seem to respond better to the mother's voices after they are born.

Can the unborn cry?

Yes, unborn babies, at least by their fifth month of development (which is only halfway to their scheduled birth) can actually cry. The only reason their cries cannot be heard outside the womb is because sound waves need air in which to travel, and the unborn float in amniotic fluid. Experiments have shown, however, that when air is present in the womb, the mother can actually hear the baby cry. On occasion, even the father sleeping next to the mother has heard the baby cry and has been awakened.[10]

Can the unborn dream?

It is believed that the unborn can dream, for the unborn have been observed to have the rapid eye movements (REM) that are associated with dreaming in adults.

At what age can an unborn entity survive outside the womb?

Babies who are only twenty weeks old (after conception) have been known to survive outside the womb. Of course, their chances are much better the longer they stay there before their scheduled birth. However, technology places viability (the age at which the unborn can survive outside the womb) earlier and earlier.

The earlier age of viability leaves proabortionists in an ironic situation. Some hospitals find that they are killing viable babies (by abortion) in one room and desperately attempting to rescue premature infants (preemies) in another. Logic demands that if the preemie is human at twenty weeks then surely the aborted baby, who may be older, is human as well. Philosopher Jane English, who takes a moderate position on abortion (neither fully prolife nor fully pro-choice), has made this observation:

> The similarity of a fetus to a baby is very significant. A fetus one week before birth is so much like a newborn baby in our psychological space that we cannot allow any cavalier treatment of the former while expecting full sympathy and nurturative support for the latter. . . . An early horror story from New York about nurses who were expected to alternate between caring for six-week premature infants and disposing of viable 24-week aborted fetuses is just that—a horror story.

English concludes that "these beings are so much alike that no one can be asked to draw a distinction and treat them so very differently."[11]

What occurs in human development month by month?

See figure 1 on the next page, "Human Development before Birth," which covers the period from actualization in the first month to viability in the fifth.

Does survivability (viability) measure humanness?

No. Viability measures only the age at which the baby can survive outside his or her mother's womb, not the point at which life begins. Furthermore, the age of viability has changed in the past couple of decades. In 1973, when the Supreme Court legalized abortion (in *Roe* v. *Wade*), viability was about twenty-four weeks. Now it is closer to twenty weeks after conception. Viability changes, not humanity. Viability is a measure of the sophistication of life-support systems, not a measure of life itself. It measures technology, not humanity.

Furthermore, even a newborn baby is not able to survive on its own outside the womb. For that matter, neither are young children, indigent adults, such as the severely handi-

Figure 1

Human Development before Birth

First Month—Actualization
Conception: all human characteristics and sex determined
Implantation ("nesting") in uterus (1 week)
Heart muscle pulsates (3 weeks)
Head, arms, legs begin to appear

Second Month—Development
Nose, eyes, ears, toes appear
Brain waves (c.40 days)
Discernable heartbeat; blood flows (its own type)
Skeleton develops; has fingerprints
Reflexes, lips sensitive to touch
All systems present

Third Month—Movement
Swallows (fluid), squints, swims
Grasps with hands, moves tongue, sucks thumb
Can feel organic pain

Fourth Month—Growth
Weight increase 6 times (to 1/2 birth weight)
Grows to 8–10" long
Can hear his/her mother's voice

Fifth Month—Viability
Skin, hair, nails develop
Dreams [REM], can hear cry (if air is present)
Can live outside the womb
(Only halfway to scheduled birth day)

capped, senile, stroke ridden, or quadriplegic, able to survive without support. But all of these are considered human beings with a full right to life. Why, then, should an unborn be considered nonhuman because it cannot survive on its own outside the womb?

If you really think about it, we are all nonviable in relation to our environment. If any one of us were to be placed naked on the North Pole or on the moon for just a couple of minutes, our nonviability would become readily apparent. Hence, just as we are nonviable in relation to our environment (certain places on the earth), unborn entities prior to twenty weeks of age are nonviable in relation to theirs.

Do physicians consider unborn entities their patients?

Yes. In modern fetology the unborn is considered the physician's "second patient" or "unborn patient." This is why Dr. Albert Liley, the father of modern fetology, noted that "this is . . . the same baby we are caring for before and after birth, who before birth can be ill and need diagnosis and treatment just like any other patient."[12] In fact, surgery has been performed on fetuses.[13] Hence, the prenatal period is now viewed as a time for diagnosis and treatment of fetal medical conditions. Here, again, is evidence that a human life from conception to death is the same person being treated by the physician.

Is the unborn an extension of his or her mother's body?

No. Each unborn entity has its own body, heartbeat, blood type, brain waves, unique genetic code, and unique fingerprints. Every mother is female; yet about half of all babies they carry are male, a clear indication that the baby is not an extension of the mother's body.

Furthermore, if a human embryo with black parents were conceived in a test tube (petri dish) and transported into the body of a white woman, the child would be born black. Just as it is absurd to say that prior to transplantation the embryo was "part of" the petri dish, it is equally absurd to say that the unborn entity is "part of" its mother. This further demonstrates beyond question that the unborn entity is not the extension of the mother's body.

Genetic Deformities and Human Life[14]
Are the deformed unborn human?

If the unborn are fully human, they are fully human for reasons other than that they lack deformity. After all, are adults with the same deformities human? Then so are smaller people, too. A handicapped unborn, if it is fully human, should stir in us as much compassion and care (if not more) than an adult with the same handicap. Since when do we declare someone subhuman simply because of a handicap? Hence, it is not the question of whether the unborn entity is deformed but whether it is fully human. This is not to deny the fact that there are tragedies in life and that having and rearing a deformed child is a difficult burden. But it is important to realize that if the unborn entity is fully human, homicide cannot be justified simply because it relieves parents or society of a burden. Furthermore, although it is not a reason against abortion, a handicapped child can give both society and the family into which it has been born an opportunity to exercise true compassion, love, charity, and kindness. Thus, it is fair to say that those who advocate the abortion of the deformed assault our common humanity by denying our capacity to attain virtue in the presence of suffering.[15]

As we have pointed out throughout this chapter, the prochoice position on abortion is that abortion is a right which a woman may exercise during the pregnancy for any reason she deems fit, not limited to cases of physical deformity. Hence, even if abortion were morally justified in the case of deformity, this would not support the prochoice advocacy of abortion on demand.

Do organizations for handicapped people support abortion?

It is interesting to note there is not a single organization serving handicapped children which has gone on record in favor of abortion. In fact, statistics show a lower suicide rate among the handicapped than among so-called normal people.[16] This is why former Surgeon General C. Everett Koop, who worked for years with severely deformed infants as a pediatric surgeon at Philadelphia's Children's Hospital, made this observation: "It has been my constant experience that disability and unhappiness do not necessarily go together."[17] He goes on to state:

Some of the most unhappy children whom I have known have all of their physical and mental faculties, and on the other hand some of the happiest youngsters have borne burdens which I myself would find very difficult to bear. Our obligation in such circumstances is to find alternatives for the problems our patients face. I don't consider death an acceptable alternative. With our technology and creativity, we are merely at the beginning of what we can do educationally and in the field of leisure activities for such youngsters. And who knows what happiness is for another person?[18]

Many handicapped people, for obvious reasons, strongly oppose the use of abortion to rid society of the handicapped. Surgeon General Koop cites the following letter, which appeared in the London *Daily Telegraph* (Dec. 8, 1962) at a time when European newspapers were seriously discussing the use of abortion as an effective means by which to avoid the birth of children who became defective in the womb through their mothers' use of thalidomide (a tranquilizer used by European women in the 1950s and 1960s but never approved by the FDA for sale in the United States).

Trowbridge
Kent
Dec. 8, 1962

Sirs:

We were disabled from causes other than Thalidomide, the first of us having useless arms and hands; the second, two useless legs; and the third, the use of neither arms nor legs.
We were fortunate . . . in having been allowed to live and we want to say with strong conviction how thankful we are that none took it upon themselves to destroy us as useless cripples.

Here at the Debarue School of Spastics, one of the schools of the National Spastic Society, we have found worthwhile and happy lives and we face our future with confidence. Despite our disability, life still has much to offer and we are more than anxious, if only metaphorically, to reach out toward the future. This, we hope, will give comfort and hope to the parents of the Thalidomide babies, and at the same time serve to condemn those who would contemplate the destruction of even a limbless baby.

Yours faithfully,

Elaine Duckett
Glynn Verdon
Caryl Hodges[19]

Are teratomas human?

No, they are tumors with some human genetic material that has gone awry. They may have some hair, skin, teeth, or even fingers, but they are not human embryos and do not develop under any conditions into human fetuses or ultimately into children. They are part of the woman's bodily tissue and not separate human individuals.

What about an anencephalic baby?

Anencephalic babies have a brain stem but no brain. This deformity is thought to be a result of the failure of the neural tube to close. This leads to degenerative changes in which the brain does not develop. We should view the anencephalic child as we would an individual who has had his head blown off by a shotgun.[20] A damaged human is not a nonhuman.

Anencephalic babies generally die within a few days after birth. There is no reason to kill them. Again, even if abortion were justified in the case of anencephalic babies, this would be far from supporting the prochoice position that it is not wrong to kill healthy unborns for any reason.

Do the unborn go through a "fish" stage?

At no time in the development of an embryo or fetus is it a fish. It begins as a human being at conception and remains one throughout its life. At no time does it have gills like a fish (a fish breathes through its gills), although the visceral furrows by the ears were once mistakenly thought by some scientists to be gills. A human being is always conceived of human parents, begins at conception as fully human, and develops in accordance with its human nature.

How many zygotes die before an implantation takes place?

Estimates of how many fertilized ova die before birth range from 20 to 50 percent, so about 30 percent die before implantation. This large number, however, no more establishes the nonhumanity of the unborn than that a high infant mortality rate in underdeveloped countries establishes that little children are not human. Even if there were 100 percent mortality in the first week of life this would not prove that the ova were not human. After all, there is a 100 percent mortality rate in the last week of life, and all of these are human.

Abortion Methods, Artificial Contraception, and Birth Control

What are some of the common methods used in performing an abortion and at what point in pregnancy is each most frequently used?

Although some forms of birth control result in abortion (the killing of the embryo or early fetus), such as the IUD and RU-486, there are really only six common methods of abortion used by physicians at abortion clinics and hospitals: (1) dilation and curettage (D & C), (2) suction abortion, (3) saline abortion, (4) hysterotomy, (5) dilation and evacuation (D & E), and (6) prostaglandin.

Former Surgeon General C. Everett Koop, M.D., outlines four of these popular methods:

The technique used most often to end early pregnancies is called D & C or *dilation and curettage*. In this procedure, usually before the twelfth or thirteenth week of pregnancy, the uterus is approached through the vagina. The cervix is stretched to permit the insertion of a curette, a tiny hoelike instrument. The surgeon then scrapes the wall of the uterus, cutting the baby's body to pieces and scraping the placenta from its attachments on the uterine wall. Bleeding is considerable.

An alternate method which is used during the same period of pregnancy is called *suction abortion*. The principle is the same as in the D & C. A powerful suction tube is inserted through the dilated cervix into the uterus. This tears apart the body of the developing baby and the placenta, sucking the pieces into a jar. The smaller parts of the body are recognizable as arms, legs, head, and so on. More than two-thirds of all abortions performed in the United States and Canada apparently are done by this method.

Later in pregnancy, when the D & C or suction abortion might produce too much bleeding in the expectant mother, doctors employ the second most common abortion technique, called the *saline abortion,* or "salting out." This method is usually carried out after sixteen weeks of pregnancy, when enough amniotic fluid has accumulated in the sac around the baby. A long needle is inserted through the mother's abdomen directly into the sac, and a solution of concentrated salt is injected into the amniotic fluid. The salt solution is absorbed both through the lungs and the gastrointestinal tract, producing changes in the osmotic pressure. The outer layer of skin is burned off by the high concentration of salt. It takes about an hour to kill the baby by this slow method. The mother usually goes into labor about a day later and delivers a dead, shriveled baby.

If abortion is decided on too late to be accomplished by either D & C, suction, or saline procedure, physicians resort to a final technique called *hysterotomy.* A hysterotomy is exactly the same as a Cesarean section with one difference—in a Cesarean section the operation is usually performed to save the life of the baby, whereas a hysterotomy is performed to kill the baby. These babies look very much like other babies except that they are small and weigh, for example, about two pounds at the end of a twenty-four week pregnancy. They are truly alive, but they are allowed to die through neglect or sometimes killed by a direct act.[21]

University of Rhode Island ethicist, Dr. Stephen Schwarz, explains *D & E or Dilation and Evacuation:*

Used between 12 and 24 weeks. Here, too, the child is cut to pieces by a sharp knife, as in D & C, only is a much larger and far more developed child, weighing as much as a pound, and measuring as much as a foot in length.[22]

Prostaglandin abortions, which are performed after the twelfth week of pregnancy, involve the "uses of chemicals developed and sold by the Upjohn Pharmaceutical Company. . . . The hormone-like compounds are injected or otherwise applied to the muscle of the uterus, causing it to contract intensely, thereby pushing out the developing baby. Babies have been decapitated during these abnormal contractions. Many have been born alive."[23]

Do these abortion methods cause the unborn to feel pain?

With no doubt by the thirteenth week and quite possibly as early as eight weeks after conception a fetus has pain receptors. According to one study, "induced abortion will cause pain to a fetus with a functioning nervous system if the method used stimulates the pain receptors, excites the neural pathways, and the impulse reaches the thalamus." Hence abortions which occur after the thirteenth week, when we are medically certain that pain can occur because the requisite conditions are in place, will cause pain if the methods employed are capable of stimulating pain receptors and exciting neural pathways. Dilation and evacuation (D & E), abortion by saline amnio-infusion, and prostaglandin abortions—the methods used after the twelfth week—are all capable of stimulating pain receptors as well as exciting neural pathways.[24]

D & E abortions would obviously excite pain receptors and

excite neural pathways since it involves the slicing, crushing, and dismemberment of the unborn. Saline abortions, which result in the expulsion of the unborn within forty-eight hours after sodium chloride (salt) is injected in the amniotic sac, burn "away the upper skin layers of the fetus. The esophagus and mouth are also burned when the fetus swallows amniotic fluid polluted by the saline. By the time the fetus is expelled there is extensive edema and submembranous degeneration." That is to say "by damaging the surface of the fetus in this fashion, saline would excite pain receptors and stimulate the neural pathways of a functioning central nervous system during the course of the abortion until the fetus dies. It is well-known that the fetus reacts with aversive responses when saline is introduced into amniotic fluid," as evidenced by the fact that the "aborting mother can feel her baby thrashing in the uterus during the approximately two hours it usually takes for the saline solution to kill the fetus." Prostaglandin abortions, by introducing the hormone into the mother's system, "may bring about death of the fetus by constricting the circulation of the blood and/or impairing the heart function." It can be assumed that this pain is analogous to that which is experienced by a person having a heart attack.[25]

How many of these pain-causing abortions are performed every year?

In 1980 alone approximately 113,500 abortions were performed during the second and third trimesters of pregnancy (after the thirteenth week), using the D & E, saline amnio-infusion, and prostaglandin methods. Approximately 9,600 of them were prostaglandin abortions, 24,000 were abortions by the saline amnio-infusion method, and 80,000 were D & E abortions.[26] The 1980 statistics are typical.

How many abortions were performed between the eighth and thirteenth weeks when there is a good chance the unborn may be capable of feeling pain?

About 480,500 were performed during this time in 1980.[27]

What is RU-486?

It is a pill developed in France which is not now approved for use in the United States. It is *not* a contraceptive, since it does not prevent conception, but is a drug which induces an abortion. It is simply another abortion method.

How effective is RU-486 and how does it work?

It is 95 percent effective if taken within seven weeks of the pregnant woman's last menstrual period. According to abortion-rights supporter Laurence Tribe, RU-486 "is extremely effective in causing shedding of the fertilized embryo [sic] after implantation in the uterine wall. It is taken in conjunction with the hormone prostaglandin, which causes uterine contractions. . . . In France a pregnant woman can get RU-486 at a clinic. She returns forty-eight hours later to receive a prostaglandin injection. She stays three hours, since prostaglandin may cause nausea, vomiting, and in a small number of cases, heavy bleeding."[28] Schwarz provides even greater detail of the procedure:

> If the pill succeeds . . . , a dead, bloody baby will be washed out. If not, she must repeat. She takes three pills, waits two days while the child dies, then takes prostaglandin and waits five to eight days for the bloody remains of the child to flow out. In about 5 percent of the cases she is not successful even then, and a surgical abortion is needed to complete the killing. The anxious wait, the uncertainty, the length of time cannot but heighten the agonizing drama of this experience. This is no "get it over and done with" method of killing the child. The woman is drawn into the death process at a time when she is particularly sensitive and susceptible to psychological stress and trauma.[29]

Is there a difference between birth control and contraception?

Yes. Although all contraceptives are a form of birth control, not every form of birth control is a contraceptive. The word *contraceptive* literally means "to prevent conception." Therefore, since they simply prevent conception, men or women who use contraceptives should not fear that they are killing human life.

On the other hand, *birth control* means "to prevent birth," so by preventing conception, contraceptives are a form of birth control. There are, however, noncontraceptive forms of birth control which kill the conceptus. These are a means of abortion.

What are the major forms of artificial contraception and birth control?

Forms of contraceptive birth control, which do not result in the death of the conceptus, include the condom, diaphragm, some forms of the Pill, spermicides, and sterilization. Forms of noncontraceptive birth control, which do result in ordinary death of the conceptus, include the IUD, the "morning-after" pill (RU-486), and abortion.

Is abortion really a form of artificial birth control?

Yes. Any artificial (nonnatural) procedure which prevents birth and results in the death of the conceptus is a form of birth control, since that is exactly what both the IUD and the "morning-after" pill do, two methods described as forms of "birth control" by the *American Medical Association Encyclopedia of Medicine*.[30] This same text also refers to abortion as a form of birth control.[31]

Will prolifers try to make contraception illegal?

No. One of the great myths perpetuated by the prochoice movement is that prolifers will eventually want to strip everyone of their contraceptives. Although some prolifers, such as Roman Catholics, may not use contraceptives for religious reasons and may encourage other Christians to do likewise, they make a moral distinction between preventing a pregnancy and killing a conceptus (abortion). Abortion is to kill a conceptus and hence rob a person (the unborn) of the right to life. Hence, the state has an obligation to interfere and protect this life. But if one believes contraception is wrong, the harm in using it is only to one's own soul. Hence, the state has an obligation not to interfere in one's personal decision in this area since it does not result in the death or severe physical harm of another. For this reason, anticontraceptive prolifers, although they may try to persuade others by preaching and writing fervently against the use of contraception, have no desire to enact their view into law. However, most prolifers do not share this Roman Catholic conviction, for they find nothing morally wrong with contraception. Among the many prolife leaders and scholars who find no problem with contraception are John Warwick Montgomery, Bernard Nathanson, M.D., Don Marquis, and James Humber.[32]

In any event, the prolifers who do not agree with each other about the morality of contraception do agree both that the state should not interfere with one's personal decision on contraception and that the state should forbid abortion since it results in the death of innocent human life.

Medical Groups and Abortion

What is the AMA's stand on abortion?

The American Medical Association is presently on record as favoring a woman's right to an abortion. They believe it is a decision that should be left to a woman and her physician.

Has the AMA always held this position?

No. They were once strongly opposed to abortion. A book by Dr. Franklin Heard and Dr. Horatio Storer published in 1868 *(Criminal Abortion: Its Nature, Its Evidence & Its Law)* under the auspices of the AMA declared:

> Physicians have now arrived at the unanimous opinion, that the foetus in utero [in the womb] is alive from the very moment of conception. . . . (T)he wilful killing of a human being, at any stage of its existence is murder. . . . (A)bortion is, in reality, a crime against the infant, its mother, the family circle, and society.[33]

Why did the AMA change its stand on abortion?

It was certainly not because the scientific evidence convinced them otherwise. The scientific evidence for the full humanity of the unborn is stronger today than it was one hundred years ago, as we have seen above. What, then, changed the mind of the AMA? In brief, it was political pressure and social considerations, not scientific facts.

What percent of physicians perform abortions?

A very small percent of obstetricians/gynecologists perform abortions, estimated at only about 2 percent. This small group, however, perform a lot of abortions. Dr. Bernard Nathanson confesses to have presided over some 60,000 abortions before he was convinced of the wrongness of his actions.[34]

Are there any prolife medical groups?

Yes. The largest prolife medical group in America is the American Association of Pro-Life Obstetricians and Gynecologists (headquarters in Lauderdale-by-the-Sea, Florida). There is also an international group known as The World Federation of Doctors Who Respect Life (with headquarters in Oak Park, Illinois).

2

Legal Questions
The Constitution

What does the Declaration of Independence say about life?

On America's birth certificate the following words are inscribed:

> We hold these truths to be self-evident, that all men are cre-
> ated equal, that they are endowed by their Creator with cer-
> tain unalienable rights; that among these are life, liberty, and
> the pursuit of happiness.[1]

From this it is clear that our founding fathers believed that the right to life was an unalienable right. That is, it is some-thing to which the Declaration says, "Nature's God entitle[s] them." In short, the right to life is a God-given right which governments cannot give and governments cannot take away.

Did the founders envision this right for the unborn?

Yes. The founders of our country envisioned the right to life as extending to the unborn. This is evident from several

39

things. First, the English common law tradition, from which our laws came, had laws against abortion.[2] Second, the moral law (natural law) tradition from which Thomas Jefferson came and to which he referred as "the laws of nature" also opposed abortion.[3] Third, during the time of the founders the unborn was defined in dictionaries as a "child in the womb," and a child was defined as a "very young person."[4] Finally, as early as 1716, sixty years before the Declaration of Independence, the common council of New York passed a law forbidding midwives from performing abortions.[5]

What does the Bill of Rights say about life?

The first ten amendments to the Constitution are called the Bill of Rights. The Fifth Amendment (1791) reads (in part) as follows: "Nor [shall any person] be deprived of life, liberty, or property, without due process of law."[6] In other words, everyone has not only the right to life, liberty, and property, but also the right to due process in regards to being deprived of these rights.

Prolifers have noted that abortion is a violation of the Fifth Amendment because it both deprives the unborn of their life and it does so without a court trial on their behalf. The unborn are accused, pronounced guilty, and given capital punishment for no crime, with no lawyer, before no jury. No greater injustice could occur to any person under our Constitution.

What does the Fourteenth Amendment say about life?

With regard to the right to life, the Fourteenth Amendment says the same thing as the Fifth Amendment:

> All persons born or naturalized in the United States, and subject to the jurisdiction thereof, are citizens of the United States and of the State wherein they reside. No State shall make or enforce any law which shall abridge the privileges or immunities of citizens of the United States; nor shall any State deprive any person of life, liberty, or property, without due process of law; nor deny to any person within its jurisdiction the equal protection of the laws.[7]

In brief, it is unconstitutional to take anyone's life without due process of the law. As applied to unborn persons, this means that no abortion should occur without a trial and defense attorneys appointed to defend the right to life of the unborn.

Does the right to life extend only to those who are born?

Some proabortionists have argued that since the Fourteenth Amendment speaks only of those born in the United States as having their lives protected, the amendment does not apply to the unborn. This is clearly a misinterpretation for several reasons.

First, those "born . . . in the United States" are not contrasted with the unborn in the United States but rather with those born outside the United States, aliens who are not "citizens of the United States."

Second, if the protection of life were extended only to those born in the United States it would be permissible to kill aliens or to deprive them of a right to due process. This is obviously absurd.

Third, the amendment clearly extends the right to life "to any person within its jurisdiction," not just to those who have been born.

In the Fourteenth Amendment does person refer to the unborn ?

Yes. We know this to be true for many reasons. First, there were legal references to the unborn as a "child" during the time the Fourteenth Amendment was written.[8] Second, the dictionaries of the day defined a fetus as a "child in the womb." Third, the killing of the unborn was called manslaughter. Fourth, at that time all abortions were prohibited, except for saving the life of the mother. Fifth, at that time the laws exacted the same range of punishments for killing the baby as for killing the mother. Sixth, the punishment was greater when it was proven that the abortion killed the baby, rather than that the death resulted from some other possible means. Seventh, a federal court as late as 1970 (in *Steinberg* v. *Ohio*), only three years before *Roe* v. *Wade,* called the unborn a person protected under the Fourteenth Amendment. Eighth, some of the congressmen who voted for and helped draft the Fourteenth Amendment also approved of strong anti-abortion laws in some United States territories, which were all under the jurisdiction of the Constitution. Hence, if the Fourteenth Amendment was meant to include the right to abort and exclude the unborn from legal protection, that concept was completely unknown to those who were chiefly responsible for the amendment's existence. And finally, "the most direct piece of federal legislation relating to abortion in this period was enacted by Congress in 1873, five years after the Fourteenth Amendment was proposed." This legislation "prohibited the selling, lending, or giving away of 'any article . . . for causing unlawful abortion' as defined by the criminal law of the state in which the federal enclave was located."[9]

But I have heard some people say that although the nineteenth-century laws prohibited abortion, they were based on the danger of the medical procedure and not on the unborn's personhood. Is this true?

No, despite the fact that Justice Blackmun argued in much the same way in *Roe* v. *Wade.* The fact is that the purpose of the anti-abortion laws was to protect *both* the life of the mother *and* the life of the unborn child and the unborn child was considered a person under the law. In his important scholarly article on this subject, law professor James Witherspoon drew the following conclusions about the nineteenth-century anti-abortion laws:

That the primary purpose of the nineteenth-century anti-abortion statutes was to protect the lives of unborn children is clearly shown by the terms of the statutes themselves. This primary purpose, or legislative recognition of the personhood of the unborn child, or both, are manifested, in the following elements of these statutes, taken individually and collectively: (1) the provision of an increased range of punishment for abortion if it were proven that the attempt caused the death of the child; (2) the provision of the same range of punishment for attempted abortions killing the unborn child as for attempted abortions killing the mother; (3) the designation of attempted abortion and other acts killing the unborn child as "manslaughter"; (4) the prohibition of all abortions except those necessary to save the life of the mother; (5) the reference to the fetus as a "child"; (6) the use of the term "person" in reference to the unborn child; (7) the categorization of abortion with homicide and related offenses and offenses against born children; (8) the severity of the punishments assessed for abortions; (9) the provision that attempted abortion killing the mother is only manslaughter or a felony rather than murder as at common law [i.e., this provision is obviously taking into account the pregnant woman's consent and thus the diminished culpability of the abortionist]; (10) the requirement that the woman on whom the abortion is attempted be pregnant; (11) the requirement that abortion be attempted with intent to produce abortion or to "destroy the child"; and (12) the incrimination of the woman's participation in her own abortion. Legislative recognition of the personhood of the unborn child is also known by the legislative history of these statutes.[10]

As we will see below, Justice Harry Blackmun seemed to have missed these points entirely in his majority opinion in *Roe* v. *Wade*. Scholars contend that the reason for Blackmun's historical gaffe is that he relied almost entirely on two articles by Professor Cyril Means,[11] who served as counsel for the National Association for the Repeal of Abortion Laws (NARAL; now known as the National Abortion Rights Action League). Means' work has been criticized by both abortion rights and prolife scholars to such an extent that Means' case is no longer taken seriously in the scholarly community,[12] although it is sometimes cited positively in the writings of those who ought to know better.[13]

But didn't the nineteenth-century laws as well as the common law use "quickening" as a criterion to determine when human life begins in the womb?

No. Quickening—the time at which the pregnant woman first feels the unborn's movements (which occurs at sixteen or seventeen weeks)—was used as the point at which the law could *know* for certain that human life existed, since one could not be prosecuted for abortion if no living human person was present in the womb.

Legal scholar and theologian John Warwick Montgomery has pointed out that when the nineteenth-century statutes and common law talked about quickening as the time at which abortion should be forbidden, "they were just identifying the first evidence of life they could conclusively detect. . . . They were saying that as soon as you had life, there must be protection. Now we know that life starts at the moment of conception with nothing superadded."[14] Witherspoon adds: "Clearly, the quickening doctrine was not based on an absurd belief that a living fetus is worthy of protection by virtue of its capacity for movement or its mother's perception of such movement. The occurrence of quickening was deemed significant *only* because it showed that the fetus was alive, and because it was *alive* and *human,* it was protected by criminal law."[15] And as medical science's knowledge of the unborn increased and it came to realize that human life was present from conception, the nineteenth-century laws eventually extended legal protection to the unborn child from the moment of conception.

How does the Dred Scott *decision apply to abortion?*

On March 6, 1857, the United States Supreme Court voted seven-to-two that "The enslaved African race was not intended to be included in, and formed no part of, the people who framed and adopted the Declaration of Independence." It further states that "the Constitution of the United States does not act upon one of the negro race whenever he shall be made free under the laws of a state, and raise him to the rank of a citizen, and immediately clothe him with all the privileges of a citizen of any other state, and in its own courts."[16]

In short, blacks were not considered persons under the

Constitution and had no rights as citizens. Blacks were looked upon as the chattel (property) of their owners. Similarly, the unborn (in *Roe* v. *Wade*) are considered the property of their mothers with no rights of their own under the Constitution. For this reason, the unborn can be disposed of in any way their mothers see fit.[17]

Can you outline the comparison between **Dred Scott** *and* **Roe** *v.* **Wade?**[18]

Slavery	Abortion
Dred Scott (1857)	*Roe* v. *Wade* (1973)
7-to-2 decision	7-to-2 decision
slaves are nonpersons	unborn are nonpersons
property of owner (master)	property of owner (mother)
abolitionists should not impose morality on slave owner	Prolifers should not impose morality on mother
slavery is legal	abortion is legal

Were the lives of blacks protected under the law?

It is a mistake to assume that because *Dred Scott* declared blacks not to be legal "persons" with rights as citizens under the Constitution that they thereby had no rights as humans under the Constitution. There was no open season, for example, to kill blacks. When blacks were murdered, the cases were to be tried in court and the murderers punished if found guilty. While justice was lacking in practice, the Constitution in principle protected the blacks' right to life. The Texas case of *Nix* v. *State* (1855) says "slaves are persons [regarding] . . . crimes; . . . as if committed upon a free person." Also in *Callihan's Exec'r* v. *Johnson* (1858) the Texas Supreme Court recognized the slave's "right to life."[19] Other states made similar decisions.

This can be applied to the abortion issue, for just because *Roe* v. *Wade* (1973) declared the unborn not to be legal persons does not mean they are not actual persons whose lives should be protected under the Constitution. After all, even aliens who are not citizens are still human and their lives are protected by United States law. Why should not the same protection be given to unborn humans who will automatically become citizens at birth?

Has the word person ever been applied to nonhumans?

The *Roe* Supreme Court decided that unborn humans (which it called potential humans) are not protected by the Fifth and Fourteenth Amendments, which guarantee the protection of the life of all "persons" in the United States. This was a tragic error for several reasons.

First, as already noted, the word *person* is used in constitutional law in a legal sense, not in an actual sense. That is, it is used to define one's legal status as a citizen, not one's human status as an individual.

Second, even nonhuman entities have been declared persons with rights under the Fourteenth Amendment. For example, in the *Santa Clara* case (1886) the Court declared unanimously that a corporation was a "person" with Fourteenth Amendment rights.[20] If a nonliving corporation is a person with these rights, then surely a living unborn human being is also a person with the right to life.

The History of Legal Abortion
What was the status of abortion in the United States before Roe?

Six years before the Supreme Court legalized abortion in 1973 all fifty states had laws prohibiting abortion except to save the life of the mother. Then, some states began to make exceptions for "hard cases," such as when a pregnancy is the result of either rape or incest. With the possible exception of New York State, prior to *Roe* all states opposed abortion on demand, the prochoice position that a woman should be free to obtain an abortion for any reason she deems fit. Hence the *Roe* decision reversed centuries of anti-abortion legislation and common law tradition in one fell swoop.

What was the status of abortion in early English common law?[21]

In the English common law tradition the unborn were protected since the thirteenth century by laws prohibiting abortion, when it could be proved a living human person was present in the womb. They were protected against battery since the seventeenth century. In the nineteenth-century U.S. statutes protecting the unborn and prohibiting abortion replaced the common law. These included laws against maternal neglect and loss-of-inheritance. It is interesting to note that the legal protection of the unborn increased as our medical knowledge of the unborn also increased.

Although Justice Blackmun argues in *Roe* that abortion was a common law liberty, his conclusion was based on false premises and invalid inferences which have been pointed out *ad infinitum* in the literature. The overwhelming weight of legal and historical scholarship since *Roe* has come out against Blackmun's psuedo-history. (See note 15.)

What was the history of abortion since ancient times?

Most cultures since ancient times have opposed abortion. The ancient Canaanite Code of Hammurabi (1727/28 B.C.) exacted a penalty for even unintentionally causing a miscarriage. The Jewish law gave the same penalty for causing the death of an unborn as for any other person (Exod. 21:22–23).[22] The Assyrian king Tiglath-Pileser I (twelfth century B.C.) punished a woman who caused herself to miscarry. The famous Greek physician Hippocrates (fourth century B.C.) opposed abortion by oath, insisting that doctors pledge: "I will not give a woman an abortive remedy."[23]

In spite of the fact that the Stoics generally favored abortion, their Roman philosopher Seneca (first century A.D.) praised his mother for not aborting him. In the same century, the poet Ovid pronounced those who abort as worthy of death. In the second century, Refus insisted that abortion was a "danger to the commonwealth." During the same period the

Roman thinker Soranus opposed abortion, claiming that physicians should save lives, not kill them.[24]

In the fourth century A.D. St. Augustine opposed all abortions as a violation of the moral law of God. Likewise, at the end of the middle ages St. Thomas Aquinas strongly opposed the abortion of all human fetuses, although he did not believe that the human (rational) soul entered the body until several weeks after conception. The reformer John Calvin (sixteenth century A.D.) called abortion abominable. English common law punished abortion when it could be shown it actually resulted in the death of the unborn. And early American law (1716) forbade midwives from performing an abortion.[25]

In brief, there has been a nearly unanimous prohibition against abortion on demand in the great cultures through legal, moral, and medical codes down through the centuries. The present policy of the United States and most industrial nations stands to stark contrast to this long moral tradition.

What does the Hippocratic oath say about abortion?

The Hippocratic oath is opposed to abortion. By it the physician pledges this:

> I will neither give a deadly drug to anyone if asked for it, nor will I make a suggestion to this effect. Similarly I will not give to a woman an abortive remedy.[26]

Do doctors have to take the Hippocratic oath?

No. The Hippocratic oath is not required for graduation from state medical schools. If it were, it would be the *hypocritical oath,* since the American Medical Association is on record in favor of abortion. Indeed, most doctors are taught in medical school how to perform abortions unless they request to be excused.

The Supreme Court's *Roe* v. *Wade* Decision
What does **Roe** v. **Wade** say about abortion, and how does the **Doe** v. **Bolton** decision affect it?

In *Roe* the Supreme Court divided pregnancy into three trimesters. In the first three months there can be no legal restrictions on abortion in any state. During the second trimester there can be legal restrictions only to make the procedure safer for the mother. During the last three-month period before scheduled birth the state may prohibit abortion to protect "potential life" unless the health or life of the mother is in danger, although the state has no obligation to do so. Hence, it is obvious that the *Roe* decision asserts that the unborn entity does not become fully human until birth, since the state has no obligation to protect it prior to that time.

On January 11, 1973 (eleven days before the *Roe* decision) the Supreme Court in *Doe* v. *Bolton* defined health by asserting that an abortion can be performed "in the light of all factors—physical, emotional, psychological, familial, and the woman's age—relevant to the well-being of the patient. All these factors may relate to health."[27] This means that an abortion, even when the unborn is seven, eight, or nine months old (after conception), can be performed for virtually any reason, including the mother's emotional stress caused by her pregnancy.

Does Roe v. Wade *permit abortion on demand?*

Yes. The *Roe* decision taken together with the *Doe* decision permits abortion on demand. The bottom line of the *Roe* and *Doe* rulings is that any woman for virtually any reason (whether social, financial, psychological, or personal) can have an abortion at any time during the nine months of pregnancy, provided it is done by a licensed physician.

A study by the Senate Judiciary Committee, which evaluated the legal and social ramifications of the Supreme Court's abortion decision, concluded that "no significant legal barriers of any kind whatsoever exist today in the United States for a woman to obtain an abortion for any reason during any stage of her pregnancy" (June 7, 1983).

Is this the opinion of legal scholars?

Yes. The following quotations, written by some of the leading legal scholars in the field, should leave no doubt in any skeptic's mind.

Victor Rosemblum, Ll.B., Ph.D., professor of political science and law, Northwestern University, and Thomas Marzen, J.D., general counsel, National Legal Center for the Medically Handicapped and Disabled:

> The concept of "health," as defined by the Supreme Court in *Doe* v. *Bolton,* includes all medical, psychological, social, familial, and economic factors which might potentially inspire a decision to procure an abortion. As such, "health" abortion is indistinguishable from elective abortion. Thus, until a more narrow definition of "health" is obtained, it may not be possible to limit effectively the number of abortions performed.[28]

United States Judiciary Committee:

> The apparently restrictive standard for the third trimester has in fact proved no different from the standard of abortion on demand expressly allowed during the first six months of the unborn child's life. The exception for maternal health has been so broad in practice as to swallow the rule. The Supreme Court has defined "health" in this context to include "all factors—physical, emotional, familial, and the woman's age— relevant to the well-being of the patient" (*Doe* v. *Bolton,* 410 U.S. 179, 192 [1973]). Since there is nothing to stop an abortionist from certifying that a third-trimester abortion is beneficial to the health of the mother—in this broad sense—the Supreme Court's decision has in fact made abortion available on demand throughout the prenatal life of the child, from conception to birth.[29]

Thomas O'Meara, J.D., dean emeritus, Notre Dame Law School:

> According to the Court's opinion, not only physical but emotional, psychological and familial factors, as well as the woman's age, are relevant for diagnostic purposes. So the

pressure is very great to perform the abortion she insists on. And remember, too, that "[i]nduced abortions are a source of easy income for doctors." All this adds up to abortion on demand.[30]

Stanley M. Harrison, Ph.D., assistant professor of philosophy, Le Moyne College:

As it turns out, a state has scant power to proscribe [forbid] the abortion of a viable fetus because of the broad manner in which the Court defines the legitimate dangers to the mother's health, including all factors—"physical, emotional, psychological, familial, and the woman's age—relevant to the well-being of the patient. . . ." Thus, although the Court affirmed that "the State may assert interests beyond the protection of the pregnant woman alone," it is indeed difficult to determine what fetal interest is protected since a pregnant woman now has sufficient latitude to obtain a legal abortion for virtually any reason.[31]

Robert A. Destro, J.D., professor of law, Boalt Hall School of Law:

Since, under the Court's expansive definition of "health" virtually all maternal interest may be sufficient to overcome the state's compelling interest in preserving prenatal life, it cannot be argued that the Court considered such life important enough even to be included in the balancing which did take place.[32]

Jacqueline Nolan Haley, J.D., associate professor of law, Fordham Law School:

Under *Roe*, abortion is always permissible when a woman's life or health is at stake. The Court never clearly articulated what it meant by "health," but it is a word which effectively transcends any authority which might have been given to the state to proscribe [that is, forbid] post-viability abortions.[33]

John Hart Ely, J.D., Robert E. Lang, professor and dean, Stanford Law School:

[A]fter viability the mother's life or health (which presumably is to be defined very broadly indeed, so as to include what many might regard as the mother's convenience . . .) must, as a matter of constitutional law, take precedence over . . . the fetus' life.[34]

Judge John T. Noonan, Jr., Ll.B., Ph.D., Ninth Circuit Court of Appeals, San Francisco, California:

Abortion-on-demand after the first six or seven months of fetal existence has been effected by the Court through its denial of personhood to the viable fetus, on the one hand, and through its broad definition of health, on the other.[35]

Charles E. Rice, Ll.M., S.J.D., professor of law, Notre Dame Law School:

The health of the mother, said the Court in *Bolton,* includes "psychological as well as physical well-being" and "the medical judgment may be exercised in light of all factors—physical, emotional, psychological, familial, and the woman's age—relevant to the well-being" of the mother. The mental health of the mother is such an elastic ground for abortion that the Supreme Court decisions effectively permit elective abortion right up until the time of normal delivery.[36]

Lynn Wardle, J.D., and Mary Anne Q. Wood, J.D., professors of law, Brigham Young University:

Since *Roe,* the Supreme Court's interpretation of the Constitution, requiring the national legalization of abortion on demand, has created the swelling abortion dispute.[37]

William R. Hopkin, Jr., J.D.:

Roe . . . allows abortion when the fetus is viable, if necessary for the preservation of the life or health of the mother. The result of this standard could be that which Chief Justice Burger assured us would not occur: abortion on demand. . . . We get a better idea of what "health" means when the Court in *Roe* discusses the potential harm to a pregnant woman of a strict abortion statute: "There is also the distress, for all concerned, associated with the unwanted child, and there is the problem of bringing a child into a family already unable, psychologically and otherwise, to care for it. . . . [T]he stigma of unwed motherhood may be involved." We are thus left with the specter of an unwed mother bearing a child capable of now living outside its mother's womb obtaining an abortion because she fears the stigma of unwed motherhood.[38]

John Warwick Montgomery, M.Phil, Th.D. Ph.D., former dean of the Simon Greenleaf School of Law:

> In actual effect, *Roe* v. *Wade* judicially created abortion on demand in the United States.[39]

Roger Wertheimer, Ph.D., visiting professor of philosophy, University of Houston:

> I would not deny that the use of viability [in *Roe*] as a compelling point is defensible and reasonable, though I defy anyone to show it to be uniquely so. Nor would I deny the propriety of abortion to prevent the mother's death or injury to her health if the state's interest in protecting maternal health is superior to its interest in protecting potential life. Of course, many will protest when Justice Douglas informs us in his concurring opinion, which refers to the *Vuitch* decision, that "health" must here be construed to "give full sweep to the 'psychological as well as the physical well-being' of women patients." With that construal, a woman who wants a late-term abortion will usually be able to find a physician willing to certify it as necessary for her health.[40]

What was the story behind Roe v. Wade?

Jane Roe (a pseudonym for Norma McCorvey), a resident of Texas, claimed to have become pregnant as a result of a gang rape. According to Texas law (enacted in 1854 but essentially unchanged since 1856), a woman can have an abortion only if it is performed to save her life. Since Roe's pregnancy was not life-threatening, she sued the state of Texas. In 1970, the unmarried Roe filed a class action suit in federal district court in Dallas. The federal court ruled that the Texas law was unconstitutionally vague and overbroad and infringed upon a person's right to reproductive freedom. The state of Texas appealed to the Supreme Court of the United States. After the case was argued twice before the Court, on January 22, 1973, the Court agreed with the federal district court and ruled that the Texas law was unconstitutional and that not only must states other than Texas permit women to have abortions in cases of rape but in all cases in accordance with the woman's own choice.

Wasn't Roe's rape story a lie?

Yes. Harvard law professor, Laurence Tribe, a proponent of abortion rights, admits: "A decade and a half after the Court handed down its decision in *Roe* v. *Wade* McCorvey explained, with embarrassment, that she had not been raped after all; she made up the story to hide the fact she had gotten 'in trouble' in the more usual way."[41]

Why did the Court rule the way it did in Roe v. Wade? In other words, how did the Court reason in Roe?

Justice Harry Blackmun, who wrote the majority opinion in *Roe*, argued that the Texas' abortion statute, as well as those in other states, is unconstitutional for five major reasons (see chart 2.1):

1. *A woman has a right to privacy based on the Fourteenth Amendment of the Constitution.* Relying on reasoning set forth in the famous contraception case, *Griswold* v. *Connecticut* (381 [1965] 479), in which the Court ruled that state laws prohibiting contraceptive use are unconstitutional, Blackmun argued that no state can prohibit a woman's right to an abortion.

2. *The Fourteenth Amendment does not include the fetus as a person protected by it.* That is to say, since the Fourteenth Amendment makes no clear reference to prenatal life, one cannot apply it to the unborn to say that they are protected as persons under the law.

3. *There is no clear historical consensus on abortion and contemporary prohibitions of abortion are of recent vintage.* According to Blackmun, neither the common law nor most ancient attitudes treated abortion as a form of homicide. The truth is that abortion was forbidden to protect the woman from a dangerous operation.

4. *The purpose of nineteenth-century abortion laws was to protect the woman from a dangerous operation rather than to protect the unborn child.* And since the operation of abortion, according to the Court, was in 1973 relatively safe in comparison to most routine elective surgeries, the nineteenth-century abortion statutes no longer served any purpose.

5. *No one knows when life begins.* As Blackmun puts it, "We need not resolve the difficult question of when life begins. When those trained in the respective disciplines of medicine, philosophy and theology are unable to arrive at any consensus, the judiciary at this point in the development of man's knowledge, is not in a position to speculate as to the answer."[42]

Based on these five points, the Court ruled that state laws prohibiting abortion were unconstitutional.

Chart 2.1[43]
The U. S. Supreme Court's Reasoning in *Roe v. Wade*

Abortion was historically toler-ated and was a common law liberty and the purpose of the nineteenth century statutes was to protect the woman's life and health

There is a constitutionally-protected right of privacy (established by Supreme Court's past decisions)

Abortion is medically safe today

This right of privacy applies to abortion (established by harms and lower court decisions)

There is a basis under our Constitution for a right to abortion

Conclusion: The right to abortion is a currently protected constitutional right.

Thus, there is no longer a purpose for the statutes.

Limitation:	**Counter-Arguments:**
Woman does not have right to do with her body as she pleases	1) Unborn child is a "person" under the Constitution 2) Unborn child is a "person" in other areas of law 3) Unborn child is a living human being at all stages (All rejected by Court)

Holding: Abortion is a constitutional liberty subject to increasing restrictions as pregnancy progresses.

Exception at all stages of pregnancy for woman's life and health ("health" is broadly defined)

Extent of right in practical terms:
Abortion is legal until time of birth

But some scholars say that **Roe v. Wade** *is built on a "foundation of lies." Is this true?*

Yes. Blackmun's opinion was based on some very questionable, if not clearly false, premises. Consider the following points in light of our responses to some of the above questions.

False Premise #1: Jane Roe, the woman who brought the case to court claimed to have been gang raped. She was not gang raped but had willingly engaged in sexual intercourse.

False Premise #2: According to the Court, the nineteenth-century abortion laws were intended to protect the woman from a dangerous medical procedure rather than to protect the unborn child's life. But as we noted above, the nineteenth-century abortion laws were intended to protect both the woman and the unborn child (who was considered a person under the law).

False Premise #3: The Court argued that abortion was not a common-law crime. Hence, its criminal status is of recent vintage. But as we saw above, abortion was a common-law crime, but was not often prosecuted because of the difficulty of proving that the child was alive at the time of the abortion. Because of evidentiary problems, some states initially made abortion a felony only after "quickening," when it can be more clearly proven that the unborn was alive. "Quickening" was never a legal criterion to decide the unborn's full humanity.

False Premise #4: According to the Court, the Fourteenth Amendment of the Constitution supports the right to privacy and hence the right to abortion. But as we noted above, the drafters of the Fourteenth Amendment as well as the other congressmen who voted on it supported prolife legislation either in their own states or in American territories or both. Furthermore, the state laws at that time were strongly antiabortion and asserted the personhood of the unborn. Hence, it is safe to say that it did not even cross their minds that the Fourteenth Amendment could support abortion rights and deny the personhood of the unborn.

False Premise #5: The Court claimed that "no one knows when life begins" and hence it could not decide the question. As we pointed out in chapter 1 and will point out in chapter 3, this claim is empty and is not supported by either scientific facts or sound philosophical reasoning. In addition, if "no one knows when life begins," that is as good a reason as any to *prohibit abortion,* for when an abortion is performed it is *possible* that a person is killed, since "no one knows when life begins." Consider the following example. If one demolishes a building without checking if a person is inside and finds out later that a person was inside and died as a result of the demolition, one is still legally negligent even if one argues that "no one knew that there was a life in there."

False Premise #6: The Court claimed that prohibition of abortion was rather recent in history in Western civilization. But as we noted above, this is clearly false. Ancient attitudes, as well as the common law and the Judeo-Christian tradition, all prohibited abortion at the point at which each believed that individual human life could be recognized. And, of course, as medical science acquired more knowledge about fetal development, legal recognition of the unborn's right to life eventually was extended back to the moment of conception.

Since *Roe* is based on these six false premises as well as others,[44] there is nothing preventing the Court, except maybe political pressure, from overturning this poorly argued Supreme Court decision.

What has the legal community thought about the reasoning in Roe?

They have been for the most part critical, with a few rare exceptions, such as Tribe, who, in his recent book in which he defends the Court's decision with only minor criticisms (*Abortion: The Clash of Absolutes*), seems to be oblivious to the literally hundreds of scholarly articles, books, and reviews, written by both abortion-rights and right-to-life scholars, criticizing the reasoning of Blackmun in *Roe*. Although Tribe does cite Robert Bork's and John Hart Ely's criticisms of *Roe*,[45] these are easy targets and relative lightweights in abortion-scholarship, despite the fact they have a better chance to be pitted against Professor Tribe on "Nightline." In essence, Tribe ignores the hundreds of works which have undermined *Roe*'s historical foundation and presents Blackmun's version of abortion law and history with no hint that the scholarly community has tarred and feathered it.

To get a good idea of what legal scholars think of *Roe*, consider the comments of the editors of the *Michigan Law Review*, who, after surveying the decision in an issue dedicated to a Symposium on the Law and Politics of Abortion, wrote that "the consensus among legal academics seems to be that, whatever one thinks of the holding, the opinion is unsatisfying."[46] Legal scholars Dennis J. Horan and Thomas J. Balch point out that "virtually every aspect of the historical, sociological, medical, and legal arguments Justice Harry Blackmun used to support the *Roe* holdings has been subjected to intense scholarly criticism."[47] This is why Supreme Court Justice Sandra Day

O'Connor has written that "*Roe* . . . is clearly on a collision course with itself. . . . [It has] no justification in law or logic."[48]

But what if Blackmun was right about the history of abortion law, would Roe v. Wade's conclusion—abortion is a constitutional right and the unborn are not legally persons—have followed?

No, since virtually any *moral* conclusion can be "proven" by appealing to historical fact. Take the following analogy employed by Wright State University history professor, Dr. Martin Abargi:

Let us assume a lawsuit seeking to reinstate slavery in the United States is heard before the Supreme Court. Of course, no one would be forced to own slaves; it would be a matter of personal choice. The majority opinion declares that history and what history reveals about man's attitude toward slavery will receive proper emphasis [as Blackmun did with the history of abortion in *Roe*]. The decision notes that laws banning and restricting slavery are of recent origin. Laws proscribing slavery were not of ancient nor common law beginnings. Instead, they were derived from changes occurring in the latter half of the nineteenth century. The Court announces that slavery was practiced by both Greeks and Romans, and that it was resorted to without scruple. Ancient religions did not bar slavery.

There was opposition, but it originated among the Pythagoreans, as well as among the Stoics in the Hellenistic and Roman periods. These were small and isolated groups. No other stratum of Greek or Roman opinion held such views with the same spirit of uncompromising austerity. In fact, most Greek thinkers commended slavery. The apparent rigidity of the Pythagorean and Stoic opposition to slavery can thus be explained in historical context. With the end of antiquity, a decided change took place. Christianity considered slavery unethical, at least in theory, but opposition to slavery was confined primarily to ecclesiastical circles. Slavery in mediaeval Western Europe declined, but it never disappeared. Even the common law recognized slavery. After 1500, slavery revived and in America it became an integral part of the American tradition. The commonly held view that the American Civil War was fought to abolish slavery is a misinterpretation of history. Actually, conflicts over tariff policy and geographical sectionalism were the primary causes of the war. President Lincoln promulgated his Emancipation Proclamation as a wartime punitive measure against the Confederacy, not because he had a commitment to human rights.

Given the division of opinion, the Court concludes, all official bans on slavery, including federal, state, and local laws, must be regarded as an unconstitutional imposition of private religious or ethical beliefs upon the general public. Therefore, all such laws must be immediately repealed.[49]

If you think this analogy is absurd, you are right, for such reasoning is morally shallow and confuses "what is" (how people *actually* act) with "what ought to be" (how people *should* morally act). But if you accept the reasoning of Justice Blackmun in *Roe,* which relies on identical historical arguments for abortion rights, then you must accept Professor Abargi's absurd analogy. Hence, not only are Justice Blackmun's premises false (see above answers), his conclusion does not follow from his premises *even if* they are true.

What other Supreme Court rulings favor abortion?

Subsequent to the 1973 *Roe* decision legalizing abortion the Supreme Court has ruled against spousal or parental consent laws (*Planned Parenthood of Central Missouri* v. *Danforth* [1976]), informed consent for abortion (*City of Akron* v. *Akron Center for Reproductive Health* [1983]), and even laws demanding the humane disposal of the aborted unborn (*City of Akron* v. *Akron Center for Reproductive Health* [1983]).

There is a bitter irony in the rulings against parental consent. According to the law, a child needs parental consent for such things as going with her school class to the zoo but absolutely no consent for such a physical risk to her as having an artificially induced abortion.

More recently (in *Ohio* v. *Akron,* June 25, 1990) the high court ruled that states may (if they wish but not necessarily must) enact laws that demand parental notification (but not consent) before an abortion.

What are the results of the Supreme Court decisions?

The result of the Supreme Court rulings legalizing abortion have yielded a net total of some 1.5 million unborn killed each year since 1973.[50] At that rate by 1993 there will have been 30 million tiny human beings killed by abortion. It is sobering to remember by comparison that Hitler killed 12 million and Stalin 29 million.[51]

When we consider that we lost 1.2 million personnel in all the wars in the history of the United States, it is sobering indeed to realize that we kill that many unborn human beings in less than a year. Likewise, many Americans, such as those who have started organizations like SADD (Students Against Drunk Driving) and MADD (Mothers Against Drunk Driving), are rightfully upset about the deaths which result from drunk driving. About 25,000 such deaths are recorded each year, whereas that many unborn are killed by abortion every six days.

A breakdown of the abortion statistics will help us to get a handle on them:

1.5 million abortions per year
4,300 abortions per day
3 abortions every minute
1 abortion every 20 seconds

John Donne wrote, "Never send to know for whom the bell tolls. It tolls for thee." The bell of death will toll for the unborn 4,300 times today in the United States!

Recent Supreme Court Decisions

Has the Supreme Court
in the recent Webster case overturned Roe?

No. Unfortunately the Supreme Court has not yet overturned *Roe* v. *Wade*, although many on both sides of the *Web-*

ster decision see it as the beginning of the dismantling. Justice Scalia called it the beginning of the process of tearing down *Roe* "doorjamb by doorjamb."[52] However, it was only the first "doorjamb." It simply modified *Roe* and gave the states more power to regulate abortion.

How has the Supreme Court modified Roe?

The *Webster* case (July 3, 1989) was the first significant victory in the Supreme Court for the prolife forces. It modified *Roe* in at least two ways.

First, it rejected *Roe*'s trimester breakdown, which divided pregnancy into three distinct three-month periods. Thus the Court's decision permits legislation on abortion that goes all the way to the moment of conception, whereas *Roe* limited legislation to only the last trimester.

Second, it rejected the demand for government funded abortions, claiming that although a woman still has a legal right to an abortion, the government has no obligation to fund it.

However, the *Webster* court did not overturn *Roe* and rule abortion unconstitutional, nor did it rule on whether there is a right to privacy that overrides the unborn's right to life, which was central to Justice Blackmun's decision in *Roe*.

How do the various Supreme Court justices stand?

When the *Roe v. Wade* decision was handed down (in 1973) the court had a seven-to-two majority in favor of abortion (Justices William Rehnquist and Byron White dissenting). In the 1989 *Webster* decision the Court voted five-to-four in favor of the state's right to regulate abortion. This change was primarily effected by President Reagan's appointees to the Supreme Court who have tended to be more prolife (Justices Sandra Day O'Connor, Atonio Scalia, and Anthony Kennedy).

At present there is not a decisive majority in the Court to completely overturn *Roe*. The Court seems to be split four-to-four with O'Connor being the swing vote. It is not yet known how David Souter will vote on *Roe*, although in the recent decision which said that health clinics receiving federal funds could not counsel women to have abortions, Souter voted with the majority (*Rust* v. *Sullivan* [1991]). Justice Clarence Thomas, who replaced proabortion Justice Thurgood Marshall, shows every indication of being prolife, based on his support of natural law theory. Thus the Court could be 7-2 or 6-3 prolife.

Didn't Supreme Court Justice Harry Blackmun use the viability argument in his dissent in Webster as he did in his majority opinion in Roe v. Wade?

Yes. He argued that the state has only an interest, not an obligation, in protecting the unborn entity when it reaches the point of viability. This is why he said that the state could restrict abortions after the second trimester (approximately twenty-four weeks), but a woman could still get an abortion after this time if the continued pregnancy endangered her health. However, health was so broadly defined in *Doe* v. *Bolton* (1973) as to include "all factors—physical, emotional, psychological, familial, and the woman's age—relevant to the well-being of the patient. All these factors may relate to health."[53] Hence, for all intents and purposes this decision, when combined with *Roe,* legalized abortion on demand.

How did Justice Blackmun argue for the viability criterion?

In his dissenting opinion in the recent *Webster* case (July 3, 1989), Blackmun repeats the viability argument he used in *Roe:*

> For my part, I remain convinced, as six other members of this Court 16 years ago were convinced, that the *Roe* framework, and the viability standard in particular, fairly, sensibly, and effectively functions to safeguard the constitutional liberties of the pregnant woman while recognizing and accommodating the State's interest in potential human life. The viability line reflects the biological facts and truths of fetal development; it marks the threshold moment prior to which a fetus cannot survive separate from the woman and cannot reasonably and objectively be regarded as a subject of rights or interests dis-

tinct from, or paramount to, those of the pregnant woman. At the same time, the viability standard takes account of the undeniable fact that as the fetus evolves into its postnatal form, and as it loses its dependence on the uterine environment, the State's interest in the fetus' potential human life, and in fostering a regard for human life in general, becomes compelling.[54]

Are Justice Blackmun's arguments valid?

Despite being defended by no less an individual than a Supreme Court justice, this argument is completely circular. That is, it assumes what it is trying to prove without providing any reason for that assumption. Blackmun tells us that viability is the time at which the state has interest in protecting potential human life because the fetus has no interests or rights prior to being able to survive outside the womb. But then we are told that viability is the best standard for the state's interest in protecting fetal life, because prior to being able to live outside the womb the fetus has no interests or rights. He does not tell us why viability is important apart from saying that prior to it the fetus has no rights. But then viability is used as the criterion to determine when the fetus has rights. This is completely circular.

Blackmun's argument is no more logically compelling than the one put forth by the zealous Chicago Bull fan who claims that the Bulls are the best team because no team is better. Or the one given by the anti-supernaturalist who argues that miracles can never happen because all the witnesses to miracles are either deceived or deceiving, and the reason he knows that these witnesses are either deceived or deceiving is because miracles can never happen.

What is the meaning of the Supreme Court's **Rust v. Sullivan** *(1991)* decision?

In 1988 the Reagan administration enacted rules which forbade the use of Title X federal money to be used in clinics which provide counseling which present abortion as more than a therapeutic option (i.e., abortion in cases other than when the mother's life is at risk). Abortion-rights groups sued the government, and eventually argued their case before the U.S. Supreme Court.

In *Rust* v. *Sullivan* (1991) the court ruled five (Rehnquist, White, Souter, Scalia, and Kennedy) to four (O'Connor, Blackmun, Marshall, and Stevens) that it is constitutional for the federal government to withhold taxpayer-derived funds from clinics which counsel women to have abortions. Basically the court employed the same reasoning it used when it ruled in *Harris* v. *McRae* 448 U.S. 297 (1980) that the Hyde Amendment, which forbade the federal government to subsidize nontherapeutic abortions with taxpayers' money, is constitutional: the right to an abortion is a negative right—a right which one can choose to exercise without government interference—not a positive one—a right for which the state is obligated to support (such as the right to public education and the right to due process). Thus Chief Justice Rehnquist writes in his majority opinion in *Rust:* "The government has no constitutional duty to subsidize an activity merely because the activity is constitutionally protected and may validly choose to fund childbirth over abortion."[55]

Doesn't the Rust decision limit a physician's First Amendment right to free speech?

Not at all, for the Court did *not* rule on what a physician may or may not say to a patient, but rather, it ruled whether the federal government has a right to define the limits of the sort of speech it wishes to subsidize. A physician has a right to say what he wants but he has no right to expect the government to subsidize it.

It is interesting to note that freedom of religion is also in the First Amendment, yet it would be difficult to find a pro-choicer who would seriously argue that since the federal government does not subsidize our driving to church, by reimbursing our gas money, thereby that it is limiting our First Amendment right to freedom of religion.

The Future of Abortion

How can abortion legally be eliminated in the United States?

Basically, there are four legal ways by which abortion can be stopped in the United States. All of them have merit and should be pursued.

1. *Education.* By educating the populace about the fully human status of the unborn and the moral wrongness of intentionally taking an innocent human life, abortion could be strongly curtailed. Few people believe it is right to intentionally take the life of an innocent human being, but apparently many people are not certain that the unborn are fully human. We are constantly surprised at how little people know about fetal development and the status of the unborn. In fact, it is our experience that many people who are informed of these facts either become ardently prolife or significantly modify their proabortion positions.

2. *Legislation.* Under the present Supreme Court rulings (especially *Webster,* 1989) it is not possible to eliminate all legal abortion. It is possible, however, by passing legislation state by state, to minimize the number of abortions that can be performed legally. For example, parental consent laws and informed consent laws would significantly affect the number of abortions.

3. *Supreme Court reversal.* The Supreme Court could reverse itself on *Roe* v. *Wade* and define abortion as being wrong under the Fifth and Fourteenth Amendments, which protect the right to life. The court has reversed itself in the past and could do so in the future. One more solidly prolife appointee to the high court would provide a clear majority to overturn *Roe.*

4. *A right-to-life amendment.* The only sure way to make abortion illegal and protect the unborn is with a constitutional amendment. Amendments have been proposed, such as this one:

The National Right to Life Committee
Human Life Amendment

Section 1: The right to life is a paramount and most fundamental right of a person.

Section 2: With respect to the right to life, the word "person" as used in this article and in the Fifth and Fourteenth Articles of Amendment to the Constitution of the United States applies to all human beings irrespective of age, health, function, or condition of dependency, including their unborn offspring at every stage of their biologic development.

Section 3: No unborn person shall be deprived of life by any person; provided, however, that nothing in this article shall prohibit a law permitting only those medical procedures required to prevent the death of the mother.

Section 4: The Congress and the several States shall have power to enforce this article by appropriate legislation.[56]

It would take two-thirds majority of all the states to ratify such an amendment. This is very difficult to do, as the Equal Rights Amendment (ERA) people discovered. It does not look like a near-view possibility. The best short-range possibility to make abortion illegal seems to be a Supreme Court reversal of *Roe* v. *Wade* which then allows each state to have its own abortion law.

What are the prospects of a reversal of Roe?

As we stated above, the present Court is divided. A number of the proabortion judges are in or near their eighties. President Bush has already had the opportunity to appoint two, David Souter and Clarence Thomas, the replacement for Thurgood Marshall. He also may have an opportunity to appoint another justice. David Souter has already voted on the prolife side and it is believed that Clarence Thomas will also. Recent decisions by the court show a tendency to dismantle *Roe* "doorjamb by doorjamb," as Justice Scalia put it (in *Webster*).

If Roe is reversed, will abortion go underground?

Not immediately. The question of abortion will be fought state by state in legislatures. In those states where it becomes illegal, some illegal abortions will no doubt be performed. But this is true of all illegal acts. For example, since both child pornography and hiring a hit man are illegal, they must be purchased "underground" or on the black market. But their illegality does prevent a large number of Americans from purchasing them. Concerning abortion, since the vast majority of Americans obey the law, making abortion illegal will severely limit the number of abortions performed. Before abortion became legal in 1973, it is estimated that there were between 100,000 and 200,000 illegal abortions per year.[57] Soon after it became legal, this figure jumped to an astronomical 1.5 million a year. Presumably the figures will soon reverse if abortion is made illegal again.

Do prochoicers believe outlawing abortion will result in thousands of women dying of illegal abortions?

Yes, they do. Anyone who has kept up with the many prochoice demonstrations in the United States could not help but see on prochoice placards and buttons a drawing of the infamous coat hanger. This symbol of the prochoice movement represents the many women who were either harmed or killed because they either performed illegal abortions on themselves (the surgery was performed with a "rusty coat hanger") or went to unscrupulous physicians (or "back alley butchers"). Hence, as the argument goes, if abortion is made illegal, then women will once again be killed, as the 5,000 to 10,000 women per year were killed prior to *Roe*.[58] Needless to say, this argument serves a powerful rhetorical purpose.

Is this a good argument against making abortion illegal?

Not really. First, this argument fails because it commits the fallacy of begging the question. One begs the question when one assumes what one is trying to prove. Another way of putting it is to say that the arguer is reasoning in a circle. For example, if one concludes that the Chicago Bulls are the best team because no team is better, one is not giving any reasons for this belief other than the conclusion one is trying to prove, since to claim that a team is the best team is the same as saying that no team is better. Sometimes this fallacy is committed in a more subtle way. For instance, an unsophisticated Christian may argue that he believes in God because the Bible says that God exists and the Bible is God's Word. Such a Christian is assuming that there is a God who inspired the Bible, but this is the Being whose existence is in question ("Does God exist?"). Hence, by implicitly assuming his conclusion to be true in his appeal to the Bible's authority, this Christian commits the logical fallacy of begging the question.

The question-begging nature of the coat hanger argument is easy to discern. That is to say, only by assuming that the unborn are not fully human does the argument work. For if the unborn are not fully human, then the prochoice advocate has a legitimate concern, as one would have in overturning a law forbidding appendectomies if countless people were needlessly dying of both appendicitis and illegal operations. But if the unborn are fully human, the prochoice argument is tantamount to saying that because people die or are harmed when killing other people, the state should make it safe for them to do so, which would mean that legal abortions result in a greater number of deaths of innocent people than illegal ones. Hence, only by assuming that the unborn are not fully human does the prochoice advocate's argument work. Therefore, the prochoice advocate begs the question.

Do prochoicers recognize the circularity of their argument?

Yes. Even some prochoice advocates, who argue for their position in other ways, admit that the coat hanger/back alley argument is fallacious. For example, prochoice philosopher Mary Anne Warren clearly recognizes that her position on abortion cannot rest on this argument if it is not first demonstrated that the unborn entity is not fully human. She writes that "the fact that restricting access to abortion has tragic side effects does not, in itself, show that the restrictions are unjustified, since murder is wrong regardless of the consequences of prohibiting it."[59]

Is there any other fallacy in the prochoice argument?

Yes. One of the original leaders of the proabortion movement, who has since converted to the prolife position, Dr. Bernard Nathanson, has confessed that he and others in the proabortion movement knowingly fabricated the deaths caused by illegal abortions.

> How many deaths were we talking about when abortion was illegal? In N.A.R.A.L. [National Association for Repeal of Abortion Laws, now known as the National Abortion Rights Action League] we generally emphasized the drama of the individual case, not the mass statistics, but when we spoke of the latter it was always "5,000 to 10,000 deaths a year." I confess that I knew the figures were totally false, and I suppose the others did too if they stopped to think of it. But in the "morality" of the revolution, it was a useful figure, widely accepted, so why go out of our way to correct it with honest statistics? The overriding concern was to get the laws eliminated, and anything within reason that had to be done was permissible.[60]

How many women were dying from illegal abortions?

According to the United States Bureau of Vital Statistics, the best official record available, in the year before *Roe* v. *Wade* thirty-nine died from abortion.[61]

Who were these "back alley butchers"?

Medical doctors. While she was president of Planned Parenthood, Dr. Mary Calderone admitted in a 1960 article in the *American Journal of Public Health* that Dr. Kinsey's research concluded that 84 percent to 87 percent of all illegal abortions were performed by licensed physicians in good standing. Dr. Calderone's own research concluded that "90 percent of all illegal abortions are presently done by physicians."[62]

Will thousands of women die if abortion is made illegal?

Probably not. Because of pharmacological and technological advancement it is extremely unlikely that many women will be harmed if abortion becomes illegal. As Nathanson points out:

> The practice of abortion was revolutionized at virtually the same moment that the laws were revolutionized, through the widespread introduction of suction currettage in 1970. (Even before this, antibiotics and other advances had already dramatically lowered the abortion death rate.) . . . Though it is preferable that this be done by a licensed physician, one can expect that if abortion is ever driven underground again, even non-physicians will be able to perform this procedure with remarkable safety. No woman need die if she chooses to abort during the first twelve weeks of pregnancy. . . . As for self-induced abortion, by thrusting a coat hanger or other dangerous object into the womb, this will also be a thing of the past. Compounds known as prostaglandins can now be used to bring on contractions and expel alpha [the unborn], and would readily be available for do-it-yourself abortions in vaginal suppository form. . . . This may sound rather cynical, but this is what would now happen in practice if abortion were illegal.[63]

While it is not certain that even hundreds of women will die if abortion is made illegal, it is certain that millions of babies will continue to die if it is not made illegal.

The Consequences of Making Abortion Illegal
If abortion was murder, why were not abortionists punished?

As already noted, before 1967 abortion was illegal in all fifty states. It had been illegal in England and America for centuries. Why, then, were not more people punished for performing abortions? This is a good question, and there is a good answer to it. No one should be punished unless the evidence of crime is beyond reasonable doubt—very difficult to produce in the case of abortion.

To prove that anyone is guilty of homicide by abortion, several things must be demonstrated. First, it must be shown that the mother was really pregnant at the time of the abortion, and that the aborted individual (the unborn) was living at the time of the intervention. Shooting a dead corpse is not murder. Second, it must be demonstrated that the intention of the procedure was to take the life of the unborn. Accidental or incidental homicides are not murders. Third, it must be proven that it was the abortion procedure and not something else which took the unborn's life. It is difficult to prove all of these in the case of an abortion. Finally, who was there to press the charges and to be the witnesses? The only witnesses (the mother, doctor, and nurse) were all in favor of abortion. For the above reasons the punishments for performing illegal abortions over the years have been less than consistent with the magnitude of the crime.

If abortion was murder, why were not mothers given capital punishment?

A similar question was posed to presidential candidate George Bush during one of his debates with Michael Dukakis. In response to this question, one must understand that there are two victims of abortion: the unborn and the mother. The unborn has already been deprived of life. We certainly do not need another victim being further destroyed. Women who have had abortions need compassion, not incarceration. They need information, not condemnation. If most pregnant women had the facts they would never have an abortion. Indeed, those who listen to the heartbeats of their unborn babies and see sonograms of their movements almost never opt for abortion. But does not this response treat the unborn as less than human? Not at all, for courts have historically not severely punished the pregnant woman, and in many cases granted her immunity from prosecution because it will help convict the abortionist. Furthermore, the courts presumed, and rightfully so, that a woman seeking an illegal abortion, in many cases, is in a desperate situation. By prudently balancing the unborn's right-to-life, the evil of abortion, and the desperation of the woman, legislators and judges of the past concluded that the best way to stop abortion and uphold the sanctity of human life is to prohibit abortion, prosecute the abortionist, and show compassion for abortion's other victim, the pregnant woman. Undoubtedly, if abortion becomes illegal again the law will once again reflect this sentiment. Another important point to be made is that it is debatable whether capital punishment should be given to guilty murderers; some say yes and some say no.[64] So actually there are two questions here.

If we cannot stop abortion, then why make it illegal?

The fallacy of this reasoning can be easily seen by applying the same logic to some other areas. For example, there are about one million car thefts in the United States every year; should we legalize car theft to control it? About 25,000 people a year are killed by drunk driving; surely, no one would suggest we legalize drunk driving to control it. Likewise, child abuse, rape, and incest are widespread problems in our society. Should we legalize them?

But to repeat, if abortion is made illegal, there will likely be a significant reduction in the number of total abortions, for a vast majority of Americans are law-abiding citizens. Soon after abortion became legal the number of abortions a year jumped to an astronomical figure, and presumably the figures will soon reverse if abortion is made illegal again.[65]

Furthermore, the function of law is not always to reflect the behavior and attitudes of society. Sometimes laws "are also a mechanism by which people are encouraged to do what they know is right, even when it is difficult to do."[66] David C. Reardon points out that "studies in the psychology of morality reveal that the law is truly the teacher. One of the most significant conclusions of these studies shows that existing laws and customs are the most important criteria for deciding what is right and wrong for most adults in a given culture."[67] Citing legal philosopher John Finnis, Nathanson writes that "sometimes the law is ahead of public morality. Laws against dueling and racial bias preceded popular support for these attitudes."[68]

In a recent study, Reardon found that the law influences

women's perceptions of abortion and plays a major role in the decision-making process:

> Given their doubts about the morality of abortion, most aborting women are strongly influenced by the legal status of the abortion option. When asked "Did the knowledge that abortion was legal influence your opinion about the morality of choosing abortion?" 70 percent said that the law had played a major role in their moral perceptions.[69]

What is more interesting is that 75 percent said that they would not have sought an illegal abortion if legal abortions were not available.[70] Given the above studies and statistics, it seems rather clear that legal abortion has resulted in a *ten*-to-*fifteenfold* increase in the total number of abortions performed.

If something is legal, does that not make it moral?

Definitely not. In 1944 German physicians could legally participate in the genocide of Jews. That did not make it moral. In 1857 Americans could legally own slaves. That did not make slavery moral. Actually, something is not moral because it is legal; it should be legal because it is moral. The civil laws should be based on the moral law, not the reverse.

3

Moral Questions

Pluralism, Tolerance, and Religion

Who is to say what is right and wrong?
Is morality not relative?

Morality is not relative. Moral values are objective and can be employed in making moral judgments. There are several reasons why this is true. First, the above questions seem to presuppose that it is morally "wrong" to say that something is objectively right or wrong. But such a claim is self-refuting. That is, one cannot affirm that "it is morally wrong to say that something is objectively right or wrong" without denying it, just as one cannot say that "language cannot accurately convey ideas" without conveying that very idea by language and hence denying that idea.

Second, even people who believe that abortion ought to be permissible believe there is an objective value in human liberty. If they deny such a value, they have no right to oppose anti-abortionists.

Third, there are many moral values that we intuitively know

to be objectively true, and to deny them is irrational. Take the following as examples: (1) Taking innocent human life is morally wrong; (2) truth-telling is good; and (3) people ought to treat others fairly. If these basic moral values are not objectively true, there is no objective basis for our Constitution (equal rights under the law), civil rights (race is an unfair standard by which to judge persons), and criminal law. Prochoice advocates often appeal to all three in their arguments.

Fourth, the moral relativist cannot objectively condemn tyrants of history such as Adolf Hitler and Josef Stalin. In addition, critics of organized religion who espouse moral relativism cannot say, as they do, that the Salem Witch Trials and the Crusades were unjust.[1] In sum, the moral relativist must reluctantly admit that Mother Teresa is no more and no less virtuous than Hitler. We believe these examples are sufficient to show that moral relativism is bankrupt.

Do objective moral values sometimes conflict? And if so, does it disprove the existence of objective values?

Objective values sometimes do conflict, but that certainly does not disprove they do not exist, since not all objective moral values are of equal value. For example, in the case of a pregnancy in which the mother's life is in significant danger unless she gets an abortion, two values conflict: the unborn's right to life and the mother's right to life. For if the woman gets an abortion, her unborn offspring will be killed; if she does not get an abortion, she will forfeit her own life. The way to resolve this supposed conflict is to ask which course of action will be most consistent with the highest good. Since an abortion results in the death of only one life, and if the woman continues with her pregnancy two lives may be snuffed out (both mother's and child's), it follows that to undergo an abortion is the course of action most consistent with the highest good. For it is better that one human being should live rather than two die.

Are prolifers inconsistent in favoring abortion to save the mother's life?

Not at all. The unborn depends on the mother to sustain life, but if abortion were not justified to save the mother's life, two humans might die rather than one. Although the death of one human being is tragic, the death of two is far worse. Therefore, by employing the principle that one should always perform the higher good, the prolifer reasons that the mother's life should be saved even if it means that the unborn will die.

Are prolifers forcing their morality on others?

First of all, it is not only their morality, as though it were not everyone's duty to preserve life. As a matter of fact, it is the prochoicers who want to permit mothers to force their moral perspectives on the unborn by killing them.

Further, this question makes two dubious assumptions: (1) that it is always wrong to impose moral standards on others; and (2) the unborn are not fully human. The first assumption is obviously false. Laws against murdering, smoking crack, stealing, child molesting, and drunk driving all impose a particular moral view on others. The second assumption presupposes that the prochoice position on abortion is correct and that the prolife position is incorrect, but this presupposes that the unborn are not fully human. This is the very controversy under question. Think about it. If the unborn are fully human, a woman who obtains an abortion forces her morality on another, her unborn offspring. On the other hand, if the unborn are not fully human, then the prochoicer correctly claims that the prolifer forces morality on the woman who seeks an abortion. Therefore, only if the prochoice advocate assumes that the unborn are not fully human is he or she correct in claiming that the prolifer is forcing personal morality on others. Hence, the prochoicer begs the question by assuming the unborn are not really human.

Before we can answer the question of who is forcing morality upon whom we must first answer the question of whether or not the unborn are fully human. And since we have already seen that there is overwhelming evidence that the unborn are fully human, the prolifer in fact advocates the protection of life and not the elimination of a woman's freedom. For there can be no legitimate freedom to kill another unjustly.

Furthermore, it is interesting to note that some prochoicers openly advocate the imposition of their moral perspective on prolife taxpayers when they demand the use of their tax dollars to help fund abortions for poor women.[2]

Is the prolife position essentially religious and hence a violation of the separation of church and state?

If this were true, an atheist could not hold the prolife position, which would mean that the prochoicer who says that the prolife position is essentially religious is being intolerant of the prolife atheist. For the prochoicer is in fact saying to the atheist, "You can't be prolife unless you believe in God." But here the prochoicer is forcing a personal view of religion on the atheist.

It is true, however, that the prolife position is consistent with many of the theological beliefs of the great religions.[3] But this does not mean that it is exclusively religious (such as the Christian doctrine of the Trinity) or in violation of the separation of church and state. For example, many prochoice advocates, such as Virginia Ramey Mollenkott,[4] argue that their position is supported by the Hebrew-Christian Scriptures, while many prolife advocates defend their position by appealing to nontheological arguments.[5] Therefore, the prolifer could argue that just because that position may also be found in religious literature, such as the Bible, does not make the prolife position exclusively religious, since that stance is also supported by many nontheological arguments that have both philosophical and scientific plausibility.

Should we legislate moral principles found in religious books?

If one could not put into law moral values that are consistent with religious doctrines, then our society would have to get rid of laws prohibiting crimes such as robbery and murder simply because such actions are forbidden by the Hebrew-Christian Bible. Moreover, some public policies, such as elimination of nuclear testing and civil rights legislation, which are supported by many priests and ministers who find these policies consistent with and supported by their theological convictions, would have to be abolished simply because they are believed by these clergymen to be in agreement with their particular religious viewpoints. In fact, most good laws, including those against murder, rape, and theft, are based on moral principles in religions. So, if one could not base laws on moral principles in religions, there would be very few, if any, good laws.

Even abortion rights advocate Laurence H. Tribe, a Harvard law professor, agrees with this perspective:

> But as a matter of constitutional law, a question such as this [abortion], having an irreducibly moral dimension, cannot properly be kept out of the political realm merely because many religions and organized religious groups inevitably take strong positions on it. . . . The participation of the religious groups in political dialogue has never been constitutional anathema in the United States. Quite the contrary. The values reflected in the constitutional guarantees of freedom of religion and political expression argue strongly for the inclusion of church and religious groups, and of religious beliefs and arguments, in public life.[6]

Rape
Should abortions be allowed in cases of rape?

No. Since hardship does not justify homicide, the real issue is whether the unborn are fully human. And if they are, the murder of the child is not justified by the rape of the mother. Appealing to pity for the rape victim does not avoid the question of justice for the abortion victim, the unborn child.

The evil of rape is not removed by abortion. Abortion just compounds the evil by adding another. Killing the unborn will not solve the rape problem. The guilty rapist should be punished, not the innocent baby.

Furthermore, even if abortion were morally justified in extreme cases such as rape, this would not justify the abortion on demand which was permitted by the *Roe* v. *Wade* (1973) and *Doe* v. *Bolton* (1973) Supreme Court decisions. After all, if the prochoice advocate would still support a woman's choice to abortion even if pregnancy due to rape never occurred, then appeals to rape are not relevant to the prochoice cause, since prochoicers argue that abortion is permissible in *all* cases. Arguing that abortion on demand is justified because women may need abortions if they are raped is like arguing that one is justified in driving 90 mph all the time because there could be a rare occasion when one may have to rush one's spouse or child to the hospital. Showing an exception does not prove a general rule.

Are there other things I should know about rape and abortion?

First, a number of famous people have confessed that they were born of rape. The famous black singer, Ethel Waters, is among them. All are grateful that their mothers did not choose abortion. Even Seneca, the famous Roman thinker who believed in the Stoic philosophy that supported abortion, praised his mother for not aborting him.

Second, Dr. Michael Bauman, a professor of theology and culture at Hillsdale College, has made the observation that "a civilized nation does not permit the victim of a crime to pass a death sentence on the criminal's offspring. To empower the victim of a sex offense to kill the offender's child is an even more deplorable act than the rape that conceived it. The child conceived by rape or incest is a victim, too. In America, we do not execute victims."[7]

Is there any way to avoid pregnancy after rape?

Conception can be avoided in all rape cases (since conception does not immediately occur) if a rape victim gets immediate medical treatment. It is also noteworthy that, because of the understandable physical and psychological trauma a rape entails, pregnancy from rape is extremely rare, well under 1 percent. However, in those cases when rape results in pregnancy, about half of the victims want to have the baby. If the mother does not want the baby, she can release the child for adoption.

How do pregnant rape victims fare psychologically?

Professor Stephen Krason points out that "psychological studies have shown that, when given the proper support, most pregnant rape victims progressively change their attitudes about their unborn child from something repulsive to someone who is innocent and uniquely worthwhile."[8] The prolife advocate believes that government, church, and community agencies should lend support to the rape victim "to make it as easy as possible for her to give up her baby for adoption, if she desires. Dealing with the woman pregnant from rape, then, can be an opportunity for us—both as individuals and as a society—to develop true understanding and charity. Is it not better to try to develop these virtues than to countenance an ethic of destruction as the solution?"[9]

Explain in greater detail why pregnancy resulting from rape is unlikely.

There are many reasons. First, the conditions of the attack are not conducive to pregnancy. Second, a woman can conceive only a few days out of the month. Third, there is evidence that severe emotional trauma, such as forcible rape, may prevent ovulation. Fourth, emotional trauma may release hormones which set up a barrier to pregnancy. Fifth, there is evidence to show that over half of all rapists are sexually dysfunctional at the time of the attack. Considering all these factors, it is very difficult to conceive by forcible rape.

What percentage of pregnant raped women keep their babies?

About half of all victims pregnant by rape elect to keep their babies. Since the number of women who become pregnant by criminal rape is well under 1 percent, that leaves us with a problem in less than one half of 1 percent of all rape cases.

Must raped women keep their babies?

No. If the mother cannot bear the thought of raising the child, she can let someone else do it. Thousands of couples are waiting to adopt a baby. Adoption is better than abortion.

Philosophy and Moral Reasoning
How do philosophers and ethicists argue in favor of abortion rights?

Philosophers and ethicists have put forth many different arguments to defend abortion rights.[10] However, they generally argue that the unborn entity is genetically a human being, but until some stage of development before or after birth it is not a person with a full right to life. For example, some philosophers argue that prior to achieving a certain function—such as self-consciousness, sentience, brainwaves, or the ability to do complex problems—the unborn is a human being but not a person. Philosophers disagree as to which characteristics make one a person, with some appealing to sentience while others appeal to self-consciousness or other functions. Prolife ethicists do not believe that personhood can be reduced to function.

Are there problems considering the unborn humans but not persons?

Yes, there are very serious difficulties. First of all, this distinction between persons and humans may be legally irrelevant. Baby eagles are not persons, yet the government has made laws protecting them. Even if the unborn were only potential persons, not actual ones, there is no reason why laws should not be made to protect them. Indeed, there are good reasons why we should protect them, since being born is their only chance to become adult persons.

Second, making a distinction between humans and persons is arbitrary. There is no essential grounds for declaring humans nonpersons, only functional ones. To consider some humans nonpersons because they lack certain functions is to discriminate on the basis of ability, rather than to discern on the basis of their true nature.

Third, to make the distinction between humans and persons on the grounds they lack certain functions would justify killing children and adults who have lost these same functions. For example, adults sometimes suffer brain damage or lose consciousness, but they are still persons while they are temporarily comatose, the sleeping, and the unconscious. They are all persons even when not functioning as such.

Fourth, determining personhood by function confuses function with essence. Function is a result of essence, not the reverse. There is no essential difference between a human being and a human person, only a functional one. For example, no one doubts that day-old humans have fewer current abilities than day-old cows. But this does not convince us that they have less inherent worth. Thus, as philosopher A. Chadwick Ray notes, this means that "the difference in status is plausibly explained . . . only with reference to the children's humanity."[11]

Fifth, there is no agreement on when personhood begins after conception. Some say it begins at implantation (two weeks after conception); others say later at animation, when the mother feels the baby move; still others insist it is at viability, when the baby can live outside the womb. In the *Roe* decision the Supreme Court placed it at birth. But some philosophers would say it begins at the point of self-consciousness, which is not until the second year after birth. So once this arbitrary distinction between being human and being a person is made, there is no point of agreement on when personhood begins. All types of brutality, therefore, can be justified.

Sixth, if one is not a person until possession of self-consciousness, then infanticide is justified up to about a year and a half after birth. For it is not until this point that self-consciousness develops in human beings. This means that tiny, defenseless human beings could be killed before they were two years of age, simply because they were declared nonpersons. One can almost hear Rachel weeping for her children.

Finally, even corporations are considered persons under the Fourteenth Amendment. In the *Santa Clara* v. *Sanford* case (1886) the United States Supreme Court was unanimous in its declaration:

> The court does not wish to hear arguments on the question whether the provision in the Fourteenth Amendment to the Constitution, which forbids a state to deny any person within its jurisdiction the equal protection of the laws, applies to these corporations. We are all of the unanimous opinion that it does.[12]

If even corporations are persons under the Constitution, then surely unborn humans should be given the same constitutional rights.

But doesn't the fetus differ from the temporarily comatose, the sleeping, and the unconscious insofar as the latter functioned as persons in the past and will probably do so in the future whereas the fetus will probably do so in the future but has not done so in the past?

Yes, but this fact does not count against the unborn's full personhood.

First, to claim that a person, such as one who is comatose, was once functional, has become nonfunctional, and then will return to a state of function is to assume that there is some underlying personal unity to this individual which makes it intelligible for us to say that the person who will return to function as a person is the *same* person who was functional prior to becoming nonfunctional. But this would mean that personal function is a sufficient but not a necessary condition for personhood. It follows then that it is incorrect to say that a person comes into existence when function arises, but rather, it does make sense to say that a fully human entity is someone who has the natural inherent capacity to give rise to personal function. A prefunctional unborn human being *does* have this capacity. As John Jefferson Davis points out: "Our ability to have conscious experiences and recollections arises out of our personhood; the basic metaphysical reality of personhood precedes the unfolding of the conscious abilities inherent in it."[13] Therefore, an ordinary unborn human entity is a person, and hence, fully human.

Second, philosopher A. Chadwick Ray points out that to exclude many of the unborn from the class of the fully human because they have not functioned as persons "in the past" is "*ad hoc* and counterintuitive." Ray asks us to "consider the treatment of comatose patients. We would not discriminate against one merely for rarely or never having been sentient in the past while another otherwise comparable patient had been sentient. (That the presentient patient might have more catching up to do than the other is a difference that can be overcome in this thought experiment by our imagining our artificially equipping the disadvantaged one with skills and memories.) In such cases, potential counts for everything."[14]

In order to fully appreciate Ray's point, consider the example provided by University of Rhode Island philosophy professor, Dr. Stephen Schwarz:

> Imagine a case of two children. One is born comatose, and he will remain so until the age of nine. The other is healthy at birth, but as soon as she achieves the concept of a continuing self for a brief time, she, too, lapses into a coma, from which she will not emerge until she is nine. Can anyone seriously hold that the second child is a person with a right to life, while the first child is not? In one case, self-awareness will come only after nine years have elapsed, in the other, it will return. In both cases, self-awareness will grow and develop. Picture the two unconscious children lying side by side. Almost nine years have passed. Would it not be absurd to say that only one of them is a person, that there is some essential, morally relevant, difference between them. Imagine someone about to kill both of them. Consistent with his theory, [the one who denies the unborn personhood because they have not functioned as persons "in the past"] he would have to say: "You may kill the first, for he is not a person. He is

human only in the genetic sense, since he has no history of
functioning as a person. You may not kill the second, since
she does have such a history." If this distinction is absurd while
applied to the two born human beings, is it any less absurd
when applied to two human beings, one born (asleep in bed),
the other preborn (sleeping in the womb)?[15]

We agree with Schwarz when he concludes that "when it
comes to functioning as a person, there is no moral difference between 'did, but does not' (the sleeping adult) and
'does not, but will' (the small child)."[16]

But aren't there some abortion-rights philosophers who argue that even if the fetus is a person, abortion is still permissible?

Yes. They argue that the unborn's presence in the pregnant woman's body entails a conflict of rights. Just as one
does not have a right to use another's kidney if one's kidney
has failed, the unborn child, although a person, does not
have a right to life so strong that it forces the pregnant
woman to forfeit her right to personal bodily autonomy.
Hence, a pregnant woman's removal of a fetus from her body,
even though it will probably result in its death, is no more
immoral than another person's refusal to donate his kidney
to another in need of one, even though such a refusal will
most likely result in the death of the prospective recipient.

The most famous and influential argument of this type is
the one presented by Judith Jarvis Thomson, a philosophy
professor at the Massachusetts Institute of Technology.[17]

Has the Supreme Court ever relied on this sort of argument?

No. In neither *Roe* v. *Wade* nor *Doe* v. *Bolton* nor any other
decision did the Court rely on Thomson's argument. In fact,
Justice Blackmun admits in *Roe* that the unborn's personhood
makes or breaks abortion rights: "If this suggestion of personhood [of the unborn] is established, the appellant's case

[i.e., a woman's right to abortion], of course, collapses, for the fetus' right to life is then guaranteed specifically by the [Fourteenth] Amendment."[18]

This does not mean, however, that the Court may not rely on Thomson's argument in the future. For instance, in his recent book, Harvard law professor Laurence Tribe, whose influence on the Court's liberal wing is well known, suggests that the Court should have used Thomson's argument. He writes: ". . .[P]erhaps the Supreme Court's opinion in *Roe,* by gratuitously insisting that the fetus *cannot* be deemed a 'person,' needlessly insulted and alienated those for whom the view that the fetus is a person represents a fundamental article of faith or a bedrock personal commitment. . . . The Court should have instead said: Even if the fetus *is* a person, our Constitution forbids compelling a woman to carry it for nine months and become a mother."[19]

How does Thomson argue for her position?

In short, Thomson argues that even if the unborn is a person, it does not follow that the pregnant woman must be forced to use her bodily organs to sustain its life. She uses the following story—sometimes called the "story of the plugged-in violinist"—in order to make her point:

You wake up in the morning and find yourself back to back in bed with an unconscious violinist. A famous unconscious violinist. He has been found to have a fatal kidney ailment, and the Society of Music Lovers has canvassed all the available medical records and found that you alone have the right blood type to help. They have therefore kidnapped you, and last night the violinist's circulatory system was plugged into yours, so that your kidneys can be used to extract poisons from his blood as well as your own. The director of the hospital now tells you, "Look we're sorry the Society of Music Lovers did this to you—we would never have permitted it if we had known. But still, they did it, and the violinist now is plugged into you. To unplug you would be to kill him. But never mind, it's only for nine months. By then he will have recovered from his ailment, and can safely be unplugged from you." Is it morally incumbent on you to accede to this situation? No doubt it would be very nice of you if you did, a great kindness. But do you *have* to accede to it? What if it were not nine months, but nine years? Or still longer? What if the director of the hospital says, "Tough luck, I agree, but you've now got to stay in bed, with the violinist plugged into you, for the rest of your life. Because remember this. All persons have a right to life, and violinists are persons. Granted you have a right to decide what happens in and to your body, but a person's right to life outweighs your right to decide what happens in and to your body. So you cannot ever be unplugged from him." I imagine that you would regard this as outrageous. . . .[20]

What's wrong with this argument?

There are numerous problems with this argument which have been pointed out in great detail in the scholarly literature.[21] The following three, which should suffice, are among these many criticisms.

First, Thomson mistakenly infers that all true moral obligations to one's children are voluntary. That is, one does not have an obligation to one's children unless one volunteers for such a role. But consider the following story. Suppose an unmarried couple has sex, and although using many forms of birth control (condom, the Pill, etc.), the woman nevertheless conceives. Suppose the woman chooses not to abort but the father is unaware of this decision (and under current Supreme Court rulings, the father has no right to be informed or take part in the decision; see for example, *Planned Parenthood of Missouri* v. *Danforth*, 428 U.S. 52 [1976]). After the child's birth the mother asks the father for child support. Since he declines, she seeks legal action. Although he certainly did not *volunteer* for fatherhood (as evidenced by his "enlightened" use of birth control), all child support laws in the United States would demand that he accept responsibility for his child's livelihood *precisely because* of his relationship to this child.[22] As Michael Levin points out, "All child-support laws make the parental body an indirect resource for the child. If the father is a construction worker, the state will intervene unless some of his calories he extends lifting equipment go to providing food for his children."[23]

Consequently, if the born child has a natural claim on her father's body, why does not the unborn child, who Thomson assumes for the sake of argument is a full human person, have a natural claim on her mother's body as well? There is no doubt that a court will not force a parent to donate a kidney to his dying child or force a pregnant woman to carry her child to term when there is a good chance that continuing the pregnancy will kill her or seriously impair her health. But these types of "dependence" on the parent's body are highly unusual and differ radically from ordinary pregnancy, since donating one's own kidney and giving up one's life are not part of the ordinary obligations associated with the *natural* and *ordinary* process of human development and parental nurturing. Similarly, the violinist's need for a kidney does not warrant a claim on the music lover's body, since there is not the ordinary obligation on the part of the music lover as there is for the mother for her child in the normal process of growth and development.

Second, Thomson's argument, which is supposed to be consistent with feminism, is actually quite anti-feminist. In response to a similar argument from a woman's control over her own body, one feminist publication asks the question, "What kind of control are we talking about? A control that allows for violence against another human being is a macho, oppressive kind of control. Women rightly object when others try to have that kind of control over them, and the movement for women's rights asserts the moral right of women to be free from the control of others." After all, "abortion involves violence against a small, weak, and dependent child. It is macho control, the very kind the feminist movement most eloquently opposes in other contexts."[24]

Third, Thomson's position flies directly in the face of well-established family law, which presupposes parental responsibility of a child's welfare. According to legal scholars Dennis J.

Horan and Burke J. Balche, "All fifty states, the District of
Columbia, American Samoa, Guam, and the U.S. Virgin
Islands have child abuse and neglect statutes which provide
for the protection of a child who does not receive needed
medical care." They go on to point out that "a review of cases
makes it clear that these statutes are properly applied to
secure emergency medical treatment and sustenance (food
or water, whether given orally or through intravenous or nasogastic tube) for children when parents, with or without the
acquiescence of physicians, refuse to provide it."[25] Consider
the following example. In a case in New York, in which parents failed to provide medical care to a child with leukemia,
the court ruled that this constituted neglect. "The parent . . .
may not deprive a child of lifesaving treatment, however well-
intentioned. Even when the parents' decision to decline necessary treatment is based on constitutional grounds, such as
religious beliefs, it must yield to the State's interests, as parens
patriae, in protecting the health and welfare of the child."[26]
Consequently, "courts have uniformly held that a parent has
the legal responsibility of furnishing his dependent child with
adequate food and medical care."[27]

There is no doubt that these child-protection laws reflect
our deepest moral intuitions about parental responsibility
and the helplessness of infants and small children. And without these moral scruples—which Thomson's view of radical
autonomy can but only undermine—the protection of children and the natural bonds and filial obligations associated
with ordinary family life, which transcend any "brave new
notions" of a socially contracted "voluntaristic" family
(Thomson's view), will become a thing of the past.

Can someone be personally against abortion and yet be prochoice?

It is possible, but it is morally schizophrenic. For example,
some politicians, such as New York Governor Mario Cuomo
and Nevada Senator Richard Bryan, claim that they are personally against abortion, but that they will not try to legally pre-

vent others from obtaining one. The problem with this claim is that we are not told the reason why such politicians are personally against abortion. Our guess is that the politicians are probably personally against abortion for the same reason that most prolifers are: The unborn are fully human and have all the rights which go along with such a status. Now, this makes the politicians' personal opposition and public permission of abortion terribly inconsistent, since the reason why they are personally opposed to abortion is the same reason why they should be against legal permission of it, namely, that a being which they believe is fully human has a full right to life.

What would we think of a man who claimed to be personally against the genocide of a particular minority group, such as Jews, but if others considered Jews subhuman he would not force his morality on their freedom of choice to participate in the genocide? The fact is that some personal views warrant public action, while some others such as a personal dislike for spinach, do not.

What if having a child interferes with a woman's career?

If the unborn are fully human, then abortion for the sake of a woman's career is morally repugnant. For what would we think of a mother who executed her three-year-old because he obstructed her opportunity to advance in her career? We would rightfully judge such an act to be morally reprehensible. Hence, unless the prochoice advocates can show that the unborn are not fully human, the appeal to career advancement is irrelevant. Achievement of social status can never justify homicide.

Is it true that abortion-rights activists are sexist, because they believe that without abortion (a form of corrective surgery) women are naturally inferior to men?

Yes, we think so, even though most abortion-rights proponents claim to be *feminists*. Consider the following statements by leading abortion-rights activists:

Kate Michelman, president of the National Abortion Rights
Action League:

We have to remind people that abortion is the guarantor of a
woman's . . . right to participate fully in the social and political
life of society.[28]

Nancy Erickson, J.D., legal scholar:
This right [to abortion], of necessity *must* be absolute, for if
it is not, women will never truly have the ability to plan and
to control their own lives.[29]

Laurence Tribe, J.D., professor of law, Harvard Law School:
Affluent professional women . . . see access to abortion . . . as
a *right* women must have *if they are to achieve equal respect and
an equal capacity to control their own destinies* [second emphasis
added].[30]

Justice Harry Blackmun, U.S. Supreme Court:
[T]he plurality [in *Webster*] discards a landmark case of the last
generation [*Roe* v. *Wade*], and casts into darkness the hopes
and visions of every woman in this country who had come to
believe that the Constitution guaranteed her the right to exercise some control over her unique ability to bear children. The
plurality does so either oblivious or insensitive to the fact that
millions of women, and their families, have ordered their lives
around the right to reproductive choice, and that this right
has become vital to the full participation of women in the economic and political walks of American life.[31]

This is why some feminists who oppose abortion ask the
following question to those who argue like Michelman,
Erickson, Tribe, and Blackmun: "How can women ever lose
their second-class status as long as they are seen as requiring
surgery in order to avoid it?" But, as these feminists point out,
"The premise of the question is the premise of male domi-
nation throughout the millennia—that it was nature which
made men superior and women inferior. Medical technology
[i.e., abortion] is offered as the solution to achieve equality;
but the premise is wrong. Nature doesn't provide for inequal-
ity, and it's an insult to women to say women must change

their biology in order to fit into society."[32] If pregnant women are discriminated against and barriers are created to prevent them from participating fully in political and social life, it is the fault of an imperfect society which must change its ways, for we know that pregnant women are perfectly normal. Can you imagine trying to end prejudice against African-Americans by suggesting a pigmentation operation? It would rightfully be perceived as insulting.

4

Social Questions

Human Rights

Do modern human rights declarations protect the unborn?

Yes. The American Convention on Human Rights declared: "Every person has the right to have his life respected. This right shall be protected by law and, in general, from the moment of conception. No one shall be arbitrarily deprived of his life" (Nov. 22, 1969).[1] The Inter-American Convention on Human Rights also affirmed that life shall be protected by law "and, in general, from the moment of conception."[2]

Are any unborn animals protected by law?

Yes. In the United States baby eagles are protected by law. It is a federal offense to kill baby eagles or destroy their eggs.

Are unborn humans protected by law?

No. The Supreme Court's *Roe* and *Doe* decisions (1973) declared that unborn humans can be killed at any time up to birth for virtually any reason, provided the killing is done by a licensed physician. Although the court allowed some abortions only when the life and health of the mother is threatened, these were defined so broadly that virtually anything, including stress brought on by pregnancy, is included under this category. (For a more detailed presentation of the meaning of these decisions, see chapter 2.)

If the unborn are human, why are they not counted in the census?

Native Americans are not counted in the census either, but they are human! Once slaves were only counted 3/5 of a person for the purposes of the census, but they were still 100 percent human. The truth is that "if you can't see them, you can't count them." The unborn cannot be seen. There may be twins or triplets in a mother's womb. Furthermore, a census counts only the humans who have been born, not the number who are human.

Maternal Health

What percent of mothers die in childbirth?

Fewer than one in ten thousand mothers die in childbirth.[3] It is one of the safest procedures in the country. Translating this statistic to a percentage, a woman has a 99.99 percent chance of surviving childbirth; the risk of maternal death is extremely small. Even so, most mothers want to have healthy babies and feel that it is worth the risks in giving birth.

Has legalizing abortion decreased maternal deaths from abortion in the United States?

Not really. The number of deaths from abortion have been decreasing steadily since the 1940s due to improved medical conditions. The legality of abortion had no real effect on the downward curve. In 1940 there were 1,679 maternal deaths from abortion; in 1950 there were 316 (penicillin made a big difference). By 1960 there were 289, and by 1970 there were 128 maternal deaths from abortion. In 1981 there were nine deaths (United States Bureau of Vital Statistics Center for Disease Control).[4]

What are the AMA figures on maternal death? Is abortion safer than childbirth?

The American Medical Association claims that the chances of a woman dying in childbirth are nine in 100,000 while the chances of her dying when an abortion is performed before the thirteenth week of pregnancy are one in 100,000, increasing to three in 100,000 after the thirteenth week.[5]

Although it is technically true that abortion is safer than childbirth, if one assumes that the AMA statistics are accurate, the difference of risk between abortion and childbirth is statistically insignificant. Consider the following. If the chances of dying in childbirth are nine in 100,000, then a woman's chance of survival are 99.991 percent. If the chances of dying during an abortion are one in 100,000, then a woman's chance of survival are 99.999 percent. But if common sense and basic knowledge of statistics tell us anything, it is that a 00.008 difference between two percentages (in this case, 99.991 percent and 99.999 percent) is statistically insignificant.

Is there any reason to challenge these figures?

There is good reason to call them into question. David C. Reardon, in his study on the physical and psychological effects of abortion on women and their families,[6] concludes that the prochoice claim that abortion is safer than childbirth is based on dubious statistical studies, for "accurate statistics are scarce, because the reporting of complications is almost entirely at the option of abortion providers. In other words, abortionists are in the privileged position of being able to hide any information which might damage their reputation and trade." And because "federal court rulings have sheltered the practice of abortion in a 'zone of privacy,' any laws which attempt to require that deaths and complications resulting from abortion be recorded, much less reported, are unconstitutional."[7] This means that only data which are voluntarily reported are recorded and used to formulate the number of deaths and complications due to abortion. This, of course, is like asking the fox how many chickens are in the chicken coop. Reardon concludes:

> Complication records from outpatient clinics are virtually inaccessible, or nonexistent, even though these clinics provide the vast majority of all abortions. Even in Britain, where reporting requirements are much better than the United States, medical experts believe that less than 10 percent of abortion complications are actually reported to government health agencies.[8]

Fetal Burial

Is it legal to perform religious burial for aborted babies?

No. The American Civil Liberties Union has argued that since they are not human persons, we cannot insist on a religious burial for them. Sadly, the courts have agreed. In a 1982 case, 16,000 aborted babies were found in a storage container in California. The ACLU opposed any religious service or planned burial for them. The court agreed and allowed only a civil ceremony. Yet in the same state (and others) there are dog and cat cemeteries. The ACLU has not been known to protest their burial. The truth is that in America today dogs are treated like human beings and human beings are treated like dogs.

Does the lack of burial rites show the unborn are not human?

Some proabortionists have argued that the general lack of burial rites for the unborn indicates that society does not really consider them human. This does not follow for several reasons. First, some people do practice burial rites for the unborn. Second, when religious burial rites are insisted on, there is often opposition by proabortion groups such as the ACLU (see previous question). Third, burial is a social practice, and many perform this religious rite only for those who have entered into society (by birth). And fourth, if having a burial rite performed for oneself is a necessary condition for humanness, then people who were killed in the holocaust and in other atrocities or accidents who did not have the benefit of burial rites were not fully human. But this is absurd.

Why are baptismal certificates not given to the unborn?

The infant baptismal ceremony is considered (by those who practice it) not as a sign of entrance into the human family but as a sign of entrance into a spiritual family. If baptism signified the beginning of humanity, Catholic and Lutheran children would be human but Baptist and Salvation Army children would not. No one believes that.

Child Abuse
Does abortion eliminate unwanted children who will be abused?

No. There is no real evidence of this. But even if there were such evidence, the fact that a practice may eliminate a certain problem does not mean it is morally right. For instance, killing women on their wedding day would eliminate years of wife beating, and executing teenagers would eradicate death by old age. Such social "cures" are worse than the diseases they try to eliminate.

Although there is no positive evidence of a direct link between legalized abortion and the elimination of child abuse, positive evidence exists that there is no connection between unwanted pregnancy and child abuse. According to one study, 90 percent of all battered children were wanted pregnancies.[9] And some researchers have pointed out that adopted children—who were no doubt wanted by their adoptive parents—are abused more frequently than the children who live with their biological parents.[10] Reports of child abuse have gone up as much as 500 percent since abortion was legalized. Apparently, the disregard for life before birth is being carried over to life after birth as well.[11]

Furthermore, whether or not a person is unwanted is irrelevant to his or her right to protection from being killed by

others. For instance, the homeless are unwanted, but killing
them to eliminate the problem of homelessness is morally
repugnant. Not being wanted is an inadequate criterion for
judging the moral value of a particular human life.

Are there any laws against fetal abuse?

No, there are not. Abortion may be performed in any way,
as long as it does not threaten the mother's life and health.
One way is to extract the tiny babies by crushing them to
pieces with a powerful vacuum machine. Another is to dis-
sect the babies into pieces with a sharp instrument. If the
bones are developed, a pliers-like instrument is used to crush
the skull. Sometimes salt is injected for large babies who
inhale it only to have their lungs burned and their bodies
charred by it. Sometimes the babies are taken alive (by C section) and must be killed by suffocation or starvation; this is
called hysterotomy. All were made legal by the Supreme
Court's *Roe* v. *Wade* decision (1973). For more on abortion
methods, see chapter 1.

What is the irony in such laws?

The irony is that children can sue their parents for abusing them after birth, but parents may kill their children
before their birth. This is not the only irony. Mothers of crack
babies, infants born with an addiction to crack cocaine, are
being prosecuted for "child abuse" in some jurisdictions
because of the fact that the cocaine entered the babies' systems while in the mothers' wombs.

Handicapped Children[12]
Why should someone have to be born handicapped?

Let's ask the handicapped. Why do we not see them march-
ing in prochoice rallies with signs such as "Better Aborted
than Handicapped"? In fact, not a single national organization of parents of handicapped children is on record in favor
of abortion.[13] Here again, it is apparently not the handi-

capped nor their parents who want abortions, but those who are not handicapped who want abortions for the handicapped. Since it is wrong to kill the born handicapped, the question really is, "Are the unborn human persons?" Justifying abortion by appealing to the unborn's handicap begs the question as to its humanity.

Do the handicapped live miserable lives?

No. In fact, studies show that there is no significant difference in degree of life satisfaction between handicapped and nonhandicapped. In fact, the suicide rate is lower for the handicapped.[14]

Are not those with very low IQs subhuman?

According to proabortionist Joseph Fletcher, those with IQs under 20 (or perhaps 40) should be declared nonhuman. How about 60? Where do we draw the line? Who determines? This is discrimination based on intelligence.

Fetal Health

Should a Down syndrome (mongoloid) baby be aborted for "health" reasons?

No. We do not kill children for health reasons, and being mongoloid is no reason to kill little children in the womb. We should treat the patient's condition, not kill the patient.

Consider the following true story related by the world-famous geneticist, Dr. Jerome LeJeune, who discovered the chromosomal pattern of Down syndrome.

Many years ago, my father was a Jewish physician in Braunau, Austria. On one particular day, two babies had been delivered by one of his colleagues. One was a fine, healthy boy with a strong cry. His parents were extremely proud and happy. The other was a little girl, but her parents were extremely sad, for she was a mongoloid baby. I followed them both for almost fifty years. The girl grew up, living at home, and was finally destined to be the one who nursed her mother through a very long and lingering illness after a stroke. I do not remember her name. I do, however, remember the boy's name. He died in a bunker in Berlin. His name was Adolf Hitler.[15]

To abort Down syndrome children for medical or social reasons is a great mistake. They are just as human as perfectly healthy children—and often much more humane. (For further elaboration on the question of handicapped children, see chapter 1.

Prolifers

Should prolifers adopt the babies they don't want aborted?

This question really asserts that unless the prolife woman is willing to help bring up the children she does not want aborted, she has no right to prevent a woman from having an abortion. But this is a very strange moral judgment. Imagine all the unusual precepts that would result if we applied the same reasoning in other moral situations: Unless I am willing to marry my neighbor's wife, I cannot prevent her husband from beating her; unless I am willing to adopt my neighbor's daughter, I cannot prevent her mother from abusing her; unless I am willing to hire former slaves for my business, I cannot say that the slave owner is morally wrong in owning slaves.

The problem with these assertions, as with the one about abortion, is that they are claiming that one cannot make a correct moral judgment about others unless one is willing to do something. My unwillingness or willingness to adopt the unborn child of a pregnant woman who seeks an abortion does not make the act of abortion any more or less moral. In the same way, the fact that in Nazi Germany a non-Jewish German was unwilling to hide Jews from certain death in the concentration camps does not justify the holocaust.

Does this prolife response assume the unborn are humans?

Yes, but only to make the point that the prochoicer likewise assumes that the unborn are not fully human. For if the unborn are fully human, the prolifer's unwillingness to adopt unborn children would certainly not justify killing them. On the other hand, suppose that the unborn are not fully human, and the prolifer is nevertheless willing to adopt the fetus after it is born. Would this make the woman who is carrying this fetus immoral if she decided to abort? We think not. Therefore, the decision on whether abortion is moral or immoral cannot be based on the character of prolifers, but on the humanness of the unborn.

In terms of practical action, what have prolifers done?

In terms of practical action, prolifers have done much to help those women who find themselves in dire straits. Many prolifers adopt children, support and run homes for unwed mothers, provide economic aid to those poor women who decide to keep their babies, and counsel women who have crisis pregnancies (such as in Christian Action Council's Crisis Pregnancy Centers).[16] James T. Burtchael, in his book *Rachel Weeping*, cites an informal survey of the members of the Indiana Right-to-Life Organization, who were asked the question: Do "those who serve as typical activists in the movement live up to such a call," or are they "in fact, social reactionaries?" To answer this question, "they canvassed their most active members, those who came to the regional convention (229 persons),"[17] and discovered the following:

81 distributed food and clothing

nearly one-fourth donated blood regularly

37 worked in support groups (drugs, alcohol, suicide)

17 worked in programs for abused women

28 worked in hospitals, clinics, and hospices

38 worked in volunteer fire and police departments and neighborhood associations

116 worked in scouting, youth work, and meals-on-wheels

176 worked in schools (tutoring, aiding teachers)

67 worked in voter registrations

52 worked in political campaigns

100 worked in Sunday schools

45 worked on crisis pregnancy phone lines

75 worked distributing maternity and infant clothing

47 had shared their homes with pregnant strangers, elderly, refugees, sick, or foster children.[18]

Are prolifers who favor capital punishment inconsistent?

Not necessarily. The prolifer who favors capital punishment believes that the life of an *innocent* human being may not be taken. The capital offender, however, is not innocent, since he or she is *guilty* of taking the life of an innocent human being. Thus there is no conflict in favoring capital punishment and opposing abortion, since the one is a punishment for the guilty and the other destruction of the innocent.

Furthermore, for the following reasons this question is misguided. First, even if we assume that the prolifer is inconsistent (which we have already seen is not the case), it does not follow that his or her view on abortion is incorrect. Inconsistency is a personal character flaw, not evidence that both parts of the inconsistency are incorrect. For example, a person may believe that it is all right to treat black people fairly and Asian people unfairly. That does not mean he is incorrect in treating blacks fairly. In the same sense, a particular prolifer may be inconsistent in affirming capital punishment and decrying abortion; that does not mean the prolifer is incorrect about abortion.

Second, many prominent prolifers, such as Cardinal Bernadin and Ron Sider,[19] are against both abortion and capital punishment. The prochoicer who accuses the prolife movement of being inconsistent may well join the ranks of Sider and Bernadin, for this position is the most consistent for someone who opposes all killing.

Third, the accusation of inconsistency is a two-edged

sword. Is not the prochoicer who both wants to keep abortion legal and is against capital punishment also inconsistent? That person wants to protect the lives of guilty murderers and not the lives of innocent unborn children.

Since men cannot get pregnant, can they have sound opinions about abortion?

Why not? First, this question implies that only if one belongs to a certain gender can one have an intelligent opinion about abortion. But this is pure sexism. Arguments don't have genitals. The case for either the prolife or the prochoice position rests on the soundness of its arguments, not on the chromosome structure or external genitalia of the arguers. It is ironic that this question is often asked by feminists, the same people who continually inform us that prejudice based on gender is criminal.

Second, if it were true that men could not have sound opinions on abortion, then the prochoicer who uses this argument must reject the landmark 1973 *Roe* v. *Wade* decision, since it was arrived at by seven men on the Supreme Court (with two dissentions).

Third, this is an argument *ad hominem,* meaning it is a prejudicial attack on the person rather than his reasons. For until you attack your opponent's arguments, his position remains unrefuted. Drawing attention to the adversary's gender is an argument *ad hominem.*

Fourth, even the prochoice advocate must admit that simply because women can get pregnant and men cannot does not automatically mean that any woman's opinion on abortion is better than any man's. For if that were true, the prochoicer would have to become prolife after hearing a debate between Sidney Callahan, Ph.D. (a prolife feminist psychologist) and her husband, Daniel Callahan, Ph.D. (a prochoice philosopher).

Fifth, the appeal to gender is a two-edged sword, for one could argue just as well that because men don't get pregnant their opinion concerning abortion is more objective.

Is being anti-abortion the same as being prolife?

No, since the prolife advocate would have no problem with abortion rights if the pregnant woman's choice to abort did not result in the death of her unborn offspring. Thus, it is not abortion per se the prolifer is against, but the killing of unborn human beings who have a full right to life.

Furthermore, we may reach a day at which our technology will make it possible for a physician to safely abort an unborn entity, place it in an artificial womb, and let it grow until its nine-month gestation is completed. If and when that day arrives, the prolifer could accept such abortions that would not result in the death of the unborn. But where will the pro-choicer stand on the issue of unborn human life? Will the prochoicer claim that a woman has a right to the death of the fetus, in addition to her right to an abortion?

We should also mention that most prolifers do not oppose abortion when the life of the mother is in serious danger, since it is better that one should live (the mother) rather than two die (both mother and child). In brief, it is incorrect to call the prolife position anti-abortion.

Why then do the media consistently refer to prolifers as anti-abortionists?

We cannot say for sure, but there are several good reasons to believe that the media are biased against the prolife movement. First, even though the prolife movement prefers to be described as prolife rather than anti-abortion, the media continue to call the movement anti-abortion (a negative label). In contrast, the supporter of abortion rights prefers to be called prochoice (a positive label), and is granted this courtesy by the media. It is only fair to call the prolifers what they want to be called, if the prochoicers are called what they want to be called.

Second, the media will often bring out the religious and/or ideological backgrounds of particular prolifers, seemingly to discredit their positions, while prochoicers are rarely if ever identified in the same way. As Dr. John Willke points out: "It is okay to identify those who oppose abortion as Catholics and in recent years, as evangelicals, fundamentalists, or members of Moral Majority. But who has ever heard of a proabortion person being identified as a Jew, an atheist, or a homosexual, if such they were?"[20]

Do any in the media acknowledge the bias?

Some are beginning to admit it. A study based on hour-long interviews with 240 newspaper and broadcast journalists from the most influential media centers in the United States—*New York Times, Washington Post, Wall Street Journal, Time* (magazine), *Newsweek* (magazine), *U.S. News and World Report,* CBS, NBC, ABC, PBS—found that 90 percent think that a woman has a right to choose abortion. Among the other findings: 50 percent had no religious affiliation; 8 percent attended synagogue or church every week, while 86 percent seldom or never attended; 15 percent felt strongly that adultery was wrong; 20 percent identified themselves as Protestant; one in eight claimed to be Catholic; 85 percent believed that homosexuals have a right to teach in the public schools.[21] With such a large number of journalists who have a predisposition against traditional values, it stretches credibility to the limit to suppose that the media will paint a friendly picture of those who support the values they oppose.

A typical example of media bias occurred in the 1990 Nevada election. On the ballot was question 7. If Nevadans had voted no on 7 it would have revoked the current Nevada law, which allows abortion on demand, and would have permitted the state legislature to pass a more restrictive abortion statute. Unfortunately, Nevadans voted 61 percent to 39 percent to keep the current law. During the campaign both sides produced television commercials, which were either approved or rejected by the three major network affiliates in southern Nevada. One commercial, which featured attorney Danny Tarkanian (son of UNLV basketball coach, Jerry Tarkanian), was rejected by the general manager of the southern Nevada CBS affiliate (KLAS, channel 8), Richard

Fraim. Fraim's rejection of the commercial was based on Tarkanian's claim in the piece both that abortion on demand is legal through all nine months of pregnancy and that sex-selection abortions are also legal. According to Fraim, both claims were false and inflammatory.

One of the authors (Francis Beckwith) wrote Fraim (letter hand-delivered on November 3, 1990) and informed him that the near unanimous weight of legal scholarship clearly establishes that abortion on demand is legal through all nine months of pregnancy. He even gave Fraim a list of quotations from legal scholars, almost all of which appeared in assorted scholarly law journals and books (an edited version of the list is included in chapter 2 of this book). He also informed Fraim that a recent article in the nonpartisan and highly respected *Hastings Center Report* ("Fatal Knowledge?: Prenatal Diagnosis and Sex Selection," by medical doctors Dorothy C. Wetz and John C. Fletcher [May/June 1989]: 21–27) clearly shows that sex-selection abortions do happen and are perfectly legal under *Roe,* the abortion decision which is currently in force in Nevada. Citing authors Wetz and Fletcher, Beckwith pointed out to Fraim that some geneticists argue "that as long as abortion is available on demand, it should not be denied for specific purposes [such as sex selection]" (p. 21). Although he clearly refuted the station's objections to the Tarkanian commercial, and even offered to send the sex-selection article to Fraim on request, Beckwith is still waiting for a response.

On the other hand, when it comes to accepting prochoice commercials careful scrutiny is abandoned. For example, Fraim and KLAS accepted a Campaign for Choice commercial which featured a woman who said that the current abortion law keeps the abortion decision between a pregnant woman, her physician, and her family. Now, that is false. For one thing, a woman can have an abortion performed on her by a doctor she has never met. The law does not stipulate that it must be performed by "her" physician. Second, the Supreme Court has consistently struck down state statutes that have required involvement by other family members in the abortion decision of an adult female (see, for example,

Planned Parenthood of Missouri v. *Danforth,* 428 U.S. 52 [1976]).
Despite the blatant falsity of the claims in the prochoice ad,
the station ran it.

Why are prolifers so against others having abortions, since no one is forcing the prolifer to have one?

The prolifers are against others having abortions because
abortions result in the deaths of unborn human beings who
have a full right to life. Prolifers believe it is the obligation of
the government to protect all human life from the moment
of conception. Thus it is no consolation to the prolifer to be
told that she does not have to have an abortion if she does
not want one.

An abortion rights bumper sticker reads, "Don't like abortion, don't have one." This makes about as much sense as
"Don't like slavery, don't own one," or "Don't like murder,
don't kill one." "The right to choice" has about as much to
do with the legitimacy of permitting abortion as "the right to
property" has to do with the legitimacy of permitting slavery.
Philosopher George Mavrodes provides a story which bril-
liantly illustrates these points:

> Let us imagine a person who believes that Jews are human per-
> sons, and that the extermination of Jews is murder. Many of
> us will find that exercise fairly easy, because we are people of
> that sort ourselves. So we may as well take ourselves to be the
> people in question. And let us now go on to imagine that we
> live in a society in which the "termination" of Jews is an every-
> day routine procedure, a society in which public facilities are
> provided in every community for this operation, and one in
> which any citizen is free to identify and denounce Jews and to
> arrange for their arrest and termination. In that imaginary
> society, many of us will know people who have themselves par-
> ticipated in these procedures, many of us will drive past the
> termination centers daily on our way to work, we can often see
> the smoke rising gently in the late afternoon sky, and so on.
> And now imagine that someone tells us that if we happen to
> believe that Jews are human beings then that's okay, we
> needn't fear any coercion, nobody requires us to participate

in the termination procedure ourselves. We need not work in the gas chamber, we don't have to denounce a Jew, and so on. We can simply mind our own business, walk quietly past the well-trimmed lawns, and (of course) pay our taxes.

Can we get some feel for what it would be like to live in that context? . . . And maybe we can then have some understanding of why they [the right-to-lifers] are unlikely to be satisfied by being told that they don't have to get abortions themselves.[22]

In essence, the prochoice advocate is asking the prolifer to act as if his or her value of human life is false. Thus the prolifer may legitimately view the prochoicer's position as a patronizing and subtle form of intolerance.

Social Benefits of Abortion

Would rich women still get abortions if abortions were made illegal?

Some would, but not all. The great majority of Americans, rich, poor, and middle class, are law-abiding citizens. However, prochoice advocates often argue that prior to abortion being legalized, pregnant women who did not go to unscrupulous physicians or "back alley butchers" traveled to foreign nations where abortions were legal. This was an option open only to rich women who could afford such an expense. Hence, *Roe* v. *Wade* has made the current situation fairer for poor women. If abortion is prohibited, again rich women will still have safe illegal (or legal) abortions.

But there is something fundamentally wrong with this argument. It assumes that legal abortion is a moral good which poor women will be denied if abortion is made illegal. But since the morality of abortion is the point under question, the prochoice proponent assumes what he or she is trying to prove and therefore begs the question. A number of examples help us to better understand this point. To cite one, we would consider it bizarre if someone argued that the hiring of hit men to kill our enemies should be legalized, since, after all, the poor do not have easy economic access to such a practice.

It puts the cart before the horse to appeal to the possible unfairness of unequal access to abortion before providing incontrovertible defense of the view that the choice to have an abortion is in fact a moral good. After all, since equal opportunity to eliminate an innocent human being is rarely if ever a moral good, the question of whether it is fair that certain rich people will have privileged access to abortion if it becomes illegal must be answered after we answer the question of whether abortion in fact is immoral. For it is not true that the vices of the wealthy are virtues simply because the poor are denied them.

Furthermore, the prolife advocate could turn this argument on its ear by admitting to the prochoice advocate that indeed something economically unjust will occur if abortion on demand is made illegal, namely, that rich unborn humans will not have the same right to life as poor unborn humans. The real issue, of course, is not one of economic inequity but whether the unborn are fully human.

Does abortion hold down the population explosion?

First of all, whether the population goes up or down should have nothing to do with the wrongness of taking an innocent human life. So it is not relevant whether or not the population is increasing. Further, it does not matter whether or not abortion holds down population; mass execution, nuclear warfare, suicide, and the holocaust certainly do so. Thus the question is not whether abortion limits population growth; the question is whether it is an acceptable way to achieve this goal. For if the unborn are fully human with a full right to life, then abortion to limit population is tantamount to mass execution, a method that is morally reprehensible.

There are other ways to control population that do not involve killing human beings. Contraceptives, whether natural or artificial, can control populations without killing one human being.

Furthermore, the population growth of the world's industrialized nations has been declining since the last half of the

1960s, even before abortion on demand was legal. Some European countries are experiencing a decline in population. Apart from immigration, the United States is reproducing only 1.8 percent for every two persons. We are literally a dying nation.

Since 1961 world food production has increased 43 percent while population has increased only half as much. Even India has had a surplus of food in recent years. And only one third of the world's agricultural land and one sixth of its arable land is now in use. As far as space is concerned, if the entire population of the world were divided into families of eight persons, each family could be given a small house and lot inside the state of Texas.[23]

Does abortion eliminate poverty?

There is no evidence to suggest this. Abortion on demand has been legal in the United States since 1973; yet, poverty is still a problem in many areas of this country. By saying that the elimination of poor infants will contribute to the elimination of poverty, the prochoicer assumes that the cause of poverty is poor people. But there is no real evidence for this assumption. The causes for poverty are complex, political, cultural, and economic. If people were the cause of poverty, then people in countries with small populations would be economically better off than people in countries with large populations. But this is not true. Japan is wealthier than Ethiopia, and the United States is better off than Mexico. Thus the differences in economic success cannot be explained by population differences but by the fact that Japan and the United States have political and economic systems conducive to economic growth, while Ethiopia and Mexico do not. Thus there is no correlation between population size and wealth.

But even if abortion eliminated poverty, that would not automatically make it right. After all, executing or sterilizing all the poor people who have already been born would be a more efficient way to achieve this goal. But this would not make either practice right, since each would conflict with the basic moral truth that the fundamental rights of human beings should not be gratuitously eradicated so that social problems can be eliminated. Therefore, we cannot rightfully exterminate unborn humans on the basis that it may be beneficial to those of us who have been fortunate enough to have passed through the birth canal.

It is interesting to note that it is not so much the poor who want abortions. Rather, it is the rich who want abortions for the poor. The effect of advocating abortion is in kind advocating genocide for poor and minority groups.

Since so many people disagree about abortion, is it a good idea not to pass a law forbidding it?

Some people argue that it is unwise to make a public policy decision in one direction when there is wide diversity of opinion within society. And since there is a wide diversity of opinion on abortion, we ought not to make a law against it.

First, it is false to say that there is a wide diversity of opinion about abortion. For example, the results of *The Boston Globe*/WBZ-TV nationwide poll, recently published in *The Globe,* concluded that "most Americans would ban the vast majority of abortions performed in this country. . . . While 78 percent of the nation would keep abortion legal in limited circumstances, according to the poll, these circumstances account for a tiny percentage of the reasons cited by women having abortions."[24] The poll asked people in what circumstances abortion should be banned. The results (in parentheses are the percentages of Americans who want abortion illegal in the circumstance in quotation marks): "a woman is a minor" (50 percent), "wrong time in life to have a child" (82 percent), "fetus not desired sex" (93 percent), "woman cannot afford child" (75 percent), "as a means of birth control" (89 percent), "pregnancy would cause too much emotional strain" (64 percent), "father unwilling to help raise the child" (83 percent), "father absent" (81 percent), "mother wants abortion—father wants baby" (72 percent), "father wants abortion—mother wants baby" (75 percent).[25] Hence, it is

false to say that there is widespread disagreement on the issue
of forbidding abortion on demand.

Second, disagreement about something does not mean
that the government should not act in one direction. After
all, the people could be wrong. For example, in the nineteenth century slavery was abolished, yet there was
widespread disagreement among Americans about the aboli-
tion of slavery. How many people today would claim that it
was wrong to abolish slavery? To cite another example, if we
cannot pass a law on an issue over which there is widespread
disagreement, then civil rights legislation, over which there
was much controversy, was unjust.

Third, if prochoicers were really serious about not passing
laws over which people widely disagree they would have to
abolish the laws that permit most abortions, since such laws
imply that the death of the unborn is of no moral consequence while people widely disagree about such judgments.
Why, then, do prochoicers continually insist on imposing this
view on society? If they were consistent, they would support
neither this view nor the prolife view.

If fetuses are human why not give them birth certificates?

Proabortionists sometimes argue that if the unborn were
really human, we would give them birth certificates. The fact
that we don't, they insist, is a proof that we do not consider
them fully human.

In response several things should be noted. First, at best
this merely proves prolifers are inconsistent, not that the
unborn are not human.

Second, Chinese custom does count the time in the womb
as part of the first year of life. Does that mean that the
Chinese unborn are human but not the American unborn?

Third, a birth certificate is just that, a *birth* certificate. It
signifies that a certain stage in human development has
occurred, just as a diploma signifies that one has graduated.
That is to say, a birth certificate is not a humanity certificate.
It signifies the "coming out" celebration. But the little "debu-
tante" is human before he or she comes out into society.

Should we harvest the organs from aborted babies?

Many believe that this should be done. *Reuters* (12 June, 1972) reported that fetal sex organs were harvested and transplanted on a seventeen-year-old Lebanese man. With the shortage of donor organs, farming aborted babies for harvest could become a lucrative business.

Also, brain tissue from live aborted babies is being used to treat Alzheimer's disease. Judging by the increased number of elderly people afflicted by the disease, this, too, could become a big business.

Sex-Selection Abortions

What are sex-selection abortions?

These are abortions that occur because the unborn child is not the gender the parents want. Through amniocentesis and chorionic villus sampling (a method which involves the laboratory analysis of a small sample of placenta tissue and is ordinarily employed to diagnose fetal abnormalities in the first three months of pregnancy), the unborn's gender can be discovered. And if the parents discover that it is a girl when they wanted a boy, the mother can choose to have an abortion.

Are sex-selection abortions legal in America?

Yes. Under *Roe* v. *Wade* a woman can get an abortion for *any reason*, even sex-selection. The Court did not place any restrictions on the reasons *why* a woman may get an abortion. As Dr. Mitchell Golbus of the University of California at San Francisco points out: "It is very hard to make a moral argument about terminations for sex when you can have abortions for any reason."[26]

Who are selected for death more often, unborn boys or unborn girls?

Unborn girls by far. According to Dr. Mark Evans, an obstetrician and geneticist at Wayne State University in Detroit, "Probably 99 percent of non-medical requests for prenatal diagnosis are made because people want a boy."[27] It is well known that tens of thousands of unborn children in Asia and the Third World have been killed for no reason other than being female. According to one study cited in *Newsweek*, "out of 8,000 cases of abortion in Bombay, 7,999 involved a female fetus."[28]

Is the abortion-rights movement against sex-selection abortions?

Not in principle, although many in the movement have expressed unease about them. On the other hand, many in the movement do not want to take any legal action against the practice, even though the vast majority of unborn children killed by sex-selection are female. The comments of Barbara Radford, executive director of the National Abortion Federation, are typical of this attitude: "The information about a woman's pregnancy has to be made available to her. We can't legislate what a man or woman will do with medical information. Physicians with problems with the way a patient will use information they give them should let the patient know so they can go elsewhere."[29] With even greater adamance, Patricia Brogan, director of community relations for Planned Parenthood of Lancaster County, Pennsylvania, argues: "Individuals need to be given the right—and they have the capacity to act—as their own moral agents. It would be inconsistent to say [referring to sex-selection abortions] that 'this is appropriate' or 'this is inappropriate.'"[30]

An obstetrician who performs abortions, Dr. Michael A. Roth of Detroit, says he would be more than willing to perform both the prenatal diagnosis and the abortion: "I have no ethical problems with it, absolutely not. I think abortion should be available on demand."[31]

How often do sex-selection abortions occur?

According to Dr. Lawrence Pratt, geneticist at the University of Southern California, "fewer than 1 percent of all abortions are because of sexing."[32] That may not seem like a great number, but if one considers that there are 1.5 million abortions in the United States every year, then it follows that nearly 15,000 (or less than one percent) of those abortions are performed for the reason of sex-selection. That is no small number.

Dr. Laird Jackson, Director of Thomas Jefferson University's (Philadelphia) medical genetics division, pointed out in 1987 that about 10 of the 2,500 women who underwent prenatal diagnosis chose abortion solely because the fetus was not the desired gender. Officials at the Michael Reese Medical Center in Chicago and the University of California at San Francisco each claim that about 1 out of 1,000 women who have undergone their testing programs abort for the reason of sex-selection. And Baylor University officials at the institution's Houston-based medical school state that 4 out of the 320 women who have undergone CVS procedures have had abortions solely because their unborn child was not the desired gender.[33]

What has been the reaction of the medical community to sex-selection abortions?

It has been mixed. Most physicians find the practice abhorrent. Yet those most likely to provide the information which makes sex-selection abortions possible, geneticists, are more open.

In a recent issue of the *Hastings Center Report*,[34] Drs. Dorothy C. Wetz and John C. Fletcher point out that nearly two-thirds of 295 geneticists surveyed would have no ethical qualms about performing prenatal diagnosis to determine the unborn's gender even if they had knowledge of the fact that the parents could request an abortion if the child is not the "correct" gender. Some of the geneticists argue "that as long as abortion is available on demand, it should not be denied for specific purposes."[35]

Questions about Bias and the Political Process
What must prolifers do in the political process in order to preempt bias?

First, become well-versed with the wording and nature of your state's abortion law so that you can properly convey to your neighbors and friends its radical nature (if your state legislature has not amended *Roe* such as in Pennsylvania, Louisiana, Utah, and Guam), for a vast majority of Americans do not realize that the Supreme Court in *Roe* and *Doe* opened up the door for abortion on demand for all nine months of pregnancy and that the unborn has *no constitutional rights at any time before birth.*

Second, the best way to convey this message is to bring scholarly and respectable sources to undecided politicians and ill-informed media people, but do so in a gentle yet forceful manner. Be meek but not weak.

Third, continually hammer home your points in creative ways that meet the proabortion rhetoric head-on. For example, in a debate a prolifer was confronted with the accusation, "Since the prolife position is religious, therefore, if the pro-life position becomes law it will violate the separation of church and state." He responded by saying, "This means, of course, that one cannot be prolife and an atheist. Yet I know many prolife atheists, such as Nat Hentoff, publisher of the *Village Voice.* You're not saying that Mr. Hentoff must believe in God to become prolife? How dare you try to force Mr. Hentoff to believe in God. You are so intolerant of diversity within our movement."[36] That same evening an abortion-rights defender in the audience told him, "If you don't like abortion, don't have one." He responded, "If you don't like slavery, don't own one. You see, your command lacks imagination. You really don't understand our view. We believe that prolife pregnant women as well as prochoice pregnant women carry within them beings which are fully human. Therefore, to kill any of these human beings is morally wrong, regardless of who their landlord is. Hence, just as it was no consolation to the abolitionists to be told that they don't have to own slaves if they don't want to, it is no consolation to us to be told that we don't have to kill human beings if we don't want to."

Fourth, do not be duped by the political process in your state, for it could have a built-in susceptibility to bias, such as in the case of the 1990 Nevada abortion referendum. According to Nevada law, the Secretary of State has complete authority, in consultation with the Attorney General, to write the ballot language any way he (or she) deems fit. Since in that year both the Attorney General (Brian McKay) and the Secretary of State (Frankie Sue Del Papa) were staunch abortion-rights supporters, the ballot language turned out to be extremely biased. And add to this that state judges in Nevada are elected, including those who sit on the state Supreme Court, it was apparent to prolifers that it would be nearly impossible to find a judge who will throw out the ballot language on such a volatile issue. For a judge may think that such an action would hurt his re-election chances, since throwing out a referendum (in which the electorate votes directly on a law) would probably be perceived as taking power out of the people's hands.

What exactly happened in Nevada?

The prolifers sued the Secretary of State and received a partial victory in the Nevada Supreme Court. The Court ordered Ms. Del Papa to change a very small portion of the ballot language. But the part she was ordered to change was not the part which caused voters to misunderstand the nature of the Nevada law and vote "prochoice."

Did prolifers try to meet with the Secretary of State to work something out?

Yes. But she refused to change the language and even claimed that he prolifers should have approached her during the "public comment period" prior to her completion of the ballot language,[37] even though a month earlier she denied that there existed such a public comment period when she argued against requesting official prolife input. She said that the Nevada referendum "statute does not provide for a hearing mechanism, nor is there a precedent."[38] The fact that Del Papa was caught in this lie was never pointed out by the media.

At one meeting with Nevada prolifers (July 20, 1990), she

told Dr. Beckwith in the presence of her attorney and over one dozen prolife leaders (including Jeanine Griffin, Ruth McGroarty, Helen Henderson, Jeanine Hansen, and Lucille Lusk) that the ballot language arguments were *approved* as fair and unbiased by the prestigious bioethics think tank, the Hastings Center. Out of curiosity, a letter was sent to Dr. Daniel Callahan, the Hastings Center's Founder and Director, concerning Del Papa's claim. Callahan, himself an abortion-rights supporter, responded:

> I simply don't know who might have responded to earlier inquiries here, or who might have talked with Ms. Del Papa. It may have been an individual staff member, but it is not easy to find out who that might be. *I certainly know that we don't officially endorse things of that kind, or pass an institutional judgment.* Hence, it must have been some individual staff member who might have been contacted individually. But I can find out nothing about it [emphasis ours].[39]

What exactly was the ballot language?

According to Article 19 of the Nevada Constitution, the people of Nevada can petition any law to be submitted to a vote of the people for approval or disapproval. This is the *referendum* process. If the people approve of the law, *it can never be amended, overturned, changed, or altered* by an act of the legislature, but only by another vote of the people (that is, another referendum). The law which was submitted for approval or disapproval by the people on the November 1990 ballot was Nevada Revised Statute 442.250, which is based entirely on *Roe* v. *Wade* (see chapter 2).

The following is what Ms. Del Papa composed for the ballot:

CONDENSATION [Ballot Question]
Shall the statute NRS 442.250, "Conditions under which abortion permitted," be approved?

EXPLANATION
If this proposal is approved, NRS 442.250, the existing Nevada statute regulating abortion, will remain in effect and cannot

be amended, repealed or otherwise changed, except by a direct vote of the people. If this proposal is disapproved, the existing statute will be void and of no effect, and the legislature will then have to decide what, if any, law will replace it.

The existing statute permits a woman to have an abortion performed by a physician within twenty-four weeks after the commencement of the pregnancy. A physician may perform an abortion after twenty-four weeks only to preserve the life or health of the pregnant woman.

A "yes" vote is a vote to approve the existing statute. A "no" vote is a vote to disapprove the existing statute.

ARGUMENT FOR PASSAGE

Abortion is a highly personal and private decision. It is argued that a woman should be free to make that decision without unreasonable governmental restriction or regulation. Some regulation is necessary to protect the health and safety of a pregnant woman. The existing statute provides that necessary protection. If abortion is not permitted, then women may seek illegal and potentially unsafe abortions.

The people of Nevada and not the legislature should decide how abortion is to be regulated.

ARGUMENT AGAINST PASSAGE

Abortion should not be legalized. It is argued that life begins at conception and the fetus is entitled to legal protection. The existing statute places the convenience of the pregnant woman above the protection of the fetus. There are other alternatives available to a pregnant woman who does not want to have a child.

The legislature and not the people of Nevada should decide how abortion is to be regulated.

Why did prolifers think this language was biased?[40]

If one considers just the "argument against passage" the ballot language's bias will become apparent.

The first sentence of the argument reads: "Abortion should not be legalized." This is completely false. For one reason, those who opposed the referendum have consistently affirmed that abortion is a legitimate medical procedure if it is employed to save the life of the mother, since if the abortion is not performed *both* mother and preborn child will most likely die, and it is a greater good that one should live (the mother) rather than two die (both mother and preborn child). Second, in this referendum Nevadans were not voting to criminalize abortion, but rather to make the current law incapable of being altered or eliminated by the Nevada legislature.

The second sentence of the argument tells us that in order to have opposed the referendum one must believe that "life begins at conception." This is completely wrong. For one could have very easily voted against the referendum and yet disagreed with the view that "life begins at conception." For example, some bioethicists and experts in abortion law, such as Dr. Baruch Brody (Baylor University), Dr. Bernard Nathanson (Cornell University), and Professor Ernest Van Den Haag (Fordham University),[41] along with a number of ordinary citizens, argue that full humanness is attained some time after conception and several months before birth, such as when brain waves can first be detected at about forty-two days after conception. These people would no doubt have opposed the referendum because it does not provide *full* legal protection of the unborn at *any* time during its prenatal gestation. Therefore, the language used gave a false impression to the voting public by making it seem that one must believe that "life begins at conception" in order to have voted against the referendum.

The third sentence clearly misrepresents the prolife position when it states that the prolifer opposes the existing statute because it "places the convenience of the pregnant woman above the protection of the fetus." The prolife opposition to the referendum rested on the fundamental belief that the unborn are fully human and should be legally protected just as those of us who were fortunate enough to have passed through the birth canal are legally protected. To have framed the prolife opposition to the current statute in the language of a conflict of rights skews the true nature of the prolife position. Imagine what the abolitionists would have thought if their position had been framed in similar language: "The existing statute allowing slavery places the convenience of the slave owner above the protection of the slave." Even the most simpleminded abolitionist would point out that this clearly misrepresents his view, for his opposition to slavery rests on the basic truth that blacks, who are fully human, should not be treated in a subhuman fashion. Whether or not the legal enforcement of this basic truth is convenient for the slave owner is simply not relevant.

The fourth sentence of the argument is not accurate when it states that the prolifer opposes abortion because "there are other alternatives available to a pregnant woman who does not want to have a child." The prolifer opposes abortion because it is a procedure which results in the death of a being who is fully human and has a full right to life. Thus the prolifer believes that it is wrong to kill an unborn child regardless of whether "there are other alternatives available to a pregnant woman. . ." (though, in point of fact, there are other alternatives available). Once again, can you imagine if similar wording were used in an argument supporting the abolitionists' case against slavery?: "It is wrong to enslave black human beings because there are other alternatives available to a slave owner, such as hiring them for low wages." But the simple fact is that slavery is wrong because it treats human beings in a subhuman fashion, not because there are other alternatives available to slave owners.

Finally, the fifth sentence of the argument asserts that the prolifer believes that "the Legislature and not the people of Nevada should decide how abortion is to be regulated." First off, this incorrectly implies that the referendum process itself was being decided in this referendum. But this was simply not the case, because if a majority of people had voted *against* the referendum, the people, to a certain extent, would have chosen to regulate abortion by not forbidding the Legislature from altering the statute in light of possible advances in and/or insights from medicine, science, or ethics.

Second, in terms of practical political realities, the prolifer, as well as the abortion-rights advocate, will pursue whatever legal avenues have the best chance of achieving his political ends. Hence, this last sentence gives the false impression that the prolifer and the abortion-rights advocate have competing philosophies of government, when in fact each was merely pursuing for pragmatic reasons means that he thinks will best achieve his desired ends. There is no doubt that if abortion-rights advocates knew that they would have had no chance of passing this referendum, they would not have even tried to get it on the ballot. So all the "prochoice" rhetoric about "letting the people decide" was nothing but political balderdash. Thus the last sentence in this argument is confusing political expediency with political philosophy.

What portions of the ballot language did the Nevada Supreme Court force the Secretary of State to change?

She was told to eliminate the last sentence of the "argument against passage"—"The legislature and not the people of Nevada should decide how abortion is to be regulated"—as well as the last sentence of the "argument for passage"—"The people of Nevada and not the legislature should decide how abortion is to be regulated."

Did the court address any of the other objections?

No. It never addressed any of the other arguments.

Did the court's decision help the Nevada prolife cause?

No, because the court did not make the secretary of state change the portions of the ballot language which misrepresented both the nature of Nevada's abortion law (namely, that abortion-on-demand is legal for all nine months of pregnancy; see chapter 2) and what the voter had to minimally believe in order to vote "no" on the referendum (namely, that individual human personhood begins *sometime* before birth and that the state should forbid *some* abortions, such as late-term abortions for reasons of birth-control and/or gender selection). Because the ballot language framed the conflict in terms of "total prohibition of abortion" (against the referendum) versus "no total prohibition of abortion" there was no conceivable way that the abortion-rights people could have lost the election, since even the most rigid prolifers (as well as some moderates who are by and large "prolife" and yet voted with the prochoicers in this election out of fear of "total prohibition") believe that some abortions are medically necessary.

What can prolifers learn from the Nevada referendum case?

First, understand that the political landscape is full of individuals who will manipulate the law to their own advantage, cloaking it in the euphemisms of "fairness." Second, be prepared and do your homework. Know your state law and what positions your elected and unelected officials take on the abortion issue. Third, with this knowledge, try to circumvent bias if it is possible. Alert the media as to the possibility of bias and have prolifers flood the government offices with phone calls and letters. Put the pressure on. Fourth, be prepared to handle the media. Be polite yet stern. Document everything. Any slipup will make you look like an idiot. Fifth, see whether your state judges are elected or appointed and carefully study their previous decisions, educational background, and scholarly writings (if any) in order to determine how they may rule if you decide to file suit. If your state courts seem to be just as susceptible to bias as your state government, you may take your case to the federal level and argue that your due process has been denied, since slanted ballot language will prevent you and your fellow citizens from making an intelligent and informed choice. The Nevada prolifers have not yet tried the federal courts. If they do and are victorious, their referendum loss could very well be declared illegal on constitutional grounds. It is our hope that they pursue this course.

Part TWO

Euthanasia

5

Questions about Infanticide

What is meant by infanticide?

Infanticide means infant killing. As distinguished from abortion, in ordinary usage, it means to intentionally take the life of a tiny human being after birth. Abortion means to take a life before birth.

Does infanticide occur today?

Yes, infanticide in different forms has even been approved by some courts. In 1983, a federal judge in New York gave permission to allow the death of "Baby Jane Doe" without treatment of her infections.[1]

The Indiana Supreme Court ruled that the parents of "Baby Doe" in Bloomington could allow their daughter to starve to death. She had Down syndrome and a correctable deformity but was allowed to die of starvation.[2] The parents' attorney was quoted as praising them for their act of compassion and concern for the child.

In another widely publicized case, a father apparently lost control and bashed his deformed son to death on the hospital floor twenty-nine minutes after the child's birth. Authorities said the father, a veterinarian, pounded the boy to death while alone with his thirty-four-year-old wife at Ingalls Memorial Hospital in Harvey, Illinois, near Chicago.[3]

Is infanticide common in hospitals?

Yes. A professor of pediatrics at the University of Wisconsin, a member of the American Academy of Pediatrics Ethics Committee, stated boldly, "It is common in the United States to withhold routine surgery and medical care from infants with Down syndrome for the explicit purpose of hastening death."[4]

Why do scientists recommend infanticide?

The most popular of many reasons is to avoid the tragedy of genetic deformity. A Nobel prize-winning scientist said that "no newborn infant should be declared human until it has passed certain tests regarding its genetic endowment and that if it fails these tests, it forfeits the right to live." Another Nobel laureate, James Watson, added, "If a child were not declared alive until three days after birth, then all parents could be allowed the choice . . . the doctor could allow the child to die if the parents so chose and save a lot of misery and suffering."[5] Some of his colleagues disagreed; they preferred thirty days after birth.

Newsweek carried headlines in an article which read: "Biologists say infanticide is as normal as the sex drive—and that most animals, including man, practice it (Sept. 6, 1982). Next to it was a picture of a mother baboon killing her baby. The implication is plain: Baboons are doing it; why shouldn't we?

Do these scientists consider the newly born human?

Most do not, at least not fully human. As just noted, Dr. Watson believes that the newborn should not be "declared" human until three days after birth. *Newsweek* quoted scientists referring to the newly born as "animals." Geneticist Joshua

Lederberg is explicit: "The newborn infant must undergo further development to achieve the full measure of humanity." How much more? He answers: "An operationally useful point of divergence of the developing organism would be at approximately the first year of life, when the human infant continues his intellectual development, proceeds to the acquisition of language, and then participates in a meaningful, cognitive interaction with his mother and the rest of society."[6]

What is implied by using consciousness as a test of humanity?

Some philosophers, like Michael Tooley, offer "self-consciousness" as a requirement for defining a human person. He declares: "An organism possesses a serious right to life only if it possesses the concept of a self as a continuing subject of experience and other mental states, and believes that it is itself such a continuing entity."[7]

Several implications follow from the insistence that human life does not exist unless it is self-conscious. First, this would mean that infanticide is permitted up to a year and a half after birth, which is the point at which a child becomes self-conscious. Further, it means that someone who is unconscious is not human. If a killer would knock out his victim before killing him, then presumably it would not be murder. In addition, if self-consciousness is a test for humanity, those who are in dreamless sleep are not human. And should a husband awaken his sleeping wife, he would actually call her back into a personal existence. Finally, those in a comatose state are not human, even though many awaken out of it (see chapter 3 for a more detailed response to a similar argument used to defend abortion).

Is there a logical connection between abortion and infanticide?

Yes. If we can kill tiny human beings before they are born because they are deformed or unwanted, why not after they are born for the same reasons? The famous situation ethicist

Joseph Fletcher saw the inseparable connection when he concluded that abortion is "fetal euthanasia" and infanticide is "postnatal abortion."[8] Common sense dictates that if the baby is a human person the moment after birth, then it is also a human person the moment before birth. Passing through a birth canal does not make one a human person any more than does moving across the street. A change in address is not a change in human status.

The late Princeton professor of ethics Paul Ramsey notes well that every "good" argument for abortion is unfortunately also a "good" argument for infanticide. After all, if we can kill unborn babies who might be poor, then why not kill children who are poor? Likewise, if it is right to kill babies who might be deformed, then why not kill children who are handicapped? As Professor Krason noted, "If we are prepared to say that a life should not come into this world malformed or abnormal, then tomorrow we should be prepared to say that a life already in this world which becomes malformed or abnormal should not be permitted to live."[9]

Do abortion rights advocates really admit to a connection between abortion and infanticide?

Yes, some do. To replace an essential definition of personhood with a functional one, logically leads to infanticide, many abortion-rights defenders admit either explicitly or implicitly. Consider the following:

Margaret Sanger, founder of Planned Parenthood: "The most merciful thing a large family can do for one of its infant members is *to kill it*" (emphasis ours).[10]

Peter Singer, Ph.D., philosophy professor and director of the Center for Human Bioethics, Monsah University: "*Species membership in Homo-sapiens is not morally relevant*. If we compare a dog or a pig to a severely defective infant, we often find the non-human to have superior capacities" (emphasis ours).[11]

Esther Langston, Ph.D., professor of social work, University of Nevada, Las Vegas: "What we are saying is that abortion becomes one of the choices, and the person has the right to choose whatever it is that is best that they need as necessary and best for them in the situation for which they find themselves, be it abortion, to keep, to adopt, to sell, to leave in a dumpster, to put on your porch, whatever; it's the person's right to choose."[12]

Michael Tooley, Ph.D., bioethicist and philosophy professor: "Since it is virtually certain that *an infant* at such a stage of its development does not possess the concept of a continuing self, and thus *does not possess a serious right to life, there is excellent reason to believe that infanticide is morally permissible* in most cases where it is otherwise desirable" (emphasis ours).[13]

Beverly Harrison, Ph.D., professor of Christian ethics, Union Theological Seminary: "*Infanticide is not a great wrong.* I do not want to be construed as condemning women who, under certain circumstances, quietly put their infants to death" (emphasis ours).[14]

Is the withholding or withdrawal of artificial treatment of infants ever justified?

Yes. The purpose of medicine is to help not harm. If the treatment does not help the patient (the infant) but merely perpetuates death, withdrawal (stopping treatment which has begun) or withholding (never beginning treatment) is justified. The infant who dies due to the withdrawal or withholding of useless treatment is not a victim of infanticide but a fatal ailment.

If infants are fully human, the decision to withhold artificial treatment must be made in accordance with the same guidelines we employ for adults. This problem is treated in the following chapter on euthanasia.

Can this distinction ever be abused?

Yes. Take for example the famous 1982 case of Baby Doe in Indiana, which we cited earlier. Infant Doe was born with Down syndrome and a surgically correctable condition known as tracheoesophageal fistula that prevented her from orally ingesting food and water. Her parents asked the attending physician to permit her to die by withholding surgery and withdrawing food and water. An Indiana court upheld this parental decision. The infant's problem was surgically correctable, so if she had not been "retarded," there is no doubt the parents would have asked for the necessary surgery. Hence it was not the tracheoesophageal fistula (TF) which was responsible for Infant Doe's death, but parental neglect inspired by the notion that a person with Down syndrome does not have a "life worth living."

In the case of Infant Doe, surgery would not have been useless treatment, but would have given her an opportunity to live a long life. Therefore, although one could argue that the parents and the physician merely "withheld and withdrew treatment" and that technically it was Infant Doe's TF combined with starvation which killed her, this would not be a case of justifiable withholding or withdrawal of treatment, since it was that act of neglect which was directly responsible for the death of the infant. To cite an example, if a mother were to refuse to feed her baby bottled milk when the child is allergic to mother's milk and this withholding resulted in the infant's death, the parent could not argue this was justified on the grounds that she was merely "withholding treatment," since it was that neglect which caused the infant's death.

The moving comments of columnist and political commentator George Will are worth noting:

> When a commentator has a direct personal interest in an issue, it behooves him to say so. Some of my best friends are Down syndrome citizens. (Citizens is what Down syndrome children are if they avoid being homicide victims in hospitals.)
> Jonathan Will, 10, fourth-grader and Orioles fan (and the best wiffle-ball hitter in southern Maryland), has Down syndrome. He does not "suffer from" (as newspapers are wont to say) Down syndrome. He suffers from nothing, except anxiety about the Orioles' lousy start.
> He is doing nicely, thank you. But he is bound to have quite enough problems dealing with society—receiving rights, let alone empathy. He can do without people like Infant Doe's

parents, and courts like Indiana's asserting by their actions the principle that people like him are less than fully human. On the evidence, Down syndrome citizens have little to learn about being human from the people responsible for the death of Infant Doe.[15]

Is infanticide justified when the infant will have a poor quality of life?

Some people argue that if an infant has a mental or physical deformity he or she will have a poor quality of life. Thus infanticide is justified. There is a fundamental problem with this argument.

By claiming that the newborn does not have a right to life because of a mental or physical deformity, the defender of this argument implies that adults with the same handicap do not have a right to life. But we know that they do. Therefore, infants with the same handicap have the same right to life. Suppose that someone responds to this by arguing that newborns are not fully human and hence do not have the same right to life as adults. This would only prove that the newborn's right to life, like that of the unborn (see chapter 1 on medical questions about abortion), rests not on his or her handicap but on whether he or she is fully human and hence possesses all the rights which go along with such a status. If quality-of-lifers argue that the newborn is not fully human, then they must not only deal with the infanticide of handicapped children but also the infanticide of healthy newborns. As philosopher David K. Clark points out: "If infanticide is no violation of the handicapped newborn's right to life . . . then neither is infanticide a violation of the healthy newborn's right to life. But this seems counter-intuitive. If we do not protect healthy neonates, then what would prevent our society from following the logical lead of the abortion issue and allowing infanticide merely for personal reasons?"[16]

What about killing babies born prematurely?

On April 4, 1981, in Dallas, Texas, a baby was born alive and well a month and a half before its scheduled birth. The mother threw it from the seventh floor of her room in the downtown Sheraton-Dallas Hotel. The autopsy showed that the baby died on impact. The case was taken to court, but the charges were dismissed. After all, during the following two months she could have walked into any abortion clinic in Texas and killed her baby in her womb.

A bitter irony. Some time later in the same city a young girl gave birth to a live baby, which was not premature, and then left it at a local hospital. The papers reported that the police had a warrant out for her arrest on child abuse charges. If she had killed it a day earlier, the act would have been called a woman's right to privacy.

Have experiments been performed on live aborted babies?

Tragically, yes. Heads have been severed from live aborted babies and experimented with. Hearts have been removed and kept alive. Kidneys and sex organs have been transplanted. Stomachs have been opened and studied—all without any anesthesia for the baby in spite of the known fact that by at least thirteen weeks after conception they have nervous systems that can feel organic pain. Consider the following examples:

Robert C. Goodlin, M.D., opened the chests of live aborted babies and observed their hearts directly. The babies died within eleven hours.[17]

Dalhouse University researchers (Halifax, Canada) conducted three studies. The first involved live, normally delivered babies whose abdomens were opened and their sex and adrenal glands examined. The second study involved seventy-nine babies aborted alive and later killed by heart puncture. The third study involved 116 babies also aborted alive. Their skulls were opened and their pituitary glands removed. They were later killed by heart puncture.[18]

Dr. Philipson gave mothers drugs and studied the effects on their aborted babies.[19]

Testicles were successfully transplanted from a six-month-old aborted fetus to a twenty-eight-year-old Lebanese man. The donor baby was then killed.[20]

Peter A. J. Adams, M.D., severed the heads of twelve live aborted babies, pumped blood to the brains, and kept them alive by machine to observe them.[21]

Bela A. Resch, M.D., removed hearts of aborted babies and observed them beating for hours outside the body.[22]

Dr. Reyes opened the stomachs and skulls of live aborted babies and studied them. He killed some by heart puncture (at the University of Manitoba, 1973, 1974, 1976).

Martti Kekomaki, M.D., opened stomachs and severed heads of live aborted babies.[23]

The irony of fetal experimentation and organ transplant is that they produce accurate findings and are successful, which are qualitatively and quantitatively better than those resulting from experiments performed on non-human animals. Hence one could argue that their success can be accounted for by the fact that the fetuses are human. That is, our best data about the human body comes from studying humans. But if the unborn are human, then much of the above experimentation is unethical. On the other hand, if they are not human, it is difficult to explain the scientific success of the experiments and transplants.

What about the social "benefits" of infanticide, such as reduction of poverty, handicap, parental anguish, etc.?

These are the same points brought up by prochoice advocates who defend abortion rights, which we have responded to in chapters 1–4. The reader need only apply the same reasoning to infanticide to clearly see that the bad arguments for abortion rights are no better when applied to infanticide.

6

Questions about Adult Euthanasia

The Morality of Euthanasia

What is euthanasia?

Literally *euthanasia* means good death. It is the intentional taking of a human life for some good purpose, such as to relieve suffering or pain. Commonly the word denotes the taking of an adult life, though it can refer generally to taking any life after birth for supposed benevolent purposes.

How does euthanasia differ from infanticide?

Infanticide is the killing of an infant or child, for supposed benevolent ends. Euthanasia usually connotes the intentional taking of the life of an adult, although infant deaths may also be euthanasia.

What is the difference between active and passive euthanasia?

Active euthanasia refers to taking a life, whereas passive euthanasia is allowing a death to occur without intervening.

The former produces the death; the latter permits the death. In a medical context, active euthanasia usually involves the injection of a drug aimed at inducing death. Passive euthanasia, on the other hand, usually involves withdrawal of extraordinary or burdensome medical treatment, which then results in the disease or sickness taking its natural course and causing death.

Is active euthanasia morally right?

Active euthanasia falls in the same category as any other form of intentional homicide of a human being; it is morally wrong. This is the judgment of most of the great moral codes down through the centuries, including Judaism, Christianity, Islam, and others. Active euthanasia, however good the motives, is in the same category as shooting someone with a gun or slitting the throat with a knife. Most moral people recognize it as a form of murder, regardless of the alleged merciful motives. Hitler thought he had good motives in attempting genocide on the Jewish race—he perceived it would help the German nation. Yet who would say his acts were right because his purpose was, in his mind, good?

Is passive euthanasia morally right?

Passive euthanasia can be as wrong as active euthanasia; it all depends. For example, starving a small child to death is just as much a murder as is shooting him or her. In fact, it is a more cruel form of death. So just because one allows another to die (say by withholding food) does not mean the act is morally good. Intentional withholding of natural means to effect another's death is a morally culpable act.

Is it ever right to withhold food and water?

Food, water, and air are absolutely necessary for life. We can only live a few minutes without air, a few days without water, and a few weeks without food. To withdraw these natural means of sustaining life is to starve a person to death.

Intentional starvation is never right. It is a deliberate form of homicide just as tying a plastic bag over someone's head or wiring someone's jaw shut so food cannot be consumed is murder.

A distinction must be made between natural means of sustaining life and artificial means. Natural means include food, air, and water. These should never be intentionally withdrawn, which will always produce death, except when the way in which these things are administered is too overly burdensome for the patient (but this rarely happens). However, artificial means of sustaining life are another matter. It is not always necessary to keep a person on machines or even medication if the physical condition is irreversible and death is imminent. Sometimes heroic or artificial means of sustaining life are unnecessary.

Is it necessary to provide artificial means of getting food, air, and water?

Normally, we should use every means available to preserve life, whether it is a respirator, feeding tube, or whatever. But there is a difference between preserving life and prolonging death. It is unnecessary and undesirable to artificially prolong the agony of those who are terminally ill and do not want the artificial means of prolonging their dying process. While mercy-killing is wrong, mercy dying in these circumstances is not. That is, *taking* a life is always wrong, but *allowing* a natural death is not always wrong.

Is it ever right to withhold medical treatment?

If withdrawing food and/or water to starve someone to death is wrong, then what about refusing to put a person on a lung, heart, or kidney machine, knowing he or she will otherwise die? If the patient wants to be treated and the life-saving treatment is available, it is generally morally wrong to refuse to do so. We should save a life when it is in our power to do so and with the technology that is available to us, and if the patient wants it.

Is there a moral obligation to accept all treatment?

Not always. For example, if a person is terminally ill, he or she may opt not to prolong death. There is no moral obligation for the caregivers to prolong death if it only prolongs suffering. The moral duty is only to prolong life, not to prolong death.

When should heroic means be withdrawn?

There is a difference between prolonging life and prolonging death. When a person is dying and nothing can be done to reverse the process, it is unnecessary to use heroic or artificial means to prolong death. If the patient wants to die and would die naturally without the medical or mechanical means of keeping life going, then it is unmerciful to prolong agony by artificial means. However, this does not mean that food, air, or water should be withdrawn. These are not artificial means of prolonging death; they are natural means of sustaining life. And there is a significant difference between the two.

Who should decide when to refuse treatment?

If the patient is rational, he or she should decide whether he or she wants to die naturally. After all, it is the patient's life. If the patient is not rational, then the decision should be a team effort consisting of the family, their lawyers, their doctors, and pastor or rabbi. The decision should be unanimous.

However, if the patient is rational, he or she should have veto power. And the decision should only be made when death is imminent.

What about the use of "suicide machines"?

Jack Kevorkian, M.D., a Michigan physician, constructed a "suicide machine," complete with a button to release a deadly chemical into the blood, so that a suffering patient could determine for herself if and when she wanted to die.[1] Is this mercy or murder?

It is morally wrong to commit suicide (except in very rare instances, see below), and it is morally wrong to help someone commit suicide. The "suicide machine" was calculated to do exactly this. Thus it follows that both doctor and patient were morally culpable. People in desperate circumstances should not be given aid to snuff out their lives. They need help to live, not the temptation to end it all. We would no sooner give a gun to an angry person than we would give lethal weapons (whether bullets or drugs) to desperate people. They need treatment, not treachery.

What if the person has a living will?

Living wills are of different kinds. They may be wills to allow either active euthanasia or passive euthanasia. As we have already seen, no will to commit active euthanasia is morally justified. Wills to allow passive euthanasia have both legal and moral problems, although some are well done and are legally and morally sound. An example of a living will is found in appendix 5. Needless to say, even if something is legal, it is not necessarily morally right.

For a living will to be ethically justified it would have to fall into the category of passive euthanasia in cases of imminent death where only artificial or heroic means are withdrawn. It is never right to withdraw the natural means of sustaining life—food, water, and air. Artificial means should be withdrawn only when physical death is imminent and the patient or responsible parties (patient's family or guardian, doctor, and lawyer) have agreed. A person (potential patient) may sign a living will for this, since it allows inevitable death but not the taking of a viable life. It allows the caregivers to avoid prolonging the patient's death but not to terminate the patient's life.

Does the end justify the means?

The ends never justify the means. The means must justify themselves. Someone's good purpose does not mean the action is good. As the saying goes, "The road to hell is paved with good intentions." As already noted, Hitler thought he had good intentions. To be a good act, the intended act itself has to be good.

If the end justified the means, killing the handicapped could be justified because they are perceived to be an increasing burden on society. Likewise, exterminating the poor could be done for good motives. But these are morally repulsive acts, and they are contrary to most major ethical creeds and systems. Furthermore, even the few who call for acts like these do not wish them to be performed on themselves in like situations. In fact, no national organization of the handicapped is on record favoring such action.

Would we shoot a horse trapped in a burning barn?

Some proeuthanasia advocates insist that if we would shoot a horse trapped in a burning barn, we should show the same compassion for a human being trapped in a fatal and painful disease. The response from a prolife position is that we do not treat humans like animals. It is precisely because they are human that we do not kill them. Human life is sacred and should be treated with respect. It is a gift we did not give and we do not have the right to take.

Is this a merciless attitude?

Not at all. This objection wrongly assumes that the only way to show mercy to people in desperate circumstances is to kill them. Those who respect life show mercy by helping to relieve suffering persons' pain, not by relieving them of their lives. We may shoot them with a sedative but not a bullet. Since the sick and suffering are part of the human community, helping them enhances our character as well as our ability to empathize and sympathize with another's suffering.

Is euthanasia practiced in America?

Yes, in certain forms. Generally, only passive euthanasia is permitted by law, not active euthanasia. However, active euthanasia organizations such as Exit believe it is right to practice voluntary active euthanasia to avoid painful death.

Is the euthanasia movement growing?

Yes. There are a number of euthanasia groups. In England is the Hemlock Society. In the United States Exit and its founder, Derek Humphrey, produced a book, *Let Me Die Before I Wake*. In it are case studies of those who have tried to commit suicide, along with instructions on the amount of certain drugs and alcohol it takes to end one's life. He boasts, "We have made it respectable to debate and discuss euthanasia. We've also helped a lot of people die well."[2] Humphrey's latest book *Final Exit* (1991), is a suicide instruction manual of greater sophistication than his earlier work.

Is there a logical connection between abortion and euthanasia?

Yes. Life is a continuum from conception to death. Therefore, taking a human life after birth is no different from killing before birth. Killing an older person is no different from killing a younger person. Abortion leads to infanticide, which leads to euthanasia. In America we have gone beyond abortion and are already into infanticide and passive euthanasia. Some European countries, such as Holland, already practice active euthanasia.

There is a connection between abortion and euthanasia. Indeed, as Joseph Fletcher points out, abortion is really prenatal euthanasia and euthanasia is postnatal abortion. Once a society begins killing babies (before or after birth) because they are deformed or unwanted, there is little to stop it from killing older people for the same reasons.

Did not the court approve of the death of Karen Ann Quinlan?

Karen was sustained on a respirator when the New Jersey Supreme Court ruled, at the request of her family, that there was no obligation to perpetuate her life by artificial means (a form of passive euthanasia).[3] After being removed from the respirator Karen lived for nearly ten years and died a natural death. During that time her father faithfully visited her and brought flowers, showing respect for her life, even though she never regained consciousness. Her case is scarcely a good example for those who favor active euthanasia.

Have courts ruled on euthanasia?

Courts have consistently ruled against both euthanasia and suicide. However, they have become more receptive to arguments that rational (or competent) adults have a right to decline any kind of medical treatment, even if it would significantly extend the patient's life. Nonetheless, in the case of children whose parents oppose blood transfusions for them, the Supreme Court ruled that the child be declared "the ward of the Court" and be given the lifesaving transfusions (*Jehovah's Witnesses* v. *King County Hospital Unit* 390 U. S. 598 [1968]).

Has the Supreme Court made any other ruling on euthanasia?

Yes, the case is titled *Cruzan* v. *Harmon* (1990). As a result of an accident on January 11, 1983, Nancy Beth Cruzan has been in a "persistent vegetative state (PVS)," being fed through a tube inserted in her stomach. In this state she was awake but not aware, though on occasion some nurses report that she could turn toward persons who speak and had cried on several occasions. But doctors say she was generally oblivious to the environment except for reflexive responses and painful stimuli.[4]

A state trial court ruled in favor of withdrawing the life-support system. But the Missouri Supreme Court ruled against the argument that the feeding tube was "heroically invasive" or burdensome. "We chose to err on the side of life," the court declared. The United States Supreme Court agreed (June 25, 1990) with the state supreme court, saying (in the decision's syllabus):

> While recognizing a right to refuse treatment embodied in the common-law doctrine of informed consent, the court questioned its applicability in this case. . . . It also declined to read into the State Constitution a broad right to privacy that would support an unrestricted right to refuse treatment and expressed doubt that the Federal Constitution embodied such a right. The court then decided that the State Living Will statute embodied a state policy strongly favoring the preservation of life, and that Cruzan's statements to her housemate were unreliable for the purpose of determining her intent. It rejected the argument that her parents were entitled to order the termination of her medical treatment, concluding that no person can assume that choice for an incompetent in the absence of the formalities required by the Living Will statute or clear and convincing evidence of the patient's wishes.

In other words, if she had a living will, then termination of treatment would have been justified. Interestingly enough, several months later the Cruzans obtained more evidence which a lower court believed constituted a living will and within the Supreme Court's parameters. In December 1990, physicians withdrew Nancy's feeding tubes. She died of starvation and dehydration several days later.

Is active euthanasia already practiced in some countries?

Yes, in Holland, for example. Its supreme court (Hoge Raad) declared that a doctor may engage in active euthanasia in certain cases, including medical emergencies, with rational patients and family support.[5] Fortunately, these conditions are not met in large numbers of cases, so relatively few active euthanasia cases are reported.

Is active euthanasia practiced in the United States?

More and more cases are being reported. For example, Roswell Gilbert killed his wife of fifty-one years "to terminate her suffering." He shot her twice in the head. He was later convicted, but "some observers think that he was convicted precisely because he did not cry about it on the stand."[6] Mr.

Gilbert was released on parole in August 1990, after serving five years in a Florida prison.

What is cryonics?

Cryonics is the process of freezing a body in hopes of bringing it back to life some day. Since this sometimes involves killing the person, it may be a form of assisted suicide. Often it is done by freezing the person to death. One woman, Dora Kent, had her head surgically removed from her body and frozen in the hopes that someday she could be brought back with a new body. According to the *American College of Surgeons Bulletin,* "She was apparently still alive when the procedure was started. Her son is a believer in cryonics, and he supervised the removal of his mother's head. The coroner has classified the death a homicide."[7] While thankfully this is not yet widespread it does occur and illustrates where the logic of present trends leads.

Do courts rule in favor of active euthanasia?

Sometimes. Take, for example, the case of Hans Florian (March 8, 1983) who shot his wife who was suffering from Alzheimer's disease. According to the *American College of Surgeons Bulletin,*[8] he did so because "he did not want to leave her alone when he died. The Grand Jury refused to indict him."

What arguments are advanced in favor of active euthanasia?

A good summary of the arguments for active euthanasia is given in the *American College of Surgeons Bulletin:*

1. Medical technology itself has created a crisis in dying that older generations could not have foreseen. . . . A fundamental question that must be answered is, do we not have an obligation to direct this technology to good human ends?
2. If persons suffer more pain and psychological discomfort as a consequence of the success of past medical interventions

(for example, controlling infection in burn patients), do we not have a responsibility to address the results of this success? As Kenneth Vaux observes: "If biomedical acts of life extension become acts of death prolongation, we may force some patients to outlive their deaths, and we may ultimately repudiate the primary lifesaving and merciful ethic itself."

3. If, from time to time, pain control proves fruitless, does not the quality of mercy and compassion compel us to accede to a patient's heartrending request for active euthanasia?

4. Is there any moral difference between omission and commission, if our motive is to help a patient die? Are we not just splitting hairs by arguing that omission permits the "natural course of disease" to take the patient's life, while commission actively intervenes to kill the patient?

5. If, as the courts have now consistently affirmed, patients have a constitutional right to determine their own medical care, could the right to privacy and the common law right of self-determination sustain a right to die?[9]

Are these arguments valid?

Not at all. First, they generally are based on the invalid utilitarian premise that the end justifies the means (discussed above). Second, some arguments are absurd. For example, number 1 begs the question, assuming that active euthanasia is "good." Number 2 is similar. Number 3 wrongly assumes that pain should be relieved at all cost, even if it is necessary to relieve a person of life to relieve suffering. Third, in response to number 4, there is a real difference between active and passive euthanasia. It is the difference between homicide and natural death. Finally, the right to privacy does not take precedence over the right to life.

Responses to these arguments are presented in greater detail throughout this chapter.

How do medical ethicists argue that there is no moral difference between active and passive euthanasia?

James Rachels, a philosophy professor at the University of Alabama, argues that there is no essential moral difference between active (killing) and passive (letting-die) euthanasia. But then, he concludes, if passive euthanasia is morally acceptable (as we think it is in some cases), and there is no moral difference between passive and active euthanasia, then active euthanasia must also be morally acceptable (at least in some cases). To defend this position, Rachels provides the following story:

> Smith stands to gain a large inheritance if anything should happen to his six-year-old cousin. One evening while the child is taking his bath, Smith sneaks into the bathroom and drowns the child, and then arranges things so that it will look like an accident. No one is the wiser, and Smith gets the inheritance. Jones also stands to gain if anything should happen to his six-year-old cousin. Like Smith, Jones sneaks in planning to drown the child in his bath. However, just as he enters the bathroom Jones sees the child slip, hit his head, and fall face-down in the water. Jones is delighted; he stands by, ready to push the child's head back under if necessary, but it is not necessary. With only a little thrashing about, the child drowns all by himself, "accidentally," as Jones watches and does nothing. No one is the wiser, and Jones get the inheritance.[10]

In using this example, Rachels is arguing that although Smith "killed" his cousin whereas Jones merely "let the child die," both acted from the same motive (personal gain) with identical results (death). This would make the acts morally equivalent. But since both cases are morally equivalent, and the only difference between them is that one involved "killing" while the other involved "letting die," this difference has no moral relevance. It follows then that there is no moral difference between active euthanasia (killing) and passive euthanasia (letting die). Therefore, if passive euthanasia is permissible (or at least sometimes permissible), then active euthanasia would also be permissible (or at least sometimes permissible).

What is your response to Rachels' "bare difference" argument?

Medical ethicist J. P. Moreland has pointed out, among other criticisms, that the "main difficulty with the bare-difference argument lies in its inadequate analysis of a human moral act."[11] That is to say, the reason why Rachels can find no moral distinction between the acts of Jones and Smith is simply because he ignores the important fact that each had the same *intention:* to kill his cousin for the sake of greed. What makes an act passive or active cannot be reduced to only the refraining (i.e., not saving the drowning cousin when it could be easily done) or the moving (i.e., pushing the cousin's head under water) of certain body parts (such as one's hands), but must include the intention of the agent. Consequently, Jones and Smith were both engaged in an active (not passive) deed of killing, since it was clearly their intention to commit the murder. Smith used his hands to commit murder whereas Jones, in order to successfully commit the murder, refrained from using his hands. Yet each was actively, not passively, engaged in murder. Hence, Rachels did not make a true comparison between active and passive euthanasia, but merely presented us with two examples of active "euthanasia" (if it really can be called euthanasia, since the cousin was not "suffering" from any fatal ailment).

How are intentions an integral part of decision making in medical ethics?

In decisions concerning the withdrawing or withholding of treatment, intentions in many cases are an integral part in judging the morality of the act. For example, if a man receiving chemotherapy which will extend his life for only a few months chooses to withdraw treatment for the sake of not undergoing the physical pain and agony which almost always accompanies the treatment, then he has chosen passive euthanasia, for his intention is not to die but to relieve pain, although the decision to withdraw treatment will most certainly hasten death. On the other hand, suppose another man in a similar situation requests a lethal injection in addition to withdrawing treatment. In this case, he has chosen death, and hence has chosen active euthanasia, for his intention is to end his life prematurely rather than to merely relieve pain. The difference between the first man and the second man is a difference between choosing life without pain (although the *cancer* will eventually kill the first man) and choosing death (i.e., it is the lethal injection and *not* the cancer which kills the second man). Although not all so-called cases of passive and active euthanasia are as clear-cut, we believe that these cases clearly show that there is a fundamental moral difference between some forms of passive and active euthanasia.

Can this distinction be applied to other decisions in medical ethics?

Yes. For instance, when one undergoes surgery to remove a cancerous tumor or have a heart bypass, one risks death by simply undergoing such delicate surgery. However, one's *intention* in choosing such a surgery is to avoid death and to extend life. If one dies while undergoing such surgery with such a specific intention, it would be ludicrous for someone to call that death suicide simply because the result of the surgery—death—is the same result which occurs when a person takes a lethal injection with the specific *intention* to kill himself.

To cite another example, a man who is suffering tremendous pain and is given large dosages of a painkiller, such as morphine, is *intending* to relieve pain when in fact a side effect may be that he is increasing his risk of death. And if this person is critically ill and death is imminent, it may be that the morphine will actually hasten death. But in either case, the suffering person is not committing suicide, since his intention is to relieve pain and not to kill himself. If one contrasts this with the person who swallows a bottle of painkillers with the specific intention of committing suicide, it is apparent that intention is extremely important in evaluating the morality of an act.

Are these philosophical distinctions just a waste of time when real people are suffering?

Not at all. In fact, because *real* people are suffering, it is important that we do the morally right thing. But this involves using the unique qualities which humans possess and distinguish us from those which inhabit the animal kingdom: rationality and moral perspective. Now if we made all these philosophical distinctions when deciding whether to kill a cockroach in our kitchen, *that* would be a waste of time, since cockroaches are not human beings who have dignity and ultimate value. Hence, if one does not care about philosophical distinctions when making moral decisions, we can throw the ball back in his court: If people are valuable and worth helping, why don't you seriously consider what is the correct and moral way to treat them by employing the abilities God has given you (rationality and moral perspective) which make you qualitatively different than the cockroach that resides underneath your sink?

Suicide and Euthanasia
What is the difference between euthanasia and suicide?

Euthanasia is either the taking of someone's life (active euthanasia) or letting someone die (passive euthanasia) when that individual is dying of a terminal illness and/or when death is imminent. Suicide is an individual's intentional ending of life, either by one's own hand, another's assistance, or by another's hand. It is suicide when someone intentionally kills himself or herself while dying of a terminal illness and/or when death is imminent. Consequently, some suicides are incidents of euthanasia. On the other hand, some incidents of euthanasia are not suicides. For example, an individual may refuse painful treatment of a terminal illness (such as chemotherapy for cancer) so as to live the last days in relative comfort. Suppose the cancer will take a life within six months if one undergoes the painful treatment, but if one refuses the treatment the life span will be two months shorter. For at least two reasons we do not believe this person commits suicide when he or she refuses treatment: the person does not intend to bring about death (although he or she welcomes it) but merely intends to relieve pain; and it is the cancer which is killing the person, not something the person has initiated.

Is the withholding or withdrawal of treatment sometimes suicide?

Yes. For example, if while driving my car on a dangerous curve I intentionally withdraw my hands from the steering wheel so that I may plunge to a fiery death, I in fact commit suicide. In addition, if an otherwise healthy person who is diabetic intentionally withdraws from taking insulin to bring about death, that person commits suicide.

These examples, of course, also apply in cases of passive euthanasia that are solely intended to bring about someone's death when that death is neither imminent nor unavoidable, these would be cases of suicide. For instance, if after triple-bypass heart surgery an otherwise healthy man instructs his physician to turn off the respirator, thereby "withdrawing" treatment, this man in effect participates in physician-assisted suicide.

Is martyrdom the same as committing suicide?

No. A martyr is commanded to renounce his/her faith or face execution. It is not the martyr's intent to die but to stand firm for personal belief against the threat of death. Since suicide is the intentional killing of oneself either by one's own hand or with the assistance of another, martyrdom is not suicide. As Wennberg puts it, the martyr "is not a suicide solely because her decision to affirm her faith in such circumstances was not one she made in order to bring about her death—or to use Kluge's terminology, she did not make her decision for 'the express purpose' of bringing about her death. In other words, although she expected her death, she did not intend it."[12]

Is suicide ever morally justified?

Yes, but in very rare circumstances when a higher good is at stake. Take the following case as an example. Suppose a

CIA agent is captured by the enemy and he knows that they will give him sodium-penathol (a drug which will make him tell the truth). And on taking this drug the agent knows that he will reveal secrets whose exposure to the enemy will result in the death of ten thousand innocent women and children. In such a situation, it seems that the agent is morally justified in taking a cyanide tablet so that these ten thousand lives can be saved. We are not saying that the end (ten thousand lives will be saved) justifies the means (the agent taking a cyanide tablet). Rather, we are saying that since it is a higher moral obligation to save ten thousand, to take the cyanide tablet is to act in accordance with a higher law. Preserving life is good in itself; it needs no outside justification.

The Western History of Euthanasia[13]

What did the classical world think about euthanasia and suicide?

The ancient world was somewhat divided about euthanasia. Among the Greek upper classes suicide and euthanasia were widely accepted.[14] However, not everyone shared this view. For example, the Pythagoreans condemned the practice of suicide. The Pythagorean movement, which was founded by the philosopher and mathematician Pythagoras (ca. 580–ca. 500 B.C.), probably influenced the formation of the Hippocratic oath, which reads in one section: "I will neither give a deadly drug to anybody if asked for it, nor will I make a suggestion to this effect. Similarly, I will not give to a woman an abortive remedy. In purity and holiness I will guard my life and my art."

Plato (428–348 B.C.) was generally negative in his attitude toward suicide, although he was sympathetic to the individual whose "cruel and inevitable calamity [had] driven him to the act."[15] Aristotle (384–322 B.C.), a pupil of Plato, took an even stronger position than his master. He argued that it is cowardice to flee life on the grounds of "cruel and inevitable calamity."[16]

However, the Pythagoreans, Plato, and Aristotle were more

the exception rather than the rule in the ancient world. Typical of the ancient view of suicide and euthanasia was the position of Seneca (4 B.C.–A.D. 65), a Roman philosopher:

> Against all the injuries of life I have the refuge of death. If I can choose between a death of torture and one that is simple and easy, why should I not select the latter? As I choose the ship in which I sail and the house which I shall inhabit, so I will choose the death by which I leave life. In no matter more than in death should we act according to our desire. . . . Why should I endure the agonies of disease when I can emancipate myself from all my torments.[17]

The Stoics did not advocate suicide for "any reason," but only when there is terminal illness or other extreme circumstances. In fact, one scholar interprets their position this way: "It is a man's duty to bear the pains that God sends him: only if deprived of life's necessities does he know that God is sounding the recall."[18] And when this occurred, they believed suicide or some form of euthanasia was justified. Although this is far from the traditional prolife position, it is even further from the position advocated by radical euthanasia groups who seem to approve of suicide for nearly any reason.

What conclusions can be drawn from the Hippocratic oath?

First, the oath places euthanasia in the same category as abortion. As already noted, they deal with the same patient, have the same procedure, and have the same result: death. Second, this time-honored medical oath insists that even the suggestion of suicide to dying persons is wrong, to say nothing of the attempt to give the drug to them.

What does the Bible teach about euthanasia and suicide?

The Bible does not mention the words *suicide* or *euthanasia,* but it seems apparent that its teachings do condemn both suicide and most forms of euthanasia.

First, since the Bible specifically condemns murder (Exod.

20:13), and suicide is a form of homicide, it is reasonable to conclude that the Bible also prohibits suicide.

Second, even the most desperate believer in the Bible who desired death never considered suicide a morally valid option. Take for example Jonah's prayer: "O Lord, please take my life from me, for death is better to me than life" (Jonah 4:3 NASB; see also Job 3).

Third, the Bible records five cases of suicide: Abimelech (Judg. 9:50–56); Saul and his armor bearer (1 Sam. 31:1–6; 2 Sam. 1:1–15; 1 Chron. 10:1–13); Zimri (1 Kings 16:18–19); Ahithophel (2 Sam. 17:23); and Judas (Matt. 27:3–10; Acts 1:15–19). But, as Wennberg has pointed out, "in each case of suicide recorded in Scripture, death represents a tragic end to a life that did not (at least in its latter stages) meet with God's approval."

The Bible, however, does not teach that people have an absolute moral obligation to always accept treatment that would sustain life artificially. For example, it does not seem inconsistent with the Bible for someone to refuse to take a pill (were it available) which would double a life span. Likewise, there does not appear to be an absolute moral obligation to undergo chemotherapy or to receive kidney dialysis, although it may be wise or desirable to accept such treatment. Since the Bible does teach that God has appointed that all will eventually suffer the natural consequences of disease and mortality (Gen. 3; Rom. 5), it is consistent with biblical teaching to accept them. After all, we must all do so eventually.

What does common law say about active euthanasia?

According to legal scholars Victor G. Rosemblum and Clarke Forsythe, "the current campaign for the legalization of assisted suicide runs directly counter to the long history of Anglo-American common law." The reason for this rejection "has been grounded in the common law's solicitousness toward vulnerable persons—including older persons and persons who are mentally incompetent—through the criminal law."[19] Cyril Means, though a defender of abortion rights, has nevertheless concluded that "throughout its long history, the common law has always set its face against suicide."[20]

Although the common law has supported a patient's right to refuse treatment (passive euthanasia),[21] it has not supported any so-called right to die (active euthanasia). It is unfortunate that the broadcast and print media often confuse refusal of treatment with active euthanasia and inaccurately describe both as instances of individuals exercising their right to die. For "to transmute a right to refuse medical treatment into a 'right to die' . . . switches the focus from the burden of nonbeneficial medical treatment to the desire for death itself."[22]

Medical Aspects of Euthanasia

What is the American Medical Association's official stance?

One of the most important statements on euthanasia by the American Medical Association was endorsed by the AMA's house of delegates on December 4, 1973:

> The intentional termination of life of one human being by another—mercy killing—is contrary to that for which the medical profession stands and is contrary to the policy of the American Medical Association.
>
> The cessation of the employment of extraordinary means to prolong the life of the body when there is irrefutable evidence that biological death is imminent is the decision of the patient and/or his immediate family. The advice and judgment of the physician should be freely available to the patient and/or his immediate family.[23]

In 1982 the AMA's judicial council endorsed the following conclusions, which differ slightly from the 1973 guidelines on euthanasia:

> In the making of decisions for the treatment of seriously deformed newborns or persons who are severely deteriorated

victims of injury, illness or advanced age, the primary consideration should be what is best for the individual patient and not the avoidance of a burden to the family or to society. Quality of life is a factor to be considered in determining what is best for the individual. Life should be cherished despite disabilities and handicaps, except when prolongation would be inhumane and unconscionable. Under these circumstances, withholding or removing life supporting means is ethical provided that the normal care given an individual who is ill is not discontinued. The social commitment of the physician is to prolong life and relieve suffering. Where the observance of one conflicts with the other, the physician, patient, and/or family of the patient have discretion to resolve the conflict.

For humane reasons, with informed consent a physician may do what is medically necessary to alleviate severe pain, or cease or omit treatment to let a terminally ill patient die, but he should not intentionally cause death. In determining whether the administration of potentially life-prolonging medical treatment is in the best interest of the patient, the physician should consider what the possibility is for extending life under humane and comfortable conditions and what are the wishes and attitudes of the family or those who have responsibility for the custody of the patient.

Where a terminally ill patient's coma is beyond doubt irreversible and there are adequate safeguards to confirm the accuracy of the diagnosis, all means of life support may be discontinued. If death does not occur when life support systems are discontinued, the comfort and dignity of the patient should be maintained.[24]

What is the difference between a persistent vegetative state (PVS) and brain death?

Brain death occurs when an individual lacks both lower and higher brain functions and whose bodily functions can be sustained only by use of machines, such as a respirator. In a great majority of the states in the United States such a person is declared clinically and legally dead.[25] Someone in a persistent vegetative state (PVS) has lower brain functions (that is, the brain stem may be the only part of the brain which is functioning, the part which controls many normal bodily functions such as respiration and heartbeat) but no higher brain functions (that is, the cerebral cortex may not be functioning, the part of the brain whose function is associated with thought, intellect, and personality).[26] The President's Commission for the Study of Ethical Problems in Medicine and Biomedical and Behavioral Research defined someone in a PVS in the following way:

> Personality, memory, purposive action, social interaction, sentience, thought, and even emotional states are gone. Only vegetative functions and reflexes persist. If food is supplied, the digestive system functions and uncontrolled evacuation occurs; the kidneys produce urine; the heart, lungs, and blood vessels continue to move air and blood; and nutrients are distributed in the body.[27]

For this reason, the individual in a PVS can, in most cases, live apart from being hooked up to a machine, although the patient has to be cared for by others in many ways (fed, clothed, cleaned). Hence, the individual in a PVS is not brain dead. Some people who are in a PVS do come out of it, although in not a few cases they suffer irreparable brain damage of varying degrees.[28]

Should we remove food and water or administer lethal injections to patients in a PVS?

First, despite his condition, the person who is PVS is still a person, albeit a broken one. It enhances our humanity as well as our sympathy for others, by helping those who are incapable of helping themselves.

Second, knowledge of the fact that physicians are killing helpless patients can undermine the trust patients have in health professionals.

Third, food and water are not *treatments* but necessary sustenance for life itself. To remove them is to *kill.* Although the question assumes there is nothing wrong with such killings, we should not ignore the chilling effect on health care which will occur if such killings become commonplace. Patients, especially elderly ones, will feel compelled "to move aside" in such a climate which condones easy death. The whole practice of medicine as a virtuous activity practiced for the sake of the community, which responds in love to the suffering of others, will be seriously compromised.

7

Conclusion: Social Activism

Civil Disobedience and Prolife Activism

The purpose of this chapter is to inform Christians as to the two main views concerning civil disobedience and abortion. Each author has his own view on the subject.

Since the subject matter of this chapter is theological, it should not be inferred from this that the prolife position is "religious." In fact, we have gone to great lengths in Part 1 of this book to make a secular non-religious case for the prolife position.

However, since the dispute over civil disobedience and abortion is among those in the Christian community, and those on all sides of the debate appeal to theological and/or biblical arguments, our focus in this chapter is primarily theological.

Are prolifers arrested for protesting abortions?

Yes. Many are dragged away to jail for disobeying the law. Why are they violating civil statutes? They believe a higher

165

moral law impels them to rescue babies whose mothers are headed for "abortuaries" (abortion clinics). They believe it is justified to disobey laws when it is necessary to save lives.

Do all prolifers accept this reasoning?

No. Many believe that efforts to save unborn lives should be done within the law but not in disobedience to it.

On what points do prolifers agree?

Almost all prolifers agree on the following major points. First, they agree that the law must be changed to protect the unborn from death by abortion. Second, they agree that everything morally and legally possible to accomplish this should be done. Third, they believe that a person should disobey laws that compel a person to have an abortion or to die by euthanasia against his or her will (none of which currently exist). Fourth, all reputable prolife groups, including Operation Rescue, which advocates civil disobedience, repudiate violence as a means of saving lives. Unfortunately, however, some of the radical fringe have engaged in bombing or burning abortion clinics; however, almost all prolifers agree that these are undesirable and unethical means.

In short, while there is some disagreement about the means, prolifers agree about the end of saving unborn human lives. General agreement exists that there are times citizens should employ civil disobedience.

What is the main point of disagreement?

The real problem is defining precisely when civil disobedience is justified. Basically, there are two positions, although it is possible to find at least six views which derive from these two.[1] One view contends that we should disobey the government when it promulgates a law contrary to God's moral law. The other view contends that laws should be disregarded only when government compels the Christian to do evil.

What is the antipromulgation view of civil disobedience?

The antipromulgation view insists that a person has the right to resist government when it promulgates laws and thereby allows or even encourages actions that are contrary to God's moral law. Those who hold this view believe that governments are under obligation to a higher moral law and that when governments make laws or take actions contrary to these moral laws citizens have the right to disobey or at least resist them.

Who has held the antipromulgation view?

Some have argued that Thomas Jefferson espoused a form of this view which he incorporated into the Declaration of Independence. Samuel Rutherford articulated this position in his famous book, *Lex Rex*[2] (*The Law Is King*). The late Francis Schaeffer adopted an antipromulgation view in his widely circulated *Christian Manifesto*.[3] Some prolife groups, such as Operation Rescue, also agree with this position.[4]

What justification did Schaeffer give for civil disobedience?

Following Rutherford, Francis Schaeffer maintained that "kings then have not an absolute power in their regiment to do what pleases them; but their power is limited by God's Word." In other words, "all men, even the king, are under the law and not above it."[5] The law is king; the king is not the law. Government is under God's law; government is not God's law.

Schaeffer claimed that "the law is king, and if the king and the government disobey the law they are to be disobeyed."[6] The Christian's obedience, then, is to God's law, then to government only insofar as it is in accord with God's law.

According to this view, when should citizens disobey laws?

According to Schaeffer, "the law is founded on the law of God." Hence, "tyranny was defined as ruling without the sanctions of God."[7] In other words, whenever a government rules contrary to God's Word it rules tyrannically. In such cases the Christian should not obey the government.

Not only should citizens disobey a tyrannical government, they should also actively resist it. Schaeffer declares that "citizens have a moral obligation to resist unjust and tyrannical government." For "when any office commands that which is contrary to the Word of God, those who hold that office abrogate their authority and they are not to be obeyed, and that includes the state."[8]

How should government be resisted according to this view?

First the citizens should protest the laws that go contrary to God's Word. If this fails, force may be necessary. "Force," according to Schaeffer, "means compulsion or constraint exerted upon a person (or persons) or on an entity such as a state."[9] Force can be used by the local government, or even by a church, against an oppressive state. For "when the state commits illegitimate acts against a corporate body—such as a duly constituted state or local body, or even a church . . . there are two levels of resistance: demonstration (or protest) and then, if necessary, force employed in self-defense."[10]

Does Schaeffer give examples of tyranny?

Schaeffer believed laws that take tax money to support abortion are tyrannical, and hence Christians should refuse to pay such taxes. He also believed that disallowing the teaching of creation in the public schools exemplified tyranny. He declared emphatically, "If there was ever a clearer example of the lower 'magistrates' being treated with tyranny, it would be hard to find. And this would be the time, if the courts do rule tyrannically, for the state government to protest and refuse to submit."[11]

What is the anticompulsion view on civil disobedience?

Those who hold this position agree with the antipromulgationists' view that some occasions demand Christian disobedience to civil laws. They differ only on what those occasions are. The former believe we should protest and resist all laws that permit people to do what is contrary to God's moral law, such as kill innocent lives. The latter hold that we should disobey only laws that compel citizens to act contrary to the moral law.

For example, agreeing that abortion is contrary to the moral law of God, the antipromulgation view insists that a citizen has the right to engage in civil disobedience to oppose abortion. Here the antipromulgationists split into two camps: those who favor violent action (such as bombing clinics) and others who favor only nonviolent disobedience (such as illegal clinic sit-ins or rescues).

Anticompulsionists, on the other hand, believe that it is wrong to transgress the law to protest abortion. This is because of the difference between a law that permits abortions and one that commands abortions. Unjust laws should be legally protested but not illegally. It is one thing for a government to allow others to do evil, but it is another thing for them to force an individual to do evil. Only in the latter case is civil disobedience justified. As was stated earlier, there are now no laws that compel abortion or euthanasia.

However, some anticompulsionists believe that rescuing is justified and argue in the following way. Since, according to Jesus, the second greatest commandment is to "love your neighbor as yourself," and since saving your neighbor's life is a way to obey this command, and since the unborn, if he or she is fully human, is your neighbor, a government which uses its trespassing laws to force Christians to disobey this command of Christ's can be justly disobeyed. Others believe that one can show love in other ways than disobeying the law.

Prorescue anticompulsionists argue that the trespassing laws are being used to force Christians to disobey a clear command of God, just as the perjury laws were used in Nazi Germany to force those hiding Jews from certain death to "tell the truth" under oath as to the Jews' whereabouts. Consequently, they believe it is incorrect, they argue, to say that the "government was just forbidding those hiding Jews to disobey perjury laws but not forbidding them to rescue Jews." Other anticompulsionists respond by noting that the Nazi law compelled death whereas present United States laws allowing abortion do not.

The Biblical Basis for Prolife Activism

Is there a biblical basis for the anticompulsionist view?

There are several biblical instances of divinely approved civil disobedience. In Exodus 1:15–21 Pharaoh commanded the midwives to slay every male Hebrew baby. But Hebrew midwives Shiphrah and Puah "feared God and did not do what the king of Egypt had told them to do; they let the boys live" (v. 17). As a result "God was kind to the midwives and the people increased and became even more numerous. And because the midwives feared God, he gave them families of their own" (vv. 20–21).

Also, Moses requested of Pharaoh, "Let my people go, so that they may hold a festival to me in the desert" (Exod. 5:1). Pharaoh responded, "Who is the LORD, that I should obey him and let Israel go? I do not know the LORD, and I will not let Israel go." But the children of Israel left Egypt with a spectacular display of divine interventions on their behalf (Exod. 7–12).

In 1 Kings 18:3–4 wicked queen Jezebel "was killing off the LORD's prophets." In defiance of her orders the prophet Obadiah "had taken a hundred prophets and hid them in two caves . . . and had supplied them with food and water" (v. 4). Although explicit approval of his act is not stated, the whole context and manner of the Bible's presentation implies that God condoned his action (see vv. 13–15).

In Daniel 3 the government commanded that everyone in the kingdom "must fall down and worship the image of gold that King Nebuchadnezzar has set up" (Dan. 3:5). But the three Hebrew friends of Daniel defiantly replied, "We want you to know, O king, that we will not serve your gods or worship the image of gold you have set up" (v. 18). As a result God blessed them and miraculously preserved them from the fiery furnace into which they were thrown (3:25–30).

Another example of divinely approved civil disobedience is found in the famous story of Daniel and the lions. The king ruled that "anyone who prays to any god or man [except him] during the next thirty days shall be thrown into the lions' den" (Dan. 6:7). Daniel defied the order and, with his window open, "three times a day he got down on his knees and prayed, giving thanks to his God, just as he had done before" (v. 10). Here again God richly blessed the civil disobedience of Daniel, who emerged from the lions' den confidently proclaiming, "My God sent his angel, and he shut the mouths of the lions. They have not hurt me, because I was found innocent in his sight" (6:22).

One more instance of disobedience to authorities, though not civil authorities, is that of the apostles. The religious authorities "commanded them [the apostles] not to speak or teach at all in the name of Jesus" (Acts 4:18). But Peter and John replied, "Judge for yourselves whether it is right in God's sight to obey you rather than God" (v. 19). The text goes on to say that "the people were praising God for what had happened" (v. 21), thereby indicating God's approval on their refusal to obey this mandate not to preach Christ.

Finally, during the tribulation period the faithful remnant of believers will refuse to worship the Antichrist or his image. John said the false prophet "ordered them to set up an image in honor of the beast who was wounded by the sword and yet lived" (Rev. 13:14). But they refused and "overcame him by the blood of the Lamb and by the word of their testimony; they did not love their lives so much as to shrink from death" (Rev. 12:11). God rewarded them with "a crown of life" (Rev. 2:10).

What do these biblical cases of civil disobedience have in common?

In each case there are three essential elements: first, a command by divinely appointed authorities that is contrary to the word of God; second, an act of disobedience to that command; third, some kind of divine approval (explicit or implicit) of the refusal to obey the authorities. And basic to these divinely approved cases of civil disobedience was that the believers were compelled to act contrary to their adherence to God's commands, which in the above cases were to worship him not idols, not to kill innocent people, to pray only to him, and to proclaim the gospel. Each civil injunction did not simply allow others to act contrary to God's law; it forced believers to disobey God's law. Such laws were oppressive and should be disobeyed.

Does anyone object to this version of the anticompulsionist view?

Yes. Some have argued that it overlooks the biblical command to rescue the innocent. Proverbs 24:11 says: "Rescue those being led away to death." On this basis the objectors insist that it is right to disobey government when innocent lives are at stake, such as the Jews in Nazi Germany or the unborn in legalized abortion.

Are there any problems with this interpretation?

Yes, several have been pointed out by critics. First, Proverbs 24:11 does not support civil disobedience to prevent legal abortion. In fact, in this very chapter God enjoins civil obedience on the believers and warns against even associating with lawbreakers (v. 21). Furthermore, those being led away to death (v. 11) are probably victims of lawbreakers, not those being put to death in accordance with the law. There is no indication at all in the text or its context that the command is to interrupt the God-ordained adjudication of the law, even in capital cases. But others have argued that neither does the text affirm that *no* civil disobedience is permissible to save lives. Hence, the text, some argue, is inconclusive for either position.

Second, comparing German Jews and the unborn is invalid based on a significant difference. For one thing, the holocaust was state commanded, whereas legalized abortion in America is only state permitted. The former would allow for civil disobedience but the latter would not. In addition, failure to disobey the law to kill unwilling Jews or failure to disobey the law to aid those who are charged with killing Jews is tantamount to assisting in the crime. However, failure to interfere with the law that permits abortion is not tantamount to assisting in the crime. On the other hand, defenders of rescuing have argued that breaking the law to stop abortion, although not obligated, fulfills Jesus' command to "love your neighbor as yourself." And since the state's trespassing laws are used to compel Christians to disobey this command, it is argued, civil disobedience is justified. Here again, the response is that loving one's neighbor does not necessitate disobeying the law.

The Nature of Prolife Activism

Where does the logic of the antipromulgation view lead?

Critics of rescuing argue that the same logic that justifies blocking clinic doors to prevent abortions would justify blocking the doors to Hindus' or Buddhists' temples so as to prevent them from committing idolatry. It would also justify snatching alcohol and cigarettes out of unbelievers' hands so as to prevent their (and others') deaths. Likewise, it would justify civil disobedience to hinder a state-executed capital punishment if the disobeyer believed the person to be innocent. Such acts are based on the presumption that one's personal belief can override God-ordained governmental process of civil justice (Rom. 13:1).

On the other hand, supporters of rescuing argue that this example commits a category mistake, such as when one asks the question, "What sound is blue?" That is to say, they claim that the antirescuer mistakenly applies that which is an appropriate response to prevent imminent murder ("immediate physical interference") to the question of what is appropriate to stop self-inflicted spiritual death. But these result from different causes, the first is physically inflicted on the victim by another person and is irreversible while the second is a decision made by the victim himself and can be reversed prior to his physical death. Hence, the best way to prevent spiritual death is to share with the unbeliever the truth about

God and pray that he makes a correct decision. Blocking the door to his "church" will do no good. In response, it is pointed out that the two cases are morally the same, since both prevent others from doing an evil to a person.

Some critics of rescuing say that the logic of nonviolent civil disobedience to rescue the unborn may lead to violent activity. John Whitehead urged, "Surely if you witnessed your father, mother, brother or sister being carried into a euthanasia clinic on a stretcher you would act, and radically if necessary."[12] Randall Terry of Operation Rescue utilizes the same kind of argument, comparing his efforts to the rescue of Jews in Hitler's Germany. However, by this same logic violent activity could be employed. For sometimes delivering the innocent demands that we shoot to kill a murderer who has already killed hundreds of little children and is aiming a weapon at more. Therefore, to be consistent with their own logic they would bomb abortion clinics and even assassinate doctors and nurses performing abortions.

In response to this objection, rescuers point out that it is wrong to assume that rescuers believe that any violation of the law—moral, civil, or criminal—is justified if it results in "saving lives." As the rescuers' view is expressed, they believe in *nonviolent* civil disobedience, which means that they would object to any violence. Opponents affirm that this avoids facing up to the logic of where their position leads.

It has also been argued that the opponents of Operation Rescue mistakenly assume that the rescuers believe that the "end justifies the means," which is not O.R.'s position. They believe that they are obeying a "higher law" by saving lives. They believe that the command for "life preserving" carries with it a greater moral obligation than the command for "no trespassing." Rescuers argue that many of the great Christian philosophers—Augustine, Thomas Aquinas, and Martin Luther King, Jr.—taught similar doctrines, which they believed are supported by the Bible. Others, however, note that neither the Bible nor good moral argument justifies interfering with someone else's legal rights.

The point the nonviolent rescuer is making is that blow-ing up clinics and committing acts of violence against physicians would seriously compromise his higher-law view, since the acts in question seriously jeopardize innocent lives as well as making the rescuers the judge, jury, and executioner of others, which is what physicians who perform abortions are doing to the unborn. By nonviolently blocking clinics they claim to be saving lives without seriously compromising their higher-law view.

Opponents to O.R. respond by emphasizing their point that the same logic which justifies blocking doors to save lives also justifies more radical action, even killing those who are performing the abortion. They point out that it would be justified by this same logic to shoot a would-be murderer to save a life. So, why not, then, kill doctors who are performing abortions since they are "would-be murderers"?

Is there agreement on how to disobey civil laws?

Not really. Here again two views need to be distinguished: One recommends revolt and the other merely refusal. The former promotes an active attack on the government, whereas the latter recommends a more passive resistance. The biblical model is to refuse to obey a government's compulsive commands, but not to revolt against it.

What can we learn from the biblical examples of disobedience?

First of all, in each case God's people engaged in refusal but not revolt. The midwives, for example, refused to obey Pharaoh's order to kill the boy babies, but they did not lead a revolt against Egypt's oppressive government.

Second, their civil disobedience was nonviolent resistance, not violent rebellion. For example, the midwives did not return violence on Egypt for the violence of Egypt. Nor did Israel start a revolution against Pharaoh's oppression; rather they accepted God's salvation from it.

Third, they did not reject the government's punishment but accepted the penalties for disobeying the law. For example, the three Hebrew friends refused to worship the idol, but they did not refuse to go into the fiery furnace. Likewise, Daniel rejected the order to pray to the king, but he accepted the consequent punishment of being cast into the lion's den. And the apostles refused to stop preaching Christ but accepted the penalty of prison. In modern times, Martin Luther King, Jr. argued that one who is involved in nonviolent civil disobedience must be willing to accept the punishment.[13]

Fourth, when possible they would flee from an oppressive command, but they did not fight it. Israel fled from Egypt, and Obadiah and Elijah fled from wicked Queen Jezebel. But none of them engaged in war against the government. So, some argue, whenever a government is tyrannical a Christian should refuse to obey its compulsive commands to do evil but should not revolt against its unbiblical commands that permit evil. This does not mean, of course, that we should neglect to engage in peaceful and legal means to overcome oppression. It does mean that we should not take the law into our own hands, since the authorities that exist have been established by God (Rom. 13:1). And when we cannot accept their command to do evil we must either flee or submit to the government's punishment. "It is mine to avenge; I will repay" (Deut. 32:35). Others argue that a political revolution, such as America's Revolutionary War, is justified differently from civil disobedience for religious oppression, as we find in the above biblical examples.

Questions from Those
Favoring the Antipromulgation View

Should we not obey God's higher law against abortion?

Yes, but God has also commanded that we obey human government (Rom. 13:1, 5). In fact, the Bible commands us to submit to every ordinance of man for the Lord's sake (1 Peter 2:13). As was shown above, man's laws should be disobeyed only when they compel the Christian to do evil, not when the laws permit evil (see Dan. 3:4–7), and we cannot really disobey a law that permits evil unless we break other laws to prevent others from making a legal choice. Others, however, argue that since the state is compelling Christians to *not* "love their neighbor as themselves" by use of the trespassing laws, rescuers are really resisting an unjust law. But the response again is that the love command does not embrace doing evil to demonstrate love.

But doesn't Romans 13 say obey government only when it does good?

No. On the contrary, Romans 13:1 states that the governments "which exist" (de facto) are ordained of God. And in many cases these are evil governments. Indeed, the civil government that existed at the time Paul wrote this was the Roman Empire, which had imposed itself by force on most of the known world. The apostle Paul was well aware of the laws of the pagan civil government which allowed evils like idolatry and sexual immorality to take place. Nevertheless, Paul says that government is ordained by God.

To say (as some Christians do) that Romans 13 applies only when a government acts in accordance with God's Word ignores the circumstances under which the Book of Romans was written, namely an evil monarchy. Finally, if Christians had to obey only those governments that were operating under biblical principles there would be very few governments that Christians would have to obey anywhere in the world. It should not be forgotten, however, that all agree that Christians are justified in disobeying government if it *compels* them to disobey a command of God.

Did Esther disobey the law to save lives?

Esther said, "I will go to the king, even though it is against the law" (Esther 4:16), but she did not really disobey the law. For what the complete law said was that "any man or woman who approaches the king in the inner court without being summoned by the king that he be put to death." The only exception to this is for the king to extend the gold scepter to him and spare his life (Esther 4:11). In short, it was risky to go in before the king unannounced, but it was not absolutely against the law. The law provided only that "any man or woman" could go in at his or her own risk. So the law provided its own exception. No such exception is provided by the Supreme Court ruling on abortion. It does not say we can stop women from going into abortion clinics if we don't believe in abortion. But those who favor rescuing would say that this is why rescuing is justified, since by not allowing Christians to obey Christ's command to love their neighbor (the unborn), the Supreme Court's decision implicitly *supports* abortion. In response, it is noted that lives can be rescued without disobeying the laws.

It is also argued that no one can rightfully force a woman into an abortion clinic against her conviction, but neither should we forcefully prevent anyone from going into a clinic in accordance with her convictions. As long as the government ordained of God permits abortion, we should respect the rights of others to practice it. The same government permits us the freedom to worship, and we expect unbelievers to respect it.

Does this mean Hitler's laws and Stalin's laws were God's laws?

Insofar as Hitler's and Stalin's governments were "ordained of God" (Rom. 13:1), their laws were "God's laws." However, this does not mean that all the laws and actions of Hitler and Stalin were approved by God, any more than all the laws and actions of our government are approved by God. Indeed, there are limits on obedience to these laws. This is why whenever these laws compel a believer to sin, such as killing an unborn child, they should be disobeyed (see Exod. 1:15ff.). Others would say that this includes any government law which forbids Christians from loving their neighbor (the unborn).

Did Corrie ten Boom break the law of Nazi Germany?

Corrie ten Boom broke a law that compelled the Jews to go to their deaths. But, as some point out, in the case of abortions in our country, the law permits, but does not compel, the mother to have an abortion. We have already noted that the Christian must not obey a law that commands them to do evil, such as helping the Nazis find unwilling Jews. But Christians must also not break the law to prevent people from committing evil acts which are permitted under the law. But defenders of rescuing argue that the unborn, not their mothers, should be compared with the Jews. Their critics, however, still insist there is an important difference—Nazi laws were compulsive, not just permissive, demanding death.

Is opposing prolife civil disobedience acting like a Pharisee?

This is a personal attack, not an argument. The comparison with the Pharisees is not valid, since the law the Pharisees accused Jesus of breaking was a law that already had provisions for doing good on the Sabbath. Jesus refused to follow their false interpretation of it. Further, we put God's Word and God's standard above our own personal moral outrage, and we trust God to work all things through the means he has determined. Furthermore, in opposition to breaking laws to rescue, it is argued that the rescuers are like the unbiblical zealots. Hence such biblical analogies do not help to justify or not justify the blocking of doors of abortion clinics.

Doesn't the fact that a law is immoral make disobedience legitimate?

Yes, if it commands us to be immoral, but not if it merely permits others to do what is not moral. Some argue that just because the government makes an immoral act legal, such as the murder of the unborn, it does not follow that the Christian should therefore violate other laws, such as trespassing on private property. They point out that this kind of reasoning would lead us to conclude that if a state passes a law making an immoral act legal, for example prostitution, then we could violate the traffic laws if we believed it would help change the law allowing prostitution. The point is that simply because a government violates God-ordained morality and allows evil to take place does not mean that Christians may violate other civil laws. Rescuers, however, argue that the analogy with prostitution is invalid since prostitutes choose for themselves their profession, whereas the unborn's right to life is violated by others. Furthermore, they argue that the trespassing laws are used to forbid Christians from obeying Christ's command for neighbor-love. The state, then, is compelling Christians to disobey. Hence, disobedience is justified. In response, those who oppose law-breaking as a means of expressing their Christian love insist that there is a more excellent way.

Would it not be right to trespass on private property to save a two-year-old from being killed? Then why not for abortion, too?

Some say that the analogy is invalid, since the murder of the two-year-old is both immoral and illegal. In the case of a mother going to the abortion clinic, she has the legal right to kill her unborn child. They claim that analogy fails because there is no parallel relationship between the example and the present situation.

Further, if it were a good analogy, then the most expedient way to stop the murder would be to kill the person who was about to kill the child. But if this reasoning were applied to the abortion issue, Christiasns would have the moral right (even duty) to kill the doctors and nurses who are doing the abortions. Clearly such actions would be biblically and morally unjustifiable.

Rescuers, however, would argue that the analogy with the mother and two-year-old is more like the Nazi killing of Jews (which was *legal* murder). Hence they claim that just as it was morally alright for the German Christians to rescue the Jew, it is alright for the American Christian to rescue the unborn.

Concerning possible physical force used against medical personnel who perform abortions, some rescuers argue that such force, even if it results in the death of the personnel, is only justified if the rescuer catches the personnel "in the act of murder." Aside from this rare case, wanton killing of medical personnel would be no different than what the abortionist does; he is the judge, jury, and executioner of the child. Thus rescuers do only that which is sufficient to save lives but which is also consistent with their view of higher law.

Opponents of rescuing reply by pointing out that this argument implicitly admits that the obligation to save a life (by the rescuer's logic) is not limited to those caught in the act of murder, since they do know where and when the murder is occurring. For if they knew that three-year-olds were being killed regularly at 3 o'clock in the neighbor's basement, surely they would be duty-bound to use force if necessary to stop it.

Hasn't working within the system failed?

Opponents of rescuing argue that that question implies that the past decade of peaceful, lawful protest, the successful efforts to elect prolife presidents and get prolife Supreme Court justices, as well as efforts to cut off federal and state funding of abortion were all for nothing. On the contrary, all of these successes, including the recent victory in the Supreme Court *Webster* case (July 3, 1989), came prior to the impact of prolife civil disobedience, not as a result of it. It is true that abortion is not yet illegal, but there is progress in that direction. Therefore, to imply that all these efforts within the system have been ineffective is an insult to all who have worked to save lives by peaceful and legal means.

Furthermore, this question implies that whatever works is right. But just because something works does not make it right. Lying and cheating on one's income tax works, but that does not make these actions right. Eliminating the poor would eliminate poverty, but this "good" end certainly would not justify mass murder.

On the other hand, rescuers argue that *greater* progress in the prolife cause would have occurred if prolifers had been consistently resisting the law. In any event, simply appealing to results by either side does not justify *either* position morally.

Isn't it a fact of history that bad governments don't change until they are disobeyed?

Not necessarily. Often governments change lawfully and peacefully. Canada got its freedom from England without a revolution. Martin Luther King's civil rights movement was both nonviolent and within the limits of the Constitution. Communism crumbled in much of Eastern Europe peacefully and legally. On the other hand, the American and French Revolutions were acts of total resistance to government.

This question, some argue, implies that God's work cannot be done in God's way. Further, Christians should get their ethical principles from Scripture rather than from what has proven pragmatically "successful" for unbelievers. Christians should not use illegal means to accomplish moral ends, unless the state compels us to disobey a clear command of God.

Does saving lives justify civil disobedience?

Whether or not one agrees with rescuers, the right end does not sufficiently justify using the wrong means. This is just another end-justifies-the-means argument. Although some do use the excuse of the good end (saving babies) to justify the illegal means (breaking the law), nevertheless, good ends never justify evil means. The means must justify themselves. Even in the saving of a life the Christian cannot use wrong means to accomplish this good end. God gives life and ultimately he is responsible to punish those who take it. Of course, the more sophisticated rescuers try to ground their position on Scripture and reason, not simply on an ends-justify-the-means argument.

Is opposing civil disobedience to rescue abortion victims also opposing their right to live?

Not at all. Those who do not support rescuing do not argue against the children themselves who may be saved by illegal means, but can and do argue against the means by which they may be saved. For example, we could celebrate the birth of a child conceived by rape while at the same time disapproving of the means by which it was conceived. Furthermore, the number of lives actually saved through civil disobedience is minimal, according to some. In fact, some say that if the same effort were exerted biblically and legally, it is entirely possible that more lives could be saved. A Christian police chief in a large city recently noted that the numbers of lives lost due to drugs and crime while police efforts were being diverted to prolifers disobeying the law were probably greater than of those saved by the "rescues." Of course, none of this means that rescuers can or cannot be *morally* justified on other grounds. It simply disputes whether in fact more lives are being saved than lost.

Does the government command us to do evil by not allowing us to rescue the innocent from death?

Some answer no. They claim the government commands us not to trespass on private property and not to block entryways to buildings. The government has not said that we must do evil. It has not said we may not peacefully protest, hand out literature, try to persuade women not to kill their babies, or many of the other legal means to change the law. While the government does not command us to do evil, it does not allow illegal means to accomplish the good which we are allowed to do.

Rescuers, however, argue that the fact the state uses trespassing laws to forbid Christians from loving their neighbors (the unborn) is more insidious than a direct ban. And, in this sense, the government is commanding us to do evil and forbidding us to do good. In response, the antirescuer notes that disobeying laws is not the only way one can work to save the unborn. Working within the law to change the law is the most appropriate way for Christians to express their love to others.

Will God hold us responsible for the sins of omission in not rescuing unborn babies?

This question often has the effect of placing a guilt trip on those who disagree with Operation Rescue. The implication behind this question is that if you are not involved in rescues you are not doing enough to help the prolife movement. In response to this, Christians who disagree with rescuing must continue to do all they can, both morally and legally, to stop abortions and change the laws. Furthermore, even if rescuing is justified, this does not mean one is *obligated* to participate. It can be argued that it is possible not to participate in a rescue, because one believes that God has led one to be involved in another area, and at the same time think rescuing is *justified.* Consequently, one would not be guilty of a sin of omission if one is not obligated to perform the action in question.

Do those who do nothing have a right to criticize those who do something to save lives?

God alone knows the heart, and he will judge accordingly. Those who do nothing are in no position to criticize those who sincerely and conscientiously do something they believe is right to save lives, even if their method is not right. Saying this, of course, is not to justify someone doing a wrong to achieve a right. But it does say that it is better to be wrong in doing something one believes is right to save lives than be in the wrong position of doing nothing to save lives.

If we don't use civil disobedience to fight abortion, what should we do?

There are many things that we can do and should do. First and foremost we should *pray.* God is not deaf; he actually hears and answers prayer. Further, we should *write.* Contrary to popular opinion, senators, legislators, and judges can and do read. Then, we can *speak.* It is amazing what a fitting word in favor of life can do at the appropriate moment. Further, we can and should *give* financially to support prolife groups. Also, we can *act.* We can help local crisis pregnancy centers. We can legally picket local abortion clinics. We can also work to pass prolife legislation. It is better to light one candle than to curse the darkness. Finally, we can and should *vote.* Yes, we can still do that in America, and it works. Vote for prolife candidates. These are some of the positive and legal ways citizens can turn the tide of the abortion holocaust.

Treatment of Rescuers

Have the rescuers been treated fairly by the police?

Not really, in many instances. Some police have treated the rescuers in ways they would not dream of treating those arrested for burglary, rape, or drug dealing, for the police fear violating the Supreme Court's *Miranda* decision and/or inviting a lawsuit from any of a number of citizen advocacy groups such as the American Civil Liberties Union.[14] The nature and degree of the police brutality has been adequately summarized by Armando Valladares, U.S. Ambassador to the United Nations Commission on Human Rights:

> Rescuers are acting to protect the rights of unborn babies . . . in a completely peaceful and non-violent manner. They merely sit (or kneel) and pray or sing religious hymns. They even pray for the police officers who arrest and/or abuse them.
> Yet, in many cases, "pain compliance" was inflicted on rescuers after they had been removed from the site, had agreed to leave the site, or were unable to leave because they were pinned to the pavement by police officers. In one instance, 900 peaceful citizens were subjected to such punitive violence.
>
> In another instance, a Catholic priest, former U.S. Army colonel and associate of Mother Teresa, was, under the police chief's orders, manhandled with such force that his own friends could not recognize him; his eyes were swollen shut and his reddened face was covered with cuts and abrasions.[15]

Unfortunately, this sort of police abuse fuels and justifies an already smoldering hatred in the hearts of those who politically oppose the prolife movement. As one news magazine reports, "On an available videotape showing police violence toward Operation Rescue demonstrators, pro-abortion counter-demonstrators are heard urging the police, 'Make it hurt.' As one Christian protestor is dragged off, a man taunts him, 'So long, Nazi boy. Take your mind control somewhere else.'"[16] Another news magazine reported that "Calvary Baptist Church in Knoxville, Tennessee, recently paid a price for its prolife activities. Worshipers arriving at church on Sunday, July 30 [1989], were greeted with the spray-painted message 'I-4-N-I' (eye for an eye) on both the church bus and a nearby sidewalk."[17] At a rescue which took place in Las Vegas, Nevada, in 1989, an incident went unreported by the media and unprevented by the police present at the scene. The physician who owns the abortion clinic gave prochoice demonstrators receptacles of urine which they subsequently poured on the rescuers while jeering at them; the rescuers took the abuse as they continued to pray and sing hymns.

Probably most police departments treat rescuers with respect, and some do not arrest them at all. It should be stressed that though one may have grave doubts about the moral justification of rescuing, one should not condone the treatment rescuers have received at the hands of some law-enforcement personnel in certain cities.

Have the rescuers been treated fairly by the courts?

Not really, in many instances. For example, United States District Judge Robert J. Ward ordered Randall Terry, founder of Operation Rescue, to pay over $50,000 in fines directly to the coffers of a major prochoice organization, the National Organization for Women, which in turn was required to distribute these funds to other abortion defenders, including Planned Parenthood of New York City. Joseph Secola, Terry's attorney, has pointed out that such a penalty is unprecedented. Even the judge admitted that the fines would be the most effective means by which to encourage Operation Rescue compliance; justice didn't seem to be at issue for the judge. Commenting on the judge's decision, Terry stated, "That's like asking civil rights leaders to pay $50,000 to the Klu Klux Klan, or the Jewish Defense League to pay $50,000 to the Young Nazis."[18]

To give the reader an idea of the unjust penalties given to convicted rescuers, consider the following chart which compares the jail sentences of Operation Rescue participants with those for common misdemeanors brought before Los Angeles Municipal Court Judge Patti Jo McKay:[19]

Operation Rescue Defendants	**Defendants for Other Misdemeanor Crimes**
Second Time Offenders	*Second Time Offenders*
Defendant 1 (180 months)	Burglary defendant (30 months)
	Prostitution defendant (45 mos.)
	Trespass defendant (0 months)
First Time Offenders	*First Time Offenders*
Defendant 2 (120 months)	Burglary defendant (5 months)
Defendant 3 (90 months)	Prostitution defendant (5 mos.)
Defendant 4 (45 months)	Trespass defendant (0 months)

Conclusion

We have briefly gone over the arguments for and against rescuing, with responses some have given to these arguments. It is our hope that the reader will draw a thoughtful and balanced conclusion. While there is disagreement about means, all prolifers agree on the end—abortion laws must be changed; the lives of innocent unborn children must be saved. Every person concerned about life should use every moral means at their disposal to resist the slaughter of the innocent.

Notes

Chapter 1 — Medical Questions

1. Testimony given at Congressional Hearings, Washington, D.C., April 23, 1981.

2. Peter Singer and Helga Kuhse, "On Letting Handicapped Infants Die," in ed. Rachels, *The Right Thing to Do* (New York: Random House, 1989), p. 146.

3. Andrew Varga, *The Main Issues in Bioethics,* rev. ed. (New York: Paulist Press, 1984), p. 65.

4. Robert Wennberg, *Life in the Balance: Exploring the Abortion Controversy* (Grand Rapids: Eerdmans, 1985), p. 71.

5. See Watson M. Laetsch, *Plants Basic Concepts of Botany,* (Boston: Little Brown, and Co., 1979).

6. The sources used in this section, which include standard medical school textbooks on prenatal development, are the following: F. Beck, D. B. Moffat, and D. P. Davies, *Human Embryology,* 2nd ed. (Oxford: Blackwell, 1985); Keith Moore, *The Developing Human: Clinically Oriented Embryology,* 2nd ed. (Philadelphia: W. B. Saunders, 1977); Andre E. Hellegers, "Fetal Development," in eds. Mappes and Zembaty, *Biomedical Ethics* (New York: McGraw-Hill, 1981), pp. 405–409; and Stephen M. Krason, *Abortion: Politics, Morality and the Constitution* (Lanham, Md.: University Press of America, 1984), pp. 337–49.

7. See John T. Noonan, "The Experience of Pain by the Unborn," in ed. Hensley, *The Zero People* (Ann Arbor: Servant Books, 1983), pp. 141–56; A. William Liley, "Experiments with Uterine and Fetal Instrumentation," in eds. Kuback and Valenti, *Intrauterine Fetal Visualization* (Oxford: Excerpta Medica; New York: American Elsevier Publishing, 1976); and Mortimer Rosen, "The Secret Brain: Learning Before Birth," in *Harper's* (April 1978): 46.

8. Vincent J. Collins, M.D., Steven R. Zielinski, M.D., and Thomas J. Marzen, Esq., *Fetal Pain and Abortion: The Medical Evidence,* Studies in Law & Medicine, No. 8 (Chicago: Americans United for Life, 1984), p. 8.

9. Ernest Van Den Haag, "Is There a Middle Ground?" *National Review* (December 22, 1989): 29–31.

10. Beth Day and Albert W. Liley, *Modern Motherhood* (New York: Random House, 1969), pp. 50–51.

11. Jane English, "Abortion and the Concept of Personhood," in *Biomedical Ethics*, p. 430.

12. Albert Liley, *A Case Against Abortion*, Liberal Studies (Whitcombe & Tombs, Inc., 1971), as quoted in Dr. and Mrs. J. C. Willke, *Abortion: Questions and Answers*, rev. ed. (Cincinnati: Hayes, 1988), p. 52.

13. See Blakeslee, "Fetus Returned to Womb Following Surgery," *New York Times* (October 7, 1986): C1, col. 5.

14. For an excellent overview of major birth defects, causes, and chances of occurring (for every 100,000 babies born alive), see "Birth Defects," in ed. Charles B. Clayman, M.D., *The American Medical Association Encyclopedia of Medicine* (New York: Random House, 1989), pp. 172–73.

15. See Stanley Hauerwas, *Suffering Presence* (Notre Dame, Ind.: University of Notre Dame Press, 1987).

16. Citing a study of the late Dr. Andre Hellegers of Georgetown University's Kennedy Institute for Bioethics and Human Reproduction, Krason writes that "of 200 consecutive suicides at the Baltimore Morgue . . . none had been committed by people with congenital anomalies" (Krason, *Abortion*, p. 295).

17. As quoted in Bernard Nathanson, M.D., *Aborting America* (New York: Doubleday, 1979), p. 235.

18. *Ibid.*, pp. 235–36.

19. C. Everett Koop, *The Right to Live: The Right to Die* (Wheaton, Ill.: Tyndale House, 1976), pp. 51–52.

20. This point was brought out by Germain Grisez, *Abortion: The Myths, the Realities, and the Arguments* (New York: Corpus Books, 1970), pp. 28–30.

21. Francis A. Schaeffer and C. Everett Koop, M.D. *Whatever Happened to the Human Race?* (Old Tappan, N.J.: Fleming H. Revell, 1979), pp. 41–42.

22. Stephen D. Schwarz, *The Moral Question of Abortion* (Chicago: Loyola University Press, 1990), p. 20.

23. Gary Bergel, *When You Were Formed in Secret* (Elyria, Ohio: Intercessors for America, 1980), p. II–4, as quoted in *Ibid.*, pp. 21–22.

24. Collins, Zielinski, and Marzen, *Fetal Pain*, p. 8.

25. *Ibid.*

26. *Ibid.*, p. 9. These statistics are based on calculations from the Centers for Disease Control—Abortion Surveillance, Annual Summary 1979–80. U.S. Department of Health and Human Services, May 1983.

27. *Ibid.*

28. Laurence Tribe, *Abortion: The Clash Absolutes* (New York: W. W. Norton, 1990), p. 215. The term used by Tribe to describe the unborn, "fertilized embryo," makes about as much sense as calling today "a now-present tomorrow," since only an ovum is capable of being fertilized and only tomorrow is capable of becoming today, but when the ovum is fertilized it ceases to be an ovum and becomes an individual member of the

human species in its youngest stage of development, a zygote, and when tomorrow becomes today it ceases to be tomorrow.

29. Schwarz, *The Moral Question of Abortion*, pp. 142–43.

30. *AMA Encyclopedia of Medicine*, pp. 303–6.

31. *Ibid.*, p. 172.

32. Norman L. Geisler, *Christian Ethics: Options and Issues* (Grand Rapids: Baker Book House, 1989); Nathanson, *Aborting America*, pp. 284–85; John Warwick Montgomery, "How to Decide the Birth Control Question," in his *Slaughter of the Innocents: Abortion, Birth Control, and Divorce in Light of Science, Law, and Theology* (Westchester, Ill.: Crossway Books, 1981), pp. 17–27; James M. Humber, "Abortion: The Avoidable Moral Dilemma," in *Journal of Value Inquiry* 9 (1975): 302; and Don Marquis, "Why Abortion Is Immoral," *Journal of Philosophy* 86 (April 1989): 201–202.

33. Horatio R. Storer and Franklin F. Heard, *Criminal Abortion: Its Nature, Its Evidence, & Its Law* (Boston: Little, Brown & Co., 1868), pp. 28–29, 79, as quoted in Krason, *Abortion*, p. 171.

34. Nathanson, *ibid.*, p. 164.

Chapter 2 — Legal Questions

1. Citation from the Declaration of Independence.

2. On English common law and abortion, Stephen M. Krason, *Abortion: Politics, Morality, and the Constitution* (Lanham, Md.: University Press of America, 1984), pp. 134–48; and John Warwick Montgomery, "The Rights of Unborn Children," in *Simon Greenleaf Law Review* 5 (1985–86): 27–31.

3. See Krason, *Abortion*, p. 400; and John T. Noonan, "An Almost Absolute Value in History," in ed. Noonan, *The Morality of Abortion* (Cambridge: Harvard University Press, 1970), pp. 23–26.

4. See the citations of the American dictionaries in John S. Putka, "The Supreme Court and Abortion: The Socio-Political Impact of Judicial Activism," unpublished Ph.D. dissertation, University of Cincinnati, 1979, pp. 33–34.

5. See Dennis J. Horan and Thomas J. Marzen, "Abortion and Midwifery: A Footnote in Legal History," in eds. Hilgers, Horan, and Mall, *New Perspective on Human Abortion* (Frederick, Md.: University Publications of America, 1981), p. 199.

6. Portion of Fifth Amendment of the United States Constitution.

7. Fourteenth Amendment of the United States Constitution.

8. For contemporary legal references to the unborn child as "person" when Fourteenth Amendment was written, see Krason, *Abortion*, pp. 164–66.

9. Krason, *Abortion*, pp. 170–71. For documentation of the facts about the Fourteenth Amendment cited in the text, see pp. 168–73.

10. Quoted from *Dred Scott v. Standford* 60 U.S. (19 How.) 393 (1857).

11. For an excellent overview of the parallels between slavery and abor-

tion, see James Tunstead Burtchaell, *Rachel Weeping: The Case Against Abortion* (San Francisco: Harper & Row, 1984), pp. 239–87.

12. This outline is taken from Dr. and Mrs. J. C. Willke, *Abortion: Questions & Answers,* rev. ed. (Cincinnati: Hayes, 1988), p. 18.

13. See *Rachel Weeping,* pp. 239–87.

14. *Santa Clara County* v. *South Pacific R.* 118 U.S. 394 (1886).

15. For an historical overview of Great Britain's abortion laws, see Krason, *Abortion,* pp. 134–50; and Montgomery, "The Rights of Unborn Children," pp. 23–72.

16. For a defense of this interpretation of Exodus 21:22–23, see Gleason Archer, *Encyclopedia of Bible Difficulties* (Grand Rapids: Zondervan, 1982), pp. 246–49; Francis J. Beckwith, "Abortion and Public Policy: A Response to Some Arguments," *Journal for the Evangelical Theological Society* 32 (Dec. 1989): 503–18; and Norman L. Geisler, *Christian Ethics: Options and Issues* (Grand Rapids: Baker Book House, 1989), p. 145.

17. Quoted in Krason, *Abortion,* p. 132.

18. For the documentation of these historical references, see *ibid.,* pp. 120–34.

19. See Noonan, "An Almost Absolute Value," pp. 15–26; Michael J. Gorman, *Abortion and the Early Church* (Downers Grove, Ill.: InterVarsity Press, 1982), pp. 70–73; George Hunston Williams, "The Sacred Condominium," in *The Morality of Abortion,* p. 169; Horan and Marzen, "Abortion and Midwifery," p. 199; and Krason, *Abortion,* pp. 134–73.

20. James Witherspoon, "Reexamining *Roe:* Nineteenth-Century Abortion Statutes and the Fourteenth Amendment," *St. Mary's Law Journal* 17 (1985): 70.

21. Cyril Means, "The Phoenix of Abortional Freedom: Is a Penumbral or Ninth Amendment Right About to Arise from the Nineteenth-Century Legislative Ashes of a Fourteenth-Century Common Law Liberty," *New York Law Forum* 17 (1971); and Cyril Means, "The Law of New York Concerning Abortion and the Status of the Foetus: 1664–1968," *New York Law Forum* 14 (1968).

22. In addition to Witherspoon's article, see Krason, *Abortion,* pp. 134–57; Dennis J. Horan and Thomas J. Balch, *"Roe* v. *Wade:* No Justification in History, Law, or Logic," eds. Horan, Grant, Cunningham in *Abortion and the Constitution: Reversing Roe* v. *Wade Through The Courts* (Washington, D.C.: Georgetown University Press, 1987), pp. 57–88; Joseph W. Dellapenna, "Abortion and the Law: Blackmun's Distortion of the Historical Record," in *Abortion and the Constitution,* pp. 137–58; and Joseph W. Dellapenna, "The History of Abortion: Technology, Morality, and Law," in *University of Pittsburgh Law Review* 40 (1979).

23. See, for example, Laurence Tribe, *Abortion: The Clash of Absolutes* (New York: W. W. Norton, 1990), pp. 27–41, 119–20; and Susan Estrich and Kathleen Sullivan, "Abortion Politics: Writing for an Audience of One," *University of Pennsylvania Law Review* 138 (1989): 152–54.

24. John Warwick Montgomery, *Slaughter of the Innocents* (Westchester, Ill.: Crossway, 1981), p. 37.

25. Witherspoon, "Reexamining *Roe,*" p. 32.

26. Quoted in Krason, *Abortion,* p. 132.

27. *Doe* v. *Bolton* 410 U.S. 179, 192 (1973).

28. Victor Rosemblum and Thomas Marzen, "Strategies for Reversing *Roe* v. *Wade* Through the Courts," in eds. Horan, Grant, and Cunningham, *Abortion and the Constitution,* pp. 199–200.

29. Report on the Human Life Bill—S. 158; Committee on the Judiciary, United States Senate, December 1981, p. 5.

30. Thomas O'Meara, "Abortion: The Court Decides a Non-Case," *The Supreme Court Review* (1974): 344.

31. Stanley M. Harrison, "The Supreme Court and Abortional Reform: Means to an End," *New York Law Forum* 19 (1974): 690.

32. Robert A. Destro, "Abortion and the Constitution: The Need for a Life-Protective Amendment," *California Law Review* 63 (1975): 1250.

33. Jacqueline Nolan Haley, "Haunting Shadows from the Rubble of Roe's Right to Privacy," *Suffolk University Law Review* 9 (1974): 152–53.

34. John Hart Ely, "The Wages of Crying Wolf: A Comment on *Roe* v. *Wade,"* *Yale Law Journal* 82 (1973): 921.

35. John T. Noonan, Jr., "Raw Judicial Power," in ed. Hensley, *The Zero People* (Ann Arbor: Servant Books, 1983), p. 18.

36. Charles E. Rice, "Overruling *Roe* v. *Wade:* An Analysis of the Proposed Constitutional Amendments," *Boston College Industrial and Commercial Law Review* 15 (December 1973): 309.

37. Lynn Wardle and Mary Anne Q. Wood, *A Lawyer Looks at Abortion* (Provo, Utah: Brigham Young University Press, 1982), p. 12.

38. William R. Hopkin, Jr., "*Roe* v. *Wade* and the Traditional Legal Standards Concerning Pregnancy," *Temple Law Quarterly* 47 (1974): 729–30.

39. John Warwick Montgomery, "The Rights of Unborn Children," *Simon Greenleaf Law Review* 5 (1985–86): 40.

40. Roger Wertheimer, "Understanding Blackmun's Argument: The Reasoning of *Roe* v. *Wade,"* in *Abortion: Moral and Legal Perspectives* (Amherst: University of Massachusetts Press, 1984), pp. 120–21.

41. Tribe, *Abortion,* p. 10.

42. *Roe* v. *Wade* 410 U.S. 113, 159 (1973).

43. Chart taken from Krason, *Abortion,* p. 93.

44. For a more thorough critique, see the appropriate artices in *Abortion and the Constitution;* and Krason, *Abortion.* For a list of the bibliographical citations of the numerous scholarly works which critique *Roe* as well as a list of other fundamental errors in the Court's decision, see Dennis J. Horan, Clark D. Forsythe, and Edward R. Grant, *Two Ships Passing in the Night: An Interpretavist Review of the White-Stevens Colloquy on* Roe *v.* Wade, Studies in Law, Medicine & Society (Chicago: Americans United for Life Legal Defense Fund, 1987), pp. 2–3, n. 8.

45. Robert Bork, *The Tempting of America: The Political Seduction of the Law* (New York: Simon and Schuster, 1990), pp. 111–17; and John Hart Ely, "The Wages of Crying Wolf: A Comment on *Roe* v. *Wade, Yale Law Review* 82 (1973). Bork and Ely are excellent legal scholars and philosophers of law whom we admire a great deal, but they are simply not currently doing the nuts and bolts dismembering of *Roe*'s historical and Constitutional foundation necessary for a complete Supreme Court reversal.

46. Editor's Preface, "Symposium on the Law and Politics of Abortion," *Michigan Law Review* 77 (1979): 1569.

47. Horan and Balch, "*Roe* v. *Wade:* No Justification in History, Law, or Logic," p. 58.

48. *City of Akron* v. *Akron Center for Reproductive Health, Inc.* 463 U.S. 416, 458 (1983) (J. O'Connor dissenting).

49. Martin Arbagi, "*Roe* and the Hippocratic Oath," in *Abortion and the Constitution*, pp. 174–75.

50. These statistics can be obtained through the Alan Guttmacher Institute, the think tank of the prochoice Planned Parenthood Federation of America.

51. See Eugene H. Methvin "Hitler & Stalin: Twentieth-Century Super Killers," *National Review* (May 31, 1985): 22–29.

52. *Webster* v. *Reproductive Health Services* (1989), as found in *The United States Law Week* 57, no. 50 (27 July, 1989): 5035.

53. *Doe* v. *Bolton*, 410 U.S. 179, 192 (1973).

54. *Webster*, 5040.

55. "Court Moves Closer to *Roe* v. *Wade* Showdown," *Christianity Today* (June 24, 1991): 50.

56. Willke, *Abortion*, pp. 27–28.

57. This is a very liberal estimate. In a recent study three researchers came to the following more conservative conclusion: "A reasonable estimate for the actual number of criminal abortions per year in the prelegalization era [prior to 1967] would be from a low of 39,000 (1950) to a high of 210,000 (1961) and a mean of 98,000 per year." (Barbara J. Syska, Thomas W. Hilgers, M.D., and Dennis O'Hare, "An Objective Model for Estimating Criminal Abortions and Its Implications for Public Policy," in *New Perspectives*, p. 178). For a detailed study of the differing statistics on this matter, see Krason, *Abortion*, pp. 300–03.

58. This is the usual claim of such groups as Planned Parenthood Federation of America. There is overwhelming evidence that this claim is grossly exaggerated. See Krason, *Abortion*, p. 304.

59. Mary Anne Warren, "On the Moral and Legal Status of Abortion," in ed. Feinberg, *The Problem of Abortion*, 2nd ed. (Belmont, Calif.: Wadsworth, 1984), p. 103.

60. Bernard Nathanson, *Aborting America* (New York: Doubleday, 1979), p. 193.

61. Willke, *Abortion*, pp. 101–2.

62. Mary Calderone, "Illegal Abortion as a Public Health Problem," in *American Journal of Public Health* 50 (July 1960): 949.

63. Nathanson, *Aborting America*, p. 194.

64. For an overview of the theological and philosophical arguments in the capital punishment debate, see Geisler, *Christian Ethics*, pp. 193–213.

65. See note 57.

66. David C. Reardon, *Aborted Women: Silent No More* (Westchester, Ill.: Crossway Books, 1987), p. 319.

67. *Ibid.*, pp. 319–20. For studies showing the plausibility of this view see works cited by Reardon.

68. Nathanson, *Aborting America*, p. 267.

69. Reardon, *Aborted Women*, p. 13.

70. *Ibid.*, p. 15.

Chapter 3—Moral Questions

1. For an evaluation of this argument against religious belief, see Francis J. Beckwith, "The Problem of Hypocrisy," *Christian Research Journal* 10 (Summer 1987): 14–17.

2. For an example of this position, see Virginia Ramey Mollenkott, "Reproductive Choice: Basic to Justice for Women," *Christian Scholars' Review* 17 (March 1988): 286–93. For a critique of this paper, see George I. Mavrodes, "Abortion and Imagination: Reflections on Mollenkott's 'Reproductive Choice,'" *Christian Scholars' Review* 18 (December 1988): 168–70. For a more detailed critique of Mollenkott's paper, see Francis J. Beckwith, "Abortion and Public Policy: A Response to Some Arguments," *Journal of the Evangelical Theological Society* 32 (Dec. 1989): 503–18.

3. See article by Rabbi Aryeh Spero, "Therefore Choose Life," in *Policy Review* (Spring 1989): 38–44. See Michael Gorman, *Abortion and the Early Church* (Downers Grove, Ill.: InterVarsity Press, 1982).

4. Mollenkott, "Reproductive Choice." pp. 286–93.

5. See especially the nontheological defense of the prolife position by former abortion-rights activist Bernard Nathanson in *Aborting America* (New York: Doubleday, 1979). For other examples of nontheological defenses of the prolife position, see Baruch Brody, *Abortion and the Sanctity of Human Life* (Cambridge: M.I.T. Press, 1975); David Clark, "An Evaluation of the Quality of Life Argument for Infanticide," *Simon Greenleaf Law Review* 5 (1985–86): 91–112; Peter Kreeft, *The Unaborted Socrates* (Downers Grove, Ill.: InterVarsity Press, 1984); Don Marquis, "Why Abortion Is Immoral," *Journal of Philosophy* 86 (April 1989): 183–202; A. Chadwick Ray, "Humanity, Personhood, and Abortion," *International Philosophical Quarterly* 25 (1985): 233–45; and Andrew Varga, *Main Issues in Bioethics*, 2nd ed. (New York: Paulist Press, 1984), pp. 59–65.

6. Laurence H. Tribe, *Abortion: The Clash of Absolutes* (New York: W. W. Norton, 1990), p. 116.

7. The facts and statistics for rape in this section are taken from Stephen Krason, *Abortion: Politics, Morality, and the Constitution* (Lanham, Md.: University Press of America, 1984), pp. 280–85, 288. It should be noted that these facts and statistics cited by Krason are taken from well-known scholarly studies fully documented in his text.

8. Michael Bauman, "Verbal Plunder: Combating the Feminist Encroachment on the Language of Religion and Morality," paper presented at the 42nd annual meeting of the Evangelical Theological Society, Southern Baptist Theological Seminary, New Orleans, Louisiana, 16–18 November, 1990, pp. 16–17.

9. *Ibid.,* p. 284. For an overview of the research, see Sandra Kathleen Mahkorn, "Pregnancy and Sexual Assault," in David Mall and Walter F. Watts, M.D., *The Psychological Aspects of Abortion* (Washington, D.C.: University Publications of America, 1979), pp. 67–68.

10. Krason, *Abortion,* p. 284.

11. See the articles in ed. Feinberg, *The Problem of Abortion,* 2nd ed. (Glencoe, Calif.: Wadsworth, 1984).

12. Ray, "Humanity and Personhood," pp. 240–41.

13. John Jefferson Davis, *Abortion and the Christian* (Phillipsburg, N.J.: Presbyterian and Reformed, 1984), p. 57.

14. Ray, "Humanity and Personhood," p. 240.

15. Stephen D. Schwarz, *The Moral Question of Abortion* (Chicago: Loyola University Press, 1990), p. 90.

16. *Ibid.*

17. Judith Jarvis Thomson, "A Defense of Abortion," in ed. Feinberg, *The Problem of Abortion,* 2nd ed. (Belmont, Calif.: Wadsworth, 1984), pp. 173–87. This article was originally published in *Philosophy and Public Affairs* 1 (1971): 47–66.

18. Justice Harry Blackmun in "The 1973 Supreme Court Decisions on State Abortion Laws: Excerpts from Opinion in *Roe v. Wade,*" in *The Problem of Abortion,* p. 195.

19. Tribe, *Abortion,* p. 135.

20. Thomson, "A Defense of Abortion," pp. 174–75.

21. See Francis J. Beckwith, "Personal Bodily Rights, Abortion, and Unplugging the Violinist: A Critical Analysis," *International Philosophical Quarterly* (March 1992): forthcoming; Schwarz, *The Moral Question of Abortion,* pp. 113–24; Stephen D. Schwarz and R. K. Tacelli, "Abortion and Some Philosophers: A Critical Examination," *Public Affairs Quarterly* 3 (April 1989): 81–98; John T. Wilcox, "Nature as Demonic in Thomson's Defense of Abortion," *The New Scholasticism* 63 (Autumn 1989): 463–84; and Celia Wolf-Devine, "Abortion and the 'Feminine Voice,'" *Public Affairs Quarterly* 3 (July 1989): 81–97.

22. See eds. Kastner and Young, *In the Best Interest of the Child: A Guide*

to State Child Support and Paternity Laws (n.p.: Child Support Enforcement Beneficial Laws Project, National Conference of State Legislatures, 1981).

23. Michael Levin, review of Wennberg, *Life in the Balance, Constitutional Commentary* 3 (Summer 1986): 511.

24. *Sound Advice for All Prolife Activists and Candidates Who Wish to Include a Concern for Women's Rights in Their Prolife Advocacy: Feminists for Life Debate Handbook* (Kansas City, Mo.: Feminists for Life of America, n.d.), pp. 15–16.

25. Dennis J. Horan and Burke J. Balch, *Infant Doe and Baby Jane Doe: Medical Treatment of the Handicapped Newborn,* Studies in Law & Medicine Series (Chicago: Americans United for Life, 1985), p. 2.

26. *In re Storar,* 53 N.Y. 2d 363, 380–81, 420 N.E. 2d 64, 73, 438 N.Y.S. 2d 266, 275 (1981), as quoted in *ibid.,* pp. 2–3.

27. Horan and Balch, *Infant Doe,* pp. 3–4.

28. Kate Michelman in *New York Times* (May 10, 1988).

29. Nancy S. Erickson, J.D., "Women and the Supreme Court: Anatomy Is Destiny," *Brooklyn Law Review* 41 (1974): 242.

30. Tribe, *Abortion,* p. 194.

31. *Webster* v. *Reproductive Health Services* 492 U.S. 490, 557 (1989) (J. Blackmun, dissenting). By totally ignoring the evidence for the unborn's humanness, Blackmun's highly emotional argument begs the question, just as it would beg the question as to a black person's humanness if it were employed in a defense of slavery:

> The Congress in passing the Fourteenth Amendment discards a landmark case of the last generation (*Dred Scott*), and casts into darkness the hopes and visions of every property owner in the South who had come to believe that the Constitution guaranteed him the right to exercise some control over his God-given right to own property. The plurality does so either oblivious or insensitive to the fact that millions of property owners, and their families, have ordered their lives around the right to ownership of property, and that this right has become vital to the full participation of Southern gentlemen in the economic and political walks of American life.

32. *Sound Advice,* p. 17.

Chapter 4 — Social Questions

1. Dr. and Mrs. J. C. Willke, *Abortion: Questions and Answers,* (Cincinnati: Hayes Publishing, 1985), p. 184.

2. *New York Times* (June 2, 1977): A5. As cited in James T. Burtchaell, *Rachel Weeping: The Case Against Abortion* (San Francisco: Harper & Row, 1984), p. 87.

3. *American Medical Association Encyclopedia of Medicine,* ed. Clayton (New York: Random House, 1989), p. 58.

4. As cited in Willke, *Abortion,* p. 101.

5. *AMA Encyclopedia,* p. 58.

6. David C. Reardon, *Aborted Women* (Westchester, Ill.: Crossway Books, 1987).

7. *Ibid.,* p. 90.

8. *Ibid.,* p. 91.

9. E. F. Lenoski, "Translating Injury Data into Preventative Health Care Services," University of Southern California Medical School, unpublished, 1976, as cited in Stephen M. Krason, *Abortion: Politics, Morality, and the Constitution* (Lanham, Md.: University Press of America, 1984), p. 320.

10. See B. D. Schmitt and C. H. Kempe, *Child Abuse: Management and Prevention of the Battered Child Syndrome* (Basel: Ciba-Geigy, 1975).

11. A. Jackson, National Center of Child Abuse and Neglect, United States Department of Health and Human Services (1973, 1982), as cited in Willke, *Abortion,* p. 139–40.

12. For more detailed responses to questions about abortion and the mentally and physically handicapped, see chapter 1, "Medical Questions."

13. See Willke, *Abortion,* pp. 208–9.

14. Citing a study of the late Dr. Andre Hellegers of Georgetown University's Kennedy Institute of Bioethics and Human Reproduction, Dr. Krason writes that "of 200 consecutive suicides at the Baltimore Morgue . . . none had been committed by people with congenital anomalies," as cited in Krason, *Abortion,* p. 295.

15. As quoted in Willke, *Abortion,* p. 208.

16. See the interview of the administrator of a religious adoption agency that provides an alternative to abortion: "Alternative to Abortion," *Pentecostal Evangel* (February 11, 1990): 14–15.

17. James T. Brutchaell, *Rachel Weeping: The Case Against Abortion* (San Francisco: Harper & Row, 1982), p. 129.

18. Ruth Ann Hanley, "Do Right-to-Lifers Care Only About the Unborn?" editorial, *The Communicator* (Indiana Right-to-Life newsletter) 5, no. 5 (June 1980): 2, as quoted in *ibid.*

19. Ron Sider, *Completely Pro-Life: Building a Consistent Stance* (Downers Grove, Ill.: InterVarsity Press, 1987).

20. Willke, *Abortion,* p. 255.

21. From S. Lichter and S. Rothman, "The Media Elite: White, Male, Secular, and Liberal," *Public Opinion* (1981), as cited in *ibid.,* 258.

22. George Mavrodes, "Abortion and Imagination: Reflections on Mollenkott's 'Reproductive Choice,'" in *Christian Scholar's Review* 18 (December 1988): 168–70.

23. Dr. Jacqueline Kasun, "The Population Bomb: A Look at the Facts," in ed. Hensley, *The Zero People* (Ann Arbor: Servant Books, 1983), pp. 33–41. This article, written by a professor of economics at Humboldt State University in northern California, originally appeared in *Intellect* (June 1977).

24. Ethan Bronner, "Most in U.S. Favor Ban on Majority of Abortions, Poll Finds," in *The Boston Globe* 235 (31 March, 1989): 1, 12.

25. *Ibid.*, p. 12.

26. Gina Kolata, "Fetal Sex Test Used as Step to Abortion," *The New York Times* (December 25, 1988): A1.

27. Christopher Farley, "The Debate over Uses of Prenatal Testing," *USA Today* (February 2, 1989).

28. Jo McGowan, "In India, They Abort Females," *Newsweek* (January 30, 1989): 12.

29. Farley, "The Debate," 1D

30. Anne Koeing, "Abortion for Gender Is Debated," *Lancaster Pennsylvania News* (January 22, 1989): A4.

31. Kolota, "Fetal Sex Test," A1.

32. Farley, "The Debate," 1D

33. Joyce Price, "Prenatal Test of Sex Sometimes Triggers Abortion Decisions," *Washington Times* (February 13, 1987): D6.

34. Dorothy C. Wetz and John C. Fletcher, "Fatal Knowledge?: Prenatal Diagnosis and Sex Selection," *Hastings Center Report*, (May/June 1989): 21–27.

35. *Ibid.*, 21.

36. See Marvin Olasky, "The Village's Prolife Voice," *Christianity Today* (June 24, 1991): 24–26.

37. An editorial in the *Reno Gazette-Journal* (June 21, 1990): A9, states: "[Del Papa] raises a very good question when she asks where the strident anti-abortionists were when the state opened a public comment period before the wording was finalized. That was the proper time for anyone to raise objections."

38. Michael L. Campbell, "Ballot Writers Face Tough Abortion Item," *Las Vegas Sun* (May 5, 1990): 1B, 4B.

39. Letter dated September 14, 1990 on official Hastings Center stationary.

40. It should be noted that the only member of the media who had the courage to acknowledge the legitimacy of these criticisms was former Nevada Governor Michael O'Callaghan (Democrat) who now writes for the *Las Vegas Sun* (see his June 5, 1990 "Where I Stand" column). The rest of the media simply did not take the criticisms very seriously.

41. See Baruch Brody, *Abortion and the Sanctity of Human Life: A Philosophical View* (Cambridge: M.I.T. Press, 1975); Bernard Nathanson, *Aborting America* (New York: Doubleday, 1979); and Ernest Van Den Haag, "Is There a Middle Ground?" *National Review* (December 12, 1989): 29–31.

Chapter 5 — Questions about Infanticide

1. Dr. and Mrs. John C. Willke, *Abortion: Questions and Answers*, (Cincinnati: Hayes Publishing, 1985), p. 205.

2. *Ibid.*

3. *Roanoke Times & World News* (30 June 1983): A4.

4. N. Fost, "Passive Euthanasia of Patients with Down's Syndrome," *Archives of Internal Medicine,* (13 Dec. 1982).

5. *AMA Prism* (May 1973), ch. 3, p. 2.

6. James Burtchaell, *Rachel Weeping: The Case Against Abortion* (San Francisco: Harper & Row, 1984), p. 85.

7. William Brennan, *The Abortion Holocaust: Today's Final Solution* (St. Louis: Landmark Press, 1983), p. 82.

8. *Ibid.*

9. Stephen Krason, *Abortion: Politics, Morality, and the Constitution* (Lanham, Md.: University Press of America, 1984), p. 34.

10. Margaret Sanger, *Woman and the New Race* (New York: Truth Publishing, 1920), p. 63.

11. Peter Singer, "Sanctity of Life or Quality of Life?" *Pediatrics* 73 (July 1973): 128–29.

12. Spoken in a debate with Francis J. Beckwith, David Day, and Glynda White, December 4, 1989, in the Hendrix Auditorium on the campus of the University of Nevada, Las Vegas. The debate was sponsored by the Black Student Association of UNLV. This section of the debate is on an audio cassette tape recorded by Mark Wiegand.

13. Michael Tooley, "Abortion and Infanticide: Abortion on Demand," in eds. Abelson and Friquegnon, *Ethics for Modern Life* (New York: St. Martin's Press, 1987), pp. 122–23.

14. *Policy Review,* no. 32 (Spring 1985): 15.

15. George Will, "The Killing Will Not Stop," in *The Zero People,* pp. 206–7. This article originally appeared as a syndicated column in the *Washington Post* (April 22, 1982).

16. David K. Clark, "An Evaluation of the Quality of Life Argument for Infanticide," *Simon Greenleaf Law Review* 5 (1985–86): 106.

17. See William Brennan, *The Abortion Holocaust: Today's Final Solution* (St. Louis: Landmark Press, 1983), pp. 58, 59.

18. *British Medical News* (2 April 1973).

19. *New England Journal of Medicine* 288, no. 23.

20. *Reuters News Agency* (12 June 1972).

21. *Medical World News* (June 1973).

22. *American Journal of Obstetrics and Gynecology* 118 (1 January 1974).

23. *National Examiner* (19 August 1980).

Chapter 6 — Questions about Adult Euthanasia

1. Reported in *The News & Daily Advance,* Lynchburg, Va. (Friday, June 8, 1990): C-2, and in all national media.

2. *Reader* June 29, 1983.

3. New Jersey Supreme Court, 70 *New Jersey Reports* 10 (March 31, 1976).

4. *Time* December 11, 1989: 80.

5. *American College of Surgeons Bulletin,* (August, 1988): 4.

6. *Ibid.*

7. *Ibid.*

8. *Ibid.*

9. *Ibid.*

10. James Rachels, *The End of Life* (Oxford: Oxford University Press, 1986), p. 112.

11. J. P. Moreland, "James Rachels and the Active Euthanasia Debate," *Journal of the Evangelical Theological Society* 31 (March 1988): 89.

12. Wennberg, *Critical Choices,* p. 24.

13. The historical facts summarized in this section are taken from Robert Wennberg's excellent work, *Critical Choices: Euthanasia, Suicide, and the Right to Die?* (Grand Rapids: Eerdmans, 1989), pp. 39–75. Although we disagree with some aspects of Wennberg's book, it has been very helpful in our study of the subject.

14. See Danielle Gourevitch, "Suicide Among the Sick in Classical Antiquity," *Bulletin of the History of Medicine* 43 (1969): 501–18.

15. Laws IX: 873 C. From eds. Hamilton and Cairns, *The Collected Dialogues of Plato,* including the letters (Princeton: Princeton University Press, 1961).

16. *Nichomachean Ethics,* pp. 111, 1115 b7.

17. Laws IX: 843, as quoted in Wennberg, *Critical Choices,* p. 43.

18. F. H. Sandbach, *The Stoics* (New York: W. W. Norton, 1975), p. 51, as quoted in Wennberg, *Critical Choices,* p. 43.

19. Victor G. Rosemblum, J.D., and Clarke D. Forsythe, J.D., "The Right to Assisted Suicide: Protection of Autonomy or an Open Door to Social Killing?" *Issues in Law & Medicine* 6 (Summer 1990): 5.

20. Cyril Means, "The Phoenix of Abortional Freedom: Is a Prenumbral or Ninth-Amendment Right About to Arise from the Nineteenth-Century Legislative Ashes of a Fourteenth-Century Common-Law Liberty?" *New York Law Forum* 17 (1971): 374.

21. See Robert Byrn, "Compulsory Lifesaving Treatment of Competent Adults," *Fordham Law Review* 44 (1975).

22. Rosemblum and Forsythe, "The Right to Assisted Suicide," p. 7.

23. As quoted in James Rachels, "Active and Passive Euthanasia," in ed. Goldberg, *Ethical Theory and Social Issues: Historical Texts and Contemporary Readings* (New York: Holt, Rinehart and Winston, 1989), pp. 411–12. This article is originally from *The New England Journal of Medicine* 292 (1975).

24. From selections from "Opinions of the Judicial Council of the American Medical Association," John H. Burkhart, chairman, American Medical Association, Chicago (1982) at 9–10, as published in *President's Commission for the Study of Ethical Problems in Medicine and Biomedical and Behavioral Research, Deciding to Forego Life-Sustaining Treatment: A Report on*

the Ethical, Medical, and Legal Issues in Treatment Decisions (Washington, D.C.: U.S. Government Printing Office, 1983), pp. 299–300.

25. President's Commission, *Deciding to Forego Life-Sustaining Treatment*, p. 10.

26. See *ibid.*, pp. 171–96; and Wennberg, *Critical Choices*, pp. 162–65.

27. President's Commission, *Deciding to Forego Life-Sustaining Treatment*, pp. 174–75.

28. Wennberg, *Critical Choices*, pp. 171–75; and President's Commission, *Deciding to Forego Life-Sustaining Treatment*, pp. 181–83.

Chapter 7 — Conclusion: Social Activism

1. See Dr. Donald P. Shoemaker, *Operation Rescue: A Critical Analysis* (Seal Beach, Calif.: Grace Community Church, n.d.). This work, by the senior pastor of Grace Community Church of Seal Beach, is very helpful in evaluating the many views concerning Operation Rescue. To get a copy, send $2 to Grace Community Church, 138 8th St., Seal Beach, Calif. 90740.

2. Samuel Rutherford, *Lex Rex (The Law Is King)*, p. 1644.

3. Francis Schaeffer, *A Christian Manifesto* (Westchester, Ill.: Crossway Books, 1981).

4. See Randall Terry, *Operation Rescue* (Birmingham, N.Y.: Whitaker House, 1988), ch. 2.

5. Schaeffer, *ibid.*, p. 100.

6. *Ibid.*, p. 99.

7. *Ibid.*, pp. 99, 100.

8. *Ibid.*, pp. 90, 101.

9. *Ibid.*, p. 106.

10. *Ibid.*, p. 104.

11. *Ibid.*, p. 110.

12. John Whitehead, *The Stealing of America* (Westchester, Ill.: Crossway Books, 1983), p. 113.

13. There are two significant differences between the kind of civil disobedience used in the civil rights movement and that utilized by some prolifers today. First, although civil rights groups did disobey local misinterpretations of their constitutional rights, they never disobeyed what the Supreme Court interpreted the law to be. Further, they never hindered anyone else exercising their rights as interpreted by the Supreme Court, as many prolifers are doing today. See Martin Luther King, "Letter from a Birmingham Jail" in ed. Pojman, *Philosophy: The Quest for Truth* (Belmont, Calif.: Wadsworth, 1989), pp. 426–33.

14. However, in a case in Portland, Oregon, the ACLU joined the Christian Legal Society in filing an amicus curiae (friend-of-the-court) brief to defend the rescuers' freedom of speech. See Ann Hibbard, "Abortionists

Wage Legal War Against Pro-Life Leaders," *Focus on the Family Citizen* 3:3 (March 1989): 5.

15. Armando Valladares, "Ambassador Condemns Abuse of 'Rescuers'," *New Dimensions* (October 1990): 62.

16. *New Dimensions* (October 1990): 60–61. For a copy of this videotape, which documents police brutality toward Operation Rescue participants, contact "Pro-Life Videos" at (213) 373–0743.

17. *Christianity Today* 33:12 (8 September 1989): 52.

18. Hibbard, "Abortionists," 4.

19. From *New Dimensions* (October 1990): 63.

Appendix 1

ROE *v.* WADE

Syllabus

ROE ᴇᴛ ᴀʟ. *v.* WADE, DISTRICT ATTORNEY OF DALLAS COUNTY
APPEAL FROM THE UNITED STATES DISTRICT COURT
FOR THE NORTHERN DISTRICT OF TEXAS

No. 70–18. Argued December 13, 1971—
Reargued October 11, 1972—
Decided January 22, 1973

A pregnant single woman (Roe) brought a class action challenging the constitutionality of the Texas criminal abortion laws, which proscribe procuring or attempting an abortion except on medical advice for the purpose of saving the mother's life. A licensed physician (Hallford), who had two state abortion prosecutions pending against him, was permitted to intervene. A childless married couple (the Does), the wife not being pregnant, separately attacked the laws, basing alleged injury on the future possibilities of contraceptive failure, pregnancy, unpreparedness for parenthood, and impairment of the wife's health. A three-judge District Court, which consolidated the actions, held that Roe and Hallford, and members of their classes, had standing to sue and presented justiciable controversies. Ruling that declaratory, though not injunctive, relief was warranted, the court declared the abortion statutes void as vague and overbroadly infringing those plaintiffs' Ninth and Fourteenth Amendment rights. The court ruled the Does' complaint not justiciable. Appellants directly appealed to this Court on the injunctive rulings, and appellee cross-appealed from the District Court's grant of declaratory relief to Roe and Hallford. *Held:*

1. While 28 U.S. C. § 1253 authorizes no direct appeal to this Court from the grant or denial of declaratory relief alone, review is not foreclosed when the case is properly before the Court on appeal from specific denial of injunctive relief and the arguments as to both injunctive and declaratory relief are necessarily identical. P. 123.

2. Roe has standing to sue; the Does and Hallford do not. Pp. 123–129.

(a) Contrary to appellee's contention, the natural termination of Roe's pregnancy did not moot her suit. Litigation involving pregnancy, which is "capable of repetition, yet evading review," is an exception to the usual federal rule that an actual controversy must exist at review stages and not simply when the action is initiated. Pp. 124–125.

(b) The district Court correctly refused injunctive, but erred in granting declaratory, relief to Hallford, who alleged no federally protected right not assertable as a defense against the good-faith state prosecutions pending against him. *Samuels* v. *Mackell,* 401 U.S. 66. Pp. 125–127.

(c) The Does' complaint, based as it is on contingencies, any one or more of which may not occur, is too speculative to present an actual case or controversy. Pp. 127–129.

3. State criminal abortion laws, like those involved here, that except from criminality only a life-saving procedure on the mother's behalf without regard to the stage of her pregnancy and other interests involved violate the Due Process Clause of the Fourteenth Amendment, which protects against state action the right to privacy, including a woman's qualified right to terminate her pregnancy. Though the State cannot override that right, it has legitimate interests in protecting both the pregnant woman's health and the potentiality of human life, each of which interests grows and reaches a "compelling" point at various stages of the woman's approach to term. Pp. 147–164.

(a) For the stage prior to approximately the end of the first trimester, the abortion decision and its effectuation must be left to the medical judgment of the pregnant woman's attending physician. Pp. 163, 164.

(b) For the stage subsequent to approximately the end of the first trimester, the State, in promoting its interest in the health of the mother, may, if it chooses, regulate the abortion procedure in ways that are reasonably related to maternal health. Pp. 163, 164.

(c) For the stage subsequent to viability the State, in promoting its interest in the potentiality of human life, may, if it chooses, regulate, and even proscribe, abortion except where necessary, in appropriate medical judgment, for the preservation of the life or health of the mother. Pp. 163–164; 164–165.

4. The State may define the term "physician" to mean only a physician currently licensed by the State, and may proscribe any abortion by a person who is not a physician as so defined. P. 165.

5. It is unnecessary to decide the injunctive relief issue since the Texas authorities will doubtless fully recognize the Court's ruling that the Texas criminal abortion statutes are unconstitutional. P. 166.

314 F. Supp. 1217 affirmed in part and reversed in part.

BLACKMUN, J., delivered the opinion of the Court, in which BURGER, C. J., and DOUGLAS, BRENNAN, STEWART, MARSHALL, and POWELL, JJ., joined. BURGER, C. J., *post,* p. 207, DOUGLAS, J., *post,* p. 209, and STEWART, J., *post,* p. 167, filed concurring opinions. WHITE, J., filed a dissenting opinion, in which REHNQUIST, J., joined, *post,* p. 221. REHNQUIST, J., filed a dissenting opinion, *post,* p. 171.

Sarah Weddington reargued the cause for appellants. With her on the briefs were *Roy Lucas, Fred Bruner, Roy L. Merrill, Jr.,* and *Norman Dorsen.*

Robert C. Flowers, Assistant Attorney General of Texas, argued the cause for appellee on the reargument. *Jay Floyd,* Assistant Attorney General, argued the cause for appellee on the original argument. With them on the brief were *Crawford C. Martin,* Attorney General, *Nola White,* First Assistant Attorney General, *Alfred Walker,* Executive Assistant Attorney General, *Henry Wade,* and *John B. Tolle.**

Opinion of the Court

MR. JUSTICE BLACKMUN delivered the opinion of the Court.

This Texas federal appeal and its Georgia companion, *Doe* v. *Bolton, post,* p. 179, present constitutional challenges to state criminal abortion legislation. The Texas statutes under attack here are typical of those that have been in effect in many States for approximately a century. The Georgia statutes, in contrast, have a modern cast and are a legislative product that, to an extent at least, obviously reflects the influences of recent attitudinal change, of advancing medical knowledge and techniques, and of new thinking about an old issue.

We forthwith acknowledge our awareness of the sensitive and emotional nature of the abortion controversy, of the vigorous opposing views, even among physicians, and of the deep and seemingly absolute convictions that the subject inspires. One's philosophy, one's experiences, one's exposure to the raw edges of human existence, one's religious training, one's attitudes toward life and family and their values, and the moral standards one establishes and seeks to observe, are all likely to influence and to color one's thinking and conclusions about abortion.

In addition, population growth, pollution, poverty, and racial overtones tend to complicate and not to simplify the problem.

Our task, of course, is to resolve the issue by constitutional measurement, free of emotion and of predilection. We seek earnestly to do this, and, because we do, we have inquired into, and in this opinion place some emphasis upon, medical and medical-legal history and what that history reveals about man's attitudes toward the abortion procedure over the centuries. We bear in mind, too, Mr. Justice Holmes' admonition in his now-vindicated dissent in *Lochner* v. *New York,* 198 U.S. 45, 76 (1905):

> "[The Constitution] is made for people of fundamentally differing views, and the accident of our finding certain opinions natural and familiar or novel and even shocking ought not to conclude our judgment upon the question whether statutes embodying them conflict with the Constitution of the United States."

*Briefs of *amici curiae* were filed by *Gary K. Nelson,* Attorney General of Arizona, *Robert K. Killian,* Attorney General of Connecticut, *Ed W. Hancock,* Attorney General of Kentucky, *Clarence A. H. Meyer,* Attorney General of Nebraska, and *Vernon B. Romney,* Attorney General of Utah; by *Joseph P. Witherspoon, Jr.,* for the Association of Texas Diocesan Attorneys; by *Charles E. Rice* for Americans United for Life; by *Eugene J. McMahon* for Women for the Unborn et al.; by *Carol Ryan* for the American College of Obstetricians and Gynecologists et al.; by *Dennis J. Horan, Jerome A. Frazel, Jr., Thomas M. Crisham,* and *Dolores V. Horan* for Certain Physicians, Professors and Fellows of the American College of Obstetrics and Gynecology; by *Harriet F. Pilpel, Nancy F. Wechsler,* and *Frederic S. Nathan* for Planned Parenthood Federation of America, Inc., et al.; by *Alan F. Charles* for the National Legal Program on Health Problems of the Poor et al.; by *Marttie L. Thompson* for State Communities Aid Assn.; by *Alfred L. Scanlan, Martin J. Flynn,* and *Robert M. Byrn* for the National Right to Life Committee; by *Helen L. Buttenwieser* for the American Ethical Union et al.; by *Norma G. Zarky* for the American Association of University Women et al.; by *Nancy Stearns* for New Women Lawyers et al.; by the California Committee to Legalize Abortion et al.; and by *Robert E. Dunne* for Robert L. Sassone.

I

The Texas statutes that concern us here are Arts. 1191–1194 and 1196 of the State's Penal Code.[1] These make it a crime to "procure an abortion," as therein defined, or to attempt one, except with respect to "an abortion procured or attempted by medical advice for the purpose of saving the life of the mother." Similar statutes are in existence in a majority of the States.[2]

Texas first enacted a criminal abortion statute in 1854. Texas Laws 1854, c. 49, § 1, set forth in 3 H. Gammel, Laws of Texas 1502 (1898). This was soon

---

1. "Article 1191. Abortion

"If any person shall designedly administer to a pregnant woman or knowingly procure to be administered with her consent any drug or medicine, or shall use towards her any violence or means whatever externally or internally applied and thereby procure an abortion, he shall be confined in the penitentiary not less than two nor more than five years; if it be done without her consent, the punishment shall be doubled. By 'abortion' is meant that the life of the fetus or embryo shall be destroyed in the woman's womb or that a premature birth thereof be caused.

"Art. 1192. Furnishing the means

"Whoever furnishes the means for procuring an abortion knowing the purpose intended is guilty as an accomplice.

"Art. 1193. Attempt at abortion

"If the means used shall fail to produce an abortion, the offender is nevertheless guilty of an attempt to produce abortion, provided it be shown that such means were calculated to produce that result, and shall be fined not less than one hundred nor more than one thousand dollars.

"Art. 1194. Murder in producing abortion

"If the death of the mother is occasioned by an abortion so produced or by an attempt to effect the same it is murder

"Art. 1196. By medical advice

"Nothing in this chapter applies to an abortion procured or attempted by medical advice for the purpose of saving the life of the mother

The foregoing Articles, together with Art. 1195, compose Chapter 9 of Title 15 of the Penal code. Article 1195, not attacked here, reads:

"Art. 1195. Destroying unborn child

"Whoever shall during parturition of the mother destroy the vitality or life in a child in a state of being born and before actual birth, which child would otherwise have been born alive, shall be confined in the penitentiary for life or for not less than five years."

2. Ariz. Rev. Stat. Ann. § 13–211 (1956); Conn. Pub. Act No. 1 (May 1972 special session) (in 4 Conn. Leg. Serv. 677 [1972]), and Conn. Gen. Stat. Rev. §§ 53–29, 53–30 (1968) (or unborn child); Idaho code § 18–601 (1948); Ill. Rev. Stat., c. 38, § 23–1 (1971); Ind. Code § 35–1–58–1 (1971); Iowa Code § 701.1 (1971); Ky. Rev. Stat. § 436.020 (1962); La. Rev. Stat. § 37:1285 (6) (1964) (loss of medical license) (but see § 14:87 [Supp. 1972] containing no exception for the life of the mother under the criminal statute); Me. Rev. Stat. Ann., Tit. 17, § 51 (1964); Mass. Gen. Laws Ann., c. 272, § 19 (1970) (using the term "unlawfully," construed to exclude an abortion to save the mother's life, Kudish v. Bd. of Registration, 356 Mass. 98, 248 N. E. 2d 264 [1969]); Mich. Comp. Laws § 750.14 (1948); Minn. Stat. § 617.18 (1971); Mo. Rev. Stat. § 559.100 (1969); Mont. Rev. Codes Ann. § 94–401 (1969); Neb. Rev. Stat. § 28–405 (1964); Nev. Rev. Stat. § 200.220 (1967); N.H. Rev. Stat. Ann. § 585:13 (1955); N.J. Stat. Ann. § 2A:87–1 (1969) ("without lawful justification"); N.D. Cent. Code §§ 12–25–01, 12–25–02 (1960); Ohio Rev. Code Ann. § 2901.16 (1953); Okla. Stat. Ann., Tit. 21, § 861 (1972–1973 Supp.); Pa. Stat. Ann., Tit. 18, §§ 4718, 4719 (1963) ("unlawful"); R.I. Gen, Laws Ann. § 11–3–1 (1969); S. D. Comp. Laws Ann. § 22–17–1 (1967); Tenn. Code Ann. §§ 39–301, 39–302 (1956); Utah Code Ann. §§ 76–2–1, 76–2–2 (1953); Vt. Stat. Ann., Tit. 13, § 101 (1958); W.Va. Code Ann. § 61–2–8 (1966); Wis. Stat. § 940.04 (1969); Wyo. Stat. Ann. §§ 6–77, 6–78 (1957).

modified into language that has remained substantially unchanged to the present time. See Texas Penal code of 1857, c. 7, Arts. 531–536; G. Paschal, Laws of Texas, Arts. 2192–2197 (1866); Texas Rev. Stat., c. 8, Arts. 536–541 (1879); Texas Rev. Crim. Stat., Arts. 1071–1076 (1911). The final article in each of these compilations provided the same exception, as does the present Article 1196, for an abortion by "medical advice for the purpose of saving the life of the mother."[3]

II

Jane Roe,[4] a single woman who was residing in Dallas County, Texas, instituted this federal action in March 1970 against the District Attorney of the county. She sought a declaratory judgment that the Texas criminal abortion statutes were unconstitutional on their face, and an injunction restraining the defendant from enforcing the statutes.

Roe alleged that she was unmarried and pregnant; that she wished to terminate her pregnancy by an abortion "performed by a competent, licensed physician, under safe, clinical conditions"; that she was unable to get a "legal" abortion in Texas because her life did not appear to be threatened by the continuation of her pregnancy; and that she could not afford to travel to another jurisdiction in order to secure a legal abortion under safe conditions. She claimed that the Texas statutes were unconstitutionally vague and that they abridged her right of personal privacy, protected by the First, Fourth, Fifth, Ninth, and Fourteenth Amendments. By an amendment to her complaint Roe purported to sue "on behalf of herself and all other women" similarly situated.

James Hubert Hallford, a licensed physician, sought and was granted leave to intervene in Roe's action. In his complaint he alleged that he has been arrested previously for violations of the Texas abortion statutes and that two such prosecutions were pending against him. He described conditions of patients who came to

---

3. Long ago, a suggestion was made that the Texas statutes were unconstitutionally vague because of definitional deficiencies. The Texas Court of Criminal Appeals disposed of that suggestion peremptorily, saying only,

"It is also insisted in the motion in arrest of judgment that the statute is unconstitutional and void in that it does not sufficiently define or describe the offense of abortion. We do not concur in respect to this question." *Jackson* v. *State,* 55 Tex. Cr. R. 79, 89, 115 S. W. 262, 268 (1908).

The same court recently has held again that the State's abortion statutes are not unconstitutionally vague or overbroad. *Thompson* v. *State* (Ct. Crim. App. Tex. 1971), appeal docketed, No. 71–1200. The court held that "the State of Texas has a compelling interest to protect fetal life"; that Art. 1191 "is designed to protect fetal life"; that the Texas homicide statutes, particularly Art. 1205 of the Penal Code, are intended to protect a person "in existence by actual birth" and thereby implicitly recognize other human life that is not "in existence by actual birth"; that the definition of human life is for the legislature and not the courts; that Art. 1196 "is more definite than the District of Columbia statute upheld in [*United States* v.] *Vuitch*" (402 U.S. 62); and that the Texas statute "is not vague and indefinite or overbroad." A physician's abortion conviction was affirmed.

In *Thompson,* n. 2, the court observed that any issue as to the burden of proof under the exemption of Art. 1196 "is not before us." But see *Veevers* v. *State,* 172 Tex. Cr. R. 162, 168–169, 354 S. W. 2d 161, 166–167 (1962). Cf. *United States* v. *Vuitch,* 402 U.S. 62, 69–71 (1971).

4. The name is a pseudonym.

him seeking abortions, and he claimed that for many cases he, as a physician, was unable to determine whether they fell within or outside the exception recognized by Article 1196. He alleged that, as a consequence, the statutes were vague and uncertain, in violation of the Fourteenth Amendment, and that they violated his own and his patients' rights to privacy in the doctor-patient relationship and his own right to practice medicine, rights he claimed were guaranteed by the First, Fourth, Fifth, Ninth, and Fourteenth Amendments.

John and Mary Doe,[5] a married couple, filed a companion complaint to that of Roe. They also named the District Attorney as defendant, claimed like constitutional deprivations, and sought declaratory and injunctive relief. The Does alleged that they were a childless couple; that Mrs. Doe was suffering from a "neural-chemical" disorder; that her physician had "advised her to avoid pregnancy until such time as her condition has materially improved" (although a pregnancy at the present time would not present "a serious risk" to her life); that, pursuant to medical advice, she had discontinued use of birth control pills; and that if she should become pregnant, she would want to terminate the pregnancy by an abortion performed by a competent, licensed physician under safe, clinical conditions. By an amendment to their complaint, the Does purported to sue "on behalf of themselves and all couples similarly situated."

The two actions were consolidated and heard together by a duly convened three-judge district court. The suits thus presented the situations of the pregnant single woman, the childless couple, with the wife not pregnant, and the licensed practicing physician, all joining in the attack on the Texas criminal abortion statutes. Upon the filing of affidavits, motions were made for dismissal and for summary judgment. The court held that Roe and members of her class, and Dr. Hallford, had standing to sue and presented justiciable controversies, but that the Does had failed to allege facts sufficient to state a present controversy and did not have standing. It concluded that, with respect to the requests for a declaratory judgment, abstention was not warranted. On the merits, the District Court held that the "fundamental right of single women and married persons to choose whether to have children is protected by the Ninth Amendment, through the Fourteenth Amendment," and that the Texas criminal abortion statutes were void on their face because they were both unconstitutionally vague and constituted an overbroad infringement of the plaintiffs' Ninth Amendment rights. The court then held that abstention was warranted with respect to the requests for an injunction. It therefore dismissed the Does' complaint, declared the abortion statutes void, and dismissed the application for injunctive relief. 314 F. Supp. 1217, 1225 (ND Tex. 1970).

The plaintiffs Roe and Doe and the intervenor Hallford, pursuant to 28 U.S.C. § 1253, have appealed to this Court from that part of the District Court's judgment denying the injunction. The defendant District Attorney has purported to cross-appeal, pursuant to the same statute, from the court's grant of declaratory relief to Roe and Hallford. Both sides also have taken protective appeals to the United States Court of Appeals for the Fifth Circuit. That court ordered the appeals held in abeyance pending decision here. We postponed decision on jurisdiction to the hearing on the merits. 402 U.S. 941 (1971).

---

5. These names are pseudonyms.

III

It might have been preferable if the defendant, pursuant to our Rule 20, had presented to us a petition for certiorari before judgment in the Court of Appeals with respect to the granting of the plaintiffs' prayer for declaratory relief. Our decisions in *Mitchell* v. *Donovan,* 398 U.S. 427 (1970), and *Gunn* v. *University Committee,* 399 U.S. 383 (1970), are to the effect that § 1253 does not authorize an appeal to this Court from the grant or denial of declaratory relief alone. We conclude, nevertheless, that those decisions do not foreclose our review of both the injunctive and the declaratory aspects of a case of this kind when it is properly here, as this one is, on appeal under § 1253 from specific denial of injunctive relief, and the arguments as to both aspects are necessarily identical. See *Carter* v. *Jury Comm'n,* 396 U.S. 320 (1970); *Florida Lime Growers* v. *Jacobsen,* 362 U.S. 73, 80–81 (1960). It would be destructive of time and energy for all concerned were we to rule otherwise. Cf. *Doe* v. *Bolton, post,* p. 179.

IV

We are next confronted with issues of justiciability, standing, and abstention. Have Roe and the Does established that "personal stake in the outcome of the controversy," *Baker* v. *Carr,* 369 U.S. 186, 204 (1962), that insures that "the dispute sought to be adjudicated will be presented in an adversary context and in a form historically viewed as capable of judicial resolution," *Flast* v. *Cohen,* 392 U.S. 83, 101 (1968), and *Sierra Club* v. *Morton,* 405 U.S. 727, 732 (1972)? And what effect did the pendency of criminal abortion charges against Dr. Hallford in state court have upon the propriety of the federal court's granting relief to him as a plaintiff-intervenor?

A. *Jane Roe.* Despite the use of the pseudonym, no suggestion is made that Roe is a fictitious person. For purposes of her case, we accept as true, and as established, her existence; her pregnant state, as of the inception of her suit in March 1970 and as late as May 21 of that year when she filed an alias affidavit with the District Court; and her inability to obtain a legal abortion in Texas.

Viewing Roe's case as of the time of its filing and thereafter until as late as May, there can be little dispute that it then presented a case or controversy and that, wholly apart from the class aspects, she, as a pregnant single woman thwarted by the Texas criminal abortion laws, had standing to challenge those statutes. *Abele* v. *Markle,* 452 F. 2d 1121, 1125 (CA2 1971); *Crossen* v. *Breckenridge,* 446 F. 2d 833, 838–839 (CA6 1971); *Poe* v. *Menghini,* 339 F. Supp. 986, 990–991 (Kan. 1972). See *Truax* v. *Raich,* 239 U.S. 33 (1915). Indeed, we do not read the appellee's brief as really asserting anything to the contrary. The "logical nexus between the status asserted and the claim sought to be adjudicated," *Flast* v. *Cohen,* 392 U.S., at 102, and the necessary degree of contentiousness, *Golden* v. *Zwickler,* 394 U.S. 103 (1969), are both present.

The appellee notes, however, that the record does not disclose that Roe was pregnant at the time of the District Court hearing on May 22, 1970[6] or on the following June 17 when the court's opinion and judgment were filed. And he suggests

---

6. The appellee twice states in his brief that the hearing before the District Court was held on July 22, 1970. Brief for Appellee 13. The docket entries, App. 2, and the transcript, App. 76, reveal this to be an error. The July date appears to be the time of the reporter's transcription. See App. 77.

that Roe's case must now be moot because she and all other members of her class are no longer subject to any 1970 pregnancy.

The usual rule in federal cases is that an actual controversy must exist at stages of appellate or certiorari review, and not simply at the date the action is initiated. *United States* v. *Munsingwear, Inc.,* 340 U.S. 36 (1950); *Golden* v. *Zwickler, supra; SEC* v. *Medical Committee for Human Rights,* 404 U.S. 403 (1972).

But when, as here, pregnancy is a significant fact in the litigation, the normal 266-day human gestation period is so short that the pregnancy will come to term before the usual appellate process is complete. If that termination makes a case moot, pregnancy litigation seldom will survive much beyond the trial stage, and appellate review will be effectively denied. Our law should not be that rigid. Pregnancy often comes more than once to the same woman, and in the general population, if man is to survive, it will always be with us. Pregnancy provides a classic justification for a conclusion of nonmootness. It truly could be "capable of repetition, yet evading review." *Southern Pacific Terminal Co.* v. *ICC,* 219 U.S. 498, 515 (1911). See *Moore* v. *Ogilvie,* 394 U.S. 814, 816 (1969); *Carroll* v. *Princess Anne,* 393 U.S. 175, 178–179 (1968); *United States* v. *W. T. Grant Co.,* 345 U.S. 629, 632–633 (1953).

We, therefore, agree with the District Court that Jane Roe had standing to undertake this litigation, that she presented a justiciable controversy, and that the termination of her 1970 pregnancy has not rendered her case moot.

B. *Dr. Hallford.* The doctor's position is different. He entered Roe's litigation as a plaintiff-intervenor, alleging in his complaint that he:

"[I]n the past has been arrested for violating the Texas Abortion Laws and at the present time stands charged by indictment with violating said laws in the Criminal District Court of Dallas County, Texas to-wit: (1) The State of Texas vs. James H. Hallford, No. C–69–5307–IH, and (2) The State of Texas vs. James H. Hallford, No. C–69–2524–H. In both cases the defendant is charged with abortion. . . ."

In his application for leave to intervene, the doctor made like representations as to the abortion charges pending in the state court. These representations were also repeated in the affidavit he executed and filed in support of his motion for summary judgment.

Dr. Hallford is, therefore, in the position of seeking, in a federal court, declaratory and injunctive relief with respect to the same statutes under which he stands charged in criminal prosecutions simultaneously pending in state court. Although he stated that he has been arrested in the past for violating the State's abortion laws, he makes no allegation of any substantial and immediate threat to any federally protected right that cannot be asserted in his defense against the state prosecutions. Neither is there any allegation of harassment or bad-faith prosecution. In order to escape the rule articulated in the cases cited in the next paragraph of this opinion that, absent harassment and bad faith, a defendant in a pending state criminal case cannot affirmatively challenge in federal court the statutes under which the State is prosecuting him, Dr. Hallford seeks to distinguish his status as a present state defendant from his status as a "potential future defendant" and to assert only the latter for standing purposes here.

We see no merit in that distinction. Our decision in *Samuels* v. *Mackell,* 401 U.S. 66 (1971), compels the conclusion that the District Court erred when it granted declaratory relief to Dr. Hallford instead of refraining from so doing. The court, of course, was correct in refusing to grant injunctive relief to the doctor. The reasons supportive of that action, however, are those expressed in *Samuels* v. *Mackell, supra,* and in *Younger* v. *Harris,* 401 U.S. 37 (1971); *Boyle* v. *Landry,* 401 U.S. 77 (1971); *Perez* v. *Ledesma,* 401 U.S. 82 (1971); and *Byrne* v. *Karalexis,* 401 U.S. 216 (1971). See also *Dombrowski* v. *Pfister,* 380 U.S. 479 (1965). We note, in passing, that *Younger* and its companion cases were decided after the three-judge District Court decision in this case.

Dr. Hallford's complaint in intervention, therefore, is to be dismissed.[7] He is remitted to his defenses in the state criminal proceedings against him. We reverse the judgment of the District Court insofar as it granted Dr. Hallford relief and failed to dismiss his complaint in intervention.

C. *The Does.* In view of our ruling as to Roe's standing in her case, the issue of the Does' standing in their case has little significance. The claims they assert are essentially the same as those of Roe, and they attack the same statutes. Nevertheless, we briefly note the Does' posture.

Their pleadings present them as a childless married couple, the woman not being pregnant, who have no desire to have children at this time because of their having received medical advice that Mrs. Doe should avoid pregnancy, and for "other highly personal reasons." But they "fear . . . they may face the prospect of becoming parents." And if pregnancy ensues, they "would want to terminate" it by an abortion. They assert an inability to obtain an abortion legally in Texas and, consequently, the prospect of obtaining an illegal abortion there or of going outside Texas to some place where the procedure could be obtained legally and competently.

We thus have as plaintiffs a married couple who have, as their asserted immediate and present injury, only an alleged "detrimental effect upon [their] marital happiness" because they are forced to "the choice of refraining from normal sexual relations or of endangering Mary Doe's health through a possible pregnancy." Their claim is that sometime in the future Mrs. Doe might become pregnant because of possible failure of contraceptive measures, and at that time in the future she might want an abortion that might then be illegal under the Texas statutes.

This very phrasing of the Does' position reveals its speculative character. Their alleged injury rests on possible future contraceptive failure, possible future pregnancy, possible future unpreparedness for parenthood, and possible future impairment of health. Any one or more of these several possibilities may not take place and all may not combine. In the Does' estimation, these possibilities might have some real or imagined impact upon their marital happiness. But we are not prepared to say that the bare allegation of so indirect an injury is sufficient to present an actual case or controversy. *Younger* v. *Harris,* 401 U.S., at 41–42; *Golden* v.

---

7. We need not consider what different result, if any, would follow if Dr. Hallford's intervention were on behalf of a class. His complaint in intervention does not purport to assert a class suit and makes no reference to any class apart from an allegation that he "and others similarly situated" must necessarily guess at the meaning of Art. 1196. His application for leave to intervene goes somewhat further, for it asserts that plaintiff Roe does not adequately protect the interest of the doctor "and the class of people who are physicians . . . [and] the class of people who are . . . patients. . . ." The leave application, however, is not the complaint. Despite the District Court's statement to the contrary, 314 F. Supp., at 1225, we fail to perceive the essentials of a class suit in the Hallford complaint.

Zwickler, 394 U.S., at 109–110; *Abele* v. *Markle,* 452 F. 2d, at 1124–1125; *Crossen* v. *Breckenridge,* 446 F. 2d, at 839. The Does' claim falls far short of those resolved otherwise in the cases that the Does urge upon us, namely, *Investment Co. Institute* v. *Camp,* 401 U.S. 617 (1971); *Data Processing Service* v. *Camp,* 397 U.S. 150 (1970); and *Epperson* v. *Arkansas,* 393 U.S. 97 (1968). See also *Truax* v. *Raich,* 239 U.S. 33 (1915).

The Does therefore are not appropriate plaintiffs in this litigation. Their complaint was properly dismissed by the District Court, and we affirm that dismissal.

V

The principal thrust of appellant's attack on the Texas statutes is that they improperly invade a right, said to be possessed by the pregnant woman, to choose to terminate her pregnancy. Appellant would discover this right in the concept of personal "liberty" embodied in the Fourteenth Amendment's Due Process Clause; or in personal, marital, familial, and sexual privacy said to be protected by the Bill of Rights or its penumbras, see *Griswold* v. *Connecticut,* 381 U.S. 479 (1965); *Eisenstadt* v. *Baird,* 405 U.S. 438 (1972); *id.,* at 460 (WHITE, J., concurring in result); or among those rights reserved to the people by the Ninth Amendment, *Griswold* v. *Connecticut,* 381 U.S., at 486 (Goldberg, J., concurring). Before addressing this claim, we feel it desirable briefly to survey, in several aspects, the history of abortion, for such insight as that history may afford us, and then to examine the state purposes and interests behind the criminal abortion laws.

VI

It perhaps is not generally appreciated that the restrictive criminal abortion laws in effect in a majority of States today are of relatively recent vintage. Those laws, generally proscribing abortion or its attempt at any time during pregnancy except when necessary to preserve the pregnant woman's life, are not of ancient or even of common-law origin. Instead, they derive from statutory changes effected, for the most part, in the latter half of the 19th century.

1. *Ancient attitudes.* These are not capable of precise determination. We are told that at the time of the Persian Empire abortifacients were known and that criminal abortions were severely punished.[8] We are also told, however, that abortion was practiced in Greek times as well as in the Roman Era,[9] and that "it was resorted to without scruple."[10] The Ephesian, Soranos, often described as the greatest of the ancient gynecologists, appears to have been generally opposed to Rome's prevailing

8. A. Castiglioni, A History of Medicine 84 (2d ed. 1947), E. Krumbhaar, translator and editor (hereinafter Castiglioni).

9. J. Ricci, The Genealogy of Gynaecology 52, 84, 113, 149 (2d ed. 1950) (hereinafter Ricci); L. Lader, Abortion 75–77 (1966) (hereinafter Lader); K. Niswander, Medical Abortion Practices in the United States, in Abortion and the Law 37, 38–40 (D. Smith ed. 1967) G. Williams, The Sanctity of Life and the Criminal Law 148 (1957) (hereinafter Williams); J. Noonan, An Almost Absolute Value in History, in The Morality of Abortion, 1, 3–7 (J. Noonan ed. 1970) (hereinafter Noonan); Quay, Justifiable Abortion—Medical and Legal Foundations (pt. 2), 49 Geo. L. J. 395, 406–422 (1961) (hereinafter Quay).

10. L. Edelstein, The Hippocratic Oath 10 (1943) (hereinafter Edelstein). But see Castiglioni 227.

free-abortion practices. He found it necessary to think first of the life of the mother, and he resorted to abortion when, upon this standard, he felt the procedure advisable.[11] Greek and Roman law afforded little protection to the unborn. If abortion was prosecuted in some places, it seems to have been based on a concept of a violation of the father's right to his offspring. Ancient religion did not bar abortion.[12]

2. *The Hippocratic Oath.* What then of the famous Oath that has stood so long as the ethical guide of the medical profession and that bears the name of the great Greek (460(?)–377(?) B.C.), who has been described as the Father of Medicine, the "wisest and the greatest practitioner of his art," and the "most important and most complete medical personality of antiquity," who dominated the medical schools of his time, and who typified the sum of the medical knowledge of the past?[13] The Oath varies somewhat according to the particular translation, but in any translation the content is clear: "I will give no deadly medicine to anyone if asked, nor suggest any such counsel; and in like manner I will not give to a woman a pessary to produce abortion,"[14] or "I will neither give a deadly drug to anybody if asked for it, nor will I make a suggestion to this effect. Similarly, I will not give to a woman an abortive remedy."[15]

Although the Oath is not mentioned in any of the principal briefs in this case or in *Doe* v. *Bolton, post,* p. 179, it represents the apex of the development of strict ethical concepts in medicine, and its influence endures to this day. Why did not the authority of Hippocrates dissuade abortion practice in his time and that of Rome? The late Dr. Edelstein provides us with a theory:[16] The Oath was not uncontested even in Hippocrates' day; only the Pythagorean school of philosophers frowned upon the related act of suicide. Most Greek thinkers, on the other hand, commended abortion, at least prior to viability. See Plato, Republic, V, 461; Aristotle, Politics, VII, 1335b 25. For the Pythagoreans, however, it was a matter of dogma. For them the embryo was animate from the moment of conception, and abortion meant destruction of a living being. The abortion clause of the Oath, therefore, "echoes Pythagorean doctrines," and "[i]n no other stratum of Greek opinion were such views held or proposed in the same spirit of uncompromising austerity."[17]

Dr. Edelstein then concludes that the Oath originated in a group representing only a small segment of Greek opinion and that it certainly was not accepted by all ancient physicians. He points out that medical writings down to Galen (A.D. 130–200) "give evidence of the violation of almost every one of its injunctions."[18] But with the end of antiquity a decided change took place. Resistance against suicide and against abortion became common. The Oath came to be popular. The emerging teachings of Christianity were in agreement with the Pythagorean ethic. The Oath "became the nucleus of all medical ethics" and "was applauded as the embodiment of truth." Thus, suggests Dr. Edelstein, it is "a Pythagorean manifesto and not the expression of an absolute standard of medical conduct."[19]

---

11. Edelstein 12; Ricci 113–114, 118–119; Noonan 5.
12. Edelstein 13–14.
13. Castiglioni 148.
14. *Id.,* at 154.
15. Edelstein 3.
16. *Id.,* at 12, 15–18.
17. *Id.,* at 18; Lader 76.
18. Edelstein 63.
19. Id., at 64.

This, it seems to us, is a satisfactory and acceptable explanation of the Hippocratic Oath's apparent rigidity. It enables us to understand, in historical context, a long-accepted and revered statement of medical ethics.

3. *The common law.* It is undisputed that at common law, abortion performed *before* "quickening"—the first recognizable movement of the fetus *in utero,* appearing usually from the 16th to the 18th week of pregnancy[20]—was not an indictable offense.[21] The absence of a common-law crime for pre-quickening abortion appears to have developed from a confluence of earlier philosophical, theological, and civil and canon law concepts of when life begins. These disciplines variously approached the question in terms of the point at which the embryo or fetus became "formed" or recognizably human, or in terms of when a "person" came into being, that is, infused with a "soul" or "animated." A loose consensus evolved in early English law that these events occurred at some point between conception and live birth.[22] This was "mediate animation." Although Christian theology and the canon law came to fix the point of animation at 40 days for a male and 80 days for a female, a view that persisted until the 19th century, there was otherwise little agreement about the precise time of formation or animation. There was agreement, however, that prior to this point the fetus was to be regarded as part of the mother, and its destruction, therefore, was not homicide. Due to continued uncertainty about the precise time when animation occurred, to the lack of any empirical basis for the 40–80-day view, and perhaps to Aquinas' definition of movement as one of the two first principles of

20. Dorland's Illustrated Medical Dictionary 1261 (24th ed. 1965).

21. E. Coke, Institutes III *50; 1 W. Hawkins, Pleas of the Crown, c. 31, § 16 (4th ed. 1762); 1 W. Blackstone, Commentaries *129-130; M. Hale, Pleas of the Crown 433 (1st Amer. ed. 1847). For discussions of the role of the quickening concept in English common law, see Lader 78; Noonan 223–226; Means, The Law of New York Concerning Abortion and the Status of the Foetus, 1664–1968: A Case of Cessation of Constitutionality (pt. 1), 14 N. Y. L. F. 411, 418–428 (1968) (hereinafter Means I); Stern Abortion: Reform and the Law, 59 J. Crim. L. C. & P. S. 84 (1968) (hereinafter Stern); Quay 430–432; Williams 152.

22. Early philosophers believed that the embryo or fetus did not become formed and begin to live until at least 40 days after conception for a male, and 80 to 90 days for a female. See, for example, Aristotle, Hist. Anim. 7.3.583b; Gen. Anim. 2.3.736, 2.5.741; Hippocrates, Lib. de Nat. Puer., No. 10. Aristotle's thinking derived from his three-stage theory of life: vegetable, animal, rational. The vegetable stage was reached at conception, the animal at "animation," and the rational soon after live birth. This theory, together with the 40/80 day view, came to be accepted by early Christian thinkers.

The theological debate was reflected in the writings of St. Augustine, who made a distinction between *embryo inanimatus,* not yet endowed with a soul, and *embryo animatus.* He may have drawn upon Exodus 21:22. At one point, however, he expressed the view that human powers cannot determine the point during fetal development at which the critical change occurs. See Augustine, De Origine Animae 4.4 (Pub. Law 44.527). See also W. Reany, The Creation of the Human Soul, c. 2 and 83–86 (1932); Huser, The Crime of Abortion in Canon Law 15 (Catholic Univ. of America, Canon Law Studies No. 162, Washington, D. C., 1942).

Galen, in three treatises related to embryology, accepted the thinking of Aristotle and his followers. Quay 426–427. Later, Augustine on aborton was incorporated by Gratian into the Decretum, published about 1140. Decretum Magistri Gratiani 2.32.2.7 to 2.32.2.10, in 1 Corpus Juris Canonici 1122, 1123 (A. Friedburg, 2d ed. 1879). This Decretal and the Decretals that followed were recognized as the definitive body of canon law until the new Code of 1917.

For discussions of the canon-law treatment, see Means I, pp. 411–412; Noonan 20–26; Quay 426–430; see also J. Noonan, Contraception: A History of Its Treatment by the Catholic Theologians and Canonists 18–29 (1965).

life, Bracton focused upon quickening as the critical point. The significance of quickening was echoed by later common-law scholars and found its way into the received common law in this country.

Whether abortion of a *quick* fetus was a felony at common law, or even a lesser crime, is still disputed. Bracton, writing early in the 13th century, thought it homicide.[23] But the later and predominant view, following the great common-law scholars, has been that it was, at most, a lesser offense. In a frequently cited passage, Coke took the position that abortion of a woman "quick with childe" is "a great misprision, and no murder."[24] Blackstone followed, saying that while abortion after quickening had once been considered manslaughter (though not murder), "modern law" took a less severe view.[25] A recent review of the common-law precedents argues, however, that those precedents contradict Coke and that even post-quickening abortion was never established as a common-law crime.[26] This is of some importance because while most American courts ruled, in holding or dictum, that abortion of an unquickened fetus was not criminal under their received common law,[27] others followed Coke in stating that abortion of a quick fetus was a "misprision," a term they translated to mean "misdemeanor."[28] That their reliance on Coke on this aspect of the law was uncritical and, apparently in all the reported cases, dictum (due probably to the paucity of common-law prosecutions for post-quickening abor-

---

23. Bracton took the position that abortion by blow or poison was homicide "if the foetus be already formed and animated, and particularly if it be animated." 2 II. Bracton, De Legibus et Consuetudinibus Angliae 279 (T. Twiss ed. 1879), or, as a later translation puts it, "if the foetus is already formed or quickened, especially if it is quickened," 2 H. Bracton, On the Laws and Customs of England 341 (S. Thorne ed. 1968). See Quay 431; see also 2 Fleta 60–61 (Book 1, c. 23) (Selden Society ed. 1955).

24. E. Coke, Institutes III *50.

25. 1 W. Blackstone, Commentaries *129–130.

26. Means, The Phoenix of Abortional Freedom: Is a Penumbral or Ninth-Amendment Right About to Arise from the Nineteenth-Century Legislative Ashes of a Fourteenth-Century Common-Law Liberty?, 17 N. Y. L. F. 335 (1971) (hereinafter Means II). The author examines the two principal precedents cited marginally by Coke, both contrary to his dictum, and traces the treatment of these and other cases by earlier commentators. He concludes that Coke, who himself participated as an advocate in an abortion case in 1601, may have intentionally misstated the law. The author even suggests a reason: Coke's strong feelings against abortion, coupled with his determination to assert common-law (secular) jurisdiction to assess penalties for an offense that traditionally had been an exclusively ecclesiastical or canon-law crime. See also Lader 78–79, who notes that some scholars doubt that the common law ever was applied to abortion; that the English ecclesiastical courts seem to have lost interest in the problem after 1527; and that the preamble to the English legislation of 1803, 43 Geo. 3, c. 58, § 1, referred to in the text, *infra*, at 136, states that "no adequate means have been hitherto provided for the prevention and punishment of such offenses."

27. *Commonwealth* v. *Bangs,* 9 Mass. 387, 388 (1812); *Commonwealth* v. *Parker,* 50 Mass. (9 Metc.) 263, 265–266 (1845); *State* v. *Cooper,* 22 N. J. L. 52, 58 (1849); *Abrams* v. *Foshee,* 3 Iowa 274, 278–280 (1856); *Smith* v. *Gaffard,* 31 Ala. 45, 51 (1857); *Mitchell* v. *Commonwealth,* 78 Ky. 204, 210 (1879); *Eggart* v. *State,* 40 Fla. 527, 532, 25 So. 144, 145 (1898); *State* v. *Alcorn,* 7 Idaho 599, 606, 64 P. 1014, 1016 (1901); *Edwards* v. *State,* 79 Neb. 251, 252, 112 N. W. 611, 612 (1907); *Gray* v. *State,* 77 Tex. Cr. R. 221, 224, 178 S. W. 337, 338 (1915); *Miller* v. *Bennett,* 190 Va. 162, 169, 56 S. E. 2d 217, 221 (1949). Contra, *Mills* v. *Commonwealth,* 13 Pa. 631, 633 (1850); *State* v. *Slagle,* 83 N. C. 630, 632 (1880).

28. See *Smith* v. *State,* 33 Me. 48, 55 (1851); *Evans* v. *People,* 49 N. Y. 86, 88 (1872); *Lamb* v. *State,* 67 Md. 524, 533, 10 A. 208 (1887).

tion), makes it now appear doubtful that abortion was ever firmly established as a common-law crime even with respect to the destruction of a quick fetus.

4. *The English statutory law.* England's first criminal abortion statute, Lord Ellenborough's Act, 43 Geo. 3, c. 58, came in 1803. It made abortion of a quick fetus, § 1, a capital crime, but in § 2 it provided lesser penalties for the felony of abortion before quickening, and thus preserved the "quickening" distinction. This contrast was continued in the general revision of 1828, 9 Geo. 4, c. 31, § 13. It disappeared, however, together with the death penalty, in 1837, 7 Will. 4 & 1 Vict., c. 85, § 6, and did not reappear in the Offenses Against the Person Act of 1861, 24 & 25 Vict., c. 100, § 59, that formed the core of English anti-abortion law until the liberalizing reforms of 1967. In 1929, the Infant Life (Preservation) Act, 19 & 20 Geo. 5, c. 34, came into being. Its emphasis was upon the destruction of "the life of a child capable of being born alive." It made a willful act performed with the necessary intent a felony. It contained a proviso that one was not to be found guilty of the offense "unless it is proved that the act which caused the death of the child was not done in good faith for the purpose only of preserving the life of the mother."

A seemingly notable development in the English law was the case of *Rex* v. *Bourne,* [1939] 1 K. B. 687. This case apparently answered in the affirmative the question whether an abortion necessary to preserve the life of the pregnant woman was excepted from the criminal penalties of the 1861 Act. In his instructions to the jury, Judge Macnaghten referred to the 1929 Act, and observed that that Act related to "the case where a child is killed by a wilful act at the time when it is being delivered in the ordinary course of nature." *Id.,* at 691. He concluded that the 1861 Act's use of the word "unlawfully," imported the same meaning expressed by the specific proviso in the 1929 Act, even though there was no mention of preserving the mother's life in the 1861 Act. He then construed the phrase "preserving the life of the mother" broadly, that is, "in a reasonable sense," to include a serious and permanent threat to the mother's *health,* and instructed the jury to acquit Dr. Bourne if it found he had acted in a good-faith belief that the abortion was necessary for this purpose. *Id.,* at 693–694. The jury did acquit.

Recently, Parliament enacted a new abortion law. This is the Abortion Act of 1967, 15 & 16 Eliz. 2, c. 87. The Act permits a licensed physician to perform an abortion where two other licensed physicians agree (a) "that the continuance of the pregnancy would involve risk to the life of the pregnant woman, or of injury to the physical or mental health of the pregnant woman or any existing children of her family, greater than if the pregnancy were terminated," or (b) "that there is a substantial risk that if the child were born it would suffer from such physical or mental abnormalities as to be seriously handicapped." The Act also provides that, in making this determination, "account may be taken of the pregnant woman's actual or reasonably foreseeable environment." It also permits a physician, without the concurrence of others, to terminate a pregnancy where he is of the good-faith opinion that the abortion "is immediately necessary to save the life or to prevent grave permanent injury to the physical or mental health of the pregnant woman."

5. *The American law.* In this country, the law in effect in all but a few States until mid-19th century was the pre-existing English common law. Connecticut, the first State to enact abortion legislation, adopted in 1821 that part of Lord Ellenborough's Act that related to a woman "quick with child."[29] The death penalty

29. Conn. Stat., Tit. 20, § 14 (1821).

was not imposed. Abortion before quickening was made a crime in that State only in 1860.[30] In 1828, New York enacted legislation[31] that, in two respects, was to serve as a model for early anti-abortion statutes. First, while barring destruction of an unquickened fetus as well as a quick fetus, it made the former only a misdemeanor, but the latter second-degree manslaughter. Second, it incorporated a concept of therapeutic abortion by providing that an abortion was excused if it "shall have been necessary to preserve the life of such mother, or shall have been advised by two physicians to be necessary for such purpose." By 1840, when Texas had received the common law,[32] only eight American States had statutes dealing with abortion.[33] It was not until after the War Between the States that legislation began generally to replace the common law. Most of these initial statutes dealt severely with abortion after quickening but were lenient with it before quickening. Most punished attempts equally with completed abortions. While many statutes included the exception for an abortion thought by one or more physicians to be necessary to save the mother's life, that provision soon disappeared and the typical law required that the procedure actually be necessary for that purpose.

Gradually, in the middle and late 19th century the quickening distinction disappeared from the statutory law of most States and the degree of the offense and the penalties were increased. By the end of the 1950's, a large majority of the jurisdictions banned abortion, however and whenever performed, unless done to save or preserve the life of the mother.[34] The exceptions, Alabama and the District of Columbia, permitted abortion to preserve the mother's health.[35] Three States permitted abortions that were not "unlawfully" performed or that were not "without lawful justification," leaving interpretation of those standards to the courts.[36] In the past several years, however, a trend toward liberalization of abortion statutes has resulted in adoption, by about one-third of the States, of less stringent laws, most of them patterned after the ALI Model Penal Code, § 230.3,[37] set forth as Appendix B to the opinion in *Doe* v. *Bolton, post,* p. 205.

---

30. Conn. Pub. Acts, c. 71, § 1 (1860).

31. N. Y. Rev. Stat., pt. 4, c. 1, Tit. 2, Art. 1, § 9, p. 661, and Tit. 6, § 21, p. 694 (1829).

32. Act of Jan. 20, 1840, § 1, set forth in 2 H. Gammel, Laws of Texas 177–178 (1898); see *Grigsby* v. *Reib*, 105 Tex. 597, 600, 153 S. W. 1124, 1125 (1913).

33. The early statutes are discussed in Quay 435–438. See also Lader 85–88; Stern 85–86; and Means II 375–376.

34. Criminal abortion statutes in effect in the States as of 1961, together with historical statutory development and important judicial interpretations of the state statutes, are cited and quoted in Quay 447–520. See Comment, A Survey of the Present Statutory and Case Law on Abortion: The Contradictions and the Problems, 1972 U. Ill. L. F. 177, 179, classifying the abortion statutes and listing 25 States as permitting abortion only if necessary to save or preserve the mother's life.

35. Ala. Code, Tit. 14, § 9 (1958); D. C. Code Ann. § 22–201 (1967).

36. Mass. Gen. Laws Ann., c. 272, § 19 (1970); N. J. Stat. Ann. § 2A:87–1 (1969); Pa. Stat. Ann., Tit. 18, §§ 4718, 4719 (1963).

37. Fourteen States have adopted some form of the ALI statute. See Ark. Stat. Ann. §§ 41–303 to 41–310 (Supp. 1971); Calif. Health & Safety Code §§ 25950–25955.5 (Supp. 1972); Colo. Rev. Stat. Ann. §§ 40–2–50 to 40–2–53 (Cum. Supp. 1967); Del. Code Ann., Tit. 24, §§ 1790–1793 (Supp. 1972); Florida Law of Apr. 13, 1972, c. 72–196, 1972 Fla. Sess. Law Serv., pp. 380–382; Ga. Code §§ 26–1201 to 26–1203 (1972); Kan. Stat. Ann. § 21–3407 (Supp. 1971); Md. Ann. Code, Art. 43, §§ 137–139 (1971); Miss. Code Ann. § 2223 (Supp. 1972); N. M. Stat. Ann. §§ 40A–5–1 to 40A–5–3 (1972); N. C. Gen. Stat. § 14–45.1

It is thus apparent that at common law, at the time of the adoption of our Constitution, and throughout the major portion of the 19th century, abortion was viewed with less disfavor than under most American statutes currently in effect. Phrasing it another way, a woman enjoyed a substantially broader right to terminate a pregnancy than she does in most States today. At least with respect to the early stage of pregnancy, and very possibly without such a limitation, the opportunity to make this choice was present in this country well into the 19th century. Even later, the law continued for some time to treat less punitively an abortion procured in early pregnancy.

6. *The position of the American Medical Association.* The anti-abortion mood prevalent in this country in the late 19th century was shared by the medical profession. Indeed, the attitude of the profession may have played a significant role in the enactment of stringent criminal abortion legislation during that period.

An AMA Committee on Criminal Abortion was appointed in May 1857. It presented its report, 12 Trans. of the Am. Med. Assn. 73–78 (1859), to the Twelfth Annual Meeting. That report observed that the Committee had been appointed to investigate criminal abortion "with a view to its general suppression." It deplored abortion and its frequency and it listed three causes of "this general demoralization":

"The first of these causes is a wide-spread popular ignorance of the true character of the crime—a belief, even among mothers themselves, that the foetus is not alive till after the period of quickening.

"The second of the agents alluded to is the fact that the profession themselves are frequently supposed careless of foetal life. . . .

"The third reason of the frightful extent of this crime is found in the grave defects of our laws, both common and statute, as regards the independent and actual existence of the child before birth, as a living being. These errors, which are sufficient in most instances to prevent conviction, are based, and only based, upon mistaken and exploded medical dogmas. With strange inconsistency, the law fully acknowledges the foetus in utero and its inherent rights, for civil purposes; while personally and as criminally affected, it fails to recognize it, and to its life as yet denies all protection." *Id.,* at 75–76.

The Committee then offered, and the Association adopted, resolutions protesting "against such unwarrantable destruction of human life," calling upon state legislatures to revise their abortion laws, and requesting the cooperation of state medical societies "in pressing the subject." *Id.,* at 28, 78.

In 1871 a long and vivid report was submitted by the Committee on Criminal Abortion. It ended with the observation, "We had to deal with human life. In a matter of less importance we could entertain no compromise. An honest judge on the bench

---

(Supp. 1971); Ore. Rev. Stat. §§ 435.405 to 435.495 (1971); S. C. Code Ann. §§ 16– 82 to 16–89 (1962 and Supp. 1971); Va. Code Ann. §§ 18.1–62 to 18.1–62.3 (Supp. 1972). Mr. Justice Clark described some of these States as having "led the way." Religion, Morality, and Abortion: A Constitutional Appraisal, 2 Loyola U. (L. A.) L. Rev. 1, 11 (1969).

By the end of 1970, four other States had repealed criminal penalties for abortions performed in early pregnancy by a licensed physician, subject to stated procedural and health requirements. Alaska Stat. § 11.15.060 (1970); Haw. Rev. Stat. § 453–16 (Supp. 1971); N. Y. Penal Code § 125.05, subd. 3 (Supp. 1972–1973); Wash. Rev. Code §§ 9.02.060 to 9.02.080 (Supp. 1972). The precise status of criminal abortion laws in some States is made unclear by recent decisions in state and federal courts striking down existing state laws, in whole or in part.

would call things by their proper names. We could do no less." 22 Trans. of the Am. Med. Assn. 258 (1871). It proffered resolutions, adopted by the Association, *id.,* at 38–39, recommending, among other things, that it "be unlawful and unprofessional for any physician to induce abortion or premature labor, without the concurrent opinion of at least one respectable consulting physician, and then always with a view to the safety of the child—if that be possible," and calling "the attention of the clergy of all denominations to the perverted views of morality entertained by a large class of females—aye, and men also, on this important question."

Except for periodic condemnation of the criminal abortionist, no further formal AMA action took place until 1967. In that year, the Committee on Human Reproduction urged the adoption of a stated policy of opposition to induced abortion, except when there is "documented medical evidence" of a threat to the health or life of the mother, or that the child "may be born with incapacitating physical deformity or mental deficiency," or that a pregnancy "resulting from legally established statutory or forcible rape or incest may constitute a threat to the mental or physical health of the patient," two other physicians "chosen because of their recognized professional competence have examined the patient and have concurred in writing," and the procedure "is performed in a hospital accredited by the Joint Commission on Accreditation of Hospitals." The providing of medical information by physicians to state legislatures in their consideration of legislation regarding therapeutic abortion was "to be considered consistent with the principles of ethics of the American Medical Association." This recommendation was adopted by the House of Delegates. Proceedings of the AMA House of Delegates 40–51 (June 1967).

In 1970, after the introduction of a variety of proposed resolutions, and of a report from its Board of Trustees, a reference committee noted "polarization of the medical profession on this controversial issue"; division among those who had testified; a difference of opinion among AMA councils and committees; "the remarkable shift in testimony" in six months, felt to be influenced "by the rapid changes in state laws and by the judicial decisions which tend to make abortion more freely available;" and a feeling "that this trend will continue." On June 25, 1970, the House of Delegates adopted preambles and most of the resolutions proposed by the reference committee. The preambles emphasized "the best interests of the patient," "sound clinical judgment," and "informed patient consent," in contrast to "mere acquiescence to the patient's demand." The resolutions asserted that abortion is a medical procedure that should be performed by a licensed physician in an accredited hospital only after consultation with two other physicians and in conformity with state law, and that no party to the procedure should be required to violate personally held moral principles.[38]

---

38. "Whereas, Abortion, like any other medical procedure, should not be performed when contrary to the best interests of the patient since good medical practice requires due consideration for the patient's welfare and not mere acquiescence to the patient's demand; and

"Whereas, the standards of sound clinical judgment, which, together with informed patient consent should be determinative according to the merits of each individual case; therefore be it

"*RESOLVED,* That abortion is a medical procedure and should be performed only by a duly licensed physician and surgeon in an accredited hospital acting only after consultation with two other physicians chosen because of their professional competency and in conformance with standards of good medical practice and the Medical Practice Act of his State; and be it further

"*RESOLVED,* That no physician or other professional personnel shall be compelled to perform any act which violates his good medical judgment. Neither physician, hospital, nor hospital personnel shall be required to perform any act violative of personally-held moral principles. In

Proceedings of the AMA House of Delegates 220 (June 1970). The AMA Judicial Council rendered a complementary opinion.[39]

7. *The position of the American Public Health Association.* In October 1970, the Executive Board of the APHA adopted Standards for Abortion Services. These were five in number:

"a. Rapid and simple abortion referral must be readily available through state and local public health departments, medical societies, or other non-profit organizations.

"b. An important function of counseling should be to simplify and expedite the provision of abortion services; it should not delay the obtaining of these services.

"c. Psychiatric consultation should not be mandatory. As in the case of other specialized medical services, psychiatric consultation should be sought for definite indications and not on a routine basis.

"d. A wide range of individuals from appropriately trained, sympathetic volunteers to highly skilled physicians may qualify as abortion counselors.

"e. Contraception and/or sterilization should be discussed with each abortion patient." Recommended Standards for Abortion Services, 61 Am. J. Pub. Health 396 (1971).

Among factors pertinent to life and health risks associated with abortion were three that "are recognized as important":

"a. the skill of the physician,

"b. the environment in which the abortion is performed, and above all

"c. the duration of pregnancy, as determined by uterine size and confirmed by menstrual history." *Id.,* at 397.

It was said that "a well-equipped hospital" offers more protection "to cope with unforeseen difficulties than an office or clinic without such resources. . . . The factor of gestational age is of overriding importance." Thus, it was recommended that abortions in the second trimester and early abortions in the presence of existing medical complications be performed in hospitals as inpatient procedures. For pregnancies in the first trimester, abortion in the hospital with or without overnight stay "is probably the safest practice." An abortion in an extramural facility, however, is an acceptable alternative "provided arrangements exist in advance to admit patients promptly if unforeseen complications develop." Standards for an abortion facility were listed. It was said that at present abortions should be performed by physicians or osteopaths who are licensed to practice and who have "adequate training." *Id.,* at 398.

---

these circumstances good medical practice requires only that the physician or other professional personnel withdraw from the case so long as the withdrawal is consistent with good medical practice." Proceedings of the AMA House of Delegates 220 (June 1970).

39. "The Principles of Medical Ethics of the AMA do not prohibit a physician from performing an abortion that is performed in accordance with good medical practice and under circumstances that do not violate the laws of the community in which he practices.

"In the matter of abortions, as of any other medical procedure, the Judicial Council becomes involved whenever there is alleged violation of the Principles of Medical Ethics as established by the House of Delegates."

8. *The position of the American Bar Association.* At its meeting in February 1972 the ABA House of Delegates approved, with 17 opposing votes, the Uniform Abortion Act that had been drafted and approved the preceding August by the Conference of Commissioners on Uniform State Laws. 58 A. B. A. J. 380 (1972). We set forth the Act in full in the margin.[40] The Conference has appended an enlightening Prefatory Note.[41]

40.   "UNIFORM ABORTION ACT

"Section 1. [*Abortion Defined; When Authorized.*]

"(a) 'Abortion' means the termination of human pregnancy with an intention other than to produce a live birth or to remove a dead fetus.

"(b) An abortion may be performed in this state only if it is performed:

"(1) by a physician licensed to practice medicine [or osteopathy] in this state or by a physician practicing medicine [or osteopathy] in the employ of the government of the United States or of this state, [and the abortion is performed [in the physician's office or in a medical clinic, or] in a hospital approved by the [Department of Health] or operated by the United States, this state, or any department, agency, or political subdivision of either;] or by a female upon herself upon the advice of the physician; and

"(2) within [20] weeks after the commencement of the pregnancy [or after [20] weeks only if the physician has reasonable cause to believe (i) there is a substantial risk that continuance of the pregnancy would endanger the life of the mother or would gravely impair the physical or mental health of the mother, (ii) that the child would be born with grave physical or mental defect, or (iii) that the pregnancy resulted from rape or incest, or illicit intercourse with a girl under the age of 16 years].

"Section 2. [*Penalty.*] Any person who performs or procures an abortion other than authorized by this Act is guilty of a [felony] and., upon conviction thereof, may be sentenced to pay a fine not exceeding [$1,000] or to imprisonment [in the state penitentiary] not exceeding [5 years], or both.

"Section 3. [*Uniformity of Interpretation.*] This Act shall be construed to effectuate its general purpose to make uniform the law with respect to the subject of this Act among those states which enact it.

"Section 4. [*Short Title.*] This Act may be cited as the Uniform Abortion Act.

"Section 5. [*Severability.*] If any provision of this Act or the application thereof to any person or circumstance is held invalid, the invalidity does not affect other provisions or applications of this Act which can be given effect without the invalid provision or application, and to this end the provisions of this Act are severable.

"Section 6. [*Repeal.*] The following acts and parts of acts are repealed:

"(1)

"(2)

"(3)

"Section 7. [*Time of Taking Effect.*] This Act shall take effect_____."

41. "This Act is based largely upon the New York abortion act following a review of the more recent laws on abortion in several states and upon recognition of a more liberal trend in laws on this subject. Recognition was given also to the several decisions in state and federal courts which show a further trend toward liberalization of abortion laws, especially during the first trimester of pregnancy.

"Recognizing that a number of problems appeared in New York, a shorter time period for 'unlimited' abortions was advisable. The time period was bracketed to permit the various states to insert a figure more in keeping with the different conditions that might exist among the states. Likewise, the language limiting the place or places in which abortions may be performed was also bracketed to account for different conditions among the states. In addition, limitations on abortions after the initial 'unlimited' period were placed in brackets so that individual states may adopt all or any of these reasons, or place further restrictions upon abortions after the initial period.

"This Act does not contain any provision relating to medical review committees or prohibitions against sanctions imposed upon medical personnel refusing to participate in abortions

VII

Three reasons have been advanced to explain historically the enactment of criminal abortion laws in the 19th century and to justify their continued existence.

It has been argued occasionally that these laws were the product of a Victorian social concern to discourage illicit sexual conduct. Texas, however, does not advance this justification in the present case, and it appears that no court or commentator has taken the argument seriously.[42] The appellants and *amici* contend, moreover, that this is not a proper state purpose at all and suggest that, if it were, the Texas statutes are overbroad in protecting it since the law fails to distinguish between married and unwed mothers.

A second reason is concerned with abortion as a medical procedure. When most criminal abortion laws were first enacted, the procedure was a hazardous one for the woman.[43] This was particularly true prior to the development of antisepsis. Antiseptic techniques, of course, were based on discoveries by Lister, Pasteur, and others first announced in 1867, but were not generally accepted and employed until about the turn of the century. Abortion mortality was high. Even after 1900, and perhaps until as late as the development of antibiotics in the 1940's, standard modern techniques such as dilation and curettage were not nearly so safe as they are today. Thus, it has been argued that a State's real concern in enacting a criminal abortion law was to protect the pregnant woman, that is, to restrain her from submitting to a procedure that placed her life in serious jeopardy.

Modern medical techniques have altered this situation. Appellants and various *amici* refer to medical data indicating that abortion in early pregnancy, that is, prior to the end of the first trimester, although not without its risk, is now relatively safe. Mortality rates for women undergoing early abortions, where the procedure is legal, appear to be as low as or lower than the rates for normal childbirth.[44] Consequently, any interest of the State in protecting the woman from an inherently hazardous procedure, except when it would be equally dangerous for her to forgo it, has largely disappeared. Of course, important state interests in the areas of health and medical standards do remain. The State has a legitimate interest in seeing to it that abortion, like any other medical procedure, is performed under circumstances that insure maximum safety for the patient. This interest obviously extends at least to the performing physician and his staff, to the facilities involved, to the availability of aftercare, and to adequate provision for any complication or emergency that might arise.

---

because of religious or other similar reasons, or the like. Such provisions, while related, do not directly pertain to when, where, or by whom abortions may be performed; however, the Act is not drafted to exclude such a provision by a state wishing to enact the same."

42. See, for example, YWCA v. *Kugler,* 342 F. Supp. 1048, 1074 (N. J. 1972); *Abele* v. *Markle,* 342 F. Supp. 800, 805–806 (Conn. 1972) (Newman, J., concurring in result), appeal docketed, No. 72–56; *Walsingham* v. *State,* 250 So. 2d 857, 863 (Ervin, J., concurring) (Fla. 1971); *State* v. *Gedicke,* 43 N. J. L. 86, 90 (1881); Means II 381–382.

43. See C. Haagensen & W. Lloyd, A Hundred Years of Medicine 19 (1943).

44. Potts, Postconceptive Control of Fertility, 8 Int'l J. of G. & O. 957, 967 (1970) (England and Wales); Abortion Mortality, 20 Morbidity and Mortality 208, 209 (June 12, 1971) (U.S. Dept. of HEW, Public Health Service) (New York City); Tietze, United States: Therapeutic Abortions, 1963–1968, 59 Studies in Family Planning 5, 7 (1970); Tietze, Mortality with Contraception and Induced Abortion, 45 Studies in Family Planning 6 (1969) (Japan, Czechoslovakia, Hungary); Tietze & Lehfeldt, Legal Abortion in Eastern Europe, 175 J. A. M. A. 1149, 1152 (April 1961). Other sources are discussed in Lader 17–23.

The prevalence of high mortality rates at illegal "abortion mills" strengthens, rather than weakens, the State's interest in regulating the conditions under which abortions are performed. Moreover, the risk to the woman increases as her pregnancy continues. Thus, the State retains a definite interest in protecting the woman's own health and safety when an abortion is proposed at a late stage of pregnancy.

The third reason is the State's interest—some phrase it in terms of duty—in protecting prenatal life. Some of the argument for this justification rests on the theory that a new human life is present from the moment of conception.[45] The State's interest and general obligation to protect life then extends, it is argued, to prenatal life. Only when the life of the pregnant mother herself is at stake, balanced against the life she carries within her, should the interest of the embryo or fetus not prevail. Logically, of course, a legitimate state interest in this area need not stand or fall on acceptance of the belief that life begins at conception or at some other point prior to live birth. In assessing the State's interest, recognition may be given to the less rigid claim that as long as at least *potential* life is involved, the State may assert interests beyond the protection of the pregnant woman alone.

Parties challenging state abortion laws have sharply disputed in some courts the contention that a purpose of these laws, when enacted, was to protect prenatal life.[46] Pointing to the absence of legislative history to support the contention, they claim that most state laws were designed solely to protect the woman. Because medical advances have lessened this concern, at least with respect to abortion in early pregnancy, they argue that with respect to such abortions the laws can no longer be justified by any state interest. There is some scholarly support for this view of original purpose.[47] The few state courts called upon to interpret their laws in the late 19th and early 20th centuries did focus on the State's interest in protecting the woman's health rather than in preserving the embryo and fetus.[48] Proponents of this view point out that in many States, including Texas,[49] by statute or judicial interpretation, the pregnant woman herself could not be prosecuted for self-abortion or for cooperating in an abortion performed upon her by another.[50] They claim that adoption of the "quickening" distinction through received common law and state statutes tacitly recognizes the greater health hazards inherent in late abortion and impliedly repudiates the theory that life begins at conception.

It is with these interests, and the weight to be attached to them, that this case is concerned.

45. See Brief of *Amicus* National Right to Life Committee; R. Drinan, The Inviolability of the Right to Be Born, in Abortion and the Law 107 (D. Smith ed. 1967); Louisell, Abortion, The Practice of Medicine and the Due Process of Law, 16 U. C. L. A. L. Rev. 233 (1969); Noonan 1.

46. See, *e. g., Abele* v. *Markle,* 342 F. Supp. 800 (Conn. 1972), appeal docketed, No. 72–56.

47. See discussions in Means I and Means II.

48. See, *e. g., State* v. *Murphy,* 27 N. J. L. 112, 114 (1858).

49. *Watson* v. *State,* 9 Tex. App. 237, 244–245 (1880); *Moore* v. *State,* 37 Tex. Cr. R. 552, 561, 40 S. W. 287, 290 (1897); *Shaw* v. *State,* 73 Tex. Cr. R. 337, 339, 165 S. W. 930, 931 (1914); *Fondren* v. *State,* 74 Tex. Cr. R. 552, 557, 169 S. W. 411, 414 (1914); *Gray* v. *State,* 77 Tex. Cr. R. 221, 229, 178 S. W. 337, 341 (1915). There is no immunity in Texas for the father who is not married to the mother. *Hammett* v. *State,* 84 Tex. Cr. R. 635, 209 S. W. 661 (1919); *Thompson* v. *State* (Ct. Crim. App. Tex. 1971), appeal docketed, No. 71–1200.

50. See *Smith* v. *State,* 33 Me., at 55; *In re Vince,* 2 N. J. 443, 450, 67 A. 2d 141, 144 (1949). A short discussion of the modern law on this issue is contained in the Comment to the ALI's Model Penal Code § 207.11, at 158 and nn. 35–37 (Tent. Draft No. 9, 1959).

VIII

The Constitution does not explicitly mention any right of privacy. In a line of decisions, however, going back perhaps as far as *Union Pacific R. Co.* v. *Botsford,* 141 U.S. 250, 251 (1891), the Court has recognized that a right of personal privacy, or a guarantee of certain areas or zones of privacy, does exist under the Constitution. In varying contexts, the Court or individual Justices have, indeed, found at least the roots of that right in the First Amendment, *Stanley* v. *Georgia,* 394 U.S. 557, 564 (1969); in the Fourth and Fifth Amendments, *Terry* v. *Ohio,* 392 U.S. 1, 8–9 (1968), *Katz* v. *United States,* 389 U.S. 347, 350 (1967), *Boyd* v. *United States,* 116 U.S. 616 (1886), see *Olmstead* v. *United States,* 277 U.S. 438, 478 (1928) (Brandeis, J., dissenting); in the penumbras of the Bill of Rights, *Griswold* v. *Connecticut,* 381 U.S., at 484–485; in the Ninth Amendment, *id.,* at 486 (Goldberg, J., concurring); or in the concept of liberty guaranteed by the first section of the Fourteenth Amendment, see *Meyer* v. *Nebraska,* 262 U.S. 390, 399 (1923). These decisions make it clear that only personal rights that can be deemed "fundamental" or "implicit in the concept of ordered liberty," *Palko* v. *Connecticut,* 302 U.S. 319, 325 (1937), are included in this guarantee of personal privacy. They also make it clear that the right has some extension to activities relating to marriage, *Loving* v. *Virginia,* 388 U.S. 1, 12 (1967); procreation, *Skinner* v. *Oklahoma,* 316 U.S. 535, 541–542 (1942); contraception, *Eisenstadt* v. *Baird,* 405 U.S., at 453–454; *id.,* at 460, 463–465 (WHITE, J., concurring in result); family relationships, *Prince* v. *Massachusetts,* 321 U.S. 158, 166 (1944); and child rearing and education, *Pierce* v. *Society of Sisters,* 268 U.S. 510, 535 (1925), *Meyer* v. *Nebraska, supra.*

This right of privacy, whether it be founded in the Fourteenth Amendment's concept of personal liberty and restrictions upon state action, as we feel it is, or, as the District Court determined, in the Ninth Amendment's reservation of rights to the people, is broad enough to encompass a woman's decision whether or not to terminate her pregnancy. The detriment that the State would impose upon the pregnant woman by denying this choice altogether is apparent. Specific and direct harm medically diagnosable even in early pregnancy may be involved. Maternity, or additional offspring, may force upon the woman a distressful life and future. Psychological harm may be imminent. Mental and physical health may be taxed by child care. There is also the distress, for all concerned, associated with the unwanted child, and there is the problem of bringing a child into a family already unable, psychologically and otherwise, to care for it. In other cases, as in this one, the additional difficulties and continuing stigma of unwed motherhood may be involved. All these are factors the woman and her responsible physician necessarily will consider in consultation.

On the basis of elements such as these, appellant and some *amici* argue that the woman's right is absolute and that she is entitled to terminate her pregnancy at whatever time, in whatever way, and for whatever reason she alone chooses. With this we do not agree. Appellant's arguments that Texas either has no valid interest at all in regulating the abortion decision, or no interest strong enough to support any limitation upon the woman's sole determination, are unpersuasive. The Court's decisions recognizing a right of privacy also acknowledge that some state regulation in areas protected by that right is appropriate. As noted above, a State may properly assert important interests in safeguarding health, in maintaining medical standards, and in protecting potential life. At some point in pregnancy, these respective interests become sufficiently compelling to sustain regulation of the factors that govern the abortion decision. The privacy right involved, therefore, cannot be said to be absolute. In fact, it is not clear to us that the claim asserted by some *amici* that one has an unlimited right to do with one's body as one pleases bears a close relationship to the right of privacy previously articulated in the Court's decisions. The Court has refused to recognize an unlimited right of this kind in the past. *Jacobson* v. *Massachusetts,* 197 U.S. 11 (1905) (vaccination); *Buck* v. *Bell,* 274 U.S. 200 (1927) (sterilization).

We, therefore, conclude that the right of personal privacy includes the abortion decision, but that this right is not unqualified and must be considered against important state interests in regulation.

We note that those federal and state courts that have recently considered abortion law challenges have reached the same conclusion. A majority, in addition to the District Court in the present case, have held state laws unconstitutional, at least in part, because of vagueness or because of overbreadth and abridgment of rights. *Abele* v. *Markle,* 342 F. Supp. 800 (Conn. 1972), appeal docketed, No. 72–56; *Abele* v. *Markle,* 351 F. Supp. 224 (Conn. 1972), appeal docketed, No. 72–730; *Doe* v. *Bolton,* 319 F. Supp. 1048 (ND Ga. 1970), appeal decided today, *post,* p. 179; *Doe* v. *Scott,* 321 F. Supp. 1385 (ND Ill. 1971), appeal docketed, No. 70–105; *Poe* v. *Menghini,* 339 F. Supp. 986 (Kan. 1972); *YWCA* v. *Kugler,* 342 F. Supp. 1048 (NJ 1972); *Babbitz* v. *McCann,* 310 F. Supp. 293 (ED Wis. 1970), appeal dismissed, 400 U.S. 1 (1970); *People* v. *Belous,* 71 Cal. 2d 954, 458 P. 2d 194 (1969), cert. denied, 397 U.S. 915 (1970); *State* v. *Barquet,* 262 So. 2d 431 (Fla. 1972).

Others have sustained state statutes. *Crossen* v. *Attorney General,* 344 F. Supp. 587 (ED Ky. 1972), appeal docketed. No. 72–256; *Rosen* v. *Louisiana State Board of Medical Examiners,* 318 F. Supp. 1217 (ED La. 1970), appeal docketed. No. 70–42; *Corkey* v. *Edwards,* 322 F. Supp. 1248 (WDNC 1971), appeal docketed, No. 71–92; *Steinberg* v. *Brown,* 321 F. Supp. 741 (ND Ohio 1970); *Doe* v. *Rampton* (Utah 1971), appeal docketed, No. 71–5666; *Cheaney* v. *State,* —Ind.—, 285 N. E. 2d 265 (1972); *Spears* v. *State,* 257 So. 2d 876 (Miss. 1972); *State* v. *Munson,* 86 S. D. 663, 201 N. W. 2d 123 (1972), appeal docketed, No. 72–631.

Although the results are divided, most of these courts have agreed that the right of privacy, however based, is broad enough to cover the abortion decision; that the right, nonetheless, is not absolute and is subject to some limitations; and that at some point the state interests as to protection of health, medical standards, and prenatal life, become dominant. We agree with this approach.

Where certain "fundamental rights" are involved, the Court has held that regulation limiting these rights may be justified only by a "compelling state interest," *Kramer* v. *Union Free School District,* 395 U.S. 621, 627 (1969); *Shapiro* v. *Thompson,* 394 U.S. 618, 634 (1969), *Sherbert* v. *Verner,* 374 U.S. 398, 406 (1963), and that legislative enactments must be narrowly drawn to express only the legitimate state interests at stake. *Griswold* v. *Connecticut,* 381, U.S., at 485; *Aptheker* v. *Secretary of State,* 378 U.S. 500, 508 (1964); *Cantwell* v. *Connecticut,* 310 U.S. 296, 307–308 (1940); see *Eisenstadt* v. *Baird,* 405 U.S., at 460, 463–464 (WHITE, J., concurring in result).

In the recent abortion cases, cited above, courts have recognized these principles. Those striking down state laws have generally scrutinized the State's interests in protecting health and potential life, and have concluded that neither interest justified broad limitations on the reasons for which a physician and his pregnant patient might decide that she should have an abortion in the early stages of pregnancy. Courts sustaining state laws have held that the State's determinations to protect health or prenatal life are dominant and constitutionally justifiable.

IX

The District Court held that the appellee failed to meet his burden demonstrating that the Texas statute's infringement upon Roe's rights was necessary to support a compelling state interest, and that, although the appellee presented "several compelling justifications for state presence in the area of abortions," the statutes outstripped these justifications and swept "far beyond any areas of compelling state interest." 314 F. Supp., at 1222–1223. Appellant and appellee both contest that holding. Appellant, as has been indicated, claims an absolute right that bars any state imposition of criminal penalties in the area. Appellee argues that the State's determination to recognize and protect prenatal life from and after conception constitutes a compelling state interest. As noted above, we do not agree fully with either formulation.

A. The appellee and certain *amici* argue that the fetus is a "person" within the language and meaning of the Fourteenth Amendment. In support of this, they outline at length and in detail the well-known facts of fetal development. If this suggestion of personhood is established, the appellant's case, of course, collapses, for the fetus' right to life would then be guaranteed specifically by the Amendment. The appellant conceded as much on reargument.[51] On the other hand, the appellee conceded on reargument[52] that no case could be cited that holds that a fetus is a person within the meaning of the Fourteenth Amendment.

The Constitution does not define "person" in so many words. Section 1 of the Fourteenth Amendment contains three references to "person." The first, in defining "citizens," speaks of "persons born or naturalized in the United States." The word also appears both in the Due Process Clause and in the Equal Protection Clause. "Person" is used in other places in the Constitution: in the listing of qualifications for Representatives and Senators, Art. I, § 2, cl. 2, and §3, cl. 3; in the Apportionment Clause, Art. I, §2, cl. 3;[53] in the Migration and Importation provision, Art. I, § 9, cl. 1; in the Emolument Clause, Art. I, § 9, cl. 8; in the Electors provisions, Art. II, § 1, cl. 2, and the superseded cl. 3; in the provision outlining qualifications for the office of President, Art. II, § 1, cl. 5; in the Extradition provisions, Art. IV, § 2, cl. 2, and the superseded Fugitive Slave Clause 3; and in the Fifth, Twelfth, and Twenty-second Amendments, as well as in §§ 2 and 3 of the Fourteenth Amendment. But in nearly all these instances, the use of the word is such that it has application only postnatally. None indicates, with any assurance, that it has any possible pre-natal application.[54]

51. Tr. of Oral Rearg. 20–21.

52. Tr. of Oral Rearg. 24.

53. We are not aware that in the taking of any census under this clause, a fetus has ever been counted.

54. When Texas urges that a fetus is entitled to Fourteenth Amendment protection as a person, it faces a dilemma. Neither in Texas nor in any other State are all abortions prohibited. Despite broad proscription, an exception always exists. The exception contained in Art. 1196, for an abortion procured or attempted by medical advice for the purpose of saving the life

All this, together with our observation, *supra,* that throughout the major portion of the 19th century prevailing legal abortion practices were far freer than they are today, persuades us that the word "person," as used in the Fourteenth Amendment, does not include the unborn.[55] This is in accord with the results reached in those few cases where the issue has been squarely presented. *McGarvey* v. *Magee-Womens Hospital,* 340 F. Supp. 751 (WD Pa. 1972); *Byrn* v. *New York City Health & Hospitals Corp.,* 31 N. Y. 2d 194, 286 N.E. 2d 887 (1972), appeal docketed, No. 72–434; *Abele* v. *Markle,* 351 F. Supp. 224 (Conn. 1972), appeal docketed, No. 72–730. Cf. *Cheaney* v. *State,*—Ind., at—, 285 N. E. 2d, at 270; *Montana* v. *Rogers,* 278 F. 2d 68, 72 (CA7 1960), aff'd *sub nom. Montana* v. *Kennedy,* 366 U.S. 308 (1961); *Keeler* v. *Superior Court,* 2 Cal. 3d 619, 470 P. 2d 617 (1970); *State* v. *Dickinson,* 28 Ohio St. 2d 65, 275 N. E. 2d 599 (1971). Indeed, our decision in *United States* v. *Vuitch,* 402 U.S. 62 (1971), inferentially is to the same effect, for we there would not have indulged in statutory interpretation favorable to abortion in specified circumstances if the necessary consequence was the termination of life entitled to Fourteenth Amendment protection.

This conclusion, however, does not of itself fully answer the contentions raised by Texas, and we pass on to other considerations.

B. The pregnant woman cannot be isolated in her privacy. She carried an ambryo and, later, a fetus, if one accepts the medical definitions of the developing young in the human uterus. See Dorland's Illustrated Medical Dictionary 478–479, 547 (24th ed. 1965). The situation therefore is inherently different from marital intimacy, or bedroom possession of obscene material, or marriage, or procreation, or education, with which *Eisenstadt* and *Griswold, Stanley, Loving, Skinner,* and *Pierce* and *Meyer* were respectively concerned. As we have intimated above, it is reasonable and appropriate for a State to decide that at some point in time another interest, that of health of the mother or that of potential human life, becomes significantly involved. The woman's privacy is no longer sole and any right of privacy she possesses must be measured accordingly.

Texas urges that, apart from the Fourteenth Amendment, life begins at conception and is present throughout pregnancy, and that, therefore, the State has a compelling interest in protecting that life from and after conception. We need not resolve the difficult question of when life begins. When those trained in the respective disciplines of medicine, philosophy, and theology are unable to arrive at any consensus,

---

of the mother, is typical. But if the fetus is a person who is not to be deprived of life without due process of law, and if the mother's condition is the sole determinant, does not the Texas exception appear to be out of line with the Amendment's command?

There are other inconsistencies between Fourteenth Amendment status and the typical abortion statute. It has already been pointed out, n. 49, *supra,* that in Texas the woman is not a principal or an accomplice with respect to an abortion upon her. If the fetus is a person, why is the woman not a principal or an accomplice? Further, the penalty for criminal abortion specified by Art. 1195 is significantly less than the maximum penalty for murder prescribed by Art. 1257 of the Texas Penal Code. If the fetus is a person, may the penalties be different?

55. Cf. the Wisconsin abortion statute, defining "unborn child" to mean "a human being from the time of conception until it is born alive," Wis. Stat. § 940.04 (6) (1969), and the new Connecticut statute, Pub. Act No. 1 (May 1972 special session), declaring it to be the public policy of the State and the legislative intent "to protect and preserve human life from the moment of conception."

the judiciary, at this point in the development of man's knowledge, is not in a position to speculate as to the answer.

It should be sufficient to note briefly the wide divergence of thinking on this most sensitive and difficult question. There has always been strong support for the view that life does not begin until live birth. This was the belief of the Stoics.[56] It appears to be the predominant, though not the unanimous, attitude of the Jewish faith.[57] It may be taken to represent also the position of a large segment of the Protestant community, insofar as that can be ascertained; organized groups that have taken a formal position on the abortion issue have generally regarded abortion as a matter for the conscience of the individual and her family.[58] As we have noted, the common law found greater significance in quickening. Physicians and their scientific colleagues have regarded that event with less interest and have tended to focus either upon conception, upon live birth, or upon the interim point at which the fetus becomes "viable," that is, potentially able to live outside the mother's womb, albeit with artificial aid.[59] Viability is usually placed at about seven months (28 weeks) but may occur earlier, even at 24 weeks.[60] The Aristotelian theory of "mediate animation," that held sway throughout the Middle Ages and the Renaissance in Europe, continued to be official Roman Catholic dogma until the 19th century, despite opposition to this "ensoulment" theory from those in the Church who would recognize the existence of life from the moment of conception.[61] The latter is now, of course, the official belief of the Catholic Church. As one brief *amicus* discloses, this is a view strongly held by many non-Catholics as well, and by many physicians. Substantial problems for precise definition of this view are posed, however, by new embryological data that purport to indicate that conception is a "process" over time, rather than an event, and by new medical techniques such as menstrual extraction, the "morning-after" pill, implantation of embryos, artificial insemination, and even artificial wombs.[62]

In areas other than criminal abortion, the law has been reluctant to endorse any theory that life, as we recognize it, begins before live birth or to accord legal rights to the unborn except in narrowly defined situations and except when the rights are contingent upon live birth. For example, the traditional rule of tort law denied recov-

56. Edelstein 16.

57. Lader 97–99; D. Feldman, Birth Control in Jewish Law 251–294 (1968). For a stricter view, see I. Jakobovits, Jewish Views on Abortion, in Abortion and the Law 124 (D. Smith ed. 1967).

58. Amicus Brief for the American Ethical Union et al. For the position of the National Council of Churches and of other denominations, see Lader 99–101.

59. L. Hellman & J. Pritchard, Williams Obstetrics 493 (14th ed. 1971); Dorland's Illustrated Medical Dictionary 1689 (24th ed. 1965).

60. Hellman & Pritchard, *supra,* n. 59, at 493.

61. For discussions of the development of the Roman Catholic position, see D. Callahan, Abortion: Law, Choice, and Morality 409–447 (1970); Noonan 1.

62. See Brodie, the New Biology and the Prenatal Child, 9 J. Family L. 391, 397 (1970); Gorney, The New Biology and the Future of Man, 15 U. C. L. A. L. Rev. 273 (1968); Note, Criminal Law—Abortion—the "Morning-After Pill" and Other Pre-Implantation Birth-Control Methods and the Law, 46 Ore. L. Rev. 211 (1967); G. Taylor, The Biological Time Bomb 32 (1968); A. Rosenfeld, The Second Genesis 138–139 (1969); Smith, Through a Test Tube Darkly: Artificial Insemination and the Law, 67 Mich. L. Rev. 127 (1968); Note, Artificial Insemination and the Law, 1968 U. Ill. L. F. 203.

ery for prenatal injuries even though the child was born alive.[63] That rule has been changed in almost every jurisdiction. In most States, recovery is said to be permitted only if the fetus was viable, or at least quick, when the injuries were sustained, though few courts have squarely so held.[64] In a recent development, generally opposed by the commentators, some States permit the parents of a stillborn child to maintain an action for wrongful death because of prenatal injuries.[65] Such an action, however, would appear to be one to vindicate the parents' interest and is thus consistent with the view that the fetus, at most, represents only the potentiality of life. Similarly, unborn children have been recognized as acquiring rights or interests by way of inheritance or other devolution of property, and have been represented by guardians _ad litem_.[66] Perfection of the interests involved, again, has generally been contingent upon live birth. In short, the unborn have never been recognized in the law as persons in the whole sense.

X

In view of all this, we do not agree that, by adopting one theory of life, Texas may override the rights of the pregnant woman that are at stake. We repeat, however, that the State does have an important and legitimate interest in preserving and protecting the health of the pregnant woman, whether she be a resident of the State or a nonresident who seeks medical consultation and treatment there, and that it has still _another_ important and legitimate interest in protecting the potentiality of human life. These interests are separate and distinct. Each grows in substantiality as the woman approaches term and, at a point during pregnancy, each becomes "compelling."

With respect to the State's important and legitimate interest in the health of the mother, the "compelling" point, in the light of present medical knowledge, is at approximately the end of the first trimester. This is so because of the now-established medical fact, referred to above at 149, that until the end of the first trimester mortality in abortion may be less than mortality in normal childbirth. It follows that, from and after this point, a State may regulate the abortion procedure to the extent that the regulation reasonably relates to the preservation and protection of maternal health. Examples of permissible state regulation in this area are requirements as to the qualifications of the person who is to perform the abortion; as to the licensure of that person; as to the facility in which the procedure is to be performed, that is, whether it must be a hospital or may be a clinic or some other place of less-than-hospital status; as to the licensing of the facility; and the like.

This means, on the other hand, that, for the period of pregnancy prior to this "compelling" point, the attending physician, in consultation with his patient, is free

63. W. Prosser, The Law of Torts 335–338 (4th ed. 1971); 2 F. Harper & F. James, The Law of Torts 1028-1031 (1956); Note, 63 Harv. L. Rev. 173 (1949).

64. See cases cited in Prosser, _supra_, n. 63, at 336–338; Annotation, Action for Death of Unborn Child, 15 A. L. R. 3d 992 (1967).

65. Prosser, _supra_, n. 63, at 338; Note, The Law and the Unborn Child: The Legal and Logical Inconsistencies, 46 Notre Dame Law. 349, 354–360 (1971).

66. Louisell, Abortion, The Practice of Medicine and the Due Process of Law, 16 U. C. L. A. L. Rev. 233, 235–238 (1969); Note, 56 Iowa L. Rev. 994, 999–1000 (1971); Note, The Law and the Unborn Child, 46 Notre Dame Law, 349, 351–354 (1971).

to determine, without regulation by the State, that, in his medical judgment, the patient's pregnancy should be terminated. If that decision is reached, the judgment may be effectuated by an abortion free of interference by the State.

With respect to the State's important and legitimate interest in potential life, the "compelling" point is at viability. This is so because the fetus then presumably has the capability of meaningful life outside the mother's womb. State regulation protective of fetal life after viability thus has both logical and biological justifications. If the State is interested in protecting fetal life after viability, it may go so far as to proscribe abortion during that period, except when it is necessary to preserve the life or health of the mother.

Measured against these standards, Art. 1196 of the Texas Penal Code, in restricting legal abortions to those "procured or attempted by medical advice for the purpose of saving the life of the mother," sweeps too broadly. The statute makes no distinction between abortions performed early in pregnancy and those performed later, and it limits to a single reason, "saving" the mother's life, the legal justification for the procedure. The statute, therefore, cannot survive the constitutional attack made upon it here.

This conclusion makes it unnecessary for us to consider the additional challenge to the Texas statute asserted on grounds of vagueness. See *United States* v. *Vuitch,* 402 U.S., at 67–72.

XI

To summarize and to repeat:

1. A state criminal abortion statute of the current Texas type, that excepts from criminality only a *lifesaving* procedure on behalf of the mother, without regard to pregnancy stage and without recognition of the other interests involved, is violative of the Due Process Clause of the Fourteenth Amendment.

(a) For the stage prior to approximately the end of the first trimester, the abortion decision and its effectuation must be left to the medical judgment of the pregnant woman's attending physician.

(b) For the stage subsequent to approximately the end of the first trimester, the State, in promoting its interest in the health of the mother, may, if it chooses, regulate the abortion procedure in ways that are reasonably related to maternal health.

(c) For the stage subsequent to viability, the State in promoting its interest in the potentiality of human life may, if it chooses, regulate, and even proscribe, abortion except where it is necessary, in appropriate medical judgment, for the preservation of the life or health of the mother.

2. The State may define the term "physician," as it has been employed in the preceding paragraphs of this Part XI of this opinion, to mean only a physician currently licensed by the State, and may proscribe any abortion by a person who is not a physician as so defined.

In *Doe* v. *Bolton, post,* p. 179, procedural requirements contained in one of the modern abortion statutes are considered. That opinion and this one, of course, are to be read together.[67]

___

67. Neither in this opinion nor in *Doe* v. *Bolton, post.* p. 179, do we discuss the father's rights, if any exist in the constitutional context, in the abortion decision. No paternal right has

This holding, we feel, is consistent with the relative weights of the respective interests involved, with the lessons and examples of medical and legal history with the lenity of the common law, and with the demands of the profound problems of the present day. The decision leaves the State free to place increasing restrictions on abortion as the period of pregnancy lengthens, so long as those restrictions are tailored to the recognized state interests. The decision vindicates the right of the physician to administer medical treatment according to his professional judgment up to the points where important state interests provide compelling justifications for intervention. Up to those points, the abortion decision in all its aspects is inherently, and primarily, a medical decision, and basic responsibility for it must rest with the physician. If an individual practitioner abuses the privilege of exercising proper medical judgment, the usual remedies, judicial and intra-professional, are available.

XII

Our conclusion that Art. 1196 is unconstitutional means, of course, that the Texas abortion statutes, as a unit, must fall. The exception of Art. 1196 cannot be struck down separately, for then the State would be left with a statute proscribing all abortion procedures no matter how medically urgent the case.

Although the District Court granted appellant Roe declaratory relief, it stopped short of issuing an injunction against enforcement of the Texas statutes. The Court has recognized that different considerations enter into a federal court's decision as to declaratory relief, on the one hand, and injunctive relief on the other. *Zwickler* v. *Koota,* 389 U.S. 241, 252–255 (1967); *Dombrowski* v. *Pfister,* 380 U.S. 479 (1965). We are not dealing with a statute that, on its face, appears to abridge free expression, an area of particular concern under *Dombrowski* and refined in *Younger* v. *Harris,* 401 U.S., at 50.

We find it unnecessary to decide whether the District Court erred in withholding injunctive relief, for we assume the Texas prosecutorial authorities will give full credence to this decision that the present criminal abortion statutes of that State are unconstitutional.

The judgment of the District Court as to intervenor Hallford is reversed, and Dr. Hallford's complaint in intervention is dismissed. In all other respects, the judgment of the District Court is affirmed. Costs are allowed to the appellee.

It is so ordered.

---

been asserted in either of the cases, and the Texas and the Georgia statutes on their face take no cognizance of the father. We are aware that some statutes recognize the father under certain circumstances. North Carolina, for example, N. C. Gen. Stat. § 14–45.1 (Supp. 1971), requires written permission for the abortion from the husband when the woman is a married minor, that is, when she is less than 18 years of age, 41 N. C. A. G. 489 (1971); if the woman is an unmarried minor, written permission from the parents is required. We need not now decide whether provisions of this kind are constitutional.

[For concurring opinion of Mr. Chief Justice Burger, see *post,* p. 207.]
[For concurring opinion of Mr. Justice Douglas, see *post,* p. 209.]
[For dissenting opinion of Mr. Justice White, see *post,* p. 221.]

Mr. Justice Stewart, concurring.

In 1963, this Court, in *Ferguson* v. *Skrupa,* 372 U.S. 726, purported to sound the death knell for the doctrine of substantive due process, a doctrine under which many state laws had in the past been held to violate the Fourteenth Amendment. As Mr. Justice Black's opinion for the Court in *Skrupa* put it: "We have returned to the original constitutional proposition that courts do not substitute their social and economic beliefs for the judgment of legislative bodies, who are elected to pass laws." *Id.,* at 730.[1]

Barely two years later, in *Griswold* v. *Connecticut,* 381 U.S. 479, the Court held a Connecticut birth control law unconstitutional. In view of what had been so recently said in *Skrupa,* the Court's opinion in *Griswold* understandably did its best to avoid reliance on the Due Process Clause of the Fourteenth Amendment as the ground for decision. Yet, the Connecticut law did not violate any provision of the Bill of Rights, nor any other specific provision of the Constitution.[2] So it was clear to me then, and it is equally clear to me now, that the *Griswold* decision can be rationally understood only as a holding that the Connecticut statute substantively invaded the "liberty" that is protected by the Due Process Clause of the Fourteenth Amendment.[3] As so understood, *Griswold* stands as one in a long line of pre-*Skrupa* cases decided under the doctrine of substantive due process, and I now accept it as such.

"In a Constitution for a free people, there can be no doubt that the meaning of 'liberty' must be broad indeed." *Board of Regents* v. *Roth,* 408 U.S. 564, 572. The Constitution nowhere mentions a specific right of personal choice in matters of marriage and family life, but the "liberty" protected by the Due Process Clause of the Fourteenth Amendment covers more than those freedoms explicitly named in the Bill of Rights. See *Schware* v. *Board of Bar Examiners,* 353 U.S. 232, 238–239; *Pierce* v. *Society of Sisters,* 268 U.S. 510, 534–535; *Meyer* v. *Nebraska,* 262 U.S. 390, 399–400. Cf. *Shapiro* v. *Thompson,* 394 U.S. 618, 629–630; *United States* v. *Guest,* 383 U.S. 745, 757–758; *Carrington* v. *Rash,* 380 U.S. 89, 96; *Aptheker* v. *Secretary of State,* 378 U.S. 500, 505; *Kent* v. *Dulles,* 357 U.S. 116, 127; *Bolling* v. *Sharpe,* 347 U.S. 497, 499–500; *Truax* v. *Raich,* 239 U.S. 33, 41.

As Mr. Justice Harlan once wrote: "[T]he full scope of the liberty guaranteed by

---

1. Only Mr. Justice Harlan failed to join the Court's opinion, 372 U.S., at 733.

2. There is no constitutional right of privacy, as such. "[The Fourth] Amendment protects individual privacy against certain kinds of governmental intrusion, but its protections go further, and often have nothing to do with privacy at all. Other provisions of the Constitution protect personal privacy from other forms of governmental invasion. But the protection of a person's *general* right to privacy—his right to be let alone by other people—is, like the protection of his property and of his very life, left largely to the law of the individual States." *Katz* v. *United States,* 389 U.S. 347, 350–351 (footnotes omitted).

3. This was also clear to Mr. Justice Black, 381 U.S., at 507 (dissenting opinion); to Mr. Justice Harlan, 381 U.S., at 499 (opinion concurring in the judgment); and to Mr. Justice White, 381 U.S., at 502 (opinion concurring in the judgment). See also Mr. Justice Harlan's thorough and thoughtful opinion dissenting from dismissal of the appeal in *Poe* v. *Ullman,* 367 U.S. 497, 522.

the Due Process Clause cannot be found in or limited by the precise terms of the specific guarantees elsewhere provided in the Constitution. This 'liberty' is not a series of isolated points pricked out in terms of the taking of property; the freedom of speech, press, and religion; the right to keep and bear arms; the freedom from unreasonable searches and seizures; and so on. It is a rational continuum which, broadly speaking, includes a freedom from all substantial arbitrary impositions and purposeless restraints . . . and which also recognizes, what a reasonable and sensitive judgment must, that certain interests require particularly careful scrutiny of the state needs asserted to justify their abridgment." *Poe* v. *Ullman,* 367 U.S. 497, 543 (opinion dissenting from dismissal of appeal) (citations omitted). In the words of Mr. Justice Frankfurter, "Great concepts like . . . 'liberty' . . . were purposely left to gather meaning from experience. For they relate to the whole domain of social and economic fact, and the statesmen who founded this Nation knew too well that only a stagnant society remains unchanged." *National Mutual Ins. Co.* v. *Tidewater Transfer Co.,* 337 U.S. 582, 646 (dissenting opinion).

Several decisions of this Court make clear that freedom of personal choice in matters of marriage and family life is one of the liberties protected by the Due Process Clause of the Fourteenth Amendment. *Loving* v. *Virginia,* 388 U.S. 1, 12; *Griswold* v. *Connecticut, supra; Pierce* v. *Society of Sisters, supra; Meyer* v. *Nebraska, supra.* See also *Prince* v. *Massachusetts,* 321 U.S. 158, 166; *Skinner* v. *Oklahoma,* 316 U.S. 535, 541. As recently as last Term, in *Eisenstadt* v. *Baird,* 405 U.S. 438, 453, we recognized "the right of the *individual,* married or single, to be free from unwarranted governmental intrusion into matters so fundamentally affecting a person as the decision whether to bear or beget a child." That right necessarily includes the right of a woman to decide whether or not to terminate her pregnancy. "Certainly the interests of a woman in giving of her physical and emotional self during pregnancy and the interests that will be affected throughout her life by the birth and raising of a child are of a far greater degree of significance and personal intimacy than the right to send a child to private school protected in Pierce v. Society of Sisters, 268 U.S. 510 (1925), or the right to teach a foreign language protected in Meyer v. Nebraska, 262 U.S. 390 (1923)." *Abele* v. *Markle,* 351 F. Supp. 224, 227 (Conn. 1972).

Clearly, therefore, the Court today is correct in holding that the right asserted by Jane Roe is embraced within the personal liberty protected by the Due Process Clause of the Fourteenth Amendment.

It is evident that the Texas abortion statute infringes that right directly. Indeed, it is difficult to imagine a more complete abridgment of a constitutional freedom than that worked by the inflexible criminal statute now in force in Texas. The question then becomes whether the state interests advanced to justify this abridgment can survive the "particularly careful scrutiny" that the Fourteenth Amendment here requires.

The asserted state interests are protection of the health and safety of the pregnant woman, and protection of the potential future human life within her. These are legitimate objectives, amply sufficient to permit a State to regulate abortions as it does other surgical procedures, and perhaps sufficient to permit a State to regulate abortions more stringently or even to prohibit them in the late stages of pregnancy. But such legislation is not before us, and I think the Court today has thoroughly demonstrated that these state interests cannot constitutionally support the broad abridgment of personal liberty worked by the existing Texas law. Accordingly, I join the Court's opinion holding that that law is invalid under the Due Process Clause of the Fourteenth Amendment.

MR. JUSTICE REHNQUIST, dissenting.

The Court's opinion brings to the decision of this troubling question both extensive historical fact and a wealth of legal scholarship. While the opinion thus commands my respect, I find myself nonetheless in fundamental disagreement with those parts of it that invalidate the Texas statute in question, and therefore dissent.

I

The Court's opinion decides that a State may impose virtually no restriction on the performance of abortions during the first trimester of pregnancy. Our previous decisions indicate that a necessary predicate for such an opinion is a plaintiff who was in her first trimester of pregnancy at some time during the pendency of her lawsuit. While a party may vindicate his own constitutional rights, he may not seek vindication for the rights of others. *Moose Lodge* v. *Irvis,* 407 U.S. 163 (1972); *Sierra Club* v. *Morton,* 405 U.S. 727 (1972). The Court's statement of facts in this case makes clear, however that the record in no way indicates the presence of such a plaintiff. We know only that plaintiff Roe at the time of filing her complaint was a pregnant woman; for aught that appears in this record, she may have been in her *last* trimester of pregnancy as of the date the complaint was filed.

Nothing in the Court's opinion indicates that Texas might not constitutionally apply its proscription of abortion as written to a woman in that stage of pregnancy. Nonetheless, the Court uses her complaint against the Texas statute as a fulcrum for deciding that States may impose virtually no restrictions on medical abortions performed during the *first* trimester of pregnancy. In deciding such a hypothetical lawsuit, the Court departs from the longstanding admonition that it should never "formulate a rule of constitutional law broader than is required by the precise facts to which it is to be applied." *Liverpool, New York & Philadelphia S. S. Co.* v. *Commissioners of Emigration,* 113 U.S. 33, 39 (1885). See also *Ashwander* v. *TVA,* 297 U.S. 288, 345 (1936) (Brandeis, J., concurring).

II

Even if there were a plaintiff in this case capable of litigating the issue which the Court decides, I would reach a conclusion opposite to that reached by the Court. I have difficulty in concluding, as the Court does, that the right of "privacy" is involved in this case. Texas, by the statute here challenged, bars the performance of a medical abortion by a licensed physician on a plaintiff such as Roe. A transaction resulting in an operation such as this is not "private" in the ordinary usage of that word. Nor is the "privacy" that the Court finds here even a distant relative of the freedom from searches and seizures protected by the Fourth Amendment to the Constitution, which the Court has referred to as embodying a right to privacy. *Katz* v. *United States,* 389 U.S. 347 (1967).

If the Court means by the term "privacy" no more than that the claim of a person to be free from unwanted state regulation of consensual transactions may be a form of "liberty" protected by the Fourteenth Amendment, there is no doubt that similar claims have been upheld in our earlier decisions on the basis of that liberty. I agree with the statement of MR. JUSTICE STEWART in his concurring opinion that the "liberty," against deprivation of which without due process the Fourteenth Amendment protects, embraces more than the rights found in the Bill of Rights. But that liberty is not guaranteed absolutely against deprivation, only against deprivation without due process of law. The test traditionally applied in the area of social and economic legislation is whether or not a law such as that challenged has a rational relation to a valid state objective. *Williamson* v. *Lee Optical Co.,* 348 U.S. 483, 491 (1955). The Due Process Clause of the Fourteenth Amendment undoubtedly does place a limit, albeit a broad one, on legislative power to enact laws such as this. If the Texas statute were to prohibit an abortion even where the mother's life is in jeopardy, I have little doubt that such a statute would lack a rational relation to a valid state objective under the test stated in *Williamson, supra.* But the Court's sweeping invalidation of any restrictions on abortion during the first trimester is impossible to justify under that standard, and the conscious weighing of competing factors that the Court's opinion apparently substitutes for the established test is far more appropriate to a legislative judgment than to a judicial one.

The Court eschews the history of the Fourteenth Amendment in its reliance on the "compelling state interest" test. See *Weber* v. *Aetna Casualty & Surety Co.,* 406 U.S. 164, 179 (1972) (dissenting opinion). But the Court adds a new wrinkle to this test by transposing it from the legal considerations associated with the Equal Protection Clause of the Fourteenth Amendment to this case arising under the Due Process Clause of the Fourteenth Amendment. Unless I misapprehend the consequences of this transplanting of the "compelling state interest test," the Court's opinion will accomplish the seemingly impossible feat of leaving this area of the law more confused than it found it.

While the Court's opinion quotes from the dissent of Mr. Justice Holmes in *Lochner* v. *New York,* 198 U.S. 45, 74 (1905), the result it reaches is more closely attuned to the majority opinion of Mr. Justice Peckham in that case. As in *Lochner* and similar cases applying substantive due process standards to economic and social welfare legislation, the adoption of the compelling state interest standard will inevitably require this Court to examine the legislative policies and pass on the wisdom of these policies in the very process of deciding whether a particular state interest put forward may or may not be "compelling." The decision here to break pregnancy into three distinct terms and to outline the permissible restrictions the State may impose in each one, for example, partakes more of judicial legislation than it does of a determination of the intent of the drafters of the Fourteenth Amendment.

The fact that a majority of the States reflecting, after all, the majority sentiment in those States, have had restrictions on abortions for at least a century is a strong indication, it seems to me, that the asserted right to an abortion is not "so rooted in the traditions and conscience of our people as to be ranked as fundamental," *Snyder* v. *Massachusetts,* 291 U.S. 97, 105 (1934). Even today, when society's views on abortion are changing the very existence of the debate is evidence that the "right" to an abortion is not so universally accepted as the appellant would have us believe.

To reach its result, the Court necessarily has had to find within the scope of the Fourteenth Amendment a right that was apparently completely unknown to the drafters of the Amendment. As early as 1821, the first state law dealing directly with abortion was enacted by the Connecticut Legislature. Conn. Stat., Tit. 22, §§ 14, 16. By the time of the adoption of the Fourteenth Amendment in 1868, there were at least 36 laws enacted by state or territorial legislatures limiting abortion.[1] While many States have amended or updated their laws, 21 of the laws on the books in 1868 remain in effect today. [2] Indeed, the Texas statute struck down today was, as the majority notes, first enacted in 1857 and "has remained substantially unchanged to the present time." *Ante,* at 119.

    1. Jurisdictions having enacted abortion laws prior to the adoption of the Fourteenth Amendment in 1868:

        1. Alabama—Ala. Acts, c. 6, § 2 (1840).
        2. Arizona—Howell Code, c. 10, § 45 (1865).
        3. Arkansas—Ark. Rev. Stat., c. 44, div. III, Art. II, § 6 (1838).
        4. California—Cal. Sess. Laws, c. 99, § 45, p. 233 (1849–1850).
        5. Colorado (Terr.)—Colo. Gen. Laws of Terr. of Colo., 1st Sess., § 42, pp. 296–297 (1861).
        6. Connecticut—Conn. Stat., Tit. 20, §§ 14, 16 (1821). By 1868, this statute had been replaced by another abortion law. Conn. Pub. Acts, c. 71, §§ 1, 2, p. 65 (1860).
        7. Florida—Fla. Acts 1st Sess., c. 1637, subc. 3, §§ 10, 11, subc. 8, §§ 9, 10, 11 (1868), as amended, now Fla. Stat. Ann. §§ 782.09, 782.10, 797.01, 797.02, 782.16 (1965).
        8. Georgia—Ga. Pen. Code, 4th Div., § 20 (1833).
        9. Kingdom of Hawaii—Hawaii Pen. Code, c. 12, §§ 1, 2, 3 (1850).
      10. Idaho (Terr.)—Idaho (Terr.) Laws, Crimes and Punishments §§ 33, 34, 42, pp. 441, 443 (1863).
      11. Illinois—Ill. Rev. Criminal Code§§ 40, 41, 46, pp. 130, 131 (1827). By 1868, this statute had been replaced by a subsequent enactment. Ill. Pub. Laws §§ 1, 2, 3, p. 89 (1867).
      12. Indiana—Ind. Rev. Stat. §§ 1, 3, p. 224 (1838). By 1868 this statute had been superseded by a subsequent enactment. Ind. Laws, c. LXXXI, § 2 (1859).
      13. Iowa (Terr.)—Iowa (Terr.) Stat., 1st Legis., 1st Sess., § 18, p. 145 (1838). By 1868, this statute had been superseded by a subsequent enactment. Iowa (Terr.) Rev. Stat., c. 49, §§ 10, 13 (1843).
      14. Kansas (Terr.)—Kan. (Terr.) Stat., c. 48, §§ 9, 10, 39 (1855). By 1868, this statute had been superseded by a subsequent enactment. Kan. (Terr.) Laws, c. 28, §§ 9, 10, 37 (1859).
      15. Louisiana—La. Rev. Stat., Crimes and Offenses § 24, p. 138 (1856).
      16. Maine—Me. Rev. Stat., c. 160, §§ 11, 12, 13, 14 (1840).
      17. Maryland—Md. Laws, c. 179, § 2, p. 315 (1868).
      18. Massachusetts—Mass. Acts & Resolves, c. 27 (1845).
      19. Michigan—Mich. Rev. Stat., c. 153, §§ 32, 33, 34, p. 662 (1846).
      20. Minnesota (Terr.)—Minn. (Terr.) Rev. Stat., c. 100, §§ 10, 11, p. 493 (1851).
      21. Mississippi—Miss. Code, c. 64, §§ 8, 9, p. 958 (1848).
      22. Missouri—Mo. Rev. Stat., Art. II, §§ 9, 10, 36, pp. 168, 172 (1835).
      23. Montana (Terr.)—Mont. (Terr.) Laws, Criminal Practice Acts § 41, p. 184 (1864).
      24. Nevada (Terr.)—Nev. (Terr.) Laws, c. 28, § 42, p. 63 (1861).
      25. New Hampshire—N. H. Laws, c. 743, § 1, p. 708 (1848).
      26. New Jersey—N. J. Laws, p. 266 (1849).
      27. New York—N. Y. Rev. Stat., pt. 4, c. 1, Tit. 2, §§ 8, 9, pp. 12–13 (1828). By 1868, this statute had been superseded. N. Y. Laws, c. 260, §§ 1–6, pp. 285–286 (1845); N. Y. Laws, c. 22, § 1, p. 19 (1846).
      28. Ohio—Ohio Gen. Stat. §§ 111 (1), 112 (2), p. 252 (1841).
      29. Oregon—Ore. Gen. Laws, Crim. Code, c. 43, § 509, p. 528 (1845–1864).
      30. Pennsylvania—Pa. Laws No. 374, §§ 87, 88, 89 (1860).

There apparently was no question concerning the validity of this provision or of any of the other state statutes when the Fourteenth Amendment was adopted. The only conclusion possible from this history is that the drafters did not intend to have the Fourteenth Amendment withdraw from the States the power to legislate with respect to this matter.

III

Even if one were to agree that the case that the Court decides were here, and that the enunciation of the substantive constitutional law in the Court's opinion were proper, the actual disposition of the case by the Court is still difficult to justify. The Texas statute is struck down *in toto,* even though the Court apparently concedes that at later periods of pregnancy Texas might impose these selfsame statutory limitations on abortion. My understanding of past practice is that a statute found to be invalid as applied to a particular plaintiff, but not unconstitutional as a whole, is not simply "struck down" but is, instead, declared unconstitutional as applied to the fact situation before the Court. *Yick Wo* v. *Hopkins,* 118 U.S. 356 (1886); *Street* v. *New York,* 394 U.S. 576 (1969).

For all of the foregoing reasons, I respectfully dissent.

31. Texas—Tex. Gen. Stat. Dig., c. VII, Arts. 531–536, p. 524 (Oldham & White 1859).
32. Vermont—Vt. Acts No. 33, § 1 (1846). By 1868, this statute had been amended. Vt. Acts No. 57, §§ 1, 3 (1867).
33. Virginia—Va. Acts, Tit. II, c. 3, § 9, p. 96 (1848).
34. Washington (Terr.)—Wash. (Terr.) Stats. c. II, §§ 37, 38, p. 81 (1854).
35. West Virginia—See Va. Acts., Tit. II, c. 3, § 9, p. 96 (1848); W. Va. Const., Art. XI, par. 8 (1863).
36. Wisconsin—Wis. Rev. Stat., c. 133, §§ 10, 11 (1849). By 1868, this statute had been superseded. Wis. Rev. Stat., c. 164, §§ 10, 11; c. 169, §§ 58, 59 (1858).
2. Abortion laws in effect in 1868 and still applicable as of August 1970:
1. Arizona (1865)
2. Connecticut (1860).
3 Florida (1868).
4. Idaho (1863).
5. Indiana (1838).
6. Iowa (1843).
7. Maine (1840).
8. Massachusetts (1845).
9. Michigan (1846).
10. Minnesota (1851).
11. Missouri (1835).
12. Montana (1864).
13. Nevada (1861).
14. New Hampshire (1848).
15. New Jersey (1849).
16. Ohio (1841).
17. Pennsylvania (1860).
18. Texas (1859).
19. Vermont (1867).
20. West Virginia (1863).
21. Wisconsin (1858).

Appendix 2

DOE *v.* BOLTON

Syllabus

DOE ET AL. *v.* BOLTON,
ATTORNEY GENERAL OF GEORGIA, ET AL.
APPEAL FROM THE UNITED STATES DISTRICT COURT
FOR THE NORTHERN DISTRICT OF GEORGIA

No. 70–40. Argued December 13, 1971—
Reargued October 11, 1972—
Decided January 22, 1973

Georgia law proscribes an abortion except as performed by a duly licensed Georgia physician when necessary in "his best clinical judgment" because continued pregnancy would endanger a pregnant woman's life or injure her health; the fetus would likely be born with a serious defect; or the pregnancy resulted from rape. § 26–1202 (a) of Ga. Criminal Code. In addition to a requirement that the patient be a Georgia resident and certain other requirements, the statutory scheme poses three procedural conditions in § 26–1202 (b): (1) that the abortion be performed in a hospital accredited by the Joint Commission on Accreditation of Hospitals (JCAH); (2) that the procedure be approved by the hospital staff abortion committee; and (3) that the performing physician's judgment be confirmed by independent examinations of the patient by two other licensed physicians. Appellant Doe, an indigent married Georgia citizen, who was denied an abortion after eight weeks of pregnancy for failure to meet any of the § 26–1202 (a) conditions, sought declaratory and injunctive relief, contending that the Georgia laws were unconstitutional. Others joining in the complaint included Georgia-licensed physicians (who claimed that the Georgia statutes "chilled and deterred" their practices), registered nurses, clergymen, and social workers. Though holding that all the plaintiffs had standing, the District Court ruled that only Doe presented a justiciable controversy. In Doe's case the court gave declaratory, but not injunctive, relief, invalidating as an infringement of privacy and personal liberty the limitation to the three situations specified in § 26-1202 (a) and certain other provisions but holding that the State's interest in health protection and the existence of a *"potential* of independent human existence" justified regulation through § 26-1202 (b) of the "manner of performance as well as the quality of the final decision to abort." The appellants, claiming entitlement to broader relief, directly appealed to this Court. *Held:*

1. Doe's case presents a live, justiciable controversy and she has standing to sue, *Roe v. Wade, anti,* p. 113, as do the physician-appellants (who, unlike the physician in *Wade,* were not charged with abortion violations), and it is therefore unnecessary to resolve the issue of the other appellants' standing. Pp. 187–189.

2. A woman's constitutional right to an abortion is not absolute. *Roe v. Wade, supra.* P. 189.

3. The requirement that a physician's decision to perform an abortion must rest upon "his best clinical judgment" of its necessity is not unconstitutionally vague, since that judgment may be made in the light of *all* the attendant circumstances. *United States v. Vuitch,* 402 U.S. 62, 71–72. Pp. 191–192.

4. The three procedural conditions in § 26-1202 (b) violate the Fourteenth Amendment. Pp. 192–200.

(a) The JCAH-accreditation requirement is invalid, since the State has not shown that only hospitals (let alone those with JCAH accreditation) meet its interest in fully protecting the patient; and a hospital requirement failing to exclude the first trimester of pregnancy would be invalid on that ground alone, see *Roe v. Wade, supra.* Pp. 193–195.

(b) The interposition of a hospital committee on abortion, a procedure not applicable as a matter of state criminal law to other surgical situations, is unduly restrictive of the patient's rights, which are already safeguarded by her personal physician. Pp. 195–198.

(c) Required acquiescence by two copractitioners also has no rational connection with a patient's needs and unduly infringes on her physician's right to practice. Pp. 198–200.

5. The Georgia residence requirement violates the Privileges and Immunities Clause by denying protection to persons who enter Georgia for medical services there. P. 200.

6. Appellants' equal protection argument centering on the three procedural conditions in § 26-1202 (b), invalidated on other grounds, is without merit. Pp. 200–201.

7. No ruling is made on the question of injunctive relief. Cf. *Roe v. Wade, supra.* P. 201.

319 F. Supp. 1048, modified and affirmed.

BLACKMUN, J., delivered the opinion of the Court, in which BURGER, C. J., and DOUGLAS, BRENNAN, STEWART, MARSHALL, and POWELL, JJ., joined. BURGER, C. J., *post,* p. 207, and DOUGLAS, J., *post,* p. 209, filed concurring opinions. WHITE, J., filed a dissenting opinion, in which REHNQUIST, J., joined, *post,* p. 221. REHNQUIST, J., filed a dissenting opinion, *post,* p. 223.

Margie Pitts Hames reargued the cause for appellants. With her on the briefs were *Reber F. Boult, Jr., Charles Morgan, Jr., Elizabeth Roediger Rindskopf,* and *Tobiane Schwartz.*

Dorothy T. Beasley reargued the cause for appellees. With her on the brief were *Arthur K. Bolton,* Attorney General of Georgia, *Harold N. Hill, Jr.,* Executive Assistant Attorney General, *Courtney Wilder Stanton,* Assistant Attorney General, *Joel Feldman, Henry L. Bowden,* and *Ralph H. Witt.**

MR. JUSTICE BLACKMUN delivered the opinion of the Court.

In this appeal, the criminal abortion statutes recently enacted in Georgia are challenged on constitutional grounds. The statutes are § § 26–1201 through 26–1203 of the State's Criminal Code, formulated by Georgia Laws, 1968 Session, pp. 1249, 1277–1280. In *Roe* v. *Wade, ante,* p. 113, we today have struck down, as constitutionally defective, the Texas criminal abortion statutes that are representative of provisions long in effect in a majority of our States. The Georgia legislation, however, is different and merits separate consideration.

I

The statutes in question are reproduced as Appendix A, *post,* p. 202.[1] As the appellants acknowledge,[2] the 1968 statutes are patterned upon the American Law Institute's Model Penal Code, § 230.3 (Proposed Official Draft, 1962), reproduced as Appendix B, *post,* p. 205. The ALI proposal has served as the model for recent legislation in approximately one-fourth of our States.[3] The new Georgia provisions replaced statutory law that had been in effect for more than 90 years. Georgia Laws 1876, No. 130, § 2, at 113.[4] The predecessor statute paralleled the Texas legislation considered in *Roe* v. *Wade, supra,* and made all abortions criminal except those necessary "to preserve the life" of the pregnant woman. The new statutes have not been tested on constitutional grounds in the Georgia state courts.

---

*Briefs of *amici curiae* were filed by *Roy Lucas* for the American College of Obstetricians and Gynecologists et al.; by *Dennis J. Horan, Jerome A. Frazel, Jr., Thomas M. Crisham,* and *Delores V. Horan* for Certain Physicians, Professors and Fellows of the American College of Obstetrics and Gynecology; by *Harriet F. Pilpel, Nancy F. Wechsler,* and *Frederic S. Nathan* for Planned Parenthood Federation of America, Inc., et al.; by *Alan F. Charles* for the National Legal Program on Health Problems of the Poor et al.; by *Marttie L. Thompson* for State Communities Aid Assn.; by *Alfred L. Scanlan, Martin J. Flynn,* and *Robert M. Byrn* for the National Right to Life Committee; by *Helen L. Buttenwieser* for the American Ethical Union et al.; by *Norma G. Zarky* for the American Association of University Women et al.; by *Nancy Stearns* for New Women Lawyers et al.; by the California Committee to Legalize Abortion et al.; by *Robert E. Dunne* for Robert L. Sassone; and by *Ferdinand Buckley pro se.*

1. The portions italicized in Appendix A are those held unconstitutional by the District Court.

2. Brief for Appellants 25 n. 5; Tr. of Oral Arg. 9.

3. See *Roe* v. *Wade, ante,* p. 113, at 140 n. 37.

4. The pertinent provisions of the 1876 statute were:

"Section I. *Be it enacted, etc.,* That from and after the passage of this Act, the willful killing of an unborn child, so far developed as to be ordinarily called 'quick,' by any injury to the mother of such child, which would be murder if it resulted in the death of such mother, shall be guilty of a felony, and punishable by death or imprisonment for life, as the jury trying the case may recommend.

"Sec. II. *Be it further enacted,* That every person who shall administer to any woman pregnant with a child, any medicine, drug, or substance whatever, or shall use or employ any instrument or other means, with intent thereby to destroy such child, unless the same shall have been necessary to preserve the life of such mother, or shall have been advised by two physicians to be necessary for such purpose, shall, in case the death of such child or mother be thereby produced, be declared guilty of an assault with intent to murder.

Section 26–1201, with a referenced exception, makes abortion a crime, and § 26–1203 provides that a person convicted of that crime shall be punished by imprisonment for not less than one nor more than 10 years. Section 26–1202 (a) states the exception and removes from § 1201's definition of criminal abortion, and thus makes noncriminal, an abortion "performed by a physician duly licensed" in Georgia when, "based upon his best clinical judgment . . . an abortion is necessary because:

"(1) A continuation of the pregnancy would endanger the life of the pregnant woman or would seriously and permanently injure her health; or

"(2) The fetus would very likely be born with a grave, permanent, and irremediable mental or physical defect; or

"(3) The pregnancy resulted from forcible or statutory rape."[5]

Section 26–1202 also requires, by numbered subdivisions of its subsection (b), that, for an abortion to be authorized or performed as a noncriminal procedure, additional conditions must be fulfilled. These are (1) and (2) residence of the woman in Georgia; (3) reduction to writing of the performing physician's medical judgment that an abortion is justified for one or more of the reasons specified by § 26–1202 (a), with written concurrence in that judgment by at least two other Georgia-licensed physicians, based upon their separate personal medical examinations of the woman; (4) performance of the abortion in a hospital licensed by the State Board of Health and also accredited by the Joint Commission on Accreditation of Hospitals; (5) advance approval by an abortion committee of not less than three members of the hospital's staff; (6) certifications in a rape situation; and (7), (8), and (9) maintenance and confidentiality of records. There is a provision (subsection (c)) for judicial determination of the legality of a proposed abortion on petition of the judicial circuit law officer or of a close relative, as therein defined, of the unborn child, and for expeditious hearing of that petition. There is also a provision (subsection (e)) giving a hospital the right not to admit an abortion patient and giving any physician and any hospital employee or staff member the right, on moral or religious grounds, not to participate in the procedure.

II

On April 16, 1970, Mary Doe,[6] 23 other individuals (nine described as Georgia-licensed physicians, seven as nurses registered in the State, five as clergymen, and two as social workers), and two nonprofit Georgia corporations that advocate

---

"Sec. III. *Be it further enacted,* That any person who shall willfully administer to any pregnant woman any medicine, drug or substance, or anything whatever, or shall employ any instrument or means whatever, with intent thereby to procure the miscarriage or abortion of any such woman, unless the same shall have been necessary to preserve the life of such woman, or shall have been advised by two physicians to be necessary for that purpose, shall, upon conviction, be punished as prescribed in section 4310 of the Revised Code of Georgia."

It should be noted that the second section, in contrast to the first, made no specific reference to quickening. The section was construed, however, to possess this line of demarcation. *Taylor* v. *State*, 105 Ga. 846, 33 S. E. 190 (1899).

5. In contrast with the ALI model, the Georgia statute makes no specific reference to pregnancy resulting from incest. We were assured by the State at reargument that this was because the statute's reference to "rape" was intended to include incest. Tr. of Oral Rearg. 32.

6. Appellants by their complaint, App. 7, allege that the name is a pseudonym.

abortion reform instituted this federal action in the Northern District of Georgia against the State's attorney general, the district attorney of Fulton County, and the chief of police of the city of Atlanta. The plaintiffs sought a declaratory judgment that the Georgia abortion statutes were unconstitutional in their entirety. They also sought injunctive relief restraining the defendants and their successors from enforcing the statutes.

Mary Doe alleged:

(1) She was a 22-year-old Georgia citizen, married, and nine weeks pregnant. She had three living children. The two older ones had been placed in a foster home because of Doe's poverty and inability to care for them. The youngest, born July 19, 1969, had been placed for adoption. Her husband had recently abandoned her and she was forced to live with her indigent parents and their eight children. She and her husband, however, had become reconciled. He was a construction worker employed only sporadically. She had been a mental patient at the State Hospital. She had been advised that an abortion could be performed on her with less danger to her health than if she gave birth to the child she was carrying. She would be unable to care for or support the new child.

(2) On March 25, 1970, she applied to the Abortion Committee of Grady Memorial Hospital, Atlanta, for a therapeutic abortion under § 26–1202. Her application was denied 16 days later, on April 10, when she was eight weeks pregnant, on the ground that her situation was not one described in § 26–1202 (a).[7]

(3) Because her application was denied, she was forced either to relinquish "her right to decide when and how many children she will bear" or to seek an abortion that was illegal under the Georgia statutes. This invaded her rights of privacy and liberty in matters related to family, marriage, and sex, and deprived her of the right to choose whether to bear children. This was a violation of rights guaranteed her by the First, Fourth, Fifth, Ninth, and Fourteenth Amendments. The statutes also denied her equal protection and procedural due process and, because they were unconstitutionally vague, deterred hospitals and doctors from performing abortions. She sued "on her own behalf and on behalf of all others similarly situated."

The other plaintiffs alleged that the Georgia statues "chilled and deterred" them from practicing their respective professions and deprived them of rights guaranteed by the First, Fourth, and Fourteenth Amendments. These plaintiffs also purported to sue on their own behalf and on behalf of others similarly situated.

A three-judge district court was convened. An offer of proof as to Doe's identity was made, but the court deemed it unnecessary to receive that proof. The case was then tried on the pleadings and interrogatories.

The District Court, *per curiam,* 319 F. Supp. 1048 (ND Ga. 1970), held that all the plaintiffs had standing but that only Doe presented a justiciable controversy. On the merits, the court concluded that the limitation in the Georgia statute of the "number of reasons for which an abortion may be sought," *id.,* at 1056, improperly restricted Doe's rights of privacy articulated in *Griswold* v. *Connecticut,* 381 U.S. 479 (1965), and of "personal liberty," both of which it thought "broad enough to include the decision to abort a pregnancy," 319 F. Supp., at 1055. As a conse-

---

7. In answers to interrogatories, Doe stated that her application for an abortion was approved at Georgia Baptist Hospital on May 5, 1970, but that she was not approved as a charity patient there and had no money to pay for an abortion. App. 64.

quence, the court held invalid those portions of § § 26–1202 (a) and (b) (3) limiting legal abortions to the three situations specified; § 26–1202 (b) (6) relating to certifications in a rape situation; and § 26–1202 (c) authorizing a court test. Declaratory relief was granted accordingly. The court, however, held that Georgia's interest in protection of health, and the existence of a *"potential* of independent human existence" (emphasis in original), *id.,* at 1055, justified state regulation of "the manner of performance as well as the quality of the final decision to abort," *id.,* at 1056, and it refused to strike down the other provisions of the statutes. It denied the request for an injunction, *id.,* at 1057.

Claiming that they were entitled to an injunction and to broader relief, the plaintiffs took a direct appeal pursuant to 28 U.S. C. § 1253. We postponed decision on jurisdiction to the hearing on the merits. 402 U.S. 941 (1971). The defendants also purported to appeal, pursuant to § 1253, but their appeal was dismissed for want of jurisdiction. 402 U.S. 936 (1971). We are advised by the appellees, Brief 42, that an alternative appeal on their part is pending in the United States Court of Appeals for the Fifth Circuit. The extent, therefore, to which the District Court decision was adverse to the defendants, that is, the extent to which portions of the Georgia statutes were held to be unconstitutional, technically is not now before us.[8] *Swarb v. Lennox,* 405 U.S. 191, 201 (1972).

III

Our decision in *Roe* v. *Wade, ante,* p. 113, establishes (1) that, despite her pseudonym, we may accept as true, for this case, Mary Doe's existence and her pregnant state on April 16, 1970; (2) that the constitutional issue is substantial; (3) that the interim termination of Doe's and all other Georgia pregnancies in existence in 1970 has not rendered the case moot; and (4) that Doe presents a justiciable controversy and has standing to maintain the action.

Inasmuch as Doe and her class are recognized, the question whether the other appellants—physicians, nurses, clergymen, social workers, and corporations—present a justiciable controversy and have standing is perhaps a matter of no great consequence. We conclude, however, that the physician-appellants, who are Georgia-licensed doctors consulted by pregnant women, also present a justiciable controversy and do have standing despite the fact that the record does not disclose that any one of them has been prosecuted, or threatened with prosecution, for violation of the State's abortion statutes. The physician is the one against whom these criminal statutes directly operate in the event he procures an abortion that does not meet the statutory exceptions and conditions. The physician-appellants, therefore, assert a sufficiently direct threat of personal detriment. They should not be required to await and undergo a criminal prosecution as the sole means of seeking relief. *Crossen* v. *Breckenridge,* 446 F. 2d 833, 839–840 (CA6 1971); *Poe v. Menghini,* 339 F. Supp. 986, 990–991 (Kan. 1972).

In holding that the physicians, while theoretically possessed of standing, did not present a justiciable controversy, the District Court seems to have relied primarily on *Poe v. Ullman,* 367 U.S. 497 (1961). There, a sharply divided Court dismissed an

---

8. What we decide today obviously has implications for the issues raised in the defendants' appeal pending in the Fifth Circuit.

appeal from a state court on the ground that it presented no real controversy justifying the adjudication of a constitutional issue. But the challenged Connecticut statute, deemed to prohibit the giving of medical advice on the use of contraceptives, had been enacted in 1879, and, apparently with a single exception, no one had ever been prosecuted under it. Georgia's statute, in contrast, is recent and not moribund. Furthermore, it is the successor to another Georgia abortion statute under which, we are told,[9] physicians were prosecuted. The present case, therefore, is closer to *Epperson* v. *Arkansas,* 393 U.S. 97 (1968), where the Court recognized the right of a school teacher, though not yet charged criminally, to challenge her State's anti-evolution statute. See also *Griswold v. Connecticut,* 381 U.S., at 481.

The parallel claims of the nurse, clergy, social worker, and corporation-appellants are another step removed and as to them, the Georgia statutes operate less directly. Not being licensed physicians, the nurses and the others are in no position to render medical advice. They would be reached by the abortion statutes only in their capacity as accessories or as counselor-conspirators. We conclude that we need not pass upon the status of these additional appellants in this suit, for the issues are sufficiently and adequately presented by Doe and the physician-appellants, and nothing is gained or lost by the presence or absence of the nurses, the clergymen, the social workers, and the corporations. See *Roe* v. *Wade, ante,* at 127.

IV

The appellants attack on several grounds those portions of the Georgia abortion statutes that remain after the District Court decision: undue restriction of a right to personal and marital privacy; vagueness; deprivation of substantive and procedural due process; improper restriction to Georgia residents; and denial of equal protection.

A. *Roe* v. *Wade, supra,* sets forth our conclusion that a pregnant woman does not have an absolute constitutional right to an abortion on her demand. What is said there is applicable here and need not be repeated.

B. The appellants go on to argue, however, that the present Georgia statutes must be viewed historically, that is, from the fact that prior to the 1968 Act an abortion in Georgia was not criminal if performed to "preserve the life" of the mother. It is suggested that the present statute, as well, has this emphasis on the mother's rights, not on those of the fetus. Appellants contend that it is thus clear that Georgia has given little, and certainly not first, consideration to the unborn child. Yet, it is the unborn child's rights that Georgia asserts in justification of the statute. Appellants assert that this justification cannot be advanced at this late date.

Appellants then argue that the statutes do not adequately protect the woman's right. This is so because it would be physically and emotionally damaging to Doe to bring a child into her poor, "fatherless"[10] family, and because advances in medicine and medical techniques have made it safer for a woman to have a medically induced abortion than for her to bear a child. Thus, "a statute that requires a woman to carry an unwanted pregnancy to term infringes not only on a fundamental right of privacy but on the right to life itself." Brief 27.

9. Tr. of Oral Arg. 21–22.
10. Brief for Appellants 25.

The appellants recognize that a century ago medical knowledge was not so advanced as it is today, that the techniques of antisepsis were not known, and that any abortion procedure was dangerous for the woman. To restrict the legality of the abortion to the situation where it was deemed necessary, in medical judgment, for the preservation of the woman's life was only a natural conclusion in the exercise of the legislative judgment of that time. A State is not to be reproached, however, for a past judgmental determination made in the light of then-existing medical knowledge. It is perhaps unfair to argue, as the appellants do, that because the early focus was on the preservation of the woman's life, the State's present professed interest in the protection of embryonic and fetal life is to be downgraded. That argument denies the State the right to readjust its views and emphases in the light of the advanced knowledge and techniques of the day.

C. Appellants argue that § 26–1202 (a) of the Georgia statutes, as it has been left by the District Court's decision, is unconstitutionally vague. This argument centers on the proposition that, with the District Court's having struck down the statutorily specified reasons, it still remains a crime for a physician to perform an abortion except when, as § 26–1202 (a) reads, it is "based upon his best clinical judgment that an abortion is necessary." The appellants contend that the word "necessary" does not warn the physician of what conduct is proscribed; that the statute is wholly without objective standards and is subject to diverse interpretation; and that doctors will choose to err on the side of caution and will be arbitrary.

The net result of the District Court's decision is that the abortion determination, so far as the physician is concerned, is made in the exercise of his professional, that is, his "best clinical," judgment in the light of *all* the attendant circumstances. He is not now restricted to the three situations originally specified. Instead, he may range farther afield wherever his medical judgment, properly and professionally exercised, so dictates and directs him.

The vagueness argument is set at rest by the decision in *United States* v. *Vuitch*, 402 U.S. 62, 71–72 (1971), where the issue was raised with respect to a District of Columbia statute making abortions criminal "unless the same were done as necessary for the preservation of the mother's life or health and under the direction of a competent licensed practitioner of medicine." That statute has been construed to bear upon psychological as well as physical well-being. This being so, the Court concluded that the term "health" presented no problem of vagueness. "Indeed, whether a particular operation is necessary for a patient's physical or mental health is a judgment that physicians are obviously called upon to make routinely whenever surgery is considered." *Id.*, at 72. This conclusion is equally applicable here. Whether, in the words of the Georgia statute, "an abortion is necessary" is a professional judgment that the Georgia physician will be called upon to make routinely.

We agree with the District Court, 319 F. Supp., at 1058, that the medical judgment may be exercised in the light of all factors—physical, emotional, psychological, familial, and the woman's age—relevant to the well-being of the patient. All these factors may relate to health. This allows the attending physician the room he needs to make his best medical judgment. And it is room that operates for the benefit, not the disadvantage, of the pregnant woman.

D. The appellants next argue that the District Court should have declared unconstitutional three procedural demands of the Georgia statute: (1) that the abortion be performed in a hospital accredited by the Joint Commission on Accreditation of

Hospitals:[11] (2) that the procedure be approved by the hospital staff abortion committee; and (3) that the performing physician's judgment be confirmed by the independent examinations of the patient by two other licensed physicians. The appellants attack these provisions not only on the ground that they unduly restrict the woman's right of privacy, but also on procedural due process and equal protection grounds. The physician-appellants also argue that, by subjecting a doctor's individual medical judgment to committee approval and to confirming consultations, the statute impermissibly restricts the physician's right to practice his profession and deprives him of due process.

   1. *JCAH accreditation.* The Joint Commission on Accreditation of Hospitals is an organization without governmental sponsorship or overtones. No question whatever is raised concerning the integrity of the organization or the high purpose of the accreditation process.[12] That process, however, has to do with hospital standards generally and has no present particularized concern with abortion as a medical or surgical procedure.[13] In Georgia, there is no restriction on the performance of non-abortion surgery in a hospital not yet accredited by the JCAH so long as other requirements imposed by the State, such as licensing of the hospital and of the operating surgeon, are met. See Georgia Code § § 88–1901 (a) and 88–1905 (1971) and 84–907 (Supp. 1971). Furthermore, accreditation by the Commission is not granted until a hospital has been in operation at least one year. The Model Penal Code, § 230.3, Appendix B hereto, contains no requirement for JCAH accreditation. And the Uniform Abortion Act (Final Draft, Aug. 1971),[14] approved by the American Bar Association in February 1972, contains no JCAH-accredited hospital specification.[15] Some courts have held that a JCAH-accreditation requirement is an overbroad infringement of fundamental rights because it does not relate to the par-

   11. We were advised at reargument, Tr. of Oral Rearg. 10, that only 54 of Georgia's 159 counties have a JCAH-accredited hospital.
   12. Since its founding, JCAH has pursued the "elusive goal" of defining the "optimal setting" for "quality of service in hospitals." JCAH, Accreditation Manual for Hospitals, Foreword (Dec. 1970). The Manual's Introduction states the organization's purpose to establish standards and conduct accreditation programs that will afford quality medical care "to give patients the optimal benefits that medical science has to offer." This ambitious and admirable goal is illustrated by JCAH's decision in 1966 "[t]o raise and strengthen the standards from their present level of minimum essential to the level of optimum achievable. . . ." Some of these "optimum achievable" standards required are: disclosure of hospital ownership and control; a dietetic service and written dietetic policies; a written disaster plan for mass emergencies; a nuclear medical services program; facilities for hematology, chemistry, microbiology, clinical microscopy, and sero-immunology; a professional library and document delivery service; a radiology program; a social services plan administered by a qualified social worker; and a special care unit.
   13. "The Joint Commission neither advocates nor opposes any particular position with respect to elective abortions." Letter dated July 9, 1971, from John I. Brewer, M. D., Commissioner, JCAH, to the Rockefeller Foundation. Brief for *amici curiae,* American College of Obstetricians and Gynecologists et al., p. A-3.
   14. See *Roe* v. *Wade, ante,* at 146–147, n. 40.
   15. Some state statutes do not have the JCAH-accreditation requirement. Alaska Stat. § 11.15.060 (1970); Hawaii Rev. Stat. § 453–16 (Supp. 1971); N. Y. Penal Code § 125.05, subd. 3 (Supp. 1972–1973). Washington has the requirement but couples it with the alternative of "a medical facility approved . . . by the state board of health." Wash. Rev. Code § 9.02.070 (Supp. 1972). Florida's new statute has a similar provision. Law of Apr. 13, 1972, c. 72–196, § 1 (2). Others contain the specification. Ark. Stat. Ann. §§ 41–303 to 41–310 (Supp. 1971);

ticular medical problems and dangers of the abortion operation. *E. g., Poe* v. *Menghini,* 339 F. Supp., at 993–994.

We hold that the JCAH-accreditation requirement does not withstand constitutional scrutiny in the present context. It is a requirement that simply is not "based on differences that are reasonably related to the purposes of the Act in which it is found." *Morey* v. *Doud,* 354 U.S. 457, 465 (1957).

This is not to say that Georgia may not or should not, from and after the end of the first trimester, adopt standards for licensing all facilities where abortions may be performed so long as those standards are legitimately related to the objective the State seeks to accomplish. The appellants contend that such a relationship would be lacking even in a lesser requirement that an abortion be performed in a licensed hospital, as opposed to a facility, such as a clinic, that may be required by the State to possess all the staffing and services necessary to perform an abortion safely (including those adequate to handle serious complications or other emergency, or arrangements with a nearby hospital to provide such services). Appellants and various *amici* have presented us with a mass of data purporting to demonstrate that some facilities other than hospitals are entirely adequate to perform abortions if they possess these qualifications. The State, on the other hand, has not presented persuasive data to show that only hospitals meet its acknowledged interest in insuring the quality of the operation and the full protection of the patient. We feel compelled to agree with appellants that the State must show more than it has in order to prove that only the full resources of a licensed hospital, rather than those of some other appropriately licensed institution, satisfy these health interests. We hold that the hospital requirement of the Georgia law, because it fails to exclude the first trimester of pregnancy, see *Roe* v. *Wade, ante,* at 163, is also invalid. In so holding we naturally express no opinion on the medical judgment involved in any particular case, that is, whether the patient's situation is such that an abortion should be performed in a hospital, rather than in some other facility.

2. *Committee approval.* The second aspect of the appellant's procedural attack relates to the hospital abortion committee and to the pregnant woman's asserted lack of access to that committee. Relying primarily on *Goldberg* v. *Kelly,* 397 U.S. 254 (1970), concerning the termination of welfare benefits, and *Wisconsin* v. *Constantineau,* 400 U.S. 433 (1971), concerning the posting of an alcoholic's name, Doe first argues that she was denied due process because she could not make a presentation to the committee. It is not clear from the record, however, whether Doe's own consulting physician was or was not a member of the committee or did or did not present her case, or, indeed, whether she herself was or was not there. We see nothing in the Georgia statute that explicitly denies access to the committee by or on behalf of the woman. If the access point alone were involved, we would not be persuaded to strike down the committee provision on the unsupported assumption that access is not provided.

Appellants attack the discretion the statute leaves to the committee. The most concrete argument they advance is their suggestion that it is still a badge of infamy

Calif. Health & Safety Code §§ 25950–25955.5 (Supp. 1972); Colo. Rev. Stat. Ann. §§ 40–2–50 to 40–2–53 (Cum. Supp. 1967); Kan. Stat. Ann. § 21–3407 (Supp. 1971); Md. Ann. Code, Art. 43, §§ 137–139 (1971). Cf. Del. Code Ann., Tit. 24, §§ 1790–1793 (Supp. 1972), specifying "a nationally recognized medical or hospital accreditation authority," § 1790 (a).

"in many minds" to bear an illegitimate child, and that the Georgia system enables the committee members' personal views as to extramarital sex relations, and punishment therefore, to govern their decisions. This approach obviously is one founded on suspicion and one that discloses a lack of confidence in the integrity of physicians. To say that physicians will be guided in their hospital committee decisions by their predilections on extramarital sex unduly narrows the issue to pregnancy outside marriage. (Doe's own situation did not involve extramarital sex and its product.) The appellants' suggestion is necessarily somewhat degrading to the conscientious physician, particularly the obstetrician, whose professional activity is concerned with the physical and mental welfare, the woes, the emotions, and the concern of his female patients. He, perhaps more than anyone else, is knowledgeable in this area of patient care, and he is aware of human frailty, so-called "error," and needs. The good physician—despite the presence of rascals in the medical profession, as in all others, we trust that most physicians are "good"—will have sympathy and understanding for the pregnant patient that probably are not exceeded by those who participate in other areas of professional counseling.

It is perhaps worth noting that the abortion committee has a function of its own. It is a committee of the hospital and it is composed of members of the institution's medical staff. The membership usually is a changing one. In this way, its work burden is shared and is more readily accepted. The committee's function is protective. It enables the hospital appropriately to be advised that its posture and activities are in accord with legal requirements. It is to be remembered that the hospital is an entity and that it, too, has legal rights and legal obligations.

Saying all this, however, does not settle the issue of the constitutional propriety of the committee requirement. Viewing the Georgia statute as a whole, we see no constitutionally justifiable pertinence in the structure for the advance approval by the abortion committee. With regard to the protection of potential life, the medical judgment is already completed prior to the committee stage, and review by a committee once removed from diagnosis is basically redundant. We are not cited to any other surgical procedure made subject to committee approval as a matter of state criminal law. The woman's right to receive medical care in accordance with her licensed physician's best judgment and the physician's right to administer it are substantially limited by this statutorily imposed overview. And the hospital itself is otherwise fully protected. Under § 26–1202 (e), the hospital is free not to admit a patient for an abortion. It is even free not to have an abortion committee. Further, a physician or any other employee has the right to refrain, for moral or religious reasons, from participating in the abortion procedure. These provisions obviously are in the statute in order to afford appropriate protection to the individual and to the denominational hospital. Section 26–1202 (e) affords adequate protection to the hospital, and little more is provided by the committee prescribed by § 26–1202 (b) (5).

We conclude that the interposition of the hospital abortion committee is unduly restrictive of the patient's rights and needs that, at this point, have already been medically delineated and substantiated by her personal physician. To ask more serves neither the hospital nor the State.

3. *Two-doctor concurrence.* The third aspect of the appellants' attack centers on the "time and availability of adequate medical facilities and personnel." It is said that the system imposes substantial and irrational roadblocks and "is patently unsuited" to prompt determination of the abortion decision. Time, of course, is crit-

ical in abortion. Risks during the first trimester of pregnancy are admittedly lower than during later months.

The appellants purport to show by a local study[16] of Grady Memorial Hospital (serving indigent residents in Fulton and DeKalb Counties) that the "mechanics of the system itself forced . . . discontinuance of the abortion process" because the median time for the work up was 15 days. The same study shows, however, that 27% of the candidates for abortion were already 13 or more weeks pregnant at the time of application, that is, they were at the end of or beyond the first trimester when they made their applications. It is too much to say, as appellants do, that these particular persons "were victims of a system over which they [had] no control." If higher risk was incurred because of abortions in the second rather than the first trimester, much of that risk was due to delay in application, and not to the alleged cumbersomeness of the system. We note, in passing, that appellant Doe had no delay problem herself; the decision in her case was made well within the first trimester.

It should be manifest that our rejection of the accredited-hospital requirement and, more important, of the abortion committee's advance approval eliminates the major grounds of the attack based on the system's delay and the lack of facilities. There remains, however, the required confirmation by two Georgia-licensed physicians in addition to the recommendation of the pregnant woman's own consultant (making under the statute, a total of six physicians involved, including the three on the hospital's abortion committee). We conclude that this provision, too, must fall.

The statute's emphasis, as has been repetitively noted, is on the attending physician's "best clinical judgment that an abortion is necessary." That should be sufficient. The reasons for the presence of the confirmation step in the statute are perhaps apparent, but they are insufficient to withstand constitutional challenge. Again, no other voluntary medical or surgical procedure for which Georgia requires confirmation by two other physicians has been cited to us. If a physician is licensed by the State, he is recognized by the State as capable of exercising acceptable clinical judgment. If he fails in this, professional censure and deprivation of his license are available remedies. Required acquiescence by co-practitioners has no rational connection with a patient's needs and unduly infringes on the physician's right to practice. The attending physicians will know when a consultation is advisable—the doubtful situation, the need for assurance when the medical decision is a delicate one, and the like. Physicians have followed this route historically and know its usefulness and benefit for all concerned. It is still true today that "[r]eliance must be placed upon the assurance given by his license, issued by an authority competent to judge in that respect, that he [the physician] possesses the requisite qualifications." Dent v. West Virginia, 129, U.S. 114, 122–123 (1889). See United States v. Vuitch, 402 U.S., at 71.

E. The appellants attack the residency requirement of the Georgia law, § § 26–1202 (b) (1) and (b) (2), as violative of the right to travel stressed in Shapiro v. Thompson, 394 U.S. 618, 629–631 (1969), and other cases. A requirement of this kind, of course, could be deemed to have some relationship to the availability of post-procedure medical care for the aborted patient.

---

16. L. Baker & M. Freeman, Abortion Surveillance at Grady Memorial Hospital Center for Disease Control (June and July 1971) (U.S. Dept. of HEW, Public Health Service).

Nevertheless, we do not uphold the constitutionality of the residence requirement. It is not based on any policy of preserving state-supported facilities for Georgia residents, for the bar also applies to private hospitals and to privately retained physicians. There is no intimation, either, that Georgia facilities are utilized to capacity in caring for Georgia residents. Just as the Privileges and Immunities Clause, Const. Art. IV, § 2, protects persons who enter other States to ply their trade, *Ward* v. *Maryland,* 12 Wall. 418, 430 (1871); *Blake* v. *McClung,* 172 U.S. 239, 248–256 (1898), so must it protect persons who enter Georgia seeking the medical services that are available there. See *Tommer* v. *Witsell,* 334 U.S. 385, 396–397 (1948). A contrary holding would mean that a State could limit to its own residents the general medical care available within its borders. This we could not approve.

F. The last argument on this phase of the case is one that often is made, namely, that the Georgia system is violative of equal protection because it discriminates against the poor. The appellants do not urge that abortions should be performed by persons other than licensed physicians, so we have no argument that because the wealthy can better afford physicians, the poor should have nonphysicians made available to them. The appellants acknowledged that the procedures are "nondiscriminatory in . . . express terms" but they suggest that they have produced invidious discriminations. The District Court rejected this approach out of hand. 319 F. Supp., at 1056. It rests primarily on the accreditation and approval and confirmation requirements, discussed above, and on the assertion that most of Georgia's counties have no accredited hospital. We have set aside the accreditation, approval, and confirmation requirements, however, and with that, the discrimination argument collapses in all significant aspects.

V

The appellants complain, finally, of the District Court's denial of injunctive relief. A like claim was made in *Roe* v. *Wade, ante,* p. 113. We declined decision there insofar as injunctive relief was concerned, and we decline it here. We assume that Georgia's prosecutorial authorities will give full recognition to the judgment of this Court.

In summary, we hold that the JCAH-accredited hospital provision and the requirements as to approval by the hospital abortion committee, as to confirmation by two independent physicians, and as to residence in Georgia are all violative of the Fourteenth Amendment. Specifically, the following portions of § 26–1202 (b), remaining after the District Court's judgment, are invalid:

(1) Subsections (1) and (2).

(2) That portion of Subsection (3) following the words "[s]uch physician's judgment is reduced to writing."

(3) Subsections (4) and (5).

The judgment of the District Court is modified accordingly and, as so modified, is affirmed. Costs are allowed to the appellants.

APPENDIX A TO OPINION OF THE COURT

Criminal Code of Georgia

(The italicized portions are those held unconstitutional by the District Court)

CHAPTER 26–12. ABORTION.

26 –1201. Criminal Abortion. Except as otherwise provided in section 26–1202, a person commits criminal abortion when he administers any medicine, drug or other substance whatever to any woman or when he uses any instrument or other means whatever upon any woman with intent to produce a miscarriage or abortion.

26–1202. Exception. (a) Section 26–1201 shall not apply to an abortion performed by a physician duly licensed to practice medicine and surgery pursuant to Chapter 84–9 or 84–12 of the Code of Georgia of 1933, as amended, based upon his best clinical judgment that an abortion is necessary *because:*

(1) A continuation of the pregnancy would endanger the life of the pregnant woman or would seriously and permanently injure her health; or

(2) The fetus would very likely be born with a grave, permanent, and irremediable mental or physical defect; or

(3) The pregnancy resulted from forcible or statutory rape.

(b) No abortion is authorized or shall be performed under this section unless each of the following conditions is met:

(1) The pregnant woman requesting the abortion certifies in writing under oath and subject to the penalties of false swearing to the physician who proposes to perform the abortion that she is a bona fide legal resident of the State of Georgia.

(2) The physician certifies that he believes the woman is a bona fide resident of this State and that he has no information which should lead him to believe otherwise.

(3) Such physician's judgment is reduced to writing and concurred in by at least two other physicians duly licensed to practice medicine and surgery pursuant to Chapter 84–9 of the Code of Georgia of 1933, as amended, who certify in writing that based upon their separate personal medical examinations of the pregnant woman, the abortion is, in their judgment, necessary *because of one or more of the reasons enumerated above.*

(4) Such abortion is performed in a hospital licensed by the State Board of Health and accredited by the Joint Commission on Accreditation of Hospitals.

(5) The performance of the abortion has been approved in advance by a committee of the medical staff of the hospital in which the operation is to be performed. This committee must be one established and maintained in accordance with the standards promulgated by the Joint Commission on the Accreditation of Hospitals, and its approval must be by a majority vote of a membership of not less than three members of the hospital's staff; the physician proposing to perform the operation may not be counted as a member of the committee for this purpose.

(6) If the proposed abortion is considered necessary because the woman has been raped, the woman makes a written statement under oath, and subject to the penalties of false swearing, of the date, time and place of the rape and the name of the rapist, if known. There must be attached to this statement a certified copy of any report of the rape made by any law enforcement officer or agency and a statement by the solicitor general of the judicial circuit where the rape occurred or allegedly occurred that, according to his best information, there is probable cause to believe that the rape did occur.

(7) Such written opinions, statements, certificates, and concurrences are maintained in the permanent files of such hospital and are available at all reasonable times to the solicitor general of the judicial circuit in which the hospital is located.

(8) A copy of such written opinions, statements, certificates, and concurrences is filed with the Director of the State Department of Public Health within 10 days after such operation is performed.

(9) All written opinions, statements, certificates, and concurrences filed and maintained pursuant to paragraphs (7) and (8) of this subsection shall be confidential records and shall not be made available for public inspection at any time.

(c) Any solicitor general of the judicial circuit in which an abortion is to be performed under this section, or any person who would be a relative of the child within the second degree of consanguinity, may petition the superior court of the county in which the abortion is to be performed for a declaratory judgment whether the performance of such abortion would violate any constitutional or other legal rights of the fetus. Such solicitor general may also petition such court for the purpose of taking issue with compliance with the requirements of this section. The physician who proposes to perform the abortion and the pregnant woman shall be respondents. The petition shall be heard expeditiously and if the court adjudges that such abortion would violate the constitutional or other legal rights of the fetus, the court shall so declare and shall restrain the physician from performing the abortion.

(d) If an abortion is performed in compliance with this section, the death of the fetus shall not give rise to any claim for wrongful death.

(e) Nothing in this section shall require a hospital to admit any patient under the provisions hereof for the purpose of performing an abortion, nor shall any hospital be required to appoint a committee such as contemplated under subsection (b) (5). A physician, or any other person who is a member of or associated with the staff of a hospital, or any employee of a hospital in which an abortion has been authorized, who shall state in writing an objection to such abortion on moral or religious grounds shall not be required to participate in the medical procedures which will result in the abortion, and the refusal of any such person to participate therein shall not form the basis of any claim for damages on account of such refusal or for any disciplinary or recriminatory action against such person.

26–1203. Punishment. A person convicted of criminal abortion shall be punished by imprisonment for not less than one nor more than 10 years.

APPENDIX B TO OPINION OF THE COURT
American Law Institute
MODEL PENAL CODE

Section 230.3. Abortion.

(1) *Unjustified Abortion.* A person who purposely and unjustifiably terminates the pregnancy of another otherwise than by a live birth commits a felony of the third degree or, where the pregnancy has continued beyond the twenty-sixth week, a felony of the second degree.

(2) *Justifiable Abortion.* A licensed physician is justified in terminating a pregnancy if he believes there is substantial risk that continuance of the pregnancy would gravely impair the physical or mental health of the mother or that the child would be born with grave physical or mental defect, or that the pregnancy resulted from rape, incest, or other felonious intercourse. All illicit intercourse with a girl below the age of 16 shall be deemed felonious for purposes of this subsection. Justifiable abortions shall be performed only in a licensed hospital except in case of emergency when hospital facilities are unavailable. [Additional exceptions from the requirement of hospitalization may be incorporated here to take account of situations in sparsely settled areas where hospitals are not generally accessible.]

(3) *Physicians' Certificates; Presumption from Non-Compliance.* No abortion shall be performed unless two physicians, one of whom may be the person performing the abortion, shall have certified in writing the circumstances which they believe to justify the abortion. Such certificate shall be submitted before the abortion to the hospital where it is to be performed and, in the case of abortion following felonious intercourse, to the prosecuting attorney or the police. Failure to comply with any of the requirements of this Subsection gives rise to a presumption that the abortion was unjustified.

(4) *Self-Abortion.* A woman whose pregnancy has continued beyond the twenty-sixth week commits a felony of the third degree if she purposely terminates her own pregnancy otherwise than by a live birth, or if she uses instruments, drugs or violence upon herself for that purpose. Except as justified under Subsection (2), a person who induces or knowingly aids a woman to use instruments, drugs or violence upon herself for the purpose of terminating her pregnancy otherwise than by a live birth commits a felony of the third degree whether or not the pregnancy has continued beyond the twenty-sixth week.

(5) *Pretended Abortion.* A person commits a felony of the third degree if, representing that it is his purpose to perform an abortion, he does an act adapted to cause abortion in a pregnant woman although the woman is in fact not pregnant, or the actor does not believe she is. A person charged with unjustified abortion under Subsection (1) or an attempt to commit that offense may be convicted thereof upon proof of conduct prohibited by this Subsection.

(6) *Distribution of Abortifacients.* A person who sells, offers to sell, possesses with intent to sell, advertises, or displays for sale anything specially designed to terminate a pregnancy, or held out by the actor as useful for that purpose, commits a misdemeanor, unless:

(a) the sale, offer or display is to a physician or druggist or to an intermediary in a chain of distribution to physicians or druggists; or

(b) the sale is made upon prescription or order of a physician; or

(c) the possession is with intent to sell as authorized in paragraphs (a) and (b); or

(d) the advertising is addressed to persons named in paragraph (a) and confined to trade or professional channels not likely to reach the general public.

(7) *Section Inapplicable to Prevention of Pregnancy.* Nothing in this Section shall be deemed applicable to the prescription, administration or distribution of drugs or other substances for avoiding pregnancy, whether by preventing implantation of a fertilized ovum or by any other method that operates before, at or immediately after fertilization.

MR. CHIEF JUSTICE BURGER, concurring*

I agree that, under the Fourteenth Amendment to the Constitution, the abortion statutes of Georgia and Texas impermissibly limit the performance of abortions necessary to protect the health of pregnant women, using the term health in its broadest medical context. See *United States* v. *Vuitch,* 402 U.S. 62, 71–72 (1971). I am somewhat troubled that the Court has taken notice of various scientific and medical data in reaching its conclusion; however, I do not believe that the Court has exceeded the scope of judicial notice accepted in other contexts.

In oral argument, counsel for the State of Texas informed the Court that early abortion procedures were routinely permitted in certain exceptional cases, such as nonconsensual pregnancies resulting from rape and incest. In the face of a rigid and narrow statute, such as that of Texas, no one in these circumstances should be placed in a posture of dependence on a prosecutorial policy or prosecutorial discretion. Of course, States must have broad power, within the limits indicated in the opinions, to regulate the subject of abortions, but where the consequences of state intervention are so severe, uncertainty must be avoided as much as possible. For my part, I would be inclined to allow a State to require the certification of two physicians to support an abortion, but the Court holds otherwise. I do not believe that such a procedure is unduly burdensome, as are the complex steps of the Georgia statute, which require as many as six doctors and the use of a hospital certified by the JCAH.

I do not read the Court's holdings today as having the sweeping consequences attributed to them by the dissenting Justices; the dissenting views discount the reality that the vast majority of physicians observe the standards of their profession, and act only on the basis of carefully deliberated medical judgments relating to life and health. Plainly, the Court today rejects any claim that the Constitution requires abortions on demand.

MR. JUSTICE DOUGLAS, concurring*

While I join the opinion of the Court,[1] I add a few words.

I

The questions presented in the present cases go far beyond the issues of vagueness, which we considered in *United States* v. *Vuitch,* 402 U.S. 62. They involve

---

*[This opinion applies also to No. 70–18, *Roe* v. *Wade, ante,*p. 113.]

*[This opinion applies also to No. 70–18, *Roe* v. *Wade, ante,* p. 113.]

1. I disagree with the dismissal of Dr. Hallford's complaint in intervention in *Roe* v. *Wade, ante,* p. 113, because my disagreement with *Younger* v. *Harris,* 401 U.S. 37, revealed in my dissent in that case, still persists and extends to the progeny of that case.

the right of privacy, one aspect of which we considered in _Griswold_ v. _Connecticut,_ 381 U.S. 479, 484, when we held that various guarantees in the Bill of Rights create zones of privacy.[2]

The _Griswold_ case involved a law forbidding the use of contraceptives. We held that law as applied to married people unconstitutional:

> "We deal with a right of privacy older than the Bill of Rights — older than our political parties, older than our school system. Marriage is a coming together for better or for worse, hopefully enduring, and intimate to the degree of being sacred." _Id.,_ at 486.

The District Court in _Doe_ held that _Griswold_ and related cases "establish a Constitutional right to privacy broad enough to encompass the right of a woman to terminate an unwanted pregnancy in its early stages, by obtaining an abortion." 319 F. Supp. 1048, 1054.

The Supreme Court of California expressed the same view in _People_ v. _Belous,_[3] 71 Cal. 2d 954, 963, 458 P. 2d 194, 199.

The Ninth Amendment obviously does not create federally enforceable rights. It merely says, "The enumeration in the Constitution, of certain rights, shall not be construed to deny or disparage others retained by the people." But a catalogue of these rights includes customary, traditional, and time-honored rights, amenities, privileges, and immunities that come within the sweep of "the Blessings of Liberty" mentioned in the preamble to the Constitution. Many of them, in my view, come within the meaning of the term "liberty" as used in the Fourteenth Amendment.

First is the autonomous control over the development and expression of one's intellect, interests, tastes, and personality.

These are rights protected by the First Amendment and, in my view, they are absolute, permitting of no exceptions. See _Terminiello_ v. _Chicago,_ 337 U.S. 1; _Roth_ v. _United States,_ 354 U.S. 476, 508 (dissent); _Kingsley Pictures Corp._ v. _Regents,_ 360 U.S. 684, 697 (concurring); _New York Times Co._ v. _Sullivan,_ 376 U.S. 254,

---

2. There is no mention of privacy in our Bill of Rights but our decisions have recognized it as one of the fundamental values those amendments were designed to protect. The fountainhead case is _Boyd_ v. _United States,_ 116 U.S. 616, holding that a federal statute which authorized a court in tax cases to require a taxpayer to produce his records or to concede the Government's allegations offended the Fourth and Fifth Amendments. Mr. Justice Bradley, for the Court, found that the measure unduly intruded into the "sanctity of a man's home and the privacies of life." _Id.,_ at 630. Prior to _Boyd,_ in _Kilbourn_ v. _Thompson,_ 103 U.S. 168, 190, Mr. Justice Miller held for the Court that neither House of Congress "possesses the general power of making inquiry into the private affairs of the citizen." Of _Kilbourn,_ Mr. Justice Field later said, "This case will stand for all time as a bulwark against the invasion of the right of the citizen to protection in his private affairs against the unlimited scrutiny of investigation by a congressional committee." _In re Pacific Railway Comm'n,_ 32 F. 241, 253 (cited with approval in _Sinclair_ v. _United States,_ 279 U.S. 263, 293). Mr. Justice Harlan, also speaking for the Court, in _ICC_ v. _Brimson,_ 154 U.S. 447, 478, thought the same was true of administrative inquiries, saying that the Constitution did not permit a "general power of making inquiry into the private affairs of the citizen." In a similar vein were _Harriman_ v. _ICC,_ 211 U.S. 407; _United States_ v. _Louisville & Nashville R. Co.,_ 236 U.S. 318, 335; and _FTC_ v. _American Tobacco Co.,_ 264 U.S. 298.

3. The California abortion statute, held unconstitutional in the _Belous_ case, made it a crime to perform or help perform an abortion "unless the same is necessary to preserve [the mother's] life." 71 Cal. 2d, at 959, 458 P. 2d, at 197.

293 (Black, J., concurring, in which I joined). The Free Exercise Clause of the First Amendment is one facet of this constitutional right. The right to remain silent as respects one's own beliefs, *Watkins* v. *United States,* 354 U.S. 178, 196–199, is protected by the First and the Fifth. The First Amendment grants the privacy of first-class mail, *United States* v. *Van Leeuwen,* 397 U.S. 249, 253. All of these aspects of the right of privacy are rights "retained by the people" in the meaning of the Ninth Amendment.

Second is freedom of choice in the basic decisions of one's life respecting marriage, divorce, procreation, contraception, and the education and upbringing of children.

These rights, unlike those protected by the First Amendment, are subject to some control by the police power. Thus, the Fourth Amendment speaks only of "unreasonable searches and seizures" and of "probable cause." These rights are "fundamental," and we have held that in order to support legislative action the statute must be narrowly and precisely drawn and that a "compelling state interest" must be shown in support of the limitation. *E. g., Kramer* v. *Union Free School District,* 395 U.S. 621; *Shapiro* v. *Thompson,* 394 U.S. 618; *Carrington* v. *Rash,* 380 U.S. 89; *Sherbert* v. *Verner,* 374 U.S. 398; *NAACP* v. *Alabama,* 357 U.S. 449.

The liberty to marry a person of one's own choosing, *Loving* v. *Virginia,* 388 U.S. 1; the right of procreation, *Skinner* v. *Oklahoma,* 316 U.S. 535; the liberty to direct the education of one's children, *Pierce* v. *Society of Sisters,* 268 U.S. 510, and the privacy of the marital relation, *Griswold* v. *Connecticut, supra,* are in this category.[4] Only last Term in *Eisenstadt* v. *Baird,* 405 U.S. 438, another contraceptive case, we expanded the concept of *Griswold* by saying:

> "It is true that in *Griswold* the right of privacy in question inhered in the marital relationship. Yet the marital couple is not an independent entity with a mind and heart of its own, but an association of two individuals each with a separate intellectual and emotional makeup. If the right of privacy means anything, it is the

4. My Brother Stewart, writing in *Roe* v. *Wade, supra,* says that our decision in *Griswold* reintroduced substantive due process that had been rejected in *Ferguson* v. *Skrupa,* 372 U.S. 726. *Skrupa* involved legislation governing a business enterprise; and the Court in that case, as had Mr. Justice Holmes on earlier occasions, rejected the idea that "liberty" within the meaning of the Due Process Clause of the Fourteenth Amendment was a vessel to be filled with one's personal choices of values, whether drawn from the *laissez faire* school, from the socialistic school, or from the technocrats. *Griswold* involved legislation touching on the marital relation and involving the conviction of a licensed physician for giving married people information concerning contraception. There is nothing specific in the Bill of Rights that covers that item. Nor is there anything in the Bill of Rights that in terms protects the right of association or the privacy in one's association. Yet we found those rights in the periphery of the First Amendment. *NAACP* v. *Alabama,* 357 U.S. 449, 462. Other peripheral rights are the right to educate one's children as one chooses, *Pierce* v. *Society of Sisters,* 268 U.S. 510, and the right to study the German language, *Meyer* v. *Nebraska,* 262 U.S. 390. These decisions, with all respect, have nothing to do with substantive due process. One may think they are not peripheral to other rights that are expressed in the Bill of Rights. But that is not enough to bring into play the protection of substantive due process.

There are, of course, those who have believed that the reach of due process in the Fourteenth Amendment included all of the Bill of Rights but went further. Such was the view of Mr. Justice Murphy and Mr. Justice Rutledge. See *Adamson* v. *California,* 332 U.S. 46, 123, 124 (dissenting opinion). Perhaps they were right; but it is a bridge that neither I nor those who joined the Court's opinion in *Griswold* crossed.

right of the *individual,* married or single, to be free from unwarranted governmental intrusion into matters so fundamentally affecting a person as the decision whether to bear or beget a child." *Id.,* at 453.

This right of privacy was called by Mr. Justice Brandeis the right "to be let alone." *Olmstead* v. *United States,* 277 U.S. 438, 478 (dissenting opinion). That right includes the privilege of an individual to plan his own affairs, for, "'outside areas of plainly harmful conduct, every American is left to shape his own life as he thinks best, do what he pleases, go where he pleases.'" *Kent* v. *Dulles,* 357 U.S. 116, 126.

Third is the freedom to care for one's health and person, freedom from bodily restraint or compulsion, freedom to walk, stroll, or loaf.

These rights, though fundamental, are likewise subject to regulation on a showing of "compelling state interest." We stated in *Papachristou* v. *City of Jacksonville,* 405 U.S. 156, 164, that walking, strolling, and wandering "are historically part of the amenities of life as we have known them." As stated in *Jacobson* v. *Massachusetts,* 197 U.S. 11, 29:

> "There is, of course, a sphere within which the individual may assert the supremacy of his own will and rightfully dispute the authority of any human government, especially of any free government existing under a written constitution, to interfere with the exercise of that will."

In *Union Pacific R. Co.* v. *Botsford,* 141 U.S. 250, 252, the Court said, "The inviolability of the person is as much invaded by a compulsory stripping and exposure as by a blow."

In *Terry* v. *Ohio,* 392 U.S. 1, 8–9, the Court, in speaking of the Fourth Amendment stated, "This inestimable right of personal security belongs as much to the citizen on the streets of our cities as to the homeowner closeted in his study to dispose of his secret affairs."

Katz v. *United States,* 389 U.S. 347, 350, emphasizes that the Fourth Amendment "protects individual privacy against certain kinds of governmental intrusion."

In *Meyer* v. *Nebraska,* 262 U.S. 390, 399, the Court said:

> "Without doubt, [liberty] denotes not merely freedom from bodily restraint but also the right of the individual to contract, to engage in any of the common occupations of life, to acquire useful knowledge, to marry, establish a home and bring up children, to worship God according to the dictates of his own conscience, and generally to enjoy those privileges long recognized at common law as essential to the orderly pursuit of happiness by free men."

The Georgia statute is at war with the clear message of these cases—that a woman is free to make the basic decision whether to bear an unwanted child. Elaborate argument is hardly necessary to demonstrate that childbirth may deprive a woman of her preferred lifestyle and force upon her a radically different and undesired future. For example, rejected applicants under the Georgia statute are required to endure the discomforts of pregnancy; to incur the pain, higher mortality rate, and aftereffects of childbirth; to abandon educational plans; to sustain loss of income; to forgo the satisfactions of careers; to tax further mental and physical health in providing child care; and, in some cases, to bear the lifelong stigma of unwed motherhood, a badge which may haunt, if not deter, later legitimate family relationships.

II

Such reasoning is, however, only the beginning of the problem. The State has interests to protect. Vaccinations to prevent epidemics are one example, as *Jacobson, supra,* holds. The Court held that compulsory sterilization of imbeciles afflicted with hereditary forms of insanity or imbecility is another. *Buch* v. *Bell,* 274 U.S. 200. Abortion affects another. While childbirth endangers the lives of some women, voluntary abortion at any time and place regardless of medical standards would impinge on a rightful concern of society. The woman's health is part of that concern; as is the life of the fetus after quickening. These concerns justify the State in treating the procedure as a medical one.

One difficulty is that this statute as construed and applied apparently does not give full sweep to the "psychological as well as physical well-being" of women patients which saved the concept "health" from being void for vagueness in *United States* v. *Vuitch,* 402 U.S., at 72. But, apart from that, Georgia's enactment has a constitutional infirmity because, as stated by the District Court, it "limits the number of reasons for which an abortion may be sought." I agree with the holding of the District Court, "This the State may not do, because such action unduly restricts a decision sheltered by the Constitutional right to privacy." 319 F. Supp., at 1056.

The vicissitudes of life produce pregnancies which may be unwanted, or which may impair "health" in the broad *Vuitch* sense of the term, or which may imperil the life of the mother, or which in the full setting of the case may create such suffering, dislocations, misery, or tragedy as to make an early abortion the only civilized step to take. These hardships may be properly embraced in the "health" factor of the mother as appraised by a person of insight. Or they may be part of a broader medical judgment based on what is "appropriate" in a given case, though perhaps not "necessary" in a strict sense.

The "liberty" of the mother, though rooted as it is in the Constitution, may be qualified by the State for the reasons we have stated. But where fundamental personal rights and liberties are involved, the corrective legislation must be "narrowly drawn to prevent the supposed evil," *Cantwell* v. *Connecticut,* 310 U.S. 296, 307, and not be dealt with in an "unlimited and indiscriminate" manner. *Shelton* v. *Tucker,* 364 U.S. 479, 490. And see *Talley* v. *California,* 362 U.S. 60. Unless regulatory measures are so confined and are addressed to the specific areas of compelling legislative concern, the police power would become the great leveler of constitutional rights and liberties.

There is no doubt that the State may require abortions to be performed by qualified medical personnel. The legitimate objective of preserving the mother's health clearly supports such laws. Their impact upon the woman's privacy is minimal. But the Georgia statute outlaws virtually all such operations—even in the earliest stages of pregnancy. In light of modern medical evidence suggesting that an early abortion is safer healthwise than childbirth itself,[5] it cannot be seriously urged that so comprehensive a ban is aimed at protecting the woman's health. Rather, this expan-

---

5. Many studies show that it is safer for a woman to have a medically induced abortion than to bear a child. In the first 11 months of operation of the New York abortion law, the mortality rate associated with such operations was six per 100,000 operations. Abortion Mortality, 20 Morbidity and Mortality 208, 209 (June 1971) (U.S. Dept. of HEW, Public Health Service). On

sive proscription of all abortions along the temporal spectrum can rest only on a public goal of preserving both embryonic and fetal life.

The present statute has struck the balance between the woman's and the State's interests wholly in favor of the latter. I am not prepared to hold that a State may equate, as Georgia has done, all phases of maturation preceding birth. We held in *Griswold* that the States may not preclude spouses from attempting to avoid the joinder of sperm and egg. If this is true, it is difficult to perceive any overriding public necessity which might attach precisely at the moment of conception. As Mr. Justice Clark has said:[6]

> "To say that life is present at conception is to give recognition to the potential, rather than the actual. The unfertilized egg has life, and if fertilized, it takes on human proportions. But the law deals in reality, not obscurity—the known rather than the unknown. When sperm meets egg life may eventually form, but quite often it does not. The law does not deal in speculation. The phenomenon of life takes time to develop, and until it is actually present, it cannot be destroyed. Its interruption prior to formation would hardly be homicide, and as we have seen, society does not regard it as such. The rites of Baptism are not performed and death certificates are not required when a miscarriage occurs. No prosecutor has ever returned a murder indictment charging the taking of the life of a fetus.[7] This would not be the case if the fetus constituted human life."

In summary, the enactment is overbroad. It is not closely correlated to the aim of preserving prenatal life. In fact, it permits its destruction in several cases, including pregnancies resulting from sex acts in which unmarried females are below the statutory age of consent. At the same time, however, the measure broadly proscribes aborting other pregnancies which may cause severe mental disorders. Additionally, the statute is overbroad because it equates the value of embryonic life immediately after conception with the worth of life immediately before birth.

III

Under the Georgia Act, the mother's physician is not the sole judge as to whether the abortion should be performed. Two other licensed physicians must concur in his judgment.[8] Moreover, the abortion must be performed in a licensed hospital;[9]

---

the other hand, the maternal mortality rate associated with childbirths other than abortions was 18 per 100,000 live births. Tietze, Mortality with Contraception and Induced Abortion, 45 Studies in Family Planning 6 (1969). See also Tietze & Lehfeldt, Legal Abortion in Eastern Europe, 175 J. A. M. A. 1149, 1152 (Apr. 1961); Kolblova, Legal Abortion in Czechoslovakia, 196 J. A. M. A. 371 (Apr. 1966); Mehland, Combating Illegal Abortion in the Socialist Countries of Europe, 13 World Med. J. 84 (1966).

6. Religion, Morality, and Abortion: A Constitutional Appraisal, 2 Loyola U. (L. A.) L. Rev. 1, 9–10 (1969).

7. In *Keeler* v. *Superior Court*, 2 Cal. 3d 619, 470 P. 2d 617, the California Supreme Court held in 1970 that the California murder statute did not cover the killing of an unborn fetus, even though the fetus be "viable," and that it was beyond judicial power to extend the statute to the killing of an unborn. It held that the child must be "born alive before a charge of homicide can be sustained." *Id.*, at 639, 470 P. 2d, at 630.

and the abortion must be approved in advance by a committee of the medical staff of that hospital.[10]

Physicians, who speak to us in *Doe* through an *amicus* brief, complain of the Georgia Act's interference with their practice of their profession.

The right of privacy has no more conspicuous place than in the physician-patient relationship, unless it be in the priest-penitent relationship.

It is one thing for a patient to agree that her physician may consult with another physician about her case. It is quite a different matter for the State compulsorily to impose on that physician-patient relationship another layer or, as in this case, still a third layer of physicians. The right of privacy—the right to care for one's health and person and to seek out a physician of one's own choice protected by the Fourteenth Amendment—becomes only a matter of theory, not a reality, when a multiple-physician-approval system is mandated by the State.

The State licenses a physician. If he is derelict or faithless, the procedures available to punish him or to deprive him of his license are well known. He is entitled to procedural due process before professional disciplinary sanctions may be imposed. See *In re Ruffalo,* 390 U.S. 544. Crucial here, however, is state-imposed control over the medical decision whether pregnancy should be interrupted. The good-faith decision of the patient's chosen physician is overridden and the final decision passed on to others in whose selection the patient has no part. This is a total destruction of the right of privacy between physician and patient and the intimacy of relation which that entails.

The right to seek advice on one's health and the right to place reliance on the physician of one's choice are basic to Fourteenth Amendment values. We deal with fundamental rights and liberties, which, as already noted, can be contained or controlled only by discretely drawn legislation that preserves the "liberty" and regulates only those phases of the problem of compelling legislative concern. The imposition by the State of group controls over the physician-patient relationship is not made on any medical procedure apart from abortion, no matter how dangerous the medical step may be. The oversight imposed on the physician and patient in abortion cases denies them their "liberty," *viz.,* their right of privacy, without any compelling, discernible state interest.

Georgia has constitutional warrant in treating abortion as a medical problem. To protect the woman's right of privacy, however, the control must be through the physician of her choice and the standards set for his performance.

The protection of the fetus when it has acquired life is a legitimate concern of the State. Georgia's law makes no rational, discernible decision on that score.[11] For under the Code, the developmental stage of the fetus is irrelevant when pregnancy is the result of rape, when the fetus will very likely be born with a permanent defect, or when a continuation of the pregnancy will endanger the life of the mother or permanently injure her health. When life is present is a question we do not try to resolve. While basically a question for medical experts, as stated by Mr. Justice

8. See Ga. Code Ann. § 26–1202 (b) (3).

9. See *id.,* § 26–1202 (b) (4).

10. *Id.,* § 26–1202 (b) (5).

11. See Rochat, Tyler, & Schoenbucher, An Epidemiological Analysis of Abortion in Georgia, 61 Am. J. of Public Health 543 (1971).

Clark,[12] it is, of course, caught up in matters of religion and morality.

In short, I agree with the Court that endangering the life of the woman or seriously and permanently injuring her health are standards too narrow for the right of privacy that is at stake.

I also agree that the superstructure of medical supervision which Georgia has erected violates the patient's right of privacy inherent in her choice of her own physician.

MR. JUSTICE WHITE, with whom MR. JUSTICE REHNQUIST joins, dissenting.*

At the heart of the controversy in these cases are those recurring pregnancies that pose no danger whatsoever to the life or health of the mother but are, nevertheless, unwanted for any one or more of a variety of reasons—convenience, family planning, economics, dislike of children, the embarrassment of illegitimacy, etc. The common claim before us is that for any one of such reasons, or for no reason at all, and without asserting or claiming any threat to life or health, any woman is entitled to an abortion at her request if she is able to find a medical advisor willing to undertake the procedure.

The Court for the most part sustains this position: During the period prior to the time the fetus becomes viable, the Constitution of the United States values the convenience, whim, or caprice of the putative mother more than the life or potential life of the fetus; the Constitution, therefore, guarantees the right to an abortion as against any state law or policy seeking to protect the fetus from an abortion not prompted by more compelling reasons of the mother.

With all due respect, I dissent. I find nothing in the language or history of the Constitution to support the Court's judgment. The Court simply fashions and announces a new constitutional right for pregnant mothers and, with scarcely any reason or authority for its action, invests that right with sufficient substance to override most existing state abortion statutes. The upshot is that the people and the legislatures of the 50 States are constitutionally disentitled to weigh the relative importance of the continued existence and development of the fetus, on the one hand, against a spectrum of possible impacts on the mother, on the other hand. As an exercise of raw judicial power, the Court perhaps has authority to do what it does today; but in my view its judgment is an improvident and extravagant exercise of the power of judicial review that the Constitution extends to this Court.

The Court apparently values the convenience of the pregnant mother more than the continued existence and development of the life or potential life that she carries. Whether or not I might agree with that marshaling of values, I can in no event join the Court's judgment because I find no constitutional warrant for imposing such an order of priorities on the people and legislatures of the States. In a sensitive area such as this, involving as it does issues over which reasonable men may easily and heatedly differ, I cannot accept the Court's exercise of its clear power of choice by interposing a constitutional barrier to state efforts to protect human life and by investing mothers and doctors with the constitutionally protected right to exterminate it. This issue, for the most part, should be left with the people and to the political processes the people have devised to govern their affairs.

It is my view, therefore, that the Texas statute is not constitutionally infirm

---

12. *Supra,* n. 6, at 10.

*[This opinion applies also to No. 70–18, *Roe* v. *Wade, ante,* p. 113.]

because it denies abortions to those who seek to serve only their convenience rather than to protect their life or health. Nor is this plaintiff, who claims no threat to her mental or physical health, entitled to assert the possible rights of those women whose pregnancy assertedly implicates their health. This, together with *United States v. Vuitch,* 402 U.S. 62 (1971), dictates reversal of the judgment of the District Court.

Likewise, because Georgia may constitutionally forbid abortions to putative mothers who, like the plaintiff in this case, do not fall within the reach of § 26–1202 (a) of its criminal code, I have no occasion, and the District Court had none, to consider the constitutionality of the procedural requirements of the Georgia statute as applied to those pregnancies posing substantial hazards to either life or health. I would reverse the judgment of the District Court in the Georgia case.

MR. JUSTICE REHNQUIST, dissenting.

The holding in *Roe* v. *Wade, ante,* p. 113, that state abortion laws can withstand constitutional scrutiny only if the State can demonstrate a compelling state interest, apparently compels the Court's close scrutiny of the various provisions in Georgia's abortion statute. Since, as indicated by my dissent in *Wade,* I view the compelling-state-interest standard as an inappropriate measure of the constitutionality of state abortion laws, I respectfully dissent from the majority's holding.

Appendix 3

WEBSTER, ATTORNEY GENERAL OF MISSOURI, ET AL. v.
REPRODUCTIVE HEALTH SERVICES ET AL.
APPEAL FROM THE UNITED STATES COURT OF APPEALS
FOR THE EIGHTH CIRCUIT

No. 88–605. Argued April 26, 1989—
Decided July 3, 1989

Appellees, state-employed health professionals and private nonprofit corporations providing abortion services, brought suit in the District Court for declaratory and injunctive relief challenging the constitutionality of a Missouri statute regulating the performance of abortions. The statute, *inter alia:* (1) sets forth "findings" in its preamble that "[t]he life of each human being begins at conception," and that "unborn children have protectable interests in life, health, and well-being," § § 1.205.1 (1) (2), and requires that all state laws be interpreted to provide unborn children with the same rights enjoyed by other persons, subject to the Federal Constitution and this Court's precedents, § 1.205.2; (2) specifies that a physician, prior to performing an abortion on any woman whom he has reason to believe is 20 or more weeks pregnant, must ascertain whether the fetus is "viable" by performing "such medical examinations and tests as are necessary to make a finding of [the fetus'] gestational age, weight, and lung maturity," § 188.029; (3) prohibits the use of public employees and facilities to perform or assist abortions not necessary to save the mother's life, § § 188.210, 188.215; and (4) makes it unlawful to use public funds, employees, or facilities for the purpose of "encouraging or counseling" a woman to have an abortion not necessary to save her life, §§ 188.205, 188.210, 188.215. The District Court struck down each of the above provisions, among others, and enjoined their enforcement. The Court of Appeals affirmed, ruling that the provisions in question violated this Court's decisions in *Roe* v. *Wade*, 410 U.S. 113, and subsequent cases.

Held: the judgment is reversed.

851 F. 2d 1071, reversed.

THE CHIEF JUSTICE delivered the opinion of the Court with respect to Parts I, II–A, II–B, and II–C, concluding that:

265

1. This Court need not pass on the constitutionality of the Missouri statute's preamble. In invalidating the preamble, the Court of Appeals misconceived the meaning of the dictum in *Akron* v. *Akron Center for Reproductive Health, Inc.,* 462 U.S. 416, 444, that "a State may not adopt one theory of when life begins to justify its regulation of abortions." That statement means only that a State could not "justify" any abortion regulation otherwise invalid under *Roe* v. *Wade* on the ground that it embodied the State's view about when life begins. The preamble does not by its terms regulate abortions or any other aspect of appellees' medical practice, and § 1.205.2 can be interpreted to do no more than offer protections to unborn children in tort and probate law, which is permissible under *Roe* v. *Wade, supra,* at 161–162. This Court has emphasized that *Roe* implies no limitation on a State's authority to make a value judgment favoring childbirth over abortion, *Maher* v. *Roe,* 432 U.S. 464, 474, and the preamble can be read simply to express that sort of value judgment. The extent to which the preamble's language might be used to interpret other state statutes or regulations is something that only the state courts can definitively decide, and, until those courts have applied the preamble to restrict appellees' activities in some concrete way, it is inappropriate for federal courts to address its meaning. *Alabama State Federation of Labor* v. *McAdory,* 325 U.S. 450, 460. Pp. 504–507.

2. The restrictions in § § 188.210 and 188.215 of the Missouri statute on the use of public employees and facilities for the performance or assistance of nontherapeutic abortions do not contravene this Court's abortion decisions. The Due Process Clauses generally confer no affirmative right to governmental aid, even where such aid may be necessary to secure life, liberty, or property interests of which the government may not deprive the individual. *DeShaney* v. *Winnebago County Dept. of Social Services,* 489 U.S. 189, 196. Thus, in *Maher* v. *Roe, supra; Poelker* v. *Doe,* 432 U.S. 519; and *Harris* v. *McRae,* 448 U.S. 297, this Court upheld governmental regulations withholding public funds for nontherapeutic abortions but allowing payments for medical services related to childbirth, recognizing that a government's decision to favor childbirth over abortion through the allocation of public funds does not violate *Roe* v. *Wade.* A State may implement that same value judgment through the allocation of other public resources, such as hospitals and medical staff. There is no merit to the claim that *Maher, Poelker,* and *McRae* must be distinguished on the grounds that preventing access to a public facility narrows or forecloses the availability of abortion. Just as in those cases, Missouri's decision to use public facilities and employees to encourage childbirth over abortion places no governmental obstacle in the path of a woman who chooses to terminate her pregnancy, but leaves her with the same choices as if the State had decided not to operate any hospitals at all. The challenged provisions restrict her ability to obtain an abortion only to the extent that she chooses to use a physician affiliated with a public hospital. Also without merit is the assertion that *Maher, Poelker,* and *McRae* must be distinguished on the ground that, since the evidence shows that all of a public facility's costs in providing abortion services are recouped when the patient pays such that no public funds are expended, the Missouri statute goes beyond expressing a preference for childbirth over abortion by creating an obstacle to the right to choose abortion that cannot stand absent a compelling state interest. Nothing in the Constitution requires States to enter or remain in the abortion business or entitles private physicians and their patients access to public facilities for the performance of abortions. Indeed, if the State does recoup all of its costs in performing abortions and no state subsidy, direct or indirect, is available, it is diffi-

cult to see how any procreational choice is burdened by the State's ban on the use of its facilities or employees for performing abortions. The cases in question all support the view that the State need not commit any resources to performing abortions, even if it can turn a profit by doing so. Pp. 507–511.

3. The controversy over § 188.205's prohibition on the use of public funds to encourage or counsel a woman to have a nontherapeutic abortion is moot. The Court of Appeals did not consider § 188.205 separately from §§ 188.210 and 188.215—which respectively prohibit the use of public employees and facilitates for such counseling—in holding all three sections unconstitutionally vague and violative of a woman's right to choose an abortion. Missouri has appealed only the invalidation of § 188.205. In light of the State's claim, which this Court accepts for purposes of decision, that § 188.205 is not directed at the primary conduct of physicians or health care providers, but is simply an instruction to the State's fiscal officers not to allocate public funds for abortion counseling, appellees contend that they are not "adversely" affected by the section and therefore that there is no longer a case or controversy before the Court on this question. Since plaintiffs are masters of their complaints even at the appellate stage, and since appellees no longer seek equitable relief on their § 188.205 claim, the Court of Appeals is directed to vacate the District Court's judgment with instructions to dismiss the relevant part of the complaint with prejudice. *Deakins* v. *Monaghan,* 484 U.S. 193, 200. Pp. 511–513.

THE CHIEF JUSTICE, joined by JUSTICE WHITE and JUSTICE KENNEDY, concluded in Parts II–D and III that:

1. Section 188.029 of the Missouri statute—which specifies, in its first sentence, that a physician, before performing an abortion on a woman he has reason to believe is carrying an unborn child of 20 or more weeks gestational age, shall first determine if the unborn child is viable by using that degree of care, skill, and proficiency that is commonly exercised by practitioners in the field; but which then provides, in its second sentence, that, in making the viability determination, the physician shall perform such medical examinations and tests as are necessary to make a finding of the unborn child's gestational age, weight, and lung maturity—is constitutional, since it permissibly furthers the State's interest in protecting potential human life. Pp. 513–521.

(a) The Court of Appeals committed plain error in reading § 188.029 as requiring that after 20 weeks the specified tests *must* be performed. That section makes sense only if its second sentence is read to require only those tests that are useful in making subsidiary viability findings. Reading the sentence to require the tests *in all circumstances,* including when the physician's reasonable professional judgment indicates that they would be irrelevant to determining viability or even dangerous to the mother and the fetus, would conflict with the first sentence's *requirement* that the physician apply his reasonable professional skill and judgment. It would also be incongruous to read the provision, especially the word "necessary," to require tests irrelevant to the expressed statutory purpose of determining viability. Pp. 514–515.

(b) Section 188.029 is reasonably designed to ensure that abortions are not performed where the fetus is viable. The section's tests are intended to determine viability, the State having chosen viability as the point at which its interest in potential human life must be safeguarded. The section creates what is essentially a presumption of viability at 20 weeks, which the physician, prior to performing an abortion, must rebut with tests—including, if feasible, those for gestational age, fetal weight, and lung capacity—indicating that the fetus is not viable. While the District Court found that uncontradicted medical evidence established that a 20-week fetus is *not*

viable, and that 23 1/2 to 24 weeks' gestation is the earliest point at which a reasonable possibility of viability exists, it also found that there may be a 4-week error in
estimating gestational age, which supports testing at 20 weeks. Pp. 515–516.

(c) Section 188.029 conflicts with *Roe* v. *Wade* and cases following it. Since
the section's tests will undoubtedly show in many cases that the fetus is not viable,
the tests will have been performed for what were in fact second-trimester abortions.
While *Roe*, 410 U.S., at 162, recognized the State's interest in protecting potential human life as "important and legitimate," it also limited state involvement in
second-trimester abortions to protecting maternal health, *id.*, at 164, and allowed
States to regulate or proscribe abortions to protect the unborn child only after viability, *id.*, at 165. Since the tests in question regulate the physician's discretion in
determining the viability of the fetus, § 188.029 conflicts with language in *Colautti*
v. *Franklin*, 439 U.S. 379, 388–389, stating that the viability determination is, and
must be, a matter for the responsible attending physician's judgment. And, in light
of District Court findings that the tests increase the expenses of abortion, their
validity may also be questioned under *Akron*, 462 U.S., at 434–435, which held
that a requirement that second-trimester abortions be performed in hospitals was
invalid because it substantially increased the expenses of those procedures. Pp.
516–517.

(d) The doubt cast on the Missouri statute by these cases is not so much a flaw
in the statute as it is a reflection of the fact that *Roe's* rigid trimester analysis has
proved to be unsound in principle and unworkable in practice. In such circumstances, this Court does not refrain from reconsidering prior constitutional rulings,
notwithstanding *stare decisis*. E. g., *Garcia* v. *San Antonio Metropolitan Transit
Authority*, 469 U.S. 528. The *Roe* framework is hardly consistent with the notion of
a Constitution like ours that is cast in general terms and usually speaks in general
principles. The framework's key elements—trimesters and viability—are not found in
the Constitution's text, and, since the bounds of the inquiry are essentially indeterminate, the result has been a web of legal rules that have become increasingly
intricate, resembling a code of regulations rather than a body of constitutional doctrine. There is also no reason why the State's compelling interest in protecting
potential human life should not extend throughout pregnancy rather than coming
into existence only at the point of viability. Thus, the *Roe* trimester framework should
be abandoned. Pp. 517–520.

(e) There is no merit to JUSTICE BLACKMUN's contention that the Court should join in
a "great issues" debate as to whether the Constitution includes an "unenumerated" general right to privacy as recognized in cases such as *Griswold* v.
Connecticut, 381 U.S. 479. Unlike *Roe*, *Griswold* did not purport to adopt a whole
framework, complete with detailed rules and distinctions, to govern the cases in
which the asserted liberty interest would apply. The *Roe* framework, sought to deal
with areas of medical practice traditionally left to the States, and to balance once
and for all, by reference only to the calendar, the State's interest in protecting potential human life against the claims of a pregnant woman to decide whether or not
to abort. The Court's experience in applying *Roe* in later cases suggests that there
is wisdom in not necessarily attempting to elaborate the differences between a
"fundamental right" to an abortion, *Akron, supra*, at 420, n. 1, a "limited fundamental constitutional right," *post*, at 555, or a liberty interest protected by the Due
Process Clause. Moreover, although this decision will undoubtedly allow more governmental regulation of abortion than was permissible before, the goal of constitu-

tional adjudication is not to remove inexorably "politically divisive" issues from the ambit of the legislative process, but is, rather, to hold true the balance between that which the Constitution puts beyond the reach of the democratic process and that which it does not. Furthermore, the suggestion that legislative bodies, in a Nation where more than half the population is female, will treat this decision as an invitation to enact abortion laws reminiscent of the dark ages misreads the decision and does scant justice to those who serve in such bodies and the people who elect them. Pp. 520–521.

2. This case affords no occasion to disturb *Roe's* holding that a Texas statute which criminalized *all* nontherapeutic abortions unconstitutionally infringed the right to an abortion derived from the Due Process Clause. *Roe* is distinguishable on its facts, since Missouri has determined that viability is the point at which its interest in potential human life must be safeguarded. P. 521.

JUSTICE O'CONNOR, agreeing that it was plain error for the Court of Appeals to interpret the second sentence of § 188.029 as meaning that doctors *must* perform tests to find gestational age, fetal weight, and lung maturity, concluded that the section was constitutional as properly interpreted by the plurality, and that the plurality should therefore not have proceeded to reconsider *Roe* v. *Wade.* This Court refrains from deciding constitutional questions where there is no need to do so, and generally does not formulate a constitutional rule broader than the precise facts to which it is to be applied. *Ashwander* v. *TVA,* 297 U.S. 288, 346, 347. Since appellees did not appeal the District Court's ruling that the first sentence of § 188.029 is constitutional, there is no dispute between the parties over the presumption of viability at 20 weeks created by that first sentence. Moreover, as properly interpreted by the plurality, the sections' second sentence does nothing more than delineate means by which the unchallenged 20-week presumption may be overcome if those means are useful in determining viability and can be prudently employed. As so interpreted, the viability testing requirements do not conflict with any of the Court's abortion decisions. As the plurality recognizes, under its interpretation of § 188.029's second sentence, the viability testing requirements promote the State's interest in potential life. This Court has recognized that a State may promote that interest when viability is possible. *Thornburgh* v. *American College of Obstetricians and Gynecologists,* 476 U.S. 747, 770–771. Similarly, the basis for reliance by the lower courts on *Colautti* v. *Franklin,* 439 U.S. 379, 388–389, disappears when § 188.029 is properly interpreted to require only *subsidiary* viability findings, since the State has not attempted to substitute its judgment for the physician's ascertainment of viability, which therefore remains "the critical point." Nor does the marginal increase in the cost of an abortion created by § 188.029's viability testing provision, as interpreted, conflict with *Akron* v. *Akron Center for Reproductive Health,* 462 U.S. 416, 434–439, since, here, such costs do not place a "heavy, and unnecessary burden" on a woman's abortion decision, whereas the statutory requirement in *Akron,* which related to previability abortions, more than doubled a woman's costs. Moreover, the statutory requirements in Akron involved second-trimester abortions generally; § 188.029 concerns only tests and examinations to determine viability when viability is possible. The State's compelling interest in potential life postviability renders its interest in determining the critical point of viability equally compelling. *Thornburgh, supra,* at 770–771. When the constitutional invalidity of a State's abortion statute actually turns upon the constitutional validity of *Roe,* there will be time enough to reexamine *Roe,* and to do so carefully. Pp. 525–531.

JUSTICE SCALIA would reconsider and explicitly overrule *Roe* v. *Wade*. Avoiding the *Roe* question by deciding this case in as narrow a manner as possible is not required by precedent and not justified by policy. To do so is needlessly to prolong this Court's involvement in a field where the answers to the central questions are political rather than juridical, and thus to make the Court the object of the sort of organized pressure that political institutions in a democracy ought to receive. It is particularly perverse to decide this case as narrowly as possible in order to avoid reading the inexpressibly "broader-than-was-required-by-the-precise-facts" structure established by *Roe* v. *Wade*. The question of *Roe's* validity is presented here, inasmuch as §188.029 constitutes a legislative imposition on the judgment of the physician concerning the point of viability and increases the cost of an abortion. It does palpable harm, if the States can and would eliminate largely unrestricted abortion, skillfully to refrain from telling them so. Pp. 532–537.

REHNQUIST, C. J., announced the judgment of the Court and delivered the opinion for a unanimous Court with respect to Part II–C, the opinion of the Court with respect to Parts I, II–A, and II–B, in which WHITE, O'CONNOR, SCALIA, and KENNEDY, JJ., joined, and an opinion with respect to Parts II–D and III, in which WHITE and KENNEDY, JJ., joined. O'CONNOR, J., *post,* p. 522, and SCALIA, J., *post,* p. 532, filed opinions concurring in part and concurring in the judgment. BLACKMUN, J., filed an opinion concurring in part and dissenting in part, in which BRENNAN and MARSHALL, JJ., joined, *post,* p. 537. STEVENS, J., filed an opinion concurring in part and dissenting in part, *post,* p. 560.

William L. Webster, Attorney General of Missouri, *pro se,* argued the cause for appellants. With him on the briefs were *Michael L. Boicourt* and *Jerry L. Short,* Assistant Attorneys General.

Charles Fried argued the cause for the United States as *amicus curiae* urging reversal. On the brief were *Acting Solicitor General Bryson, Assistant Attorney General Bolton, Deputy Solicitor General Merrill, Roger Clegg, Steven R. Valentine,* and *Michael K. Kellogg.*

Frank Susman argued the cause for appellees. With him on the brief were *Roger K. Evans, Dara Klassel, Barbara E. Otten, Thomas M. Blumenthal,* and *Janet Benshoof.**

---

*Briefs of *amici curiae* urging reversal were filed for Alabama Lawyers for Unborn Children, Inc., by *John J. Coleman III* and *Thomas E. Maxwell;* for the American Association of Prolife Obstetricians and Gynecologists et al. by *Dolores Horan* and *Paige Comstock Cunningham;* for American Family Association, Inc., by *Peggy M. Coleman;* for American Life League, Inc., by *Marion Edwyn Harrison* and *John S. Baker, Jr.;* for the Catholic Health Association of the United States by *J. Roger Edgar, David M. Harris, Kathleen M. Boozang, J. Stuart Showalter,* and *Peter E. Campbell;* for Catholic Lawyers Guild of the Archdiocese of Boston, Inc., by *Calum B. Anderson* and *Leonard F. Zandrow, Jr.;* for the Center for Judicial Studies et al. by *Jules B. Gerard;* for Covenant House et al. by *Gregory A. Loken;* for Focus On The Family et al. by *H. Robert Showers;* for the Holy Orthodox Church by *James George Jatras;* for the Knights of Columbus by *Robert J. Cynkar* and *Brendan V. Sullivan, Jr.;* for The Lutheran Church-Missouri Synod et al. by *Philip E. Draheim;* for the Missouri Catholic Conference by *David M. Harris, J. Roger Edgar, Bernard C. Huger, Kathleen M. Boozang,* and *Louis C. DeFeo, Jr.;* for the National Legal Foundation by *Douglas W. Davis* and *Robert K. Skolrood;* for Right to Life Advocates, Inc., by *Richard W. Schmude* and *Rory R. Olsen;* for the Rutherford Institute et al. by *James J. Knicely, John W. Whitehead, Thomas W. Strahan, David E. Morris, William B. Hollberg, Amy Dougherty, Randall A. Pentiuk, William Bonner, Larry L. Crain,* and *W. Charles Bundren;* for the Southern Center for Law and Ethics by *Albert L. Jordan;* for Southwest Life and Law Center, Inc., by *David Burnell Smith;* for the United States Catholic Conference by *Mark E. Chopko* and *Phillip H. Harris;* for 127 Members of the Missouri General Assembly by *Timothy Belz, Lynn D. Wardle,* and *Richard G. Wilkins;* and for James Joseph Lynch, Jr., by Mr. Lynch, *pro se.*

Briefs of *amici curiae* urging affirmance were filed for the American Civil Liberties Union et al. by *Burt Neuborne, Janet Benshoof, Rachael N. Pine,* and *Lynn M. Paltrow;* for the American Jewish Congress et al. by *Martha L. Minow;* for the American Library Association et al. by *Bruce J. Ennis* and *Mark D. Schneider;* for the American Medical Association et al. by *Jack R. Bierig, Carter G. Phillips, Elizabeth H. Esty, Stephan E. Lawton, Ann E. Allen, Laurie R. Rockett,* and *Joel I. Klein;* for the American Psychological Association by *Donald N. Bersoff;* for the American Public Health Association et al. by *John H. Hall* and *Nadine Taub;* for Americans for Democratic Action et al. by *Marsha S. Berzon;* for Americans United for Separation of Church and State by *Lee Boothby, Robert W. Nixon,* and *Robert J. Lipshutz;* for the Association of Reproductive Health Professionals et al. by *Colleen K. Connell* and *Dorothy B. Zimbrakos;* for Bioethicists for Privacy by *George J. Annas;* for Catholics for a Free Choice et al. by *Patricia Hennessey;* for the Center for Population Options et al. by *John H. Henn* and *Thomas Asher;* for the Committee on Civil Rights of the Bar of the City of New York et al. by *Jonathan Lang, Diane S. Wilner, Arthur S. Leonard, Audrey S. Feinberg,* and *Janice Goodman;* for 22 International Women's Health Organizations by *Kathryn Kolbert;* for the American Nurses' Association et al. by *E. Calvin Golumbic;* for the National Coalition Against Domestic Violence by *David A. Strauss;* for the National Family Planning and Reproductive Health Association by *James L. Feldesman, Jeffrey K. Stith, and Thomas E. Zemaitis;* for the National Association of Public Hospitals by *Alan K. Parver* and *Phyllis E. Bernard;* for Population-Environment Balance et al. by *Dina R. Lassow;* for 281 American Historians by *Sylvia A. Law;* and for 2,887 Women Who Have Had Abortions et al by *Sarah E. Burns.*

Briefs of *amici curiae* were filed for the State of California et al. by *Robert Abrams,* Attorney General of New York, *O. Peter Sherwood,* Solicitor General, *Suzanne M. Lynn* and *Marla Tepper,* Assistant Attorneys General, *James M. Shannon,* Attorney General of Massachusetts, *Suzanne E. Durrell* and *Madelyn F. Wessel,* Assistant Attorneys General, *Elizabeth Holtzman,* pro se, *Barbara D. Underwood, John K. Van de Kamp,* Attorney General of California, *Duane Woodard,* Attorney General of Colorado, *Jim Mattox,* Attorney General of Texas, and *Jeffrey L. Amestoy,* Attorney General of Vermont; for the State of Louisiana et al. by *William J. Guste, Jr.,* Attorney General of Louisiana, *Jo Ann P. Levert,* Assistant Attorney General, *Thomas A. Rayer, Robert K. Corbin,* Attorney General of Arizona, *Jim Jones,* Attorney General of Idaho, and *Ernest D. Preate, Jr.,* Attorney General of Pennsylvania; for Agudath Israel of America by *Steven D. Prager;* for the American Academy of Medical Ethics by *James Bopp, Jr.;* for the California National Organization for Women et al. by *Kathryn A. Sure;* for American Collegians for Life, Inc., et al. by *Robert A. Destro;* for the Canadian Abortion Rights Action League et al. by *Estelle Rogers;* for the Association for Public Justice et al. by *Joseph W. Dellapenna;* for Birthright, Inc., by *Joseph I. McCullough, Jr.;* for Catholics United for Life et al. by *Walter M. Weber, Michael J. Woodruff, Charles E. Rice,* and *Michael J. Laird;* for Christian Advocates Serving Evangelism by *Theodore H. Amshoff, Jr.;* for Doctors for Life et al. by *Andrew F. Puzder* and *Kenneth C. Jones;* for Feminists For Life of America et al. by *Christine Smith Torre;* for Free Speech Advocates by *Thomas Patrick Monaghan;* for Human Life International by *Robert L. Sassone;* for the International Right to Life Federation by *John J. Potts;* for the National Association of Women Lawyers et al. by *Nicholas DeB. Katzenbach, Leona Beane,* and *Estelle H. Rogers;* for National Council of Negro Women, Inc., et al. by *Rhonda Copelon;* for the National Organization for Women by *John S. L. Katz;* for National Right to Life Committee, Inc., by *James Bopp, Jr.;* for New England Christian Action Council, Inc., by *Philip D. Moran;* for Right to Life League of Southern California, Inc., by *Robert L. Sassone;* for 77 Organizations Committed to Women's Equality by *Judith L. Lichtman, Donna R. Lenhoff, Marcia Greenberger, Stephanie Ridder,* and *Wendy Webster Williams;* for Certain Members of the Congress of the United States by *Burke Marshall* and *Norman Redlich;* for Congressman *Christopher H. Smith* et al. by *Albert P. Blaustein, Edward R. Grant,* and *Ann-Louise Lohr;* for 608 State Legislators by *Herma Hill Kay, James J. Brosnahan,* and *Jack W. Londen;* for Certain Members of the General Assembly of the Commonwealth of Pennsylvania by *William Bentley Ball, Philip J. Murren,* and *Maura K. Quinlan;* for Certain American State Legislators by *Paul Benjamin Linton* and *Clarke D. Forsythe;* for A Group of American Law Professors by *Norman Redlich;* for 167 Distinguished Scientists and Physicians by *Jay Kelly Wright;* for *Edward Allen* by *Robert L. Sassone;* for *Larry Joyce* by *Thomas P. Joyce;* for *Paul Marx* by *Robert L. Sassone;* for *Bernard N. Nathanson* by *Mr. Sassone;* and for *Austin Vaughn* et al. by *Mr. Sassone.*

CHIEF JUSTICE REHNQUIST announced the judgment of the Court and delivered the opinion of the Court with respect to Parts I, II–A, II–B, and II–C, and an opinion with respect to Parts II–D and III, in which JUSTICE WHITE and JUSTICE KENNEDY join.

This appeal concerns the constitutionality of a Missouri statute regulating the performance of abortions. The United States Court of Appeals for the Eighth Circuit struck down several provisions of the statute on the ground that they violated this Court's decision in *Roe* v. *Wade,* 410 U.S. 113 (1973), and cases following it. We noted probable jurisdiction, 488 U.S. 1003 (1989), and now reverse.

I

In June 1986, the Governor of Missouri signed into law Missouri Senate Committee Substitute for House Bill No. 1596 (hereinafter Act or statute), which amended existing state law concerning unborn children and abortions.[1] The Act consisted of 20 provisions, 5 of which are now before the Court. The first provision, or preamble, contains "findings" by the state legislature that "[t]he life of each human being begins at conception," and that "unborn children have protectable interests in life, health, and well-being." Mo. Rev. Stat. § § 1.205.1 (1), (2) (1986). The Act further requires that all Missouri laws be interpreted to provide unborn children with the same rights enjoyed by other persons, subject to the Federal Constitution and this Court's precedents. § 1.205.2. Among its other provisions,

---

1. After *Roe* v. *Wade,* the State of Missouri's then-existing abortion regulations, see Mo. Rev. Stat. §§ 559.100, 542.380, and 563.300 (1969), were declared unconstitutional by a three-judge federal court. This Court summarily affirmed that judgment. *Danforth* v. *Rodgers,* 414 U.S. 1035 (1973). Those statutes, like the Texas statute at issue in *Roe,* made it a crime to perform an abortion except when the mother's life was at stake. 410 U.S., at 117–118, and n. 2.

In June 1974, the State enacted House Committee Substitute for House Bill No. 1211, which imposed new regulations on abortions during all stages of pregnancy. Among other things, the 1974 Act defined "viability," § 2(2); required the written consent of the woman prior to an abortion during the first 12 weeks of pregnancy, § 3(2); required the written consent of the woman's spouse prior to an elective abortion during the first 12 weeks of pregnancy, § 3(3); required the written consent of one parent if the woman was under 18 and unmarried prior to an elective abortion during the first 12 weeks of pregnancy, § 3(4); required a physician performing an abortion to exercise professional care to "preserve the life and health of the fetus" regardless of the stage of pregnancy and, if he should fail that duty, deemed him guilty of manslaughter and made him liable for damages, § 6(1); prohibited the use of saline amniocentesis, as a method of abortion, after the first 12 weeks of pregnancy, § 9; and required certain record-keeping for health facilities and physicians performing abortions, §§ 10, 11. In *Planned Parenthood of Central Mo.* v. *Danforth,* 428 U.S. 52 (1976), the Court upheld the definition of viability, *id.,* at 63–65, the consent provision in § 3(2), *id.,* at 65–67, and the recordkeeping requirements. *Id.,* at 79–81. It struck down the spousal consent provision, *id.,* at 67–72, the parental consent provision, *id.,* at 72–75, the prohibition on abortions by amniocentesis, *id.,* at 75–79, and the requirement that physicians exercise professional care to preserve the life of the fetus regardless of the stage of pregnancy. *Id.,* at 81–84.

In 1979, Missouri passed legislation that, *inter alia,* required abortions after 12 weeks to be performed in a hospital, Mo. Rev. Stat. § 188.025 (Supp. 1979); required a pathology report for each abortion performed, § 188.047; required the presence of a second physician during abortions performed after viability, § 188.030.3; and required minors to secure parental consent or consent from the juvenile court for an abortion, § 188.028. In *Planned Parenthood Assn. of Kansas City, Mo., Inc.* v. *Ashcroft,* 462 U.S. 476 (1983), the Court struck down the second-trimester hospitalization requirement, *id.,* at 481–482, but upheld the other provisions described above. *Id.,* at 494.

the Act requires that, prior to performing an abortion on any woman whom a physician has reason to believe is 20 or more weeks pregnant, the physician ascertain whether the fetus is viable by performing "such medical examinations and tests as are necessary to make a finding of the gestational age, weight, and lung maturity of the unborn child." § 188.029. The Act also prohibits the use of public employees and facilities to perform or assist abortions not necessary to save the mother's life, and it prohibits the use of public funds, employees, or facilities for the purpose of "encouraging or counseling" a woman to have an abortion not necessary to save her life. § § 188.205, 188.210, 188.215.

In July 1986, five health professionals employed by the State and two nonprofit corporations brought this class action in the United States District Court for the Western District of Missouri to challenge the constitutionality of the Missouri statute. Plaintiffs, appellees in this Court, sought declaratory and injunctive relief on the ground that certain statutory provisions violated the First, Fourth, Ninth, and Fourteenth Amendments to the Federal Constitution. App. A9. They asserted violations of various rights, including the "privacy rights of pregnant women seeking abortions"; the "woman's right to an abortion"; the "righ[t] to privacy in the physician-patient relationship"; the physician's righ[t] to practice medicine"; the pregnant woman's "right to life due to inherent risks involved in childbirth"; and the woman's right to "receive . . . adequate medical advice and treatment" concerning abortions. _Id.,_ at A17–A19.

Plaintiffs filed this suit "on their own behalf and on behalf of the entire class consisting of facilities and Missouri licensed physicians or other health care professionals offering abortion services or pregnancy counseling and on behalf of the entire class of pregnant females seeking abortion services or pregnancy counseling within the State of Missouri." _Id.,_ at A13. The two nonprofit corporations are Reproductive Health Services, which offers family planning and gynecological services to the public, including abortion services up to 22 weeks "gestational age,"[2] and Planned Parenthood of Kansas City, which provides abortion services up to 14 weeks gestational age. _Id.,_ at A9–A10. The individual plaintiffs are three physicians, one nurse, and a social worker. All are "public employees" at "public facilities" in Missouri, and they are paid for their services with "public funds," as those terms are defined by § 188.200. The individual plaintiffs, within the scope of their public employment, encourage and counsel pregnant women to have nontherapeutic abortions. Two of the physicians perform abortions. App. A54–A55.

Several weeks after the complaint was filed, the District Court temporarily restrained enforcement of several provisions of the Act. Following a 3-day trial in December 1986, the District Court declared seven provisions of the Act unconstitutional and enjoined their enforcement. 662 F. Supp. 407 (WD Mo. 1987). These provisions included the preamble, § 1.205; the "informed consent" provision, which required physicians to inform the pregnant woman of certain facts before performing an abortion, § 188.039; the requirement that post-16-week abortions be performed only in hospitals, § 188.025; the mandated tests to determine viability, § 188.029; and the prohibition on the use of public funds, employees, and facilities to perform or assist nontherapeutic abortions, and the restrictions on the use of public funds, employees, and facilities to encourage or counsel women to have such abortions, § § 188.205, 188.210, 188.215. _Id.,_ at 430.

---

2. The Act defines "gestational age" as the "length of pregnancy as measured from the first day of the woman's last menstrual period." Mo. Rev. Stat. § 188.015(4) (1986).

The Court of Appeals for the Eighth Circuit affirmed, with one exception not relevant to this appeal. 851 F. 2d 1071 (1988). The Court of Appeals determined that Missouri's declaration that life begins at conception was "simply an impermissible state adoption of a theory of when life begins to justify its abortion regulations." *Id.,* at 1076. Relying on *Colautti* v. *Franklin,* 439 U.S. 379, 388–389 (1979), it further held that the requirement that physicians perform viability tests was an unconstitutional legislative intrusion on a matter of medical skill and judgment. 851 F. 2d, at 1074–1075. The Court of Appeals invalidated Missouri's prohibition on the use of public facilities and employees to perform or assist abortions not necessary to save the mother's life. *Id.,* at 1081–1083. It distinguished our decisions in *Harris* v. *McRae,* 448 U.S. 297 (1980), and *Maher* v. *Roe,* 432 U.S. 464 (1977), on the ground that "'[t]here is a fundamental difference between providing direct funding to effect the abortion decision and allowing staff physicians to perform abortions at an existing publicly owned hospital.'" 851 F. 2d, at 1081, quoting *Nyberg* v. *City of Virginia,* 667 F. 2d 754, 758 (CA8 1982), appeal dism'd, 462 U.S. 1125 (1983). The Court of Appeals struck down the provision prohibiting the use of public funds for "encouraging or counseling" women to have nontherapeutic abortions, for the reason that this provision was both overly vague and inconsistent with the right to an abortion enunciated in *Roe* v. *Wade.* 851 F. 2d, at 1077–1080. The court also invalidated the hospitalization requirement for 16-week abortions, *id.,* at 1073–1074, and the prohibition on the use of public employees and facilities for abortion counseling, *id.,* at 1077–1080, but the State has not appealed those parts of the judgment below. See Juris. Statement I–II.[3]

II

Decision of this case requires us to address four sections of the Missouri Act: (a) the preamble; (b) the prohibition on the use of public facilities or employees to perform abortions; (c) the prohibition on public funding of abortion counseling; and (d) the requirement that physicians conduct viability tests prior to performing abortions. We address these *seriatim.*

A

The Act's preamble, as noted, sets forth "findings" by the Missouri legislature that "[t]he life of each human being begins at conception," and that "[u]nborn children have protectable interests in life, health, and well-being." Mo. Rev. Stat. § § 1.205.1(1), (2) (1986). The Act then mandates that state laws be interpreted to provide unborn children with "all the rights, privileges, and immunities available to other persons, citizens, and residents of this state," subject to the Constitution and this Court's precedents. § 1.205.2.[4] In invalidating the preamble, the Court of Appeals relied on this Court's dictum that "'a State may not adopt one theory of

---

3. The State did not appeal the District Court's invalidation of the Act's "informed consent" provision to the Court of Appeals, 851 F. 2d, at 1073, n. 2, and it is not before us.

4. Section 1.205 provides in full:

"1. The general assembly of this state finds that:

"(1) The life of each human being begins at conception;

"(2) Unborn children have protectable interests in life, health, and well-being;

when life begins to justify its regulation of abortions.'" 851 F. 2d, at 1075–1076, quoting _Akron_ v. _Akron Center for Reproductive Health, Inc._, 462 U.S. 416, 444 (1983), in turn citing _Roe_ v. _Wade_, 410 U.S., at 159–162. It rejected Missouri's claim that the preamble was "abortion-neutral," and "merely determine[d] when life begins in a nonabortion context, a traditional state prerogative." 851 F. 2d, at 1076. The court thought that "[t]he only plausible inference" from the fact that "every remaining section of the bill save one regulates the performance of abortions" was that "the state intended its abortion regulations to be understood against the backdrop of its theory of life." _Ibid._[5]

The State contends that the preamble itself is precatory and imposes no substantive restrictions on abortions, and that appellees therefore do not have standing to challenge it. Brief for Appellants 21–24. Appellees, on the other hand, insist that the preamble is an operative part of the Act intended to guide the interpretation of other provisions of the Act. Brief for Appellees 19–23. They maintain, for example, that the preamble's definition of life may prevent physicians in public hospitals from dispensing certain forms of contraceptives, such as the intrauterine device. _Id.,_ at 22.

In our view, the Court of Appeals misconceived the meaning of the _Akron_ dictum, which was only that a State could not "justify" an abortion regulation otherwise invalid under _Roe_ v. _Wade_ on the ground that it embodied the State's view about when life begins. Certainly the preamble does not by its terms regulate abortion or any other aspect of appellees' medical practice. The Court has emphasized that _Roe_ v. _Wade_ "implies no limitation on the authority of a State to make a value judgment favoring childbirth over abortion." _Maher_ v. _Roe_, 432 U.S., at 474. The preamble can be read simply to express that sort of value judgment.

We think the extent to which the preamble's language might be used to interpret other state statutes or regulations is something that only the courts of Missouri can definitely decide. State law has offered protections to unborn children in tort and probate law, see _Roe_ v. _Wade, supra,_ at 161–162, and § 1.205.2 can be interpreted to do no more than that. What we have, then, is much the same situation

---

"(3) the natural parents of unborn children have protectable interests in the life, health, and well-being of their unborn child.

"2. Effective January 1, 1988, the laws of this state shall be interpreted and construed to acknowledge on behalf of the unborn child at every stage of development, all the rights, privileges, and immunities available to other persons, citizens, and residents of this state, subject only to the Constitution of the United States, and decisional interpretations thereof by the United States Supreme Court and specific provisions to the contrary in the statutes and constitution of this state.

"3. As used in this section, the term 'unborn children' or 'unborn child' shall include all unborn child _[sic]_ or children or the offspring of human beings from the moment of conception until birth at every stage of biological development.

"4. Nothing in this section shall be interpreted as creating a cause of action against a woman for indirectly harming her unborn child by failing to properly care for herself or by failing to follow any particular program of prenatal care."

5. Judge Arnold dissented from this part of the Court of Appeals' decision, arguing that Missouri's declaration of when life begins should be upheld "insofar as it relates to subjects other than abortion," such as "creating causes of action against persons other than the mother" for wrongful death or extending the protection of the criminal law to fetuses. 851 F. 2d, at 1085 (opinion concurring in part and dissenting in part).

that the Court confronted in *Alabama State Federation of Labor* v. *McAdory*, 325 U.S. 450 (1945). As in that case:

> "We are thus invited to pass upon the constitutional validity of a state statute which has not yet been applied or threatened to be applied by the state courts to petitioners or others in the manner anticipated. Lacking any authoritative construction of the statute by the state courts, without which no constitutional question arises, and lacking the authority to give such a controlling construction ourselves, and with a record which presents no concrete set of facts to which the statute is to be applied, the case is plainly not one to be disposed of by the declaratory judgment procedure." *Id.*, at 460.

It will be time enough for federal courts to address the meaning of the preamble should it be applied to restrict the activities of appellees in some concrete ways. Until then, this Court "is not empowered to decide . . . abstract propositions, or to declare, for the government of future cases, principles or rules of law which cannot affect the result as to the thing in issue in the case before it." *Tyler* v. *Judges of Court of Registration*, 179 U.S. 405, 409 (1900). See also *Valley Forge Christian College* v. *Americans United for Separation of Church & State, Inc.*, 454 U.S. 464, 473 (1982).[6] We therefore need not pass on the constitutionality of the Act's preamble.

B

Section 188.210 provides that "[i]t shall be unlawful for any public employee within the scope of his employment to perform or assist an abortion, not necessary to save the life of the mother," while § 188.215 makes it "unlawful for any public facility to be used for the purpose of performing or assisting an abortion not necessary to save the life of the mother."[7] The Court of Appeals held that these provisions contravened this Court's abortion decisions. 851 F. 2d, at 1082–1083. We take the contrary view.

As we said earlier this Term in *DeShaney* v. *Winnebago County Dept. of Social Services*, 489 U.S. 189, 196 (1989): "[O]ur cases have recognized that the Due Process Clauses generally confer no affirmative right to governmental aid, even where such aid may be necessary to secure life, liberty, or property interests of which the government itself may not deprive the individual." In *Maher* v. *Roe, supra,* the Court upheld a Connecticut welfare regulation under which Medicaid recipients received payments for medical services related to childbirth, but not for nontherapeutic abortions. The Court rejected the claim that this unequal subsidization of childbirth and abortion was impermissible under *Roe* v. *Wade.* As the Court put it:

---

6. Appellees also claim that the legislature's preamble violates the Missouri Constitution. Brief for Appellees 23–26. But the considerations discussed in the text make it equally inappropriate for a federal court to pass upon this claim before the state courts have interpreted the statute.

7. The statute defines "public employee" to mean "any person employed by this state or any agency or political subdivision thereof." Mo. Rev. Stat. § 188.200(1) (1986). "Public facility" is defined as "any public institution, public facility, public equipment, or any physical asset owned, leased, or controlled by this state or any agency or political subdivisions thereof." § 188.200(2).

"The Connecticut regulation before us is different in kind from the laws invalidated in our previous abortion decisions. The Connecticut regulation places no obstacles—absolute or otherwise—in the pregnant woman's path to an abortion. An indigent woman who desires an abortion suffers no disadvantage as a consequence of Connecticut's decision to fund childbirth; she continues as before to be dependent on private sources for the service she desires. The State may have made childbirth a more attractive alternative, thereby influencing the woman's decision, but it has imposed no restriction on access to abortions that was not already there. The indigency that may make it difficult—and in some cases, perhaps, impossible—for some women to have abortions is neither created nor in any way affected by the Connecticut regulation." 432 U.S., at 474.

Relying on _Maher,_ the Court in _Poelker_ v. _Doe,_ 432 U.S. 519, 521 (1977), held that the city of St. Louis committed "no constitutional violation . . . in electing, as a policy choice, to provide publicly financed hospital services for childbirth without providing corresponding services for nontherapeutic abortions."

More recently, in _Harris_ v. _McRae,_ 448 U.S. 297 (1980), the Court upheld "the most restrictive version of the Hyde Amendment," _id.,_ at 325, n. 27, which withheld from States federal funds under the Medicaid program to reimburse the costs of abortions, "'except where the life of the mother would be endangered if the fetus were carried to term.'" _Ibid._ (quoting Pub. L. 94–439, § 209, 90 Stat. 1434). As in _Maher_ and _Poelker,_ the Court required only a showing that Congress' authorization of "reimbursement for medically necessary services generally, but not for certain medically necessary abortions" was rationally related to the legitimate governmental goal of encouraging childbirth. 448 U.S., at 325.

The Court of Appeals distinguished these cases on the ground that "[t]o prevent access to a public facility does more than demonstrate a political choice in favor of childbirth; it clearly narrows and in some cases forecloses the availability of abortion to women." 851 F. 2d, at 1081. The court reasoned that the ban on the use of public facilities "could prevent a woman's chosen doctor from performing an abortion because of his unprivileged status at other hospitals or because a private hospital adopted a similar anti-abortion stance." _Ibid._ It also thought that "[s]uch a rule could increase the cost of obtaining an abortion and delay the timing of it as well." _Ibid._

We think that this analysis is much like that which we rejected in _Maher, Poelker,_ and _McRae._ As in those cases, the State's decision here to use public facilities and staff to encourage childbirth over abortion "places no governmental obstacle in the path of a woman who chooses to terminate her pregnancy." _McRae,_ 448 U.S., at 315. Just as Congress' refusal to fund abortions in _McRae_ left "an indigent woman with at least the same range of choice in deciding whether to obtain a medically necessary abortion as she would have had if Congress had chosen to subsidize no health care costs at all," _id.,_ at 317, Missouri's refusal to allow public employees to perform abortions in public hospitals leaves a pregnant woman with the same choices as if the State had chosen not to operate any public hospitals at all. The challenged provisions only restrict a woman's ability to obtain an abortion to the extent that she chooses to use a physician affiliated with a public hospital. This circumstance is more easily remedied, and thus considerably less burdensome, than indigency, which "may make it difficult—and in some cases, perhaps, impossible—for some women to have abortions" without public funding. _Maher,_ 432 U.S., at 474. Having held that the State's refusal to fund abortions does not violate *Roe* v. *Wade,* it strains logic to reach a contrary result for the use of public facilities and employees. If the State may "make a value judgment favoring childbirth over abortion and . . . implement that judgment by the allocation of public funds," *Maher, supra,* at 474, surely it may do so through the allocations of other public resources, such as hospitals and medical staff.

The Court of Appeals sought to distinguish our cases on the additional ground that "[t]he evidence here showed that all of the public facility's costs in providing abortion services are recouped when the patient pays." 851 F. 2d, at 1083. Absent any expenditure of public funds, the court thought that Missouri was "expressing" more than "its preference for childbirth over abortions," but rather was creating an "obstacle to exercise of the right to choose an abortion [that could not] stand absent a compelling state interest." *Ibid.* We disagree.

"Constitutional concerns are greatest," we said in *Maher, supra,* at 476, "when the State attempts to impose its will by the force of law; the State's power to encourage actions deemed to be in the public interest is necessarily far broader." Nothing in the Constitution requires States to enter or remain in the business of performing abortions. Nor, as appellees suggest, do private physicians and their patients have some kind of constitutional right of access to public facilities for the performance of abortions. Brief for Appellees 46–47. Indeed, if the State does recoup all of its costs in performing abortions, and no state subsidy, direct or indirect, is available, it is difficult to see how any procreational choice is burdened by the State's ban on the use of its facilities or employees for performing abortions.[8]

Maher, Poelker, and *McRae* all support the view that the State need not commit any resources to facilitating abortions, even if it can turn a profit by doing so. In *Poelker,* the suit was filed by an indigent who could not afford to pay for an abortion, but the ban on the performance of nontherapeutic abortions in city-owned hospitals applied whether or not the pregnant woman could pay. 432 U.S., at 520; *id.,* at 524 (BRENNAN, J., dissenting).[9] The Court emphasized that the mayor's decision to prohibit abortions in city hospitals was "subject to public debate and approval or disapproval at the polls," and that "the Constitution does not forbid a State or city, pursuant to democratic processes, from expressing a preference for normal childbirth as St. Louis has done." *Id.,* at 521. Thus we uphold the Act's restrictions on the use of public employees and facilities for the performance or assistance of nontherapeutic abortions.

C

The Missouri Act contains three provisions relating to "encouraging or counseling a woman to have an abortion not necessary to save her life." Section 188.205 states that no public funds can be used for this purpose; § 188.210 states that public employees cannot, within the scope of their employment, engage in such speech;

---

8. A different analysis might apply if a particular State had socialized medicine and all of its hospitals and physicians were publicly funded. This case might also be different if the State barred doctors who performed abortions in private facilities from the use of public facilities for any purpose. See *Harris* v. *McRae,* 448 U.S. 297, 317, n. 19 (1980).

9. The suit in *Poelker* was brought by the plaintiff "on her own behalf and on behalf of the entire class of pregnant women residents of the City of St. Louis, Missouri, desiring to utilize the personnel, facilities and services of the general public hospitals within the City of St. Louis for the termination of pregnancies." *Doe* v. *Poelker,* 497 F. 2d 1063, 1065 (CA8 1974).

and § 188.215 forbids such speech in public facilities. The Court of Appeals did not consider § 188.205 separately from §§ 188.210 and 188.215. It held that all three of these provisions were unconstitutionally vague, and that "the ban on using public funds, employees, and facilities to encourage or counsel a woman to have an abortion is an unacceptable infringement of the woman's fourteenth amendment right to choose an abortion after receiving the medical information necessary to exercise the right knowingly and intelligently." 851 F. 2d, at 1079.[10]

Missouri has chosen only to appeal the Court of Appeals' invalidation of the public funding provision, § 188.205. See Juris. Statement I–II. A threshold question is whether this provision reaches primary conduct, or whether it is simply an instruction to the State's fiscal officers not to allocate funds for abortion counseling. We accept, for purposes of decision, the State's claim that § 188.205 "is not directed at the conduct of any physician or health care provider, private or public," but "is directed solely at those persons responsible for expending public funds." Brief for Appellants 43.[11]

Appellees contend that they are not "adversely" affected under the State's interpretation of § 188.205, and therefore that there is no longer a case or controversy before us on this question. Brief for Appellees 31–32. Plaintiffs are masters of their complaints and remain so at the appellate stage of a litigation. See *Caterpillar Inc. v. Williams,* 482 U.S. 386, 398–399 (1987). A majority of the Court agrees with appellees that the controversy over § 188.205 is now moot, because appellees' argument amounts to a decision to no longer seek a declaratory judgment that § 188.205 is unconstitutional and accompanying declarative relief. See *Deakins* v. *Monaghan,* 484 U.S. 193, 199–201 (1988); *United States* v. *Munsingwear, Inc.,* 340 U.S. 36, 39–40 (1950). We accordingly direct the Court of Appeals to vacate the judgment of the District Court with instructions to dismiss the relevant part of the complaint. *Deakins,* 484 U.S., at 200. "Because this [dispute] was rendered moot in part by [appellees'] willingness permanently to withdraw their equitable claims from their federal action, a dismissal with prejudice indicated." *Ibid.*

D

Section 188.029 of the Missouri Act provides:

"Before a physician performs an abortion on a woman he has reason to believe is carrying an unborn child of twenty or more weeks gestational age, the physician shall first determine if the unborn child is viable by using and exercising that degree of care, skill, and proficiency commonly exercised by the ordinarily skillful, careful, and prudent physician engaged in similar practice under the same or

10. In a separate opinion, Judge Arnold argued that Missouri's prohibition violated the First Amendment because it "sharply discriminate[s] between kinds of speech on the basis of their viewpoint: a physician, for example, could discourage an abortion, or counsel against it, while in a public facility, but he or she could not encourage or counsel in favor of it." 851 F. 2d, at 1085.

11. While the Court of Appeals did not address this issue, the District Court thought that the definition of "public funds" in Mo. Rev. Stat. § 188.200 (1986) "certainly is broad enough to make 'encouraging or counseling' unlawful for anyone who is paid from" public funds as defined in § 188.200. 662 F. Supp. 407, 426 (WD Mo. 1987).

similar conditions. In making this determination of viability, the physician shall perform or cause to be performed such medical examinations and tests as are necessary to make a finding of the gestational age, weight, and lung maturity of the unborn child and shall enter such findings and determination of viability in the medical record of the mother."[12]

As with the preamble, the parties disagree over the meaning of this statutory provision. The State emphasizes the language of the first sentence, which speaks in terms of the physician's determination of viability being made by the standards of ordinary skill in the medical profession. Brief for Appellants 32–35. Appellees stress the language of the second sentence, which prescribes such "tests as are necessary" to make a finding of gestational age, fetal weight, and lung maturity. Brief for Appellees 26–30.

The Court of Appeals read § 188.029 as requiring that after 20 weeks "doctors *must* perform tests to find gestational age, fetal weight and lung maturity." 851 F. 2d, at 1075, n. 5. The court indicated that the tests needed to determine fetal weight at 20 weeks are "unreliable and inaccurate" and would add $125 to $250 to the cost of an abortion. *Ibid.* It also stated that "amniocentesis, the only method available to determine lung maturity, is contrary to accepted medical practice until 28–30 weeks of gestation, expensive, and imposes significant health risks for both the pregnant woman and the fetus." *Ibid.*

We must first determine the meaning of § 188.029 under Missouri law. Our usual practice is to defer to the lower court's construction of a state statute, but we believe the Court of Appeals has "fallen into plain error" in this case. *Frisby* v. *Schultz,* 487 U.S. 474, 483 (1988); see *Brockett* v. *Spokane Arcades, Inc.,* 472 U.S. 491, 500, n. 9 (1985). "'In expounding a statute, we must not be guided by a single sentence or member of a sentence, but look to the provisions of the whole law, and to its object and policy.'" *Philbrook* v. *Glodgett,* 421 U.S. 707, 713 (1975), quoting *United States* v. *Heirs of Boisdoré,* 8 How. 113, 122 (1849). See *Chemehuevi Tribe of Indians* v. *FPC,* 420 U.S. 395, 402–403 (1975); *Kokoszka* v. *Belford,* 417 U.S. 642, 650 (1974). The Court of Appeals' interpretation also runs "afoul of the well-established principle that statutes will be interpreted to avoid constitutional difficulties." *Frisby, supra,* at 483.

We think the viability-testing provision makes sense only if the second sentence is read to require only those tests that are useful to making subsidiary findings as to viability. If we construe this provision to require a physician to perform those tests needed to make the three specified findings *in all circumstances,* including when the physician's reasonable professional judgment indicates that the tests would be irrelevant to determining viability or even dangerous to the mother and the fetus, the second sentence of § 188.029 would conflict with the first sentence's *requirement* that a physician apply his reasonable professional skill and judgment. It would also be incongruous to read this provision, especially the word "necessary,"[13] to

---

12. The Act's penalty provision provides that "[a]ny person who contrary to the provisions of sections 188.010 to 188.085 knowingly performs . . . any abortion or knowingly fails to perform any action required by [these] sections . . . shall be guilty of a class A misdemeanor." Mo. Rev. Stat. § 188.075 (1986).

13. See Black's Law Dictionary 928 (5th ed. 1979) ("Necessary. This word must be considered in the connection in which it is used, as it is a word susceptible of various meanings. It

require the performance of tests irrelevant to the expressed statutory purpose of determining viability. It thus seems clear to us that the Court of Appeals' construction of § 188.029 violates well-accepted canons of statutory interpretation used in the Missouri courts, see *State ex rel. Stern Brothers & Co.* v. *Stilley,* 337 S. W. 2d 934, 939 (Mo. 1960) ("The basic rule of statutory construction is to first seek the legislative intention, and to effectuate it if possible, and the law favors constructions which harmonize with reason, and which tend to avoid unjust, absurd, unreasonable or confiscatory results, or oppression."); *Bell* v. *Mid-Century Ins. Co.,* 750 S. W. 2d 708, 710 (Mo. App. 1988) ("Interpreting the phrase literally would produce an absurd result, which the Legislature is strongly presumed not to have intended"), which JUSTICE BLACKMUN ignores. *Post,* at 545–546.

The viability-testing provision of the Missouri Act is concerned with promoting the State's interest in potential human life rather than in maternal health. Section 188.029 creates what is essentially a presumption of viability at 20 weeks, which the physician must rebut with tests indicating that the fetus is not viable prior to performing an abortion. It also directs the physician's determination as to viability by specifying consideration, if feasible, of gestational age, fetal weight, and lung capacity. The District Court found that "the medical evidence is uncontradicted that a 20-week fetus is *not* viable," and that "23 1/2 to 24 weeks gestation is the earliest point in pregnancy where a reasonable possibility of viability exists." 662 F. Supp., at 420. But it also found that there may be a 4-week error in estimating gestational age, *id.,* at 421, which supports testing at 20 weeks.

In *Roe* v. *Wade,* the Court recognized that the State has "important and legitimate" interests in protecting maternal health and in the potentiality of human life. 410 U.S., at 162. During the second trimester, the State "may, if it chooses, regulate the abortion procedure in ways that are reasonably related to maternal health." *Id.,* at 164. After viability, when the State's interest in potential human life was held to become compelling, the State "may, if it chooses, regulate, and even proscribe, abortion except where it is necessary, in appropriate medical judgment, for the preservation of the life or health of the mother." *Id.,* at 165.[14]

In *Colautti* v. *Franklin,* 439 U.S. 379 (1979), upon which appellees rely, the Court held that a Pennsylvania statute regulating the standard of care to be used by a physician performing an abortion of a possibly viable fetus was void for vagueness. *Id.,* at 390–401. But in the course of reaching that conclusion, the Court reaffirmed

---

may import absolute physical necessity or inevitability, or it may import that which is only convenient, useful, appropriate, suitable, proper, or conducive to the end sought").

14. The Court's subsequent cases have reflected this understanding. See *Colautti* v. *Franklin,* 439 U.S. 379, 386 (1979) (emphasis added) ("For both logical and biological reasons, we indicated in [in *Roe*] that the State's interest in the potential life of the fetus reaches the compelling point at the stage of viability. Hence, *prior to viability, the State may not seek to further this interest by directly restricting a woman's decision whether or not to terminate her pregnancy*"); *id.,* at 389 ("Viability is the critical point. And we have recognized no attempt to stretch the point of viability one way or the other"); accord, *Planned Parenthood of Central Mo.* v. *Danforth,* 428 U.S., at 61 (State regulation designed to protect potential human life limited to period "subsequent to viability"); *Akron* v. *Akron Center for Reproductive Health, Inc.,* 462 U.S. 416, 428 (1983), quoting *Roe* v. *Wade,* 410 U.S., at 163 (emphasis added) (State's interest in protecting potential human life "becomes compelling *only* at viability, the point at which the fetus 'has the capability of meaningful life outside the mother's womb'").

its earlier statement in *Planned Parenthood of Central Mo.* v. *Danforth,* 428 U.S. 52, 64 (1976), that "the determination of whether a particular fetus is viable is, and must be, a matter for the judgment of the responsible attending physician.'" 439 U.S., at 396. JUSTICE BLACKMUN, *post,* at 545, n. 6, ignores the statement in *Colautti* that "neither the legislature nor the courts may proclaim one of the elements entering into the ascertainment of viability—be it weeks of gestation or fetal weight or any other single factor—as the determinant of when the State has a compelling interest in the life or health of the fetus." 439 U.S., at 388–389. To the extent that § 188.029 regulates the method for determining viability, it undoubtedly does superimpose state regulation on the medical determination whether a particular fetus is viable. The Court of Appeals and the District Court thought it unconstitutional for this reason. 851 F. 2d, at 1074–1075; 662 F. Supp., at 423. To the extent that the viability tests increase the cost of what are in fact second-trimester abortions, their validity may also be questioned under *Akron,* 462 U.S., at 434–435, where the Court held that a requirement that second-trimester abortions must be performed in hospitals was invalid because it substantially increased the expense of those procedures.

We think that the doubt cast upon the Missouri statute by these cases is not so much a flaw in the statute as it is a reflection of the fact that the rigid trimester analysis of the course of a pregnancy enunciated in *Roe* has resulted in subsequent cases like *Colautti* and *Akron* making constitutional law in this area a virtual Procrustean bed. Statutes specifying elements of informed consent to be provided abortion patients, for example, were invalidated if they were thought to "structur[e] . . . the dialogue between the woman and her physician." *Thornburgh* v. *American College of Obstetricians and Gynecologists,* 476 U.S. 747, 763 (1986). As the dissenters in *Thornburgh* pointed out, such a statute would have been sustained under any traditional standard of judicial review, *id.,* at 802 (WHITE, J., dissenting), or for any other surgical procedure except abortion. *Id.,* at 783 (Burger, C. J. dissenting).

Stare decisis is a cornerstone of our legal system, but it has less power in constitutional cases, where, save for constitutional amendments, this Court is the only body able to make needed changes. See *United States* v. *Scott,* 437 U.S. 82, 101 (1978). We have not refrained from reconsideration of a prior construction of the Constitution that has proved "unsound in principle and unworkable in practice." *Garcia* v. *San Antonio Metropolitan Transit Authority,* 469 U.S. 528, 546 (1985); see *Solorio* v. *United States,* 483 U.S. 435, 448–450 (1987); *Erie R. Co.* v. *Tompkins,* 304 U.S. 64, 74–78 (1938). We think the *Roe* trimester framework falls into that category.

In the first place, the rigid *Roe* framework is hardly consistent with the notion of a Constitution cast in general terms, as ours is, and usually speaking in general principles, as ours does. The key elements of the *Roe* framework—trimesters and viability—are not found in the text of the Constitution or in any place else one would expect to find a constitutional principle. Since the bounds of the inquiry are essentially indeterminate, the result has been a web of legal rules that have become increasingly intricate, resembling a code of regulations rather than a body of constitutional doctrine.[15] As JUSTICE WHITE has put it, the trimester framework has left this Court to serve as the country's "*ex officio* medical board with powers to approve

---

15. For example, the Court has held that a State may require that certain information be given to a woman by a physician or his assistant, *Akron* v. *Akron Center for Reproductive Health, Inc.,* 462 U.S., at 448, but that it may not require that such information be furnished to her

or disapprove medical and operative practices and standards throughout the United States." *Planned Parenthood of Central Mo.* v. *Danforth,* 428 U.S., at 99 (opinion concurring in part and dissenting in part). Cf. *Garcia, supra,* at 547.

In the second place, we do not see why the State's interest in protecting potential human life should come into existence only at the point of viability, and that there should therefore be a rigid line allowing state regulation after viability but prohibiting it before viability. The dissenters in *Thornburgh,* writing in the context of the *Roe* trimester analysis, would have recognized this fact by positing against the "fundamental right" recognized in *Roe* the State's "compelling interest" in protecting potential human life throughout pregnancy. "[T]he State's interest, if compelling after viability, is equally compelling before viability." *Thornburgh,* 476 U.S., at 795 (WHITE, J., dissenting); see *id.,* at 828 (O'CONNOR, J., dissenting) ("State has compelling interests in ensuring maternal health and in protecting potential human life, and these interests exist 'throughout pregnancy'") (citation omitted).

The tests that § 188.029 requires the physician to perform are designed to determine viability. The State here has chosen viability as the point at which its interest in potential human life must be safeguarded. See Mo. Rev. Stat. § 188.030 (1986) ("No abortion of a viable unborn child shall be performed unless necessary to preserve the life or health of the woman"). It is true that the tests in question increase the expense of abortion, and regulate the discretion of the physician in determining the viability of the fetus. Since the tests will undoubtedly show in many cases that the fetus is not viable, the tests will have been performed for what were in fact second-trimester abortions. But we are satisfied that the requirement of these tests permissibly furthers the State's interest in protecting potential human life, and we therefore believe § 188.029 to be constitutional.

JUSTICE BLACKMUN takes us to task for our failure to join in a "great issues" debate as to whether the Constitution includes an "unenumerated" general right to privacy as recognized in cases such as *Griswold* v. *Connecticut,* 381 U.S. 479 (1965), and *Roe.* But *Griswold* v. *Connecticut,* unlike *Roe,* did not purport to adopt a whole framework, complete with detailed rules and distinctions, to govern the cases in which the asserted liberty interest would apply. As such, it was far different from the opinion, if not the holding, of *Roe* v. *Wade,* which sought to establish a constitutional framework for judging state regulation of abortion during the entire term of pregnancy. That framework sought to deal with areas of medical practice traditionally subject to state regulation, and it sought to balance once and for all by reference only to the calendar the claims of the State to protect the fetus as a form of human life against the claims of a woman to decide for herself whether or not to abort a fetus she was carrying. The experience of the Court in applying *Roe* v. *Wade* in later cases, see *supra,* at 518, n. 15, suggests to us that there is wisdom in not unnecessarily attempting to elabo-

---

only by the physician himself. *Id.,* at 449. Likewise, a State may require that abortions in the second trimester be performed in clinics, *Simopoulos* v. *Virginia,* 462 U.S. 506 (1983), but it may not require that such abortions be performed only in hospitals. *Akron, supra,* at 437–439. We do not think these distinctions are of any constitutional import in view of our abandonment of the trimester framework. JUSTICE BLACKMUN's claim, *post,* at 539–541, n. 1, that the State goes too far, even under *Maher* v. *Roe,* 432 U.S. 464 (1977); *Poelker* v. *Doe,* 432 U.S. 519 (1977); and *Harris* v. *McRae,* 448 U.S. 297 (1980), by refusing to permit the use of public facilities, as defined in Mo. Rev. Stat. § 188.200 (1986), for the performance of abortions is another example of the fine distinctions endemic in the *Roe* framework.

rate the abstract differences between a "fundamental right" to abortion, as the Court described it in *Akron,* 462 U.S. at 420, n. 1, a "limited fundamental constitutional right," which Justice Blackmun today treats *Roe* as having established, *post,* at 555, or a liberty interest protected by the Due Process Clause, which we believe it to be. The Missouri testing requirement here is reasonably designed to ensure that abortions are not performed where the fetus is viable—an end which all concede is legitimate—and that is sufficient to sustain its constitutionality.

Justice Blackmun also accuses us, *inter alia,* of cowardice and illegitimacy in dealing with "the most politically divisive domestic legal issue of our time." *Post,* at 559. There is no doubt that our holding today will allow some governmental regulation of abortion that would have been prohibited under the language of cases such as *Colautti* v. *Franklin,* 439 U.S. 379 (1979), and *Akron* v. *Akron Center for Reproductive Health, Inc., supra.* But the goal of constitutional adjudication is surely not to remove inexorably "politically divisive" issues from the ambit of the legislative process, whereby the people through their elected representatives deal with matters of concern to them. The goal of constitutional adjudication is to hold true the balance between that which the Constitution puts beyond the reach of the democratic process and that which it does not. We think we have done that today. Justice Blackmun's suggestion, *post,* at 538, 557–558, that legislative bodies, in a Nation where more than half of our population is women, will treat our decision today as an invitation to enact abortion regulation reminiscent of the dark ages not only misreads our views but does scant justice to those who serve in such bodies and the people who elect them.

III

Both appellants and the United States as *Amicus Curiae* have urged that we overrule our decision in *Roe* v. *Wade.* Brief for Appellants 12–18; Brief for United States as *Amicus Curiae* 8–24. The facts of the present case, however, differ from those at issue in *Roe.* Here, Missouri has determined that viability is the point at which its interest in potential human life must be safeguarded. In *Roe,* on the other hand, the Texas statute criminalized the performance of *all* abortions, except when the mother's life was at stake. 410 U.S., at 117–118. This case therefore affords us no occasion to revisit the holding of *Roe,* which was that the Texas statute unconstitutionally infringed the right to an abortion derived from the Due Process Clause, *id.,* at 164, and we leave it undisturbed. To the extent indicated in our opinion, we would modify and narrow *Roe* and succeeding cases.

Because none of the challenged provisions of the Missouri Act properly before us conflict with the Constitution, the judgment of the Court of Appeals is

Reversed.

Justice O'Connor, concurring in part and concurring in the judgment.

I concur in Parts I, II–A, II–B, and II–C of the Court's opinion.

I

Nothing in the record before us or the opinions below indicates that subsections 1(1) and 1(2) of the preamble to Missouri's abortion regulation statute will affect a woman's decision to have an abortion. Justice Stevens, following appellees, see Brief for Appellees 22, suggests that the preamble may also "interfer[e] with contraceptive choices," *post,* at 564, because certain contraceptive devices act on a female ovum after it has been fertilized by a male sperm. The Missouri Act defines "conception" as "the fertilization of the ovum of a female by a sperm of a male," Mo. Rev. Stat. § 188.015(3) (1986), and invests "unborn children" with "protectable interests in life, health, and well-being," § 1.205.1(2), from "the moment of conception . . . ." § 1.205.3 JUSTICE STEVENS asserts that any possible interference with a woman's right to use such postfertilization contraceptive devices would be unconstitutional under *Griswold* v. *Connecticut,* 381 U.S. 479 (1965), and our subsequent contraception cases. *Post,* at 564–566. Similarly, certain *amici* suggest that the Missouri Act's preamble may prohibit the developing technology of *in vitro* fertilization, a technique used to aid couples otherwise unable to bear children in which a number of ova are removed from the woman and fertilized by male sperm. This process often produces excess fertilized ova ("unborn children" under the Missouri Act's definition) that are discarded rather than reinserted into the woman's uterus. Brief for Association of Reproductive Health Professionals et al. as *Amici Curiae* 38. It may be correct that the use of postfertilization contraceptive devices is constitutionally protected by *Griswold* and its progeny, but, as with a woman's abortion decision, nothing in the record or the opinions below indicates that the preamble will affect a woman's decision to practice contraception. For that matter, nothing in appellees' original complaint, App. 8–21, or their motion *in limine* to limit testimony and evidence on their challenge to the preamble, *id.,* at 57–59, indicates that appellees sought to enjoin potential violations of *Griswold.* Neither is there any indication of the possibility that the preamble might be applied to prohibit the performance of *in vitro* fertilization. I agree with the court therefore, that all of these intimations of unconstitutionality are simply too hypothetical to support the use of declaratory judgment procedures and injunctive remedies in this case.

Similarly, it seems to me to follow directly from our previous decisions concerning state or federal funding of abortions, *Harris* v. *McRae,* 448 U.S. 297 (1980), *Maher* v. *Roe,* 432 U.S. 464 (1977), and *Poelker* v. *Doe,* 432 U.S. 519 (1977), that appellees' facial challenge to the constitutionality of Missouri's ban on the utilization of public facilities and the participation of public employees in the performance of abortions not necessary to save the life of the mother, Mo. Rev. Stat. §§ 188.210, 188.215 (1986), cannot succeed. Given Missouri's definition of "public facility" as "any public institution, public facility, public equipment, or any physical asset owned, leased, or controlled by this state or any agency or political subdivisions thereof," § 188.200(2), there may be conceivable applications of the ban on the use of public facilities that would be unconstitutional. Appellees and *amici* suggest that the State could try to enforce the ban against private hospitals using public water and sewage lines, or against private hospitals leasing state-owned equipment or state land. See Brief for Appellees 49–50; Brief for National Association of Public Hospitals as *Amicus Curiae* 9–12. Whether some or all of these or other applications of § 188.215 would be constitutional need not be decided here. *Maher, Poelker,* and *McRae* stand for the proposition that some quite straightforward applications of the Missouri ban on the use of public facilities for performing abortions would be constitutional and that is enough to defeat appellees' assertion that the ban is facially unconstitutional. "A facial challenge to a legislative Act is, of course, the most difficult challenge to mount successfully, since the challenger must establish that no set of circumstances exists under which the Act would be valid. The fact that the [relevant statute] might operate unconstitutionally under some conceivable set of circumstances is insufficient to render it wholly invalid, since we have not recognized an 'overbreadth' doctrine outside the limited context of the First Amendment." *United States* v. *Salerno,* 481 U.S. 739, 745 (1987).

I also agree with the Court that, under the interpretation of § 188.205 urged by the State and adopted by the Court, there is no longer a case or controversy before us over the constitutionality of that provision. I would note, however, that this interpretation of § 188.205 is not binding on the Supreme Court of Missouri which has the final word on the meaning of that State's statutes. *Virginia* v. *American Booksellers Assn., Inc.,* 484 U.S. 383, 395 (1988); *O'Brien* v. *Skinner,* 414 U.S. 524, 531 (1974). Should it happen that § 188.205, as ultimately interpreted by the Missouri Supreme Court, does prohibit publicly employed health professionals from giving specific medical advice to pregnant women, "the vacation and dismissal of the complaint that has become moot 'clears the path for future relitigation of the issues between the parties,' should subsequent events rekindle their controversy." *Deakins* v. *Monaghan,* 484 U.S. 193, 201, n. 5 (1988), quoting *United States* v. *Munsingwear, Inc.,* 340 U.S. 36, 40 (1950). Unless such events make their appearance and give rise to relitigation, I agree that we and all federal courts are without jurisdiction to hear the merits of this moot dispute.

II

In its interpretation of Missouri's "determination of viability" provision, Mo. Rev. Stat. § 188.029 (1986), see *ante,* at 513–521, the plurality has proceeded in a manner unnecessary to deciding the question at hand. I agree with the plurality that it was plain error for the Court of Appeals to interpret the second sentence of § 188.029 as meaning that "doctors *must* perform tests to find gestational age, fetal weight and lung maturity." 851 F. 2d, at 1075, n. 5 (emphasis in original). When read together with the first sentence of § 188.029—which requires a physician to "determine if the unborn child is viable by using and exercising that degree of care, skill, and proficiency commonly exercised by the ordinary skillful, careful, and prudent physician engaged in similar practice under the same or similar conditions"—it would be contradictory nonsense to read the second sentence as requiring a physician to perform viability examinations and tests in situations where it would be careless and imprudent to do so. The plurality is quite correct: "the viability-testing provision makes sense only if the second sentence is read to require only those tests that are useful to making subsidiary findings as to viability," *ante,* at 514, and, I would add, only those examinations and tests that it would not be imprudent or careless to perform in the particular medical situation before the physician.

Unlike the plurality, I do not understand these viability testing requirements to conflict with any of the Court's past decisions concerning state regulation of abortion. Therefore, there is no necessity to accept the State's invitation to reexamine the constitutional validity of *Roe* v. *Wade,* 410 U.S. 113 (1973). Where there is no need to decide a constitutional question, it is a venerable principle of this Court's adjudicatory processes not to do so, for "[t]he Court will not 'anticipate a question of constitutional law in advance of the necessity of deciding it.'" *Ashwander* v. *TVA,* 297 U.S. 288, 346 (1936) (Brandeis, J., concurring), quoting *Liverpool, New York and Philadelphia S. S. Co.* v. *Commissioners of Emigration,* 113 U.S. 33, 39 (1885). Neither will it generally "formulate a rule of constitutional law broader than is required by the precise facts to which it is to be applied." 297 U.S., at 347. Quite simply, "[i]t is not the habit of the court to decide questions of a constitutional nature unless absolutely necessary to a decision of the case." *Burton* v. *United States*, 196 U.S. 283, 295 (1905). The Court today has accepted the State's every interpretation of its abortion statute and has upheld, under our existing precedents, every provision of that statute which is properly before us. Precisely for this reason reconsideration of *Roe* falls not into any "good-cause exception" to this "fundamental rule of judicial restraint . . . ." *Three Affiliated Tribes of Fort Berthold Reservation* v. *Wold Engineering, P. C.,* 467 U.S. 138, 157 (1984). See *post,* at 532–533 (SCALIA, J., concurring in part and concurring in judgment). When the constitutional invalidity of a State's abortion statute actually turns on the constitutional validity of *Roe* v. *Wade,* there will be time enough to reexamine *Roe.* And to do so carefully.

In assessing § 188.029 it is especially important to recognize that appellees did not appeal the District Court's ruling that the first sentence of § 188.029 is constitutional. 662 F. Supp., at 420–422. There is, accordingly, no dispute between the parties before us over the constitutionality of the "presumption of viability at 20 weeks," *ante,* at 515, created by the first sentence of § 188.029. If anything might arguably conflict with the Court's previous decisions concerning the determination of viability, I would think it is the introduction of this presumption. The plurality, see *ante,* at 515, refers to a passage from *Planned Parenthood of Central Mo.* v. *Danforth,* 428 U.S. 52, 64 (1976): "The time when viability is achieved may vary with each pregnancy, and the determination of whether a particular fetus is viable is, and must be, a matter for the judgment of the responsible attending physician." The 20-week presumption of viability in the first sentence of § 188.029, it could be argued (though, I would think, unsuccessfully), restricts "the judgment of the responsible attending physician," by imposing on that physician the burden of overcoming the presumption. This presumption may be a "superimpos[ition] [of] state regulation on the medical determination whether a particular fetus is viable," *ante,* at 517, but, if so, it is a restriction on the physician's judgment that is not before us. As the plurality properly interprets the second sentence of § 188.029, it does nothing more than delineate means by which the unchallenged 20-week presumption of viability may be overcome if those means are useful in doing so and can be prudently employed. Contrary to the plurality's suggestion, see *ante,* at 517, the District Court did not think the second sentence of § 188.029 unconstitutional for this reason. Rather, both the District Court and the Court of Appeals thought the second sentence to be unconstitutional precisely because they interpreted that sentence to impose state regulation on the determination of viability that it does not impose.

Appellees suggest that the interpretation of § 188.029 urged by the State may "virtually eliminat[e] the constitutional issue in this case." Brief for Appellees 30. Appellees therefore propose that we should abstain from deciding that provision's constitutionality "in order to allow the state courts to render the saving construction the State has proposed." *Ibid.* Where the lower court has so clearly fallen into error I do not think abstention is necessary or prudent. Accordingly, I consider the constitutionality of the second sentence of § 188.029, as interpreted by the State, to determine whether the constitutional issue is actually eliminated.

I do not think the second sentence of § 188.029, as interpreted by the Court, imposes a degree of state regulation on the medical determination of viability that in any way conflicts with prior decisions of this Court. As the plurality recognizes, the requirement that, where not imprudent, physicians perform examinations and tests useful to making subsidiary findings to determine viability "promot[es] the State's interest in potential human life rather than in maternal health." *Ante,* at 515. No decision of this Court has held that the State may not directly promote its interest in potential life when viability is possible. Quite the contrary. In *Thornburgh* v. *American College of Obstetricians and Gynecologists,* 476 U.S. 747 (1986), the Court considered a constitutional challenge to a Pennsylvania statute requiring that a second physician be present during an abortion performed "when viability is possible." *Id.,* at 769–770. For guidance, the Court looked to the earlier decision in *Planned Parenthood Assn. of Kansas City, Mo., Inc.* v. *Ashcroft,* 462 U.S. 476 (1983), upholding a Missouri statute requiring the presence of a second physician during an abortion performed after viability. *Id.,* at 482–486 (opinion of Powell, J.); *id.,* at 505 (O'CONNOR, J., concurring in judgment in part and dissenting in part). The *Thornburgh* majority struck down the Pennsylvania statute merely because the statute had no exception for emergency situations and not because it found a constitutional difference between the State's promotion of its interest in potential life when viability is possible and when viability is certain. 476 U.S., at 770–771. Despite the clear recognition by the *Thornburgh* majority that the Pennsylvania and Missouri statutes differed in this respect, there is no hint in the opinion of the *Thornburgh* Court that the State's interest in potential life differs depending on whether it seeks to further that interest postviability or when viability is possible. Thus, all nine Members of the *Thornburgh* Court appear to have agreed that it is not constitutionally impermissible for the State to enact regulations designed to protect the State's interest in potential life when viability is possible. See *id.,* at 811 (WHITE, J., dissenting); *id.,* at 832 (O'CONNOR, J., dissenting). That is exactly what Missouri has done in § 188.029.

Similarly, the basis for reliance by the District Court and the Court of Appeals below on *Colautti* v. *Franklin,* 439 U.S. 379 (1979), disappears when § 188.029 is properly interpreted. In *Colautti* the Court observed:

> "Because this point [of viability] may differ with each pregnancy, neither the legislature nor the courts may proclaim one of the elements entering into the ascertainment of viability—be it weeks of gestation or fetal weight or any other single factor—as the determinant of when the State has a compelling interest in the life or health of the fetus. Viability is the critical point." *Id.,* at 388–389.

The courts below, on the interpretation of § 188.029 rejected here, found the second sentence of that provision at odds with this passage from *Colautti.* See 851 F. 2d, at 1074; 662 F. Supp., at 423. On this Court's interpretation of § 188.029 it is clear that Missouri has not substituted any of the "elements entering into the ascertainment of viability" as "the determinant of when the State has a compelling interest in the life or health of the fetus." All the second sentence of § 188.029 does is to require, when not imprudent, the performance of "those tests that are useful to making *subsidiary* findings as to viability." *Ante,* at 514 (emphasis added). Thus, consistent with *Colautti,* viability remains the "critical point" under § 188.029.

Finally, and rather half-heartedly, the plurality suggests that the marginal increase in the cost of an abortion created by Missouri's viability testing provision may make § 188.029, even as interpreted, suspect under this Court's decision in *Akron* v.

Akron Center for Reproductive Health, Inc., 462 U.S. 416, 434–439 (1983), striking down a second-trimester hospitalization requirement. See *ante*, at 517. I dissented from the Court's opinion in *Akron* because it was my view that, even apart from *Roe's* trimester framework which I continue to consider problematic, see *Thornburgh, supra,* at 828 (dissenting opinion), the *Akron* majority had distorted and misapplied its own standard for evaluating state regulation of abortion which the Court had applied with fair consistency in the past: that, previability, "a regulation imposed on a lawful abortion is not unconstitutional unless it unduly burdens the right to seek an abortion." *Akron, supra,* at 453 (dissenting opinion) (internal quotations omitted).

It is clear to me that requiring the performance of examinations and tests useful to determining whether a fetus is viable, when viability is possible, and when it would not be medically imprudent to do so, does not impose an undue burden on a woman's abortion decision. On this ground alone I would reject the suggestion that § 188.029 as interpreted is unconstitutional. More to the point, however, just as I see no conflict between § 188.029 and *Colautti* or any decision of this Court concerning a State's ability to give effect to its interest in potential life, I see no conflict between § 188.029 and the Court's opinion in *Akron*. The second-trimester hospitalization requirement struck down in *Akron* imposed, in the majority's view, "a heavy, and unnecessary, burden," 462 U.S., at 438, more than doubling the cost of "women's access to a relatively inexpensive, otherwise accessible, and safe abortion procedure." *Ibid.,* see also *id.,* at 434. By contrast, the cost of examinations and tests that could usefully and prudently be performed when a woman is 20–24 weeks pregnant to determine whether the fetus is viable would only marginally, if at all, increase the cost of an abortion. See Brief for American Association of Prolife Obstetricians and Gynecologists et al. as *Amici Curiae* 3 ("At twenty weeks gestation, an ultrasound examination to determine gestational age is standard medical practice. It is routinely provided by the plaintiff clinics. An ultrasound examination can effectively provide all three designated findings of sec. 188.029"); *id.,* at 22 ("A finding of fetal weight can be obtained from the same ultrasound test used to determine gestational age"); *id.,* at 25 ("There are a number of different methods in standard medical practice to determine fetal lung maturity at twenty or more weeks gestation. The most simple and most obvious is by inference. It is well known that fetal lungs do not mature until 33–34 weeks gestation . . . . If an assessment of the gestational age indicates that the child is less than thirty-three weeks, a general finding can be made that the fetal lungs are not mature. This finding can then be used by the physician in making his determination of viability under section 188.029"); cf. Brief for American Medical Association et al. as *Amici Curiae* 42 (no suggestion that fetal weight and gestational age cannot be determined from the same sonogram); *id.,* at 43 (another clinical test for gestational age and, by inference, fetal weight and lung maturity, is an accurate report of the last menstrual period), citing Smith, Frey, & Johnson, Assessing Gestational Age, 33 Am. Fam. Physician 215, 219–220 (1986).

Moreover, the examinations and tests required by § 188.029 are to be performed when viability is possible. This feature of § 188.029 distinguishes it from the second-trimester hospitalization requirement struck down by the *Akron* majority. As the Court recognized in *Thornburgh,* the State's compelling interest in potential life postviability renders its interest in determining the critical point of viability equally compelling. See *supra,* at 527–528. Under the Court's precedents, the same cannot be said for the *Akron* second-trimester hospitalization requirement. As I understand the Court's opinion in *Akron,* therefore, the plurality's suggestion today that *Akron* casts doubt on the validity of § 188.029, even as the Court has interpreted it, is without foundation and cannot provide a basis for reevaluating *Roe.* Accordingly, because the Court of Appeals misinterpreted § 188.029, and because, properly interpreted, § 188.029 is not inconsistent with any of this Court's prior precedents, I would reverse the decision of the Court of Appeals.

In sum, I concur in Parts I, II–A, II–B, and II–C of the Court's opinion and concur in the judgment as to Part II–D.

JUSTICE SCALIA, concurring in part and concurring in the judgment.

I join Parts I, II–A, II–B, and II–C of the opinion of the Court. As to Part II–D, I share JUSTICE BLACKMUN's view, *post,* at 556, that it effectively would overrule *Roe* v. *Wade,* 410 U.S. 113 (1973). I think that should be done, but would do it more explicitly. Since today we contrive to avoid doing it, and indeed to avoid almost any decision of national import, I need not set forth my reasons, some of which have been well recited in dissents of my colleagues in other cases. See, *e.g., Thornburgh* v. *American College of Obstetricians and Gynecologists,* 476 U.S. 747, 786–797 (1986) (WHITE, J., dissenting); *Akron* v. *Akron Center for Reproductive Health, Inc.,* 462 U.S. 416, 453–459 (1983) (O'CONNOR, J., dissenting); *Roe* v. *Wade, supra,* at 172–178 (REHNQUIST, J., dissenting); *Doe* v. *Bolton,* 410 U.S. 179, 221–223 (1973) (WHITE, J., dissenting).

The outcome of today's case will doubtless be heralded as a triumph of judicial statesmanship. It is not that, unless it is statesmanlike needlessly to prolong this Court's self-awarded sovereignty over a field where it has little proper business since the answers to most of the cruel questions posed are political and not juridical—a sovereignty which therefore quite properly, but to the great damage of the Court, makes it the object of the sort of organized public pressure that political institutions in a democracy ought to receive.

JUSTICE O'CONNOR's assertion, *ante,* at 526, that a "'fundamental rule of judicial restraint'" requires us to avoid reconsidering *Roe,* cannot be taken seriously. By finessing *Roe* we do not, as she suggests, *ante,* at 526, adhere to the strict and venerable rule that we should avoid "'decid[ing] questions of a constitutional nature.'" We have not disposed of this case on some statutory or procedural ground, but have decided, and could not avoid deciding, whether the Missouri statute meets the requirements of the United States Constitution. The only choice available is whether, in deciding that constitutional question, we should use *Roe* v. *Wade* as the benchmark, or something else. What is involved, therefore, is not the rule of avoiding constitutional issues where possible, but the quite separate principle that we will not "'formulate a rule of constitutional law broader than is required by the precise facts to which it is to be applied.'" *Ante,* at 526. The latter is a sound general principle, but one often departed from when good reason exists. Just this Term, for example, in an opinion authored by JUSTICE O'CONNOR, despite the fact that we had already held a racially based set-aside unconstitutional because unsupported by evidence of identified discrimination, which was all that was needed to decide the case, we went on to outline the criteria for properly tailoring race-based remedies in cases where such evidence is present. *Richmond* v. *J. A. Croson Co.,* 488 U.S. 469, 506–508 (1989). Also this Term, in an opinion joined by JUSTICE O'CONNOR, we announced the constitutional rule that deprivation of the right to confer with counsel during trial violates the Sixth Amendment even if no prejudice can be shown, despite our finding that there had been no such deprivation on the facts before us—which was all that was needed to decide that case. _Perry_ v. _Leeke,_ 488 U.S. 272, 278–280 (1989); see _id., at_ 285 (KENNEDY, J., concurring in part). I have not identified with certainty the first instance of our deciding a case on broader constitutional grounds than absolutely necessary, but it is assuredly no later than _Marbury_ v. _Madison,_ 1 Cranch 137 (1803), where we held that mandamus could constitutionally issue against the Secretary of State, although that was unnecessary given our holding that the law authorizing issuance of the mandamus by this Court was unconstitutional.

The Court has often spoken more broadly than needed in precisely the fashion at issue here, announcing a new rule of constitutional law when it could have reached the identical result by applying the rule thereby displaced. To describe two recent opinions that JUSTICE O'CONNOR joined: In _Daniels_ v. _Williams,_ 474 U.S. 327 (1986), we overruled our prior holding that a "deprivation" of liberty or property could occur through negligent governmental acts, ignoring the availability of the alternative constitutional ground that, even if a deprivation had occurred, the State's postdeprivation remedies satisfied due process, see _id.,_ at 340–343 (STEVENS, J., concurring in judgment). In _Illinois_ v. _Gates,_ 462 U.S. 213 (1983), we replaced the pre-existing "two-pronged" constitutional test for probable cause with a totality-of-the-circumstances approach, ignoring the concurrence's argument that the same outcome could have been reached under the old test, see _id.,_ at 267–272 (WHITE, J., concurring in judgment). It is rare, of course, that the court goes out of its way to _acknowledge_ that its judgment could have been reached under the old constitutional rule, making its adoption of the new one unnecessary to the decision, but even such explicit acknowledgment is not unheard of. See _Commonwealth Edison Co._ v. _Montana,_ 453 U.S. 609 (1981); _Perez_ v. _Campbell,_ 402 U.S. 637 (1971). For a sampling of other cases where the availability of a narrower, well-established ground is simply ignored in the Court's opinion adopting a new constitutional rule, though pointed out in separate opinions of some Justices, see _Michelin Tire Corp._ v. _Wages,_ 423 U.S. 276 (1976); _Pointer_ v. _Texas,_ 380 U.S. 400 (1965); and _Mapp_ v. _Ohio,_ 367 U.S. 643 (1961). It would be wrong, in any decision, to ignore the reality that our policy not to "formulate a rule of constitutional law broader than is required by the precise facts" has a frequently applied good-cause exception. But it seems particularly perverse to convert the policy into an absolute in the present case, in order to place beyond reach the inexpressibly "broader-than-was-required-by-the-precise-facts" structure established by _Roe_ v. _Wade._

The real question, then, is whether there are valid reasons to go beyond the most stingy possible holding today. It seems to me there are not only valid but compelling ones. Ordinarily, speaking no more broadly than is absolutely required avoids throwing settled law into confusion; doing so today preserves a chaos that is evident to anyone who can read and count. Alone sufficient to justify a broad holding is the fact that our retaining control, through _Roe,_ of what I believe to be, and many of our citizens recognize to be, a political issue, continuously distorts the public perception of the role of this Court. We can now look forward to at least another Term with carts full of mail from the public, and streets full of demonstrators, urging us—their unelected and life-tenured judges who have been awarded those extraordinary, undemocratic characteristics precisely in order that we might follow the law despite the popular will—to follow the popular will. Indeed, I expect we can look forward to even more of that than before, given our indecisive decision today. And if these reasons for taking the unexceptional course of reaching a broader holding are not enough, then consider the nature of the constitutional question we avoid: In most cases, we do no harm by not speaking more broadly than the decision requires. Anyone affected by the conduct that the avoided holding would have prohibited will be able to challenge it himself and have his day in court to make the argument. Not so with respect to the harm that many States believed, pre-*Roe*, and many may continue to believe, is caused by largely unrestricted abortion. That will continue to occur if the States have the constitutional power to prohibit it, and would do so, but we skillfully avoid telling them so. Perhaps those abortions cannot constitutionally be proscribed. That is surely an arguable question, the question that reconsideration of *Roe* v. *Wade* entails. But what is not at all arguable, it seems to me, is that we should decide now and not insist that we be run into a corner before we grudgingly yield up our judgment. The only sound reason for the latter course is to prevent a change in the law—but to think that desirable begs the question to be decided.

It was an arguable question today whether § 188.029 of the Missouri law contravened this Court's understanding of *Roe* v. *Wade,** and I would have examined *Roe* rather than examining the contravention. Given the Court's newly contracted abstemiousness, what will it take, one must wonder, to permit us to reach that fun-

---

*That question, compared with the question whether we should reconsider and reverse *Roe,* is hardly worth a footnote, but I think JUSTICE O'CONNOR answers that incorrectly as well. In *Roe* v. *Wade,* 410 U.S. 113, 165–166 (1973), we said that "the physician [has the right] to administer medical treatment according to his professional judgment up to the points where important state interests provide compelling justifications for intervention." We have subsequently made clear that it is also a matter of medical judgment when viability (one of those points) is reached. "The time when viability is achieved may vary with each pregnancy, and the determination of whether a particular fetus is viable is, and must be, a matter for the judgment of the responsible attending physician." *Planned Parenthood of Central Mo.* v. *Danforth,* 428 U.S. 52, 64 (1976). Section 188.029 conflicts with the purpose and hence the fair import of this principle because it will sometimes require a physician to perform tests that he would not otherwise have performed to determine whether a fetus is viable. It is therefore a legislative imposition on the judgment of the physician, and one that increases the cost of an abortion.

JUSTICE O'CONNOR would nevertheless uphold the law because it "does not impose an undue burden on a woman's abortion decision." *ante,* at 530. This conclusion is supported by the observation that the required tests impose only a marginal cost on the abortion procedure, far less of an increase than the cost-doubling hospitalization requirement invalidated in *Akron* v. *Akron Center for Reproductive Health, Inc.,* 462 U.S. 416 (1983). See *ante,* at 530–531. The fact that the challenged regulation is less costly than what we struck down in *Akron* tells us only that we cannot decide the present case on the basis of that earlier decision. It does not tell us whether the present requirement is an "undue burden," and I know of no basis for determining that this particular burden (or any other for that matter) is "due." One could with equal justification conclude that it is not. To avoid the question of *Roe* v. *Wade's* validity, with the attendant costs that this will have for the Court and for the principles of self-governance, on the basis of a standard that offers "no guide but the Court's own discretion," *Baldwin* v. *Missouri,* 281 U.S. 586, 595 (1930) (Holmes, J., dissenting), merely adds to the irrationality of what we do today.

Similarly irrational is the new concept that JUSTICE O'CONNOR introduces into the law in order to achieve her result, the notion of a State's "interest in potential life when viability is possible." *Ante,* at 528. Since "viability" means the mere *possibility* (not the certainty) of survivability outside the womb, "possible viability" must mean the possibility of a possibility of survivability outside the womb. Perhaps our next opinion will expand the third trimester into the second even further, by approving state action designed to take account of "the chance of possible viability."

damental question? The result of our vote today is that we will not reconsider that prior opinion, even if most of the Justices think it is wrong, unless we have before us a statute that in fact contradicts it—and even then (under our newly discovered "no-broader-than-necessary" requirement) only minor problematical aspects of *Roe* will be reconsidered, unless one expects state legislatures to adopt provisions whose compliance with *Roe* cannot even be argued with a straight face. It thus appears that the mansion of constitutionalized abortion-law, constructed overnight in *Roe* v. *Wade,* must be disassembled doorjamb by doorjamb, and never entirely brought down, no matter how wrong it may be.

Of the four courses we might have chosen today—to reaffirm *Roe,* to overrule it explicitly, to overrule it *sub silentio,* or to avoid the question—the last is the least responsible. On the question of the constitutionality of § 188.029, I concur in the judgment of the Court and strongly dissent from the manner in which it has been reached.

JUSTICE BLACKMUN, with whom JUSTICE BRENNAN and JUSTICE MARSHALL join, concurring in part and dissenting in part.

Today, *Roe* v. *Wade,* 410 U.S. 113 (1973), and the fundamental constitutional right of women to decide whether to terminate a pregnancy, survive but are not secure. Although the Court extricates itself from this case without making a single, even incremental, change in the law of abortion, the plurality and JUSTICE SCALIA would overrule *Roe* (the first silently, the other explicitly) and would return to the States virtually unfettered authority to control the quintessentially intimate, personal, and life-directing decision whether to carry a fetus to term. Although today, no less than yesterday, the Constitution and the decisions of this Court prohibit a State from enacting laws that inhibit women from the meaningful exercise of that right, a plurality of this Court implicitly invites every state legislature to enact more and more restrictive abortion regulations in order to provoke more and more test cases, in the hope that sometime down the line the Court will return the law of procreative freedom to the severe limitations that generally prevailed in this country before January 22, 1973. Never in my memory has a plurality announced a judgment of this Court that so foments disregard for the law and for our standing decisions.

Nor in my memory has a plurality gone about its business in such a deceptive fashion. At every level of its review, from its effort to read the real meaning out of the Missouri statute, to its intended evisceration of precedents and its deafening silence about the constitutional protections that it would jettison, the plurality obscures the portent of its analysis. With feigned restraint, the plurality announces that its analysis leaves *Roe* "undisturbed," albeit "modif[ied] and narrow[ed]." *Ante,* at 521. But this disclaimer is totally meaningless. The plurality opinion is filled with winks, and nods, and knowing glances to those who would do away with *Roe* explicitly, but turns a stone face to anyone in search of what the plurality conceives as the scope of a woman's right under the Due Process Clause to terminate a pregnancy free from the coercive and brooding influence of the State. The simple truth is that *Roe* would not survive the plurality's analysis, and that the plurality provides no substitute for *Roe's* protective umbrella.

I fear for the future. I fear for the liberty and equality of the millions of women who have lived and come of age in the 16 years since *Roe* was decided. I fear for the integrity of, and public esteem for, this Court.

I dissent.

I

THE CHIEF JUSTICE parades through the four challenged sections of the Missouri statute *seriatim*. I shall not do this, but shall relegate most of my comments as to those sections to the margin.[1] Although I disagree with the Court's consideration of §§ 1.205, 188.210, and 188.215, and am especially disturbed by its misapplica-

1. Contrary to the Court, I do not see how the preamble, § 1.205, realistically may be construed as "abortion-neutral." It declares that "[t]he life of each human being begins at conception" and that "[u]nborn children have protectable interests in life, health, and well-being." Mo. Rev. Stat. §§ 1.205.1(1) and (2) (1986). By the preamble's specific terms, these declarations apply to all of Missouri's laws which, in turn, are to be interpreted to protect the rights of the unborn to the fullest extent possible under the Constitution of the United States and the decisions of this Court. § 1.205.2. As the Court of Appeals concluded, the Missouri Legislature "intended its abortion regulations to be understood against the backdrop of its theory of life." 851 F. 2d 1071, 1076 (CA8 1988). I note the Solicitor General's acknowledgment that this backdrop places "a burden of uncertain scope on the performance of abortions by supplying a general principle that would fill in whatever interstices may be present in existing abortion precedents." Brief for United States as *Amicus Curiae* on behalf of appellants 8–9, n. 5.

In my view, a State may not expand indefinitely the scope of its abortion regulations by creating interests in fetal life that are limited solely by reference to the decisional law of this Court. Such a statutory scheme, whose scope is dependent on the uncertain and disputed limits of our holdings, will have the unconstitutional effect of chilling the exercise of a woman's right to terminate a pregnancy and of burdening the freedom of health professionals to provide abortion services. In this case, moreover, because the preamble defines fetal life as beginning upon "the fertilization of the ovum of a female by a sperm of a male," § 188.015(3), the provision also unconstitutionally burdens the use of contraceptive devices, such as the IUD and the "morning after" pill, which may operate to prevent pregnancy only after conception as defined in the statute. See Brief for Association of Reproductive Health Professionals et al. as *Amici Curiae* 30–39.

The Court upholds §§ 188.210 and 188.215 on the ground that the constitutionality of these provisions follows from our holdings in *Maher* v. *Roe*, 432 U.S. 464 (1977), *Poelker* v. *Doe*, 432 U.S. 519 (1977), and *Harris* v. *McRae*, 448 U.S. 297 (1980). There were strong dissents in all those cases.

Whatever one may think of *Maher, Poelker,* and *Harris,* however, they most certainly do not control this case, where the State not only has withdrawn from the business of abortion, but has taken affirmative steps to assure that abortions are not performed by *private* physicians in *private* institutions. Specifically, by defining "public facility" as "any public institution, public facility, public equipment, or any physical asset owned, leased, or controlled by this state or any agency or political subdivisions thereof," § 188.200, the Missouri statute prohibits the performance of abortions in institutions that in all pertinent respects are private, yet are located on property owned, leased, or controlled by the government. Thus, under the statute, no abortion may be performed at Truman Medical Center in Kansas City—where, in 1985, 97 percent of all Missouri hospital abortions at 16 weeks or later were performed—even though the Center is a private hospital, staffed primarily by private doctors, and administered by a private corporation: the Center is located on ground leased from a political subdivision of the State.

The sweeping scope of Missouri's "public facility" provision sharply distinguishes this case from *Maher, Poelker,* and *Harris.* In one of those cases, it was said: "The State may have made childbirth a more attractive alternative . . . but it . . . imposed no restriction on access to abortions that was not already there." *Maher,* 432 U.S., at 474. Missouri's public facility ban, by contrast, goes far beyond merely offering incentives in favor of childbirth (as in *Maher* and *Harris*), or a straightforward disassociation of state-owned institutions and personnel from abortion services (as in *Poelker*). Here, by defining as "public" every health-care institution with some connection to the State, no matter how attenuated, Missouri has brought to bear the full force of its economic power and control over essential facilities to discourage its citizens from exercising

tion of our past decisions in upholding Missouri's ban on the performance of abortions at "public facilities," its discussion of these provisions is merely prologue to the plurality's consideration of the statute's viability-testing requirement, § 188.029—the only section of the Missouri statute that the plurality construes as implicating _Roe_ itself. There, tucked away at the end of its opinion, the plurality suggests a radical reversal of the law of abortion; and there, primarily, I direct my attention.

In the plurality's view, the viability-testing provision imposes a burden on second-trimester abortions as a way of furthering the State's interest in protecting the potential life of the fetus. Since under the _Roe_ framework, the State may not fully regulate abortion in the interest of potential life (as opposed to maternal health) until the third trimester, the plurality finds it necessary, in order to save the Missouri testing provision, to throw out _Roe's_ trimester framework. _Ante,_ at 518–520. In flat contradiction to _Roe,_ 410 U.S., at 163, the plurality concludes that the State's interest in potential life is compelling before viability, and upholds the testing provision because it "permissibly furthers" that state interest. _Ante,_ at 519.

A

At the outset, I note that in its haste to limit abortion rights, the plurality compounds the errors of its analysis by needlessly reaching out to address constitutional questions that are not actually presented. The conflict between § 188.029 and _Roe's_ trimester framework, which purportedly drives the plurality to reconsider our past decisions, is a contrived conflict: the product of an aggressive misreading

---

their constitutional rights, even where the State itself could never be understood as authorizing, supporting, or having any other positive association with the performance of an abortion. See R. Dworkin, The Great Abortion Case, New York Review of Books, June 29, 1989, p. 49.

The difference is critical. Even if the State may decline to subsidize or to participate in the exercise of a woman's right to terminate a pregnancy, and even if a State may pursue its own abortion policies in distributing public benefits, it may not affirmatively constrict the availability of abortions by defining as "public" that which in all meaningful respects is private. With the certain knowledge that a substantial percentage of private health-care providers will fall under the public facility ban, see Brief for National Association of Public Hospitals as _Amicus Curiae_ 10–11, Missouri does not "leav[e] a pregnant woman with the same choices as if the State had chosen not to operate any public hospitals at all," _ante,_ at 509; rather, the public facility ban leaves the pregnant woman with far fewer choices, or, for those too sick or too poor to travel, perhaps no choice at all. This aggressive and shameful infringement on the right of women to obtain abortions in consultation with their chosen physicians, unsupported by any state interest, much less a compelling one, violates the command of _Roe._

Indeed, Justice O'Connor appears to recognize the constitutional difficulties presented by Missouri's "public facilities" ban, and rejects respondents' "facial" challenge to the provisions on the ground that a facial challenge cannot succeed where, as here, at least some applications of the challenged law are constitutional. _Ante,_ at 523–524. While I disagree with this approach, Justice O'Connor's writing explicitly leaves open the possibility that some applications of the "public facilities" ban may be unconstitutional, regardless of _Maher, Poelker,_ and _Harris._

I concur in Part II–C of Court's opinion, holding that respondents' challenge to § 188.205 is moot, although I note that the constitutionality of this provision might become the subject of relitigation between these parties should the Supreme Court of Missouri adopt an interpretation of the provision that differs from the one accepted here. See _Deakins v. Monaghan,_ 484 U.S. 193, 201, n. 5 (1988).

of the viability-testing requirement and a needlessly wooden application of the *Roe* framework.

The plurality's reading of § 188.029 is irreconcilable with the plain language of the statute and is in derogation of this Court's settled view that "'district courts and courts of appeals are better schooled in and more able to interpret the laws of their respective States.'" *Frisby* v. *Schultz*, 487 U.S. 474, 482 (1988), quoting *Brockett* v. *Spokane Arcades, Inc.*, 472 U.S. 491, 499–500 (1985). Abruptly setting aside the construction of § 188.029 adopted by both the District Court and Court of Appeals as "plain error," the plurality reads the viability–testing provision as requiring only that before a physician may perform an abortion on a woman whom he believes to be carrying a fetus of 20 or more weeks gestational age, the doctor must determine whether the fetus is viable and, as part of that exercise, must, to the extent feasible and consistent with sound medical practice, conduct tests necessary to make findings of gestational age, weight, and lung maturity. *Ante,* at 514–517. But the plurality's reading of the provision, according to which the statute requires the physician to perform tests only in order to determine *viability*, ignores the statutory language explicitly directing that "the physician *shall* perform or cause to be performed such medical examinations and tests as are *necessary to make a finding of the gestational age, weight, and lung maturity* of the unborn child and *shall* enter such findings" in the mother's medical record. § 188.029 (emphasis added). The statute's plain language requires the physician to undertake whatever tests are necessary to determine gestational age, weight, and lung maturity, regardless of whether these tests are necessary to a finding of viability, and regardless of whether the tests subject the pregnant woman or the fetus to additional health risks or add substantially to the cost of an abortion.[2]

Had the plurality read the statute as written, it would have had no cause to reconsider the *Roe* framework. As properly construed, the viability-testing provision does not pass constitutional muster under even a rational-basis standard, the least restrictive level of review applied by this Court. See *Williamson* v. *Lee Optical Co.*, 348 U.S. 483 (1955). By mandating tests to determine fetal weight and lung maturity for every fetus thought to be more than 20 weeks gestational age, the statute requires physicians to undertake procedures, such as amniocentesis, that, in the situation presented, have no medical justification, impose significant additional health risks on both the pregnant woman and the fetus, and bear no rational relation to the State's interest in protecting fetal life.[3] As written, § 188.029 is an arbitrary imposition of discomfort, risk, and expense, furthering no discernible interest except to make the procurement of an abortion as arduous and difficult as possible. Thus,

---

2. I consider irrefutable JUSTICE STEVENS' discussion of this interpretive point. See *post,* at 560–563.

3. The District Court found that "the only method to evaluate [fetal] lung maturity is by amniocentesis," a procedure that "imposes additional significant health risks for both the pregnant woman and the fetus." 662 F. Supp. 407, 422 (WD Mo. 1987). Yet the medical literature establishes that to require amniocentesis for all abortions after 20 weeks would be contrary to sound medical practice and, moreover, would be useless for the purpose of determining lung maturity until no earlier than between 28 and 30 weeks gestational age. *Ibid.;* see also Brief for American Medical Association et al. as *Amici Curiae* 41. Thus, were § 188.029 read to require a finding of lung maturity, it would require physicians to perform a highly intrusive procedure of risk that would yield no result relevant to the question of viability.

were it not for the plurality's tortured effort to avoid the plain import of § 188.029, it could have struck down the testing provision as patently irrational irrespective of the _Roe_ framework.[4]

The plurality eschews this straightforward resolution, in the hope of precipitating a constitutional crisis. Far from avoiding constitutional difficulty, the plurality attempts to engineer a dramatic retrenchment in our jurisprudence by exaggerating the conflict between its untenable construction of § 188.029 and the _Roe_ trimester framework.

No one contests that under the _Roe_ framework the State, in order to promote its interest in potential human life, may regulate and even proscribe nontherapeutic abortions once the fetus becomes viable. _Roe,_ 410 U.S., at 164–165. If, as the plurality appears to hold, the testing provision simply requires a physician to use appropriate and medically sound tests to determine whether the fetus is actually viable when the estimated gestational age is greater than 20 weeks (and therefore within what the District Court found to be the margin of error for viability, _ante,_ at 515–516), then I see little or no conflict with _Roe._[5] Nothing in _Roe,_ or any of its progeny, holds that a State may not effectuate its compelling interest in the potential life of a viable fetus by seeking to ensure that no viable fetus is mistakenly aborted because of the inherent lack of precision in estimates of gestational age. A requirement that a physician make a finding of viability, one way or the other, for every fetus that falls within the range of possible viability does no more than preserve the State's recognized authority. Although, as the plurality correctly points out, such a testing requirement would have the effect of imposing additional costs on second-trimester abortions where the tests indicated that the fetus was not viable, these costs would be merely incidental to, and a necessary accommodation of, the State's unquestioned right to prohibit nontherapeutic abortions after the point of viability. In short, the testing provision, as construed by the plurality, is consistent with the _Roe_ framework and could be upheld effortlessly under current doctrine.[6]

4. I also agree with the Court of Appeals, 851 F. 2d, at 1074–1075, that, as written, § 188.029 is contrary to this court's decision in _Colautti_ v. _Franklin,_ 439 U.S. 379, 388–389 (1979).

5. The plurality never states precisely its construction of § 188.029. I base my synopsis of the plurality's views mainly on its assertion that the entire provision must be read in light of its requirement that the physician act only in accordance with reasonable professional judgment, and that the provision imposes no requirement that a physician perform irrelevant or dangerous tests. _Ante,_ at 514–515. To the extent that the plurality may be reading the provision to require tests other than those that a doctor, exercising reasonable professional judgment, would deem necessary to a finding of viability, the provision bears no rational relation to a legitimate governmental interest, and cannot stand.

6. As convincingly demonstrated by Justice O'Connor, _ante,_ at 527–531, the cases cited by the plurality, are not to the contrary. As noted by the plurality, in both _Colautti_ v. _Franklin,_ 439 U.S., at 388–389, and _Planned Parenthood of Central Mo._ v. _Danforth,_ 428 U.S. 52 (1976), we stressed that the determination of viability is a matter for the judgment of the responsible attending physician. But § 188.029, at least as construed by the plurality, is consistent with this requirement. The provision does nothing to remove the determination of viability from the purview of the attending physician; it merely instructs the physician to make a finding of viability using tests to determine gestational age, weight, and lung maturity when such tests are feasible and medically appropriate.

I also see no conflict with the Court's holding in _Akron_ v. _Akron Center for Reproductive Health,_

How ironic it is, then, and disingenuous, that the plurality scolds the Court of Appeals for adopting a construction of the statute that fails to avoid constitutional difficulties. *Ante,* at 514, 515. By distorting the statute, the plurality manages to avoid invalidating the testing provision on what should have been noncontroversial constitutional grounds; having done so, however, the plurality rushes headlong into a much deeper constitutional thicket, brushing past an obvious basis for upholding § 188.029 in search of a pretext for scuttling the trimester framework. Evidently, from the plurality's perspective, the real problem with the Court of Appeals' construction of § 188.029 is not that it raised a constitutional difficulty, but that it raised the wrong constitutional difficulty—one not implicating *Roe.* The plurality has remedied that, traditional canons of construction and judicial forbearance notwithstanding.

B

Having set up the conflict between § 188.029 and the *Roe* trimester framework, the plurality summarily discards *Roe's* analytic core as "'unsound in principle and unworkable in practice.'" *Ante,* at 518, quoting *Garcia* v. *San Antonio Metropolitan Transit Authority,* 469 U.S. 528, 546 (1985). This is so, the plurality claims, because the key elements of the framework do not appear in the text of the Constitution, because the framework more closely resembles a regulatory code than a body of constitutional doctrine, and because under the framework the State's interest in potential human life is considered compelling only after viability, when, in fact, that interest is equally compelling throughout pregnancy. *Ante,* at 519–520. The plurality does not bother to explain these alleged flaws in *Roe.* Bald assertion masquerades as reasoning. The object, quite clearly, is not to persuade, but to prevail.

1

The plurality opinion is far more remarkable for the arguments that it does not advance than for those that it does. The plurality does not even mention, much less join, the true jurisprudential debate underlying this case: whether the Constitution includes an "unenumerated" general right to privacy as recognized in many of our decisions, most notably *Griswold* v. *Connecticut,* 381 U.S. 479 (1965), and *Roe,* and, more specifically, whether, and to what extent, such a right to privacy extends to matters of childbearing and family life, including abortion. See, *e.g., Eisenstadt* v. *Baird,* 405 U.S. 438 (1972) (contraception); *Loving* v. *Virginia,* 388 U.S. 1 (1967) (marriage); *Skinner* v. *Oklahoma ex rel. Williamson,* 316 U.S. 535 (1942) (procreation); *Pierce* v. *Society of Sisters,* 268 U.S. 510 (1925) (childrear-

---

Inc., 462 U.S. 416 (1983), that the State may not impose "a heavy, *and unnecessary,* burden on women's access to a relatively inexpensive, otherwise accessible, and safe abortion procedure." *Id.,* at 438 (emphasis added). In *Akron,* we invalidated a city ordinance requiring that all second-trimester abortions be performed in acute-care hospitals on the ground that such a requirement was not medically necessary and would double the cost of abortions. *Id.,* at 434–439. By contrast, the viability determination at issue in this case (as read by the plurality), is necessary to the effectuation of the State's compelling interest in the potential human life of viable fetuses and applies not to all second-trimester abortions, but instead only to that small percentage of abortions performed on fetuses estimated to be of more than 20 weeks gestational age.

ing).[7] These are questions of unsurpassed significance in this Court's interpretation of the Constitution, and mark the battleground upon which this case was fought, by the parties, by the Solicitor General as *amicus* on behalf of petitioners, and by an unprecedented number of *amici.* On these grounds, abandoned by the plurality, the Court should decide this case.

But rather than arguing that the text of the Constitution makes no mention of the right to privacy, the plurality complains that the critical elements of the *Roe* framework—trimesters and viability—do not appear in the Constitution and are, therefore, somehow inconsistent with a Constitution cast in general terms. *Ante,* at 518–519. Were this a true concern, we would have to abandon most of our constitutional jurisprudence. As the plurality well knows, or should know, the "critical elements" of countless constitutional doctrines nowhere appear in the Constitution's text. The Constitution makes no mention, for example, of the First Amendment's "actual malice" standard for proving certain libels, see *New York Times Co.* v. *Sullivan,* 376 U.S. 254 (1964), or of the standard for determining when speech is obscene. See *Miller* v. *California,* 413 U.S. 15 (1973). Similarly, the Constitution makes no mention of the rational-basis test, or the specific verbal formulations of intermediate and strict scrutiny by which this Court evaluates claims under the Equal Protection Clause. The reason is simple. Like the *Roe* framework, these tests or standards are not, and do not purport to be, rights protected by the Constitution. Rather, they are judge-made methods for evaluating and measuring the strength and scope of constitutional rights or for balancing the constitutional rights of individuals against the competing interests of government.

With respect to the *Roe* framework, the general constitutional principle, indeed the fundamental constitutional right, for which it was developed is the right to privacy, see, *e.g., Griswold* v. *Connecticut,* 381 U.S. 479 (1965), a species of "liberty" protected by the Due Process Clause, which under our past decisions safeguards the right of women to exercise some control over their own role in procreation. As we recently reaffirmed in *Thornburgh* v. *American College of Obstetricians and Gynecologists,* 476 U.S. 747 (1986), few decisions are "more basic to individual dignity and autonomy" or more appropriate to that "certain private sphere of individual liberty" that the Constitution reserves from the intrusive reach of government than the right to make the uniquely personal, intimate, and self-defining

---

7. The plurality, ignoring all of the aforementioned cases except *Griswold,* responds that this case does not require consideration of the "great issues" underlying this case because *Griswold,* "unlike *Roe,* did not purport to adopt a whole framework . . . to govern the cases in which the asserted liberty interest would apply." *Ante,* at 520. This distinction is highly ironic. The Court in *Roe* adopted the framework of which the plurality complains as a mechanism necessary to give effect both to the constitutional rights of the pregnant woman and to the State's significant interests in maternal health and potential life. Concededly, *Griswold* does not adopt a framework for determining the permissible scope of state regulation of contraception. The reason is simple: in *Griswold* (and *Eisenstadt*), the Court held that the challenged statute, regulating the use of medically safe contraception, did not properly serve *any* significant state interest. Accordingly, the Court had no occasion to fashion a framework to accommodate a State's interests in regulating contraception. Surely, the plurality is not suggesting that it would find *Roe* unobjectionable if the Court had forgone the framework and, as in the contraception decisions, had left the State with little or no regulatory authority. The plurality's focus on the framework is merely an excuse for avoiding the real issues embedded in this case and a mask for its hostility to the constitutional rights that *Roe* recognized.

decision whether to end a pregnancy. *Id.,* at 772. It is this general principle, the "'moral fact that a person belongs to himself and not others nor to society as a whole,'" *id.,* at 777, n. 5 (STEVENS, J., concurring), quoting Fried, Correspondence, 6 Phil. & Pub. Aff. 288–289 (1977), that is found in the Constitution. See *Roe,* 410 U.S., at 152–153. The trimester framework simply defines and limits that right to privacy in the abortion context to accommodate, not destroy, a State's legitimate interest in protecting the health of pregnant women and in preserving potential human life. *Id.,* at 154–162. Fashioning such accommodations between individual rights and the legitimate interests of government, establishing benchmarks and standards with which to evaluate the competing claims of individuals and government, lies at the very heart of constitutional adjudication. To the extent that the trimester framework is useful in this enterprise, it is not only consistent with constitutional interpretation, but necessary to the wise and just exercise of this Court's paramount authority to define the scope of constitutional rights.

2

The plurality next alleges that the result of the trimester framework has "been a web of legal rules that have become increasingly intricate, resembling a code of regulations rather than a body of constitutional doctrine." *Ante,* at 518. Again, if this were a true and genuine concern, we would have to abandon vast areas of our constitutional jurisprudence. The plurality complains that under the trimester framework the Court has distinguished between a city ordinance requiring that second-trimester abortions be performed in clinics and a state law requiring that these abortions be performed in hospitals, or between laws requiring that certain information be furnished to a woman by a physician or his assistant and those requiring that such information be furnished by the physician exclusively. *Ante,* at 518, n. 15, citing *Simopoulos* v. *Virginia,* 462 U.S. 506 (1983), and *Akron* v. *Akron Center for Reproductive Health, Inc.,* 462 U.S. 416 (1983). Are these distinctions any finer, or more "regulatory," than the distinctions we have often drawn in our First Amendment jurisprudence, where, for example, we have held that a "release time" program permitting public-school students to leave school grounds during school hours to receive religious instruction does not violate the Establishment Clause, even though a release-time program permitting religious instruction on school grounds does violate the Clause? Compare *Zorach* v. *Clauson,* 343 U.S. 306 (1952), with *Illinois ex rel. McCollum* v. *Board of Education of School Dist. No. 71, Champaign County,* 333 U.S. 203 (1948). Our Fourth Amendment jurisprudence recognizes factual distinctions no less intricate. Just this Term, for example, we held that while an aerial observation from a helicopter hovering at 400 feet does not violate any reasonable expectation of privacy, such an expectation of privacy would be violated by a helicopter observation from an unusually low altitude. *Florida* v. *Riley,* 488 U.S. 445, 451 (1989) (O'CONNOR, J., concurring in judgment). Similarly, in a Sixth Amendment case, the Court held that although an overnight ban on attorney-client communication violated the constitutionally guaranteed right to counsel, *Geders* v. *United States,* 425 U.S. 80 (1976), that right was not violated when a trial judge separated a defendant from his lawyer during a 15-minute recess after the defendant's direct testimony. *Perry* v. *Leeke,* 488 U.S. 272 (1989).

That numerous constitutional doctrines result in narrow differentiations between similar circumstances does not mean that this Court has abandoned adjudication in favor of regulation. Rather, these careful distinctions reflect the process of constitutional adjudication itself, which is often highly fact specific, requiring such determinations as whether state laws are "unduly burdensome" or "reasonable" or bear a "rational" or "necessary" relation to asserted state interests. In a recent due process case, THE CHIEF JUSTICE wrote for the Court: "[M]any branches of the law abound in nice distinctions that may be troublesome but have been thought nonetheless necessary: 'I do not think we need trouble ourselves with the thought that my view depends upon differences of degree. The whole law does so as soon as it is civilized.'" _Daniels_ v. _Williams,_ 474 U.S. 327, 334 (1986), quoting _LeRoy Fibre Co._ v. _Chicago, M & St. P. R. Co._ 232 U.S. 340, 354 (1914) (Holmes, J., partially concurring).

These "differences of degree" fully account for our holdings in _Simopoulos, supra,_ and _Akron, supra._ Those decisions rest on this Court's reasoned and accurate judgment that hospitalization and doctor-counseling requirements unduly burdened the right of women to terminate a pregnancy and were not rationally related to the State's asserted interest in the health of pregnant women, while Virginia's _substantially less restrictive_ regulations were not unduly burdensome and did rationally serve the State's interest.[8] That the Court exercised its best judgment in evaluating these markedly different statutory schemes no more established the Court as an "'_ex officio_ medical board,'" _ante,_ at 519, quoting _Planned Parenthood of Central Mo._ v. _Danforth,_ 428 U.S. 52, 99 (1976) (opinion of WHITE, J., concurring in part and dissenting in part), than our decisions involving religion in the public schools establish the Court as a national school board, or our decisions concerning prison regulations establish the Court as a bureau of prisons. See _Thornburgh_ v. _Abbott,_ 490 U.S. 401 (1989) (adopting different standard of First Amendment review for incoming as opposed to outgoing prison mail). If, in delicate and complicated areas of constitutional law, our legal judgments "have become increasingly intricate," _ante,_ at 518, it is not, as the plurality contends, because we have overstepped our judicial role. Quite the opposite: the rules are intricate because we have remained conscientious in our duty to do justice carefully, especially when fundamental rights rise or fall with our decisions.

3

Finally, the plurality asserts that the trimester framework cannot stand because the State's interest in potential life is compelling throughout pregnancy, not merely after viability. _Ante,_ at 519. The opinion contains not one word of rationale for its view of the State's interest. This "it-is-so-because-we-say-so" jurisprudence constitutes nothing other than an attempted exercise of brute force; reason, much less persuasion, has no place.

---

8. The difference in the _Akron_ and _Simopoulos_ regulatory regimes is stark. The Court noted in _Akron_ that the city ordinance requiring that all second-trimester abortions be performed in acute-care hospitals undoubtedly would have made the procurement of legal abortions difficult and often prohibitively expensive, thereby driving the performance of abortions back underground where they would not be subject to effective regulation. Such a requirement obviously did not further the city's asserted interest in maternal health. 462 U.S., at 420, n. 1. On the other hand, the Virginia law at issue in _Simopoulos,_ by permitting the performance of abortions in licensed outpatient clinics as well as hospitals, did not similarly constrict the availability of legal abortions and, therefore, did not undermine its own stated purpose of protecting maternal health.

In answering the plurality's claim that the State's interest in the fetus is uniform and compelling throughout pregnancy, I cannot improve upon what JUSTICE STEVENS has written:

> "I should think it obvious that the State's interest in the protection of an embryo—even if that interest is defined as 'protecting those who will be citizens'. . .—increases progressively and dramatically as the organism's capacity to feel pain, to experience pleasure, to survive, and to react to its surroundings increases day by day. The development of a fetus—and pregnancy itself—are not static conditions, and the assertion that the government's interest is static simply ignores this reality . . . . [U]nless the religious view that a fetus is a 'person' is adopted . . . there is a fundamental and well–recognized difference between a fetus and a human being; indeed, if there is not such a difference, the permissibility of terminating the life of a fetus could scarcely be left to the will of the state legislatures. And if distinctions may be drawn between a fetus and a human being in terms of the state interest in their protection—even though the fetus represents one of 'those who will be citizens'—it seems to me quite odd to argue that distinctions may not also be drawn between the state interest in protecting the freshly fertilized egg and the state interest in protecting the 9-month-gestated, fully sentient fetus on the eve of birth. Recognition of this distinction is supported not only by logic, but also by history and by our shared experiences." *Thornburgh*, 476 U.S., at 778–779 (footnote omitted).

See also *Roe*, 410 U.S., at 129–147.

For my own part, I remain convinced, as six other Members of this Court 16 years ago were convinced, that the *Roe* framework, and the viability standard in particular, fairly, sensibly, and effectively functions to safeguard the constitutional liberties of pregnant women while recognizing and accommodating the State's interest in potential human life. The viability line reflects the biological facts and truths of fetal development; it marks that threshold moment prior to which a fetus cannot survive separate from the woman and cannot reasonably and objectively be regarded as a subject of rights or interests distinct from, or paramount to, those of the pregnant woman. At the same time, the viability standard takes account of the undeniable fact that as the fetus evolves into its postnatal form, and as it loses its dependence on the uterine environment, the State's interest in the fetus' potential human life, and in fostering a regard for human life in general, becomes compelling. As a practical matter, because viability follows "quickening"—the point at which a woman feels movement in her womb—and because viability occurs no earlier than 23 weeks gestational age, it establishes an easily applicable standard for regulating abortion while providing a pregnant woman ample time to exercise her fundamental right with her responsible physician to terminate her pregnancy.[9] Although I have stated

---

9. Notably, neither the plurality nor JUSTICE O'CONNOR advances the now-familiar catch-phrase criticism of the *Roe* framework that because the point of viability will recede with advances in medical technology, *Roe* "is clearly on a collision course with itself." See *Akron*, 462 U.S., at 458 (dissenting opinion). This critique has no medical foundation. As the medical literature and the *amicus* briefs filed in this case conclusively demonstrate, "there is an 'anatomic threshold' for fetal viability of about 23–24 weeks of gestation." Brief for American Medical Association et al. as *Amici Curiae* 7. See also Brief for 167 Distinguished Scientists and Physicians, including 11 Nobel Laureates, as *Amici Curiae* 8–14. Prior to that time, the crucial organs are not sufficiently mature to provide the mutually sustaining functions that are prerequisite to extrauter-

previously for a majority of this Court that "[c]onstitutional rights do not always have easily ascertainable boundaries," to seek and establish those boundaries remains the special responsibility of this Court. *Thornburgh,* 476 U.S., at 771. In *Roe,* we discharged that responsibility as logic and science compelled. The plurality today advances not one reasonable argument as to why our judgment in that case was wrong and should be abandoned.

4

Having contrived an opportunity to reconsider the *Roe* framework, and then having discarded that framework, the plurality finds the testing provision unobjectionable because it "permissibly furthers the State's interest in protecting potential human life." *Ante,* at 519–520. This newly minted standard is circular and totally meaningless. Whether a challenged abortion regulation "permissibly furthers" a legitimate state interest is the *question* that courts must answer in abortion cases, not the standard for courts to apply. In keeping with the rest of its opinion, the plurality makes no attempt to explain or to justify its new standard, either in the abstract or as applied in this case. Nor could it. The "permissibly furthers" standard has no independent meaning, and consists of nothing other than what a majority of this Court may believe at any given moment in any given case. The plurality's novel test appears to be nothing more than a dressed-up version of rational-basis review, this Court's most lenient level of scrutiny. One thing is clear, however: were the plurality's "permissibly furthers" standard adopted by the Court, for all practical purposes, *Roe* would be overruled.[10]

The "permissibly furthers" standard completely disregards the irreducible minimum of *Roe:* the Court's recognition that a woman has a limited fundamental constitutional right to decide whether to terminate a pregnancy. That right receives no meaningful recognition in the plurality's written opinion. Since, in the plurality's view, the State's interest in potential life is compelling as of the moment of conception, and is therefore served only if abortion is abolished, every hindrance to a woman's ability to obtain an abortion must be "permissible." Indeed, the more severe the hindrance, the more effectively (and permissibly) the State's interest would be furthered. A tax on abortions or a criminal prohibition would both satisfy the plurality's standard. So, for that matter, would a requirement that a pregnant woman memorize and recite today's plurality opinion before seeking an abortion.

---

ine survival, or viability. Moreover, "no technology exists to bridge the development gap between the three-day embryo culture and the 24th week of gestation." Fetal Extrauterine Survivability, Report to the New York State Task Force on Life and the Law 3 (1988). Nor does the medical community believe that the development of any such technology is possible in the foreseeable future. *Id.,* at 12. In other words, the threshold of fetal viability is, and will remain no different from what it was at the time *Roe* was decided. Predictions to the contrary are pure science fiction. See Brief for A Group of American Law Professors as *Amicus Curiae* 23–25.

10. Writing for the Court in *Akron,* Justice Powell observed the same phenomenon, though in hypothetical response to the dissent in that case: "In sum, it appears that the dissent would uphold virtually any abortion regulation under a rational-basis test. It also appears that even where heightened scrutiny is deemed appropriate, the dissent would uphold virtually any abortion-inhibiting regulation because of the State's interest in preserving potential human life. . . . This analysis is wholly incompatible with the existence of the fundamental right recognized in *Roe* v. *Wade.*" 462 U.S., at 420–421, n. 1.

The plurality pretends that *Roe* survives, explaining that the facts of this case differ from those in *Roe:* here, Missouri has chosen to assert its interest in potential life only at the point of viability, whereas, in *Roe,* Texas had asserted that interest from the point of conception, criminalizing all abortions, except where the life of the mother was at stake. *Ante,* at 521. This, of course, is a distinction without a difference. The plurality repudiates every principle for which *Roe* stands; in good conscience, it cannot possibly believe that *Roe* lies "undisturbed" merely because this case does not call upon the Court to reconsider the Texas statute, or one like it. If the Constitution permits a State to enact any statute that reasonably furthers its interest in potential life, and if that interest arises as of conception, why would the Texas statute fail to pass muster? One suspects that the plurality agrees. It is impossible to read the plurality opinion and especially its final paragraph, without recognizing its implicit invitation to every State to enact more and more restrictive abortion laws, and to assert their interest in potential life as of the moment of conception. All these laws will satisfy the plurality's nonscrutiny, until sometime, a new regime of old dissenters and new appointees will declare what the plurality intends: that *Roe* is no longer good law.[11]

5

Thus, "not with a bang, but a whimper," the plurality discards a landmark case of the last generation, and casts into darkness the hopes and visions of every woman in this country who had come to believe that the Constitution guaranteed her the right to exercise some control over her unique ability to bear children. The plurality does so either oblivious or insensitive to the fact that millions of women, and their families, have ordered their lives around the right to reproductive choice, and that this right has become vital to the full participation of women in the economic and political walks of American life. The plurality would clear the way once again for government to force upon women the physical labor and specific and direct medical and psychological harms that may accompany carrying a fetus to term. The plurality

---

11. The plurality claims that its treatment of *Roe,* and a woman's right to decide whether to terminate a pregnancy, "hold[s] true the balance between that which the Constitution puts beyond the reach of the democratic process and that which it does not." *Ante,* at 521. This is unadulterated nonsense. The plurality's balance matches a lead weight (the State's allegedly compelling interest in fetal life as of the moment of conception) against a feather (a "liberty interest" of the pregnant woman that the plurality barely mentions, much less describes). The plurality's balance—no balance at all—places nothing, or virtually nothing, beyond the reach of the democratic process.

JUSTICE SCALIA candidly argues that this is all for the best. *Ante,* at 532. I cannot agree. "The very purpose of a Bill of Rights was to withdraw certain subjects from the vicissitudes of political controversy, to place them beyond the reach of majorities and officials and to establish them as legal principles to be applied by the courts. One's right to life, liberty, and property . . . may not be submitted to vote; they depend on the outcome of no elections." *West Virginia Board of Education* v. *Barnette,* 319 U.S. 624, 638 (1943). In a Nation that cherishes liberty, the ability of a woman to control the biological operation of her body and to determine with her responsible physician whether or not to carry a fetus to term must fall within that limited sphere of individual autonomy that lies beyond the will or power of any transient majority. This Court stands as the ultimate guarantor of that zone of privacy, regardless of the bitter disputes to which our decisions may give rise. In *Roe,* and our numerous cases reaffirming *Roe,* we did no more than discharge our constitutional duty.

would clear the way again for the State to conscript a woman's body and to force upon her a "distressful life and future." *Roe,* 410 U.S., at 153.

The result, as we know from experience, see Cates & Rochat, Illegal Abortions in the United States: 1972–1974, 8 Family Planning Perspectives 86, 92 (1976), would be that every year hundreds of thousands of women, in desperation, would defy the law, and place their health and safety in the unclean and unsympathetic hands of back-alley abortionists, or they would attempt to perform abortions upon themselves, with disastrous results. Every year, many women, especially poor and minority women, would die or suffer debilitating physical trauma, all in the name of enforced morality or religious dictates or lack of compassion, as it may be.

Of the aspirations and settled understandings of American women, of the inevitable and brutal consequences of what it is doing, the tough-approach plurality utters not a word. This silence is callous. It is also profoundly destructive of this Court as an institution. To overturn a constitutional decision is a rare and grave undertaking. To overturn a constitutional decision that secured a fundamental personal liberty to millions of persons would be unprecedented in our 200 years of constitutional history. Although the doctrine of *stare decisis* applies with somewhat diminished force in constitutional cases generally, *ante,* at 518, even in ordinary constitutional cases "any departure from . . . *stare decisis* demands special justification." *Arizona* v. *Rumsey,* 467 U.S. 203, 212 (1984). See also *Vasquez* v. *Hillery,* 474 U.S. 254, 266 (1986) ("[T]he careful observer will discern that any detours from the straight path of *stare decisis* in our past have occurred for articulable reasons, and only when the Court has felt obliged 'to bring its opinions into agreement with experience and with facts newly ascertained,'" quoting *Burnet* v. *Coronado Oil & Gas Co.,* U.S. 393, 412 (1932) (Brandeis, J., dissenting)). This requirement of justification applies with unique force where, as here, the Court's abrogation of precedent would destroy people's firm belief, based on past decisions of this Court, that they possess an unabridgeable right to undertake certain conduct.[12]

As discussed at perhaps too great length above, the plurality makes no serious attempt to carry "the heavy burden of persuading . . . that changes in society or in the law dictate" the abandonment of *Roe* and its numerous progeny, *Vasquez,* 474 U.S., at 266, much less the greater burden of explaining the abrogation of a fundamental personal freedom. Instead, the plurality pretends that it leaves *Roe* standing, and

---

12. Cf. *South Carolina* v. *Gathers,* 490 U.S. 805, 824 (1989) (SCALIA, J., dissenting) ("[T]he respect accorded prior decisions increases, rather than decreases, with their antiquity, as the society adjusts itself to their existence, and the surrounding law becomes premised on their validity").

Moreover, as Justice Powell wrote for the Court in *Akron:* "There are especially compelling reasons for adhering to *stare decisis* in applying the principles of *Roe* v. *Wade.* That case was considered with special care. It was first argued during the 1971 Term, and reargued—with extensive briefing—the following term. The decision was joined by THE CHIEF JUSTICE and six other Justices. Since *Roe* was decided in January 1973, the Court repeatedly and consistently has accepted and applied the basic principle that a woman has a fundamental right to make the highly personal choice whether or not to terminate her pregnancy." 462 U.S., at 420, n. 1. See, *e. g., Planned Parenthood of Central Mo.* v. *Danforth,* 428 U.S. 52 (1976); *Bellotti* v. *Baird,* 428 U.S. 132 (1976); *Beal* v. *Doe,* 432 U.S. 438 (1977); *Maher* v. *Roe,* 432 U.S. 464 (1977); *Colautti* v. *Franklin,* 439 U.S. 379 (1979); *Bellotti* v. *Baird,* 443 U.S. 622 (1979); *Harris* v. *McRae,* 448 U.S. 297 (1980); *Akron* v. *Akron Center for Reproductive Health, Inc.,* 462 U.S. 416 (1983); *Thornburgh* v. *American College of Obstetricians and Gynecologists,* 476 U.S. 747 (1986).

refuses even to discuss the real issue underlying this case: whether the Constitution includes an unenumerated right to privacy that encompasses a woman's right to decide whether to terminate a pregnancy. To the extent that the plurality does criticize the *Roe* framework, these criticisms are pure *ipse dixit*.

This comes at a cost. The doctrine of *stare decisis* "permits society to presume that bedrock principles are founded in the law rather than in the proclivities of individuals, and thereby contributes to the integrity of our constitutional system of government, both in appearance and in fact." 474 U.S., at 265–266. Today's decision involves the most politically divisive domestic legal issue of our time. By refusing to explain or to justify its proposed revolutionary revision in the law of abortion, and by refusing to abide not only by our precedents, but also by our canons for reconsidering those precedents, the plurality invites charges of cowardice and illegitimacy to our door. I cannot say that these would be undeserved.

II

For today, at least, the law of abortion stands undisturbed. For today, the women of this Nation still retain the liberty to control their destinies. But the signs are evident and very ominous, and a chill wind blows.

Justice Stevens, concurring in part and dissenting in part.

Having joined Part II–C of the Court's opinion, I shall not comment on § 188.205 of the Missouri statute. With respect to the challenged portions of §§ 188.210 and 188.215, I agree with Justice Blackmun, *ante*, at 539–541, n. 1 (concurring in part and dissenting in part), that the record identifies a sufficient number of unconstitutional applications to support the Court of Appeals' judgment invalidating those provisions. The reasons why I would also affirm that court's invalidation of § 188.029, the viability testing provision, and §§ 1.205.1(1), (2) of the preamble,[1] require separate explanation.

I

It seems to me that in Part II–D of its opinion, the plurality strains to place a construction on § 188.029[2] that enables it to conclude: "[W]e would modify and narrow *Roe* and succeeding cases," *ante*, at 521. That statement is ill advised

---

1. The State prefers to refer to subsections (1) and (2) of § 1.205.1 as "prefatory statements with no substantive effect." Brief for Appellants 9; see *id.*, at 21; see also 851 F. 2d 1071, 1076 (CA8 1988). It is true that § 1.205 is codified in Chapter 1, Laws in Force and Construction of Statutes, of Title I, Laws and Statutes, of the Missouri Revised Statutes, while all other provisions at issue are codified in Chapter 188, Regulation of Abortions, of Title XII, Public Health and Welfare. But because § 1.205 appeared at the beginning of House Bill No. 1596, see *ante*, at 500–501, it is entirely appropriate to consider it as a preamble relevant to those regulations.

2. The testing provision states:

"188.029. Physician, determination of viability, duties

"Before a physician performs an abortion on a woman he has reason to believe is carrying an unborn child of twenty or more weeks gestational age, the physician shall first determine if the unborn child is viable by using and exercising that degree of care, skill, and proficiency commonly exercised by the ordinarily skillful, careful, and prudent physician engaged in similar practice under the same or similar conditions. In making this determination of viability, the physician

because there is no need to modify even slightly the holdings of prior cases in order to uphold § 188.029. For the most plausible nonliteral construction, as both JUSTICE BLACKMUN, *ante,* at 542–544 (concurring in part and dissenting in part), and JUSTICE O'CONNOR, *ante,* at 525–531 (concurring in part and concurring in judgment), have demonstrated, is constitutional and entirely consistent with our precedents.

I am unable to accept JUSTICE O'CONNOR'S construction of the second sentence in § 188.029, however, because I believe it is foreclosed by two controlling principles of statutory interpretation. First, it is our settled practice to accept "the interpretation of state law in which the District Court and the Court of Appeals have concurred even if an examination of the state-law issue without such guidance might have justified a different conclusion." *Bishop* v. *Wood,* 426 U.S. 341, 346 (1976).[3] Second, "[t]he fact that a particular application of the clear terms of a statute might be unconstitutional does not provide us with a justification for ignoring the plain meaning of the statute." *Public Citizen* v. *Department of Justice,* 491 U.S. 440, 481 (1989) (KENNEDY, J., concurring in judgment).[4] In this case, I agree with the Court of Appeals, 851 F. 2d 1071, 1074–1075 (CA8 1988), and the District Court, 662 F. Supp. 407, 423 (WD Mo. 1987), that the meaning of the second sentence of § 188.029 is too plain to be ignored. The sentence twice uses the mandatory term "shall," and contains no qualifying language. If it is implicitly limited to tests that are useful in determining viability, it adds nothing to the requirement imposed by the preceding sentence.

My interpretation of the plain language is supported by the structure of the statute as a whole, particularly the preamble, which "finds" that life "begins at conception" and further commands that state laws shall be construed to provide the maximum protection to "the unborn child at every stage of development." Mo. Rev. Stat. §§ 1.205.1(1), 1.205.2 (1986). I agree with the District Court that "[o]bviously, the purpose of this law is to protect the potential life of the fetus, rather than to safeguard maternal health." 662 F. Supp., at 420. A literal reading of the statute tends to accomplish that goal. Thus it is not "incongruous," *ante,* at 515, to assume that the Missouri Legislature was trying to protect the potential human life of nonviable fetuses by making the abortion decision more costly.[5] On the contrary, I am satisfied that the Court of Appeals, as well as the District Court, correctly concluded

---

shall perform or cause to be performed such medical examinations and tests as are necessary to make a finding of the gestational age, weight, and lung maturity of the unborn child and shall enter such findings and determination of viability in the medical record of the mother." Mo. Rev. Stat. § 188.029 (1986).

3. See also *United States* v. *Durham Lumber Co.,* 363 U.S. 522, 526–527 (1960); *Propper* v. *Clark,* 337 U.S. 472, 486–487 (1949); *Hillsborough* v. *Cromwell,* 326 U.S. 620, 630 (1946); *Huddleston* v. *Dwyer,* 322 U.S. 232, 237 (1944); *MacGregor* v. *State Mutual Life Ins. Co.,* 315 U.S. 280, 281 (1942) *(per curiam).*

4. We have stated that we will interpret a federal statute to avoid serious constitutional problems if "a reasonable alternative interpretation poses no constitutional question," *Gomez* v. *United States,* 490 U.S. 858, 864 (1989), or if "it is fairly possible to interpret the statute in a manner that renders it constitutionally valid," *Communications Workers* v. *Beck,* 487 U.S. 735, 762 (1988), or "unless such construction is plainly contrary to the intent of Congress," *Edward J. DeBartolo Corp.* v. *Florida Gulf Coast Building and Construction Trades Council,* 485 U.S. 568, 575 (1988).

5. As with the testing provision, the plurality opts for a construction of this statute that conflicts with those of the Court of Appeals, 851 F. 2d, at 1076–1077, and the District Court, 662 F. supp. 407, 413 (WD Mo. 1987).

that the Missouri Legislature meant exactly what it said in the second sentence of § 188.029. I am also satisfied, for the reasons stated by JUSTICE BLACKMUN, that the testing provision is manifestly unconstitutional under *Williamson* v. *Lee Optical Co.,* 348 U.S. 483 (1955), "irrespective of the *Roe* [v. *Wade,* 410 U.S. 113 (1973),] framework." *Ante,* at 544 (concurring in part and dissenting in part).

II

The Missouri statute defines "conception" as "the fertilization of the ovum of a female by a sperm of a male," Mo. Rev. Stat. § 188.015(3) (1986), even though standard medical texts equate "conception" with implantation in the uterus, occurring about six days after fertilization.[6] Missouri's declaration therefore implies regulation not only of previability abortions, but also of common forms of contraception such as the IUD and the morning-after pill.[7] Because the preamble, read in context, threatens serious encroachments upon the liberty of the pregnant woman and the health professional, I am persuaded that these plaintiffs, appellees before us, have standing to challenge its constitutionality. Accord, 851 F. 2d, at 1075–1076.

To the extent that the Missouri statute interferes with contraceptive choices, I have no doubt that it is unconstitutional under the Court's holdings in *Griswold* v. *Connecticut,* 381 U.S. 479 (1965); *Eisenstadt* v. *Baird,* 405 U.S. 438 (1972); and *Carey* v. *Population Services International,* 431 U.S. 678 (1977). The place of *Griswold* in the mosaic of decisions defining a woman's liberty interest was accurately stated by Justice Stewart in his concurring opinion in *Roe* v. *Wade,* 410 U.S. 113, 167–170 (1973):

> "[I]n *Griswold* v. *Connecticut,* 381 U.S. 479, the Court held a Connecticut birth control law unconstitutional. In view of what had been so recently said in [*Ferguson* v.] *Skrupa,* [372 U.S. 726 (1963),] the Court's opinion in *Griswold* understandably did its best to avoid reliance on the Due Process Clause of the Fourteenth Amendment as the ground for decision. Yet, the Connecticut law did not violate any provision of the Bill of Rights, nor any other specific provision of the Bill of

6. The fertilized egg remains in the woman's Fallopian tube for 72 hours, then travels to the uterus' cavity, where cell division continues for another 72 hours before implantation in the uterine wall. D. Mishell & V. Davajan, Infertility, Contraception and Reproductive Endocrinology 109–110 (2d ed. 1986); see also Brief for Association of Reproductive Health Professionals et al. as *Amici curiae* 31–32 (ARHP Brief) (citing, *inter alia,* J. Pritchard, P. MacDonald, & N. Gant, Williams Obstetrics 88–91 (17th ed. 1985)). "[O]nly 50 per cent of fertilized ova ultimately become implanted." ARHP Brief 32, n. 25 (citing Post Coital Contraception, The Lancet 856 (Apr. 16, 1983)).

7. An intrauterine device, commonly called an IUD, "Works primarily by preventing a fertilized egg from implanting." Burnhill, Intrauterine Contraception, in Fertility Control 271, 280 (S. Corson, R. Derman, & L. Tyrer eds. 1985). See also 21 CFR § 801.427, p. 32 (1988); ARHP Brief 34–35. Other contraceptive methods that may prevent implantation include "morning-after pills," high-dose estrogen pills taken after intercourse, particularly in cases of rape, ARHP Brief 33, and the French RU 486, a pill that works "during the indeterminate period between contraception and abortion," *id.,* at 37. Low-level estrogen "combined" pills—a version of the ordinary, daily ingested birth control pill—also may prevent the fertilized egg from reaching the uterine wall and implanting. *Id.,* at 35–36.

Rights, nor any other specific provision of the Constitution. So it was clear to me then, and it is equally clear to me now, that the _Griswold_ decision can be rationally understood only as a holding that the Connecticut statute substantively invaded the 'liberty' that is protected by the Due Process Clause of the Fourteenth Amendment. As so understood, _Griswold_ stands as one in a long line of pre-_Skrupa_ cases decided under the doctrine of substantive due process, and I now accept it as such.

"Several decisions of this Court make clear that freedom of personal choice in matters of marriage and family life is one of the liberties protected by the Due Process Clause of the Fourteenth Amendment. _Loving_ v. _Virginia,_ 388 U.S. 1, 12 [(1967)]; _Griswold_ v. _Connecticut, supra; Pierce_ v. _Society of Sisters,_ [268 U.S. 510 [(1925)]; _Meyer_ v. _Nebraska,_ [262 U.S. 390 (1923)]. See also _Prince_ v. _Massachusetts,_ 321 U.S. 158, 166 [(1944)]; _Skinner_ v. _Oklahoma,_ 316 U.S. 535, 541 [(1942)]. As recently as last Term, in _Eisenstadt_ v. _Baird,_ 405 U.S. 438, 453, we recognized 'the right of the _individual,_ married or single, to be free from unwarranted governmental intrusion into matters so fundamentally affecting a person as the decision whether to bear or beget a child.' That right necessarily includes the right of a woman to decide whether or not to terminate her pregnancy. 'Certainly the interests of a woman in giving of her physical and emotional self during pregnancy and the interests that will be affected throughout her life by the birth and raising of a child are of a far greater degree of significance and personal intimacy than the right to send a child to private school protected in _Pierce_ v. _Society of Sisters,_ 268 U.S. 510 (1925), or the right to teach a foreign language protected in _Meyer_ v. _Nebraska,_ 262 U.S. 390 (1923).' _Abele_ v. _Markle,_ 351 F. Supp. 224, 227 (Conn. 1972).

"Clearly, therefore, the Court today is correct in holding that the right asserted by Jane Roe is embraced within the personal liberty protected by the Due Process Clause of the Fourteenth Amendment." (Emphasis in original; footnotes omitted.)[8]

One might argue that the _Griswold_ holding applies to devices "preventing conception," 381 U.S., at 480—that is, fertilization—but not to those preventing implantation, and therefore, that _Griswold_ does not protect a woman's choice to use an IUD or take a morning-after pill. There is unquestionably a theological basis for such an argument,[9] just as there was unquestionably a theological basis for the Connecticut statute that the Court invalidated in _Griswold._ Our jurisprudence, however, has consistently required a secular basis for valid legislation. See, _e.g., Stone_ V. _Graham,_ 449 U.S. 39, 40 (1980) _(per curiam)._[10] Because I am not aware of any

8. The contrast between Justice Stewart's careful explication that our abortion precedent flowed naturally from a stream of substantive due process cases and JUSTICE SCALIA'S notion that our abortion law was "constructed overnight in _Roe_ v. _Wade,_" _ante,_ at 537 (concurring in part and concurring in judgment) is remarkable.

9. Several _amici_ state that the "sanctity of human life from conception and opposition to abortion are, in fact, sincere and deeply held religious beliefs," Brief for Lutheran Church-Missouri Synod et al. as _Amici Curiae_ 20 (on behalf of 49 "church denominations"); see Brief for Holy Orthodox Church as _Amicus Curiae_ 12–14.

10. The dissent in _Stone_ did not dispute this proposition; rather, it argued that posting the Ten Commandments on schoolroom walls has a secular purpose. 449 U.S., at 43–46 (REHNQUIST, J., dissenting).

secular basis for differentiating between contraceptive procedures that are effective immediately before and those that are effective immediately after fertilization, I believe it inescapably follows that the preamble to the Missouri statute is invalid under *Griswold* and its progeny.

Indeed, I am persuaded that the absence of any secular purpose for the legislative declarations that life begins at conception and that conception occurs at fertilization makes the relevant portion of the preamble invalid under the Establishment Clause of the First Amendment to the Federal Constitution. This conclusion does not, and could not, rest on the fact that the statement happens to coincide with the tenets of certain religions, see *McGowan* v. *Maryland,* 366 U.S. 420, 442 (1961); *Harris* v. *McRae,* 448 U.S. 297, 319–320 (1980), or on the fact that the legislators who voted to enact it may have been motivated by religious considerations, see *Washington* v. *Davis,* 426 U.S. 229, 253 (1976) (STEVENS, J., concurring). Rather, it rests on the fact that the preamble, an unequivocal endorsement of a religious tenet of some but by no means all Christian faiths,[11] serves no identifiable secular purpose. That fact alone compels a conclusion that the statute violates the Establishment Clause.[12] *Wallace* v. *Jaffree,* 472 U.S. 38, 56 (1985).

My concern can best be explained by reference to the position on this issue that was widely accepted by the leaders of the Roman Catholic Church for many years. The position is summarized in a report, entitled "Catholic Teaching On Abortion," prepared by the Congressional Research Service of the Library of Congress. It states in part:

> "The disagreement over the status of the unformed as against the formed fetus was crucial for Christian teaching on the soul. It was widely held that the soul was not present until the formation of the fetus 40 or 80 days after conception, for males and females respectively. Thus, abortion of the 'unformed' or 'inanimate' fetus (from *anima,* soul) was something less than true homicide, rather a form of anticipatory or quasi-homicide. This view received its definitive treatment in St. Thomas Aquinas and became for a time the dominant interpretation in the Latin Church.

> "For St. Thomas, as for mediaeval Christendom generally, there is a lapse of time— approximately 40 to 80 days—after conception and before the soul's infusion. . . . "For St. Thomas, 'seed and what is not seed is determined by sensation and movement.' What is destroyed in abortion of the unformed fetus is seed, not man. This distinction received its most careful analysis in St. Thomas. It was the general belief of Christendom, reflected, for example, in the Council of Trent (1545–1563), which restricted penalties for homicide to abortion of an animated fetus only." C. Whittier, Catholic Teaching on Abortion: Its Origin and Later Development (1981), reprinted in Brief for Americans United for Separation of

---

11. See, *e. g.,* Brief for Catholics for a Free Choice et al. as *Amici Curiae* 5 ("There is no constant teaching in Catholic theology on the commencement of personhood").

12. Pointing to the lack of consensus about life's onset among experts in medicine, philosophy, and theology, the Court in *Roe* v. *Wade,* 410 U.S. 113, 158, 162 (1973), established that the Constitution does not permit a State to adopt a theory of life that overrides a pregnant woman's rights. Accord, *Akron* v. *Akron Center for Reproductive Health, Inc.,* 462 U.S. 416, 444 (1983). The constitutional violation is doubly grave if, as here, the only basis for the State's "finding" is nonsecular.

Church and State as _Amicus Curiae_ 13a, 17a (quoting _In octo libros politicorum_ 7.12, attributed to St. Thomas Aquinas).

If the views of St. Thomas were held as widely today as they were in the Middle Ages, and if a state legislature were to enact a statute prefaced with a "finding" that female life begins 80 days after conception and male life begins 40 days after conception, I have no doubt that this Court would promptly conclude that such an endorsement of a particular religious tenet is violative of the Establishment Clause.

In my opinion the difference between that hypothetical statute and Missouri's preamble reflects nothing more than a difference in theological doctrine. The preamble to the Missouri statute endorses the theological position that there is the same secular interest in preserving the life of a fetus during the first 40 or 80 days of pregnancy as there is after viability—indeed, after the time when the fetus has become a "person" with legal rights protected by the Constitution.[13] To sustain that position as a matter of law, I believe Missouri has the burden of identifying the secular interests that differentiate the first 40 days of pregnancy from the period immediately before or after fertilization when, as _Griswold_ and related cases establish, the Constitution allows the use of contraceptive procedures to prevent potential life from developing into full personhood. Focusing our attention on the first several weeks of pregnancy is especially appropriate because that is the period when the vast majority of abortions are actually performed.

As a secular matter, there is an obvious difference between the state interest in protecting the freshly fertilized egg and the state interest in protecting a 9-month-gestated, fully sentient fetus on the eve of birth. There can be no interest in protecting the newly fertilized egg from physical pain or mental anguish, because the capacity for such suffering does not yet exist; respecting a developed fetus, however, that interest is valid. In fact, if one prescinds the theological concept of ensoulment—or one accepts St. Thomas Aquinas' view that ensoulment does not occur for at least 40 days—a State has no greater secular interest in protecting the potential life of an embryo that is still "seed" than in protecting the potential life of a sperm or an unfertilized ovum.

There have been times in history when military and economic interests would have been served by an increase in population. No one argues today, however, that Missouri can assert a societal interest in increasing its population as its secular reason for fostering potential life. Indeed, our national policy, as reflected in legislation the Court upheld last Term, is to prevent the potential life that is produced by "pregnancy and childbirth among unmarried adolescents." _Bowen_ v. _Kendrick,_ 487 U.S. 589, 593 (1988); accord, _id.,_ at 602. If the secular analysis were based on a strict balancing of fiscal costs and benefits, the economic costs of unlimited childbearing would outweigh those of abortion. There is, of course, an important and unquestionably valid secular

---

13. No Member of this Court has ever questioned the holding in _Roe,_ 410 U.S., at 156–159, that a fetus is not a "person" within the meaning of the Fourteenth Amendment. Even the dissenters in _Roe_ implicitly endorsed that holding by arguing that state legislatures should decide whether to prohibit or to authorize abortions. See _id.,_ at 177 (REHNQUIST, J., dissenting) (arguing that the Fourteenth Amendment did not "withdraw from the States the power to legislate with respect to this matter"); _Doe_ v. _Bolton,_ 410 U.S. 179, 222 (1973) (WHITE, J., dissenting jointly in _Doe_ and _Roe_). By characterizing the basic question as "a political issue," see _ante,_ at 535 (concurring in part and concurring in judgment), JUSTICE SCALIA likewise implicitly accepts this holding.

interest in "protecting a young pregnant woman from the consequences of an incorrect decision," *Planned Parenthood of Central Mo.* v. *Danforth,* 428 U.S. 52, 102 (1976) (STEVENS, J., concurring in part and dissenting in part). Although that interest is served by a requirement that the woman receive medical and, in appropriate circumstances, parental, advice,[14] it does not justify the state legislature's official endorsement of the theological tenet embodied in §§ 1.205.1(1), (2).

The State's suggestion that the "finding" in the preamble to its abortion statute is, in effect, an amendment to its tort, property, and criminal laws is not persuasive. The Court of Appeals concluded that the preamble "is simply an impermissible state adoption of a theory of when life begins to justify its abortion regulations." 851 F. 2d, at 1076. Supporting that construction is the state constitutional prohibition against legislative enactments pertaining to more than one subject matter. Mo. Const., Art. 3, § 23. See *In re Ray,* 83 B. R. 670 (Bkrtcy Ct., ED Mo. 1988); *Berry* v. *Majestic Milling Co.,* 223 S. W. 738 (Mo. 1920). Moreover, none of the tort, property, or criminal law cases cited by the State was either based on or buttressed by a theological answer to the question of when life begins. Rather, the Missouri courts, as well as a number of other state courts, had already concluded that a "fetus is a 'person,' 'minor,' or 'minor child' within the meaning of their particular wrongful death statutes." *O'Grady* v. *Brown,* 645 S. W. 2d 904, 910 (Mo. 1983) (en banc).[15]

Bolstering my conclusion that the preamble violates the First Amendment is the fact that the intensely divisive character of much of the national debate over the abortion issue reflects the deeply held religious convictions of many participants in the debate.[16] The Missouri Legislature may not inject its endorsement of a particular religious tradition into this debate, for "[t]he Establishment Clause does not allow

---

14. "The Court recognizes that the State may insist that the decision not be made without the benefit of medical advice. But since the most significant consequences of the decision are not medical in character, it would seem to me that the State may, with equal legitimacy, insist that the decision be made only after other appropriate counsel has been had as well. Whatever choice a pregnant young woman makes—to marry, to abort, to bear her child out of wedlock—the consequence of her decision may have a profound impact on her entire future life. A legislative determination that such a choice will be made more wisely in most cases if the advice and moral support of a parent play a part in the decisionmaking process is surely not irrational. Moreover, it is perfectly clear that the parental-consent requirement will necessarily involve a parent in the decisional process." *Planned Parenthood of Central Mo.* v. *Danforth,* 428 U.S., at 103 (STEVENS, J., concurring in part and dissenting in part).

15. The other examples cited by the State are statutes providing that unborn children are to be treated as though born within the lifetime of the decedent, see Uniform Probate code § 2–108 (1969), and statutes imposing criminal sanctions in the nature of manslaughter for the killing of a viable fetus or unborn quick child, see, *e. g.,* Ark. Stat. Ann. § 41–2223 (1947). None of the cited statutes included any "finding" on the theological question of when life begins.

16. No fewer than 67 religious organizations submitted their views as *amici curiae* on either side of this case. *Amici* briefs on both sides, moreover, frankly discuss the relation between the abortion controversy and religion. See generally, *e. g.,* Brief for Agudath Israel of America as *Amicus Curiae,* Brief for Americans United for Separation of Church and State et al. as *Amici Curiae,* Brief for Catholics for a Free Choice et al. as *Amici Curiae,* Brief for Holy Orthodox Church as *Amicus Curiae,* Brief for Lutheran Church-Missouri Synod et al. as *amici curiae,* Brief for Missouri Catholic Conference as *Amicus Curiae.* Cf. Burke, Religion and Politics in the United States, in Movements and Issues in World Religions 243, 254–256 (C. Fu & G. Spiegler eds. 1987).

public bodies to foment such disagreement." See *County of Allegheny* v. *American Civil Liberties Union, Greater Pittsburgh Chapter, post,* at 651 (STEVENS, J., concurring in part and dissenting in part).

In my opinion the preamble to the Missouri statute is unconstitutional for two reasons. To the extent that it has substantive impact on the freedom to use contraceptive procedures, it is inconsistent with the central holding in *Griswold.* To that extent that it merely makes "legislative findings without operative effect," as the State argues, Brief for Appellants 22, it violates the Establishment Clause of the First Amendment. Contrary to the theological "finding" of the Missouri Legislature, a woman's constitutionally protected liberty encompasses the right to act on her own belief that—to paraphrase St. Thomas Aquinas—until a seed has acquired the powers of sensation and movement, the life of a human being has not yet begun.[17]

17. "Just as the right to speak and the right to refrain from speaking are complementary components of a broader concept of individual freedom of mind, so also the individual's freedom to choose his own creed is the counterpart of his right to refrain from accepting the creed established by the majority. At one time it was thought that this right merely proscribed the preference of one Christian sect over another, but would not require equal respect for the conscience of the infidel, the atheist, or the adherent of a non-Christian faith such as Islam or Judaism. But when the underlying principle has been examined in the crucible of litigation, the Court has unambiguously concluded that the individual freedom of conscience protected by the First Amendment embraces the right to select any religious faith or none at all. This conclusion derives support not only from the interest in respecting the individuals' freedom of conscience, but also from the conviction that religious beliefs worthy of respect are the product of free and voluntary choice by the faithful, and from recognition of the fact that the political interest in forestalling intolerance extends beyond intolerance among Christian sects—or even intolerance among 'religions'—to encompass intolerance of the disbeliever and the uncertain. As Justice Jackson eloquently stated in *West Virginia Board of Education* v. *Barnette,* 319 U.S. 624, 642 (1943):

"'If there is any fixed star in our constitutional constellation, it is that no official, high or petty, can prescribe what shall be orthodox in politics, nationalism, religion, or other matters of opinion or force citizens to confess by word or act their faith therein.'

"The State . . . , no less than the Congress of the United States, must respect that basic truth." *Wallace* v. *Jaffree,* 472 U. S 38, 52–55 (1985) (footnotes omitted).

Appendix 4

(Slip Opinion)
NOTE: Where it is feasible, a syllabus (headnote) will be released, as is being
done in connection with this case, at the time the opinion is issued. The syllabus constitutes no part of the opinion of the Court but has been prepared
by the Reporter of Decisions for the convenience of the reader. See *United
States* v. *Detroit Lumber Co.*, 200 U.S. 321, 337.

SUPREME COURT OF THE UNITED STATES

Syllabus

CRUZAN, BY HER PARENTS AND CO-GUARDIANS, CRUZAN ET UX.
v. DIRECTOR, MISSOURI DEPARTMENT OF HEALTH, ET AL.

CERTIORARI TO THE SUPREME COURT OF MISSOURI

No. 88–1503. Argued December 6, 1989—
Decided June 25, 1990

Petitioner Nancy Cruzan is incompetent, having sustained severe injuries in an
automobile accident, and now lies in a Missouri state hospital in what is referred to
as a persistent vegetative state: generally, a condition in which a person exhibits
motor reflexes but evinces no indications of significant cognitive function. The State
is bearing the cost of her care. Hospital employees refused, without court approval,
to honor the request of Cruzan's parents, co-petitioners here, to terminate her artificial nutrition and hydration, since that would result in death. A state trial court
authorized the termination, finding that a person in Cruzan's condition has a fundamental right under the State and Federal Constitutions to direct or refuse the
withdrawal of death-prolonging procedures, and that Cruzan's expression to a former
housemate that she would not wish to continue her life if sick or injured unless she

314

could live at least halfway normally suggested that she would not wish to continue on with her nutrition and hydration. The State Supreme Court reversed. While recognizing a right to refuse treatment embodied in the commonlaw doctrine of informed consent, the court questioned its applicability in this case. It also declined to read into the State Constitution a broad right to privacy that would support an unrestricted right to refuse treatment and expressed doubt that the Federal Constitution embodied such a right. The court then decided that the State Living Will statute embodied a state policy strongly favoring the preservation of life, and that Cruzan's statements to her housemate were unreliable for the purpose of determining her intent. It rejected the argument that her parents were entitled to order the termination of her medical treatment, concluding that no person can assume that choice for an incompetent in the absence of the formalities required by the Living Will statute or clear and convincing evidence of the patient's wishes.

Held:

1. The United States Constitution does not forbid Missouri to require that evidence of an incompetent's wishes as to the withdrawal of life-sustaining treatment be proved by clear and convincing evidence. Pp. 5–20.

(a) Most state courts have based a right to refuse treatment on the common-law right to informed consent, see, _e.g., In re Storar,_ 52 N. Y. 2d 363, 420 N. E. 2d 64, or on both that right and a constitutional privacy right, see, _e. g., Superintendent of Belchertown State School_ v. _Saikewicz,_ 373 Mass. 728, 370 N. E. 2d 417. In addition to relying on state constitutions and the common law, state courts have also turned to state statutes for guidance, see, _e. g., Conservatorship of Drabick,_ 200 Cal. App. 3d 185, 245 Cal. Rptr. 840. However, these sources are not available to this Court, where the question is simply whether the Federal Constitution prohibits Missouri from choosing the rule of law which it did. Pp. 5–13.

(b) A competent person has a liberty interest under the Due Process Clause in refusing unwanted medical treatment. Cf., _e.g., Jacobson_ v. _Massachusetts,_ 197 U.S. 11, 24–30. However, the question whether that constitutional right has been violated must be determined by balancing the liberty interest against relevant state interests. For purposes of this case, it is assumed that a competent person would have a constitutionally protected right to refuse lifesaving hydration and nutrition. This does not mean that an incompetent person should possess the same right, since such a person is unable to make an informed and voluntary choice to exercise that hypothetical right or any other right. While Missouri has in effect recognized that under certain circumstances a surrogate may act for the patient in electing to withdraw hydration and nutrition and thus cause death, it has established a procedural safeguard to assure that the surrogate's action conforms as best it may to the wishes expressed by the patient while competent. Pp. 14–16.

(c) It is permissible for Missouri, in its proceedings, to apply a clear and convincing evidence standard, which is an appropriate standard when the individual interests at stake are both particularly important and more substantial than mere loss of money, _Santosky_ v. _Kramer,_ 455 U.S. 745, 756. Here, Missouri has a general interest in the protection and preservation of human life, as well as other, more particular interests, at stake. It may legitimately seek to safeguard the personal element of an individual's choice between life and death. The State is also entitled to guard against potential abuses by surrogates who may not act to protect the patient. Similarly, it is entitled to consider that a judicial proceeding regarding an incompetent's wishes may not be adversarial, with the added guarantee of accurate factfinding that the adversary process brings with it. The State may also properly decline to make judgments about the "quality" of a particular individual's life and simply assert an unqualified interest in the preservation of human life to be weighed against the constitutionally protected interests of the individual. It is self-evident that these interests are more substantial, both on an individual and societal level, than those involved in a common civil dispute. The clear and convincing evidence standard also serves as a societal judgment about how the risk of error should be distributed between the litigants. Missouri may permissibly place the increased risk of an erroneous decision on those seeking to terminate life-sustaining treatment. An erroneous decision not to terminate results in a maintenance of the status quo, with at least the potential that a wrong decision will eventually be corrected or its impact mitigated by an event such as an advancement in medical science or the patient's unexpected death. However, an erroneous decision to withdraw such treatment is not susceptible of correction. Although Missouri's proof requirement may have frustrated the effectuation of Cruzan's not-fully-expressed desires, the Constitution does not require general rules to work flawlessly. Pp. 16–20.

2. The State Supreme Court did not commit constitutional error in concluding that the evidence adduced at trial did not amount to clear and convincing proof of Cruzan's desire to have hydration and nutrition withdrawn. The trial court had not adopted a clear and convincing evidence standard, and Cruzan's observations that she did not want to live life as a "vegetable" did not deal in terms with withdrawal of medical treatment or of hydration and nutrition. Pp. 20–21.

3. The Due Process Clause does not require a State to accept the "substituted judgment" of close family members in the absence of substantial proof that their views reflect the patient's. This Court's decision upholding a State's favored treatment of traditional family relationships, *Michael H.* v. *Gerald D.,* 491 U. S ——, may not be turned into a constitutional requirement that a State must recognize the primacy of these relationships in a situation like this. Nor may a decision upholding a State's right to permit family decision making, *Parham* v. *J. R.,* 442 U.S. 584, be turned into a constitutional requirement that the State recognize such decisionmaking. Nancy Cruzan's parents would surely be qualified to exercise such a right of "substituted judgment" were it required by the Constitution. However, for the same reasons that Missouri may require clear and convincing evidence of a patient's wishes, it may also choose to defer only to those wishes rather than confide the decision to close family members. Pp. 21–22.

760 S. W. 2d 408, affirmed.

REHNQUIST, C. J., delivered the opinion of the Court, in which WHITE, O'CONNOR, SCALIA, and KENNEDY, JJ., joined. O'CONNOR, J., and SCALIA, J., filed concurring opinions. BRENNAN, J., filed a dissenting opinion, in which MARSHALL and BLACKMUN, JJ., joined. STEVENS, J., filed a dissenting opinion.

SUPREME COURT OF THE UNITED STATES

No. 88–1503

NANCY BETH CRUZAN, BY HER PARENTS AND CO-GUARDIANS, LESTER L. CRUZAN, ET UX., PETITIONERS *v.* DIRECTOR, MISSOURI DEPARTMENT OF HEALTH, ET AL.

ON WRIT OF CERTIORARI TO THE SUPREME COURT OF MISSOURI

[June 25, 1990]

CHIEF JUSTICE REHNQUIST delivered the opinion of the Court.

Petitioner Nancy Beth Cruzan was rendered incompetent as a result of severe injuries sustained during an automobile accident. Co-petitioners Lester and Joyce Cruzan, Nancy's parents and co-guardians, sought a court order directing the withdrawal of their daughter's artificial feeding and hydration equipment after it became apparent that she had virtually no chance of recovering her cognitive faculties. The Supreme Court of Missouri held that because there was no clear and convincing evidence of Nancy's desire to have life-sustaining treatment withdrawn under such circumstances, her parents lacked authority to effectuate such a request. We granted certiorari, 492 U.S. ——(1989), and now affirm.

On the night of January 11, 1983, Nancy Cruzan lost control of her car as she traveled down Elm Road in Jasper County, Missouri. The vehicle overturned, and Cruzan was discovered lying face down in a ditch without detectable respiratory or cardiac function. Paramedics were able to restore her breathing and heartbeat at the accident site, and she was transported to a hospital in an unconscious state. An attending neurosurgeon diagnosed her as having sustained probable cerebral contusions compounded by significant anoxia (lack of oxygen). The Missouri trial court in this case found that permanent brain damage generally results after 6 minutes in an anoxic state; it was estimated that Cruzan was deprived of oxygen from 12 to 14 minutes. She remained in a coma for approximately three weeks and then progressed to an unconscious state in which she was able to orally ingest some nutrition. In order to ease feeding and further the recovery, surgeons implanted a gastronomy feeding and hydration tube in Cruzan with the consent of her then husband. Subsequent rehabilitative efforts proved unavailing. She now lies in a Missouri state hospital in what is commonly referred to as a persistent vegetative state; generally, a condition in which a person exhibits motor reflexes but evinces no indications of significant cognitive function.[1] The State of Missouri is bearing the cost of her care.

---

1. The State Supreme Court, adopting much of the trial court's findings, described Nancy Cruzan's medical condition as follows:

". . . (1) [H]er respiration and circulation are not artificially maintained and are within the normal limits of a thirty-year-old female; (2) she is oblivious to her environment except for reflexive responses to sound and perhaps painful stimuli; (3) she suffered anoxia of the brain resulting in a massive enlargement of the ventricles filling with cerebrospinal fluid in the area where the

After it had become apparent that Nancy Cruzan had virtually no chance of regaining her mental faculties her parents asked hospital employees to terminate the artificial nutrition and hydration procedures. All agree that such a removal would cause her death. The employees refused to honor the request without court approval. The parents then sought and received authorization from the state trial court for termination. The court found that a person in Nancy's condition had a fundamental right under the State and Federal Constitutions to refuse or direct the withdrawal of "death prolonging procedures." App. to Pet. for Cert. A99. The court also found that Nancy's "expressed thoughts at age twenty-five in somewhat serious conversation with a housemate friend that if sick or injured she would not wish to continue her life unless she could live at least halfway normally suggests that given her present condition she would not wish to continue on with her nutrition and hydration." Id., at A97–A98.

The Supreme Court of Missouri reversed by a divided vote. The court recognized a right to refuse treatment embodied in the common-law doctrine of informed consent, but expressed skepticism about the application of that doctrine in the circumstances of this case. Cruzan v. Harmon, 760 S. W. 2d 408, 416–417 (Mo. 1988) (en banc). The court also declined to read a broad right of privacy into the

---

brain has degenerated and [her] cerebral cortical atrophy is irreversible, permanent, progressive and ongoing; (4) her highest cognitive brain function is exhibited by her grimacing perhaps in recognition of ordinarily painful stimuli, indicating the experience of pain and apparent response to sound; (5) she is a spastic quadriplegic; (6) her four extremities are contracted with irreversible muscular and tendon damage to all extremities; (7) she has no cognitive or reflexive ability to swallow food or water to maintain her daily essential needs and . . . she will never recover her ability to swallow sufficient [sic] to satisfy her needs. In sum, Nancy is diagnosed as in a persistent vegetative state. She is not dead. She is not terminally ill. Medical experts testified that she could live another thirty years." Cruzan v. Harmon, 760 S. W. 2d 408, 411 (Mo. 1989) (en banc) (quotations omitted; footnote omitted).

In observing that Cruzan was not dead, the court referred to the following Missouri statute:

"For all legal purposes, the occurrence of human death shall be determined in accordance with the usual and customary standards of medical practice, provided that death shall not be determined to have occurred unless the following minimal conditions have been met:

"(1) When respiration and circulation are not artificially maintained, there is an irreversible cessation of spontaneous respiration and circulation; or

"(2) When respiration and circulation are artificially maintained, and there is total and irreversible cessation of all brain function, including the brain stem and that such determination is made by a licensed physician." Mo. Rev. Stat. § 194.005 (1986).

Since Cruzan's respiration and circulation were not being artificially maintained, she obviously fit within the first proviso of the statute.

Dr. Fred Plum, the creator of the term "persistent vegetative state" and a renowned expert on the subject, has described the "vegetative state" in the following terms:

"'Vegetative state describes a body which is functioning entirely in terms of its internal controls. It maintains temperature. It maintains heart beat and pulmonary ventilation. It maintains digestive activity. It maintains reflex activity of muscles and nerves for low level conditioned responses. But there is no behavioral evidence of either self-awareness or awareness of the surroundings in a learned manner.'" In re Jobes, 108 N. J. 394, 403, 529 A. 2d 434, 438 (1987).

See also Brief for American Medical Association et al., as Amici Curiae, 6 ("The persistent vegetative state can best be understood as one of the conditions in which patients have suffered a loss of consciousness.").

State Constitution which would "support the right of a person to refuse medical treatment in every circumstance," and expressed doubt as to whether such a right existed under the United States Constitution. *Id.,* at 417–418. It then decided that the Missouri Living Will statute, Mo. Rev. Stat. § 459.010 *et seq.* (1986), embodied a state policy strongly favoring the preservation of life. 760 S. W. 2d, at 419–420. The court found that Cruzan's statements to her roommate regarding her desire to live or die under certain conditions were "unreliable for the purpose of determining her intent," *id.,* at 424, "and thus insufficient to support the co-guardians claim to exercise substituted judgment on Nancy's behalf." *Id.,* at 426. It rejected the argument that Cruzan's parents were entitled to order the termination of her medical treatment, concluding that "no person can assume that choice for an incompetent in the absence of the formalities required under Missouri's Living Will statutes or the clear and convincing, inherently reliable evidence absent here." *Id.,* at 425. The court also expressed its view that "[b]road policy questions bearing on life and death are more properly addressed by representative assemblies" than judicial bodies. *Id.,* at 426.

We granted certiorari to consider the question of whether Cruzan has a right under the United States Constitution which would require the hospital to withdraw life-sustaining treatment from her under these circumstances.

At common law, even the touching of one person by another without consent and without legal justification was a battery. See W. Keeton, D. Dobbs, R. Keeton, & D. Owen, Prosser and Keeton on Law of Torts § 9, pp. 39–42 (5th ed. 1984). Before the turn of the century, this Court observed that "[n]o right is held more sacred, or is more carefully guarded, by the common law, than the right of every individual to the possession and control of his own person, free from all restraint or interference of others, unless by clear and unquestionable authority of law." *Union Pacific R. Co.* v. *Botsford,* 141 U.S. 250, 251 (1891). This notion of bodily integrity has been embodied in the requirement that informed consent is generally required for medical treatment. Justice Cardozo, while on the Court of Appeals of New York, aptly described this doctrine: "Every human being of adult years and sound mind has a right to determine what shall be done with his own body; and a surgeon who performs an operation without his patient's consent commits an assault, for which he is liable in damages." *Schloendorff* v. *Society of New York Hospital,* 211 N. Y. 125, 129–30, 105 N. E. 92, 93 (1914). The informed consent doctrine has become firmly entrenched in American tort law. See Dobbs, Keeton, & Owen, *supra,* § 32, pp. 189–192; F. Rozovsky, Consent to Treatment, A Practical Guide 1–98 (2d ed. 1990).

The logical corollary of the doctrine of informed consent is that the patient generally possesses the right not to consent, that is, to refuse treatment. Until about 15 years ago and the seminal decision in *In re Quinlan,* 70 N. J. 10, 355 A. 2d 647, cert. denied *sub nom., Garger* v. *New Jersey,* 429 U.S. 922 (1976), the number of right-to-refuse-treatment decisions were relatively few.[2] Most of the earlier cases involved patients who refused medical treatment forbidden by their religious beliefs, thus implicating First Amendment rights as well as common law rights of self-

---

2. See generally Karnezis, Patient's Right to Refuse Treatment Allegedly Necessary to Sustain Life, 93 A. L. R. 3d 67 (1979) (collecting cases); Cantor, A Patient's Decision to Decline Life-Saving Medical Treatment: Bodily Integrity Versus the Preservation of Life, 26 Rutgers L. Rev. 228, 229, and n. 5 (1973) (noting paucity of cases).

determination.[3] More recently, however, with the advance of medical technology capable of sustaining life well past the point where natural forces would have brought certain death in earlier times, cases involving the right to refuse life-sustaining treatment have burgeoned. See 760 S W. 2d, at 412, n. 4 (collecting 54 reported decisions from 1976–1988).

In the *Quinlan* case, young Karen Quinlan suffered severe brain damage as the result of anoxia, and entered a persistent vegetative state. Karen's father sought judicial approval to disconnect his daughter's respirator. The New Jersey Supreme Court granted the relief, holding that Karen had a right of privacy grounded in the Federal Constitution to terminate treatment. *In re Quinlan,* 70 N. J., at 38–42, 355 A. 2d at 662–664. Recognizing that this right was not absolute, however, the court balanced it against asserted state interests. Noting that the State's interest "weakens and the individual's right to privacy grows as the degree of bodily invasion increases and the prognosis dims," the court concluded that the state interests had to give way in that case. *Id.,* at 41, 355 A. 2d, at 664. The court also concluded that the "only practical way" to prevent the loss of Karen's privacy right due to her incompetence was to allow her guardian and family to decide "whether she would exercise it in these circumstances." *Ibid.*

After *Quinlan,* however, most courts have based a right to refuse treatment either solely on the common law right to informed consent or on both the common law right and a constitutional privacy right. See L. Tribe, American Constitutional Law § 15–11, p. 1365 (2d ed. 1988). In *Superintendent of Belchertown State School* v. *Saikewicz,* 373 Mass. 728, 370 N. E. 2d 417 (1977), the Supreme Judicial Court of Massachusetts relied on both the right of privacy and the right of informed consent to permit the withholding of chemotherapy from a profoundly-retarded 67-year-old man suffering from leukemia. *Id.,* at 737–738, 370 N. E. 2d, at 424. Reasoning that an incompetent person retains the same rights as a competent individual "because the value of human dignity extends to both," the court adopted a "substituted judgment" standard whereby courts were to determine what an incompetent individual's decision would have been under the circumstances. *Id.,* at 745, 752–753, 757–758, 370 N. E. 2d, at 427, 431, 434. Distilling certain state interests from prior case law—the preservation of life, the protection of the interests of innocent third parties, the prevention of suicide, and the maintenance of the ethical integrity of the medical profession—the court recognized the first interest as paramount and noted it was greatest when an affliction was curable, "as opposed to the State interest where, as here, the issue is not whether, but when, for how long, and at what cost to the individual [a] life may be briefly extended." *Id.,* at 742, 370 N. E. 2d, at 426.

In *In re Storar* 52 N. Y. 2d 363, 420 N. E. 2d 64, cert. denied, 454 U.S. 858 (1981), the New York Court of Appeals declined to base a right to refuse treatment on a constitutional privacy right. Instead, it found such a right "adequately supported" by the informed consent doctrine. *Id.,* at 376–377, 420 N. E. 2d, at 70. In *In re Eichner* (decided with *In re Storar, supra*) an 83-year-old man who had suffered brain damage from anoxia entered a vegetative state and was thus incompe-

---

3. See Chapman, The Uniform Rights of the Terminally Ill Act: Too Little, Too Late?, 42 Ark. L. Rev. 319, 324, n. 15 (1989); see also F. Rozovsky, Consent to Treatment, A Practical Guide 415–423 (2d ed. 1984).

tent to consent to the removal of his respirator. The court, however, found it unnecessary to reach the question of whether his rights could be exercised by others since it found the evidence clear and convincing from statements made by the patient when competent that he "did not want to be maintained in a vegetative coma by use of a respirator." *Id.,* at 380, 420 N. E. 2d, at 72. In the companion *Storar* case, a 52-year-old man suffering from bladder cancer had been profoundly retarded during most of his life. Implicitly rejecting the approach taken in *Saikewicz, supra,* the court reasoned that due to such life-long incompetency, "it is unrealistic to attempt to determine whether he would want to continue potentially life prolonging treatment if he were competent." 52 N. Y. 2d, at 380, 420 N. E. 2d, at 72. As the evidence showed that the patient's required blood transfusions did not involve excessive pain and without them his mental and physical abilities would deteriorate, the court concluded that it should not "allow an incompetent patient to bleed to death because someone, even someone as close as a parent or sibling, feels that this is best for one with an incurable disease." *Id.,* at 382, 420 N. E. 2d, at 73.

Many of the later cases build on the principles established in *Quinlan, Saikewicz* and *Storar/Eichner.* For instance, in *In re Conroy,* 98 N. J. 321, 486 A. 2d 1209 (1985), the same court that decided *Quinlan* considered whether a nasogastric feeding tube could be removed from an 84-year-old incompetent nursing-home resident suffering irreversible mental and physical ailments. While recognizing that a federal right of privacy might apply in the case, the court, contrary to its approach in *Quinlan,* decided to base its decision on the common-law right to self-determination and informed consent. 98 N. J., at 348, 486 A. 2d, at 1223. "On balance, the right to self-determination ordinarily outweighs any countervailing state interests, and competent persons generally are permitted to refuse medical treatment, even at the risk of death. Most of the cases that have held otherwise, unless they involved the interest in protecting innocent third parties, have concerned the patient's competency to make a rational and considered choice." *Id.,* at 353–354, 486 A. 2d, at 1225.

Reasoning that the right of self-determination should not be lost merely because an individual is unable to sense a violation of it, the court held that incompetent individuals retain a right to refuse treatment. It also held that such a right could be exercised by a surrogate decisionmaker using a "subjective" standard when there was clear evidence that the incompetent person would have exercised it. Where such evidence was lacking, the court held that an individual's right could still be invoked in certain circumstances under objective "best interest" standards. *Id.,* at 361–368, 486 A. 2d, at 1229–1233. Thus, if some trustworthy evidence existed that the individual would have wanted to terminate treatment, but not enough to clearly establish a person's wishes for purposes of the subjective standard, and the burden of a prolonged life from the experience of pain and suffering markedly outweighed its satisfactions, treatment could be terminated under a "limited-objective" standard. Where no trustworthy evidence existed, and a person's suffering would make the administration of life-sustaining treatment inhumane, a "pure-objective" standard could be used to terminate treatment. If none of these conditions obtained, the court held it was best to err in favor of preserving life. *Id.,* at 364–368, 486 A. 2d, at 1231–1233.

The court also rejected certain categorical distinctions that had been drawn in prior refusal-of-treatment cases as lacking substance for decision purposes: the distinction between actively hastening death by terminating treatment and passively allowing a person to die of a disease; between treating individuals as an initial matter versus withdrawing treatment afterwards; between ordinary versus extraordinary treatment; and between treatment by artificial feeding versus other forms of life-sustaining medical procedures. *Id.,* at 369–374, 486 N. E. 2d, at 1233–1237. As to the last item, the court acknowledged the "emotional significance" of food, but noted that feeding by implanted tubes is a "medical procedur[e] with inherent risks and possible side effects, instituted by skilled health-care providers to compensate for impaired physical functioning" which analytically was equivalent to artificial breathing using a respirator. *Id.,* at 373, 486 A. 2d, at 1236.[4]

In contrast to *Conroy,* the Court of Appeals of New York recently refused to accept less than the clearly expressed wishes of a patient before permitting the exercise of her right to refuse treatment by a surrogate decisionmaker. *In re Westchester County Medical Center on behalf of O'Connor,* 531 N. E. 2d 607 (1988) *(O'Connor).* There, the court, over the objection of the patient's family members, granted an order to insert a feeding tube into a 77-year-old woman rendered incompetent as a result of several strokes. While continuing to recognize a common-law right to refuse treatment, the court rejected the substituted judgment approach for asserting it "because it is inconsistent with our fundamental commitment to the notion that no person or court should substitute its judgment as to what would be an acceptable quality of life for another. Consequently, we adhere to the view that, despite its pitfalls and inevitable uncertainties, the inquiry must always be narrowed to the patient's expressed intent, with every effort made to minimize the opportunity for error." *Id.,* at 530, 531 N. E. 2d, at 613 (citation omitted). The court held that the record lacked the requisite clear and convincing evidence of the patient's expressed intent to withhold life-sustaining treatment. *Id.,* at 531–534, 531 N. E. 2d, at 613–615.

Other courts have found state statutory law relevant to the resolution of these issues. In *Conservatorship of Drabick,* 200 Cal. App. 3d 185, 245 Cal. Rptr. 840, cert. denied,——U.S.——(1988), the California Court of Appeal authorized the removal of a nasogastric feeding tube from a 44-year-old man who was in a persistent vegetative state as a result of an auto accident. Noting that the right to refuse treatment was grounded in both the common law and a constitutional right of privacy, the court held that a state probate statute authorized the patient's conservator to order the withdrawal of life-sustaining treatment when such a decision was made in good faith based on medical advice and the conservatee's best interests. While acknowledging that "to claim that [a patient's] 'right to choose' survives incompetence is a legal fiction at best," the court reasoned that the respect society

---

4. In a later trilogy of cases, the New Jersey Supreme Court stressed that the analytic framework adopted in *Conroy* was limited to elderly, incompetent patients with shortened life expectancies, and established alternative approaches to deal with a different set of situations. See *In re Farrell,* 108 N. J. 335, 529 A. 2d 404 (1987) (37-year-old competent mother with terminal illness had right to removal of respirator based on common law and constitutional principles which overrode competing state interests); *In re Peter,* 108 N. J. 365, 529 A. 2d 419 (1987) (65-year-old woman in persistent vegetative state had right to removal of nasogastic feeding tube— under *Conroy* subjective test, power of attorney and hearsay testimony constituted clear and convincing proof of patient's intent to have treatment withdrawn); *In re Jobes,* 108 N. J. 394, 529 A. 2d 434 (1987) (31-year-old woman in persistent vegetative state entitled to removal of jejunostomy feeding tube—even though hearsay testimony regarding patient's intent insufficient to meet clear and convincing standard of proof, under *Quinlan,* family or close friends entitled to make a substituted judgment for patient).

accords to persons as individuals is not lost upon incompetence and is best preserved by allowing others "to make a decision that reflects [a patient's] interests more closely than would a purely technological decision to do whatever is possible"[5] *Id.*, at 208, 245 Cal. Rptr. at 854–855. See also *In re Conservatorship of Torres*, 357 N. W. 2d 332 (Minn. 1984) (Minnesota court had constitutional and statutory authority to authorize a conservator to order the removal of an incompetent individual's respirator since in patient's best interests).

In *In re Estate of Longeway*, 123 Ill. 2d 33, 549 N. E. 2d 292 (1989), the Supreme Court of Illinois considered whether a 76-year-old woman rendered incompetent from a series of strokes had a right to the discontinuance of artificial nutrition and hydration. Noting that the boundaries of a federal right of privacy were uncertain, the court found a right to refuse treatment in the doctrine of informed consent. *Id.*, at 43–45, 549 N. E. 2d, at 296–297. The court further held that the State Probate Act impliedly authorized a guardian to exercise a ward's right to refuse artificial sustenance in the event that the ward was terminally ill and irreversibly comatose. *Id.*, at 45–47, 549 N. E. 2d, at 298. Declining to adopt a best interests standard for deciding when it would be appropriate to exercise a ward's right because it "lets another make a determination of a patient's quality of life," the court opted instead for a substituted judgment standard. *Id.*, at 49, 549 N. E. 2d, at 299. Finding the "expressed intent" standard utilized in *O'Connor*, *supra*, too rigid, the court noted that other clear and convincing evidence of the patient's intent could be considered. 133 Ill. 2d, at 50–51, 549 N. E. 2d, at 300. The court also adopted the "consensus opinion [that] treats artificial nutrition and hydration as medical treatment." *Id.*, at 42, 549 N. E. 2d, at 296. Cf. *McConnell* v. *Beverly Enterprises-Connecticut, Inc.*, 209 Conn. 692, 705, 553 A. 2d 596, 603 (1989) (right to withdraw artificial nutrition and hydration found in the Connecticut Removal of Life Support Systems Act, which "provid[es] functional guidelines for the exercise of the common law and constitutional rights of self-determination"; attending physician authorized to remove treatment after finding that patient is in a terminal condition, obtaining consent of family, and considering expressed wishes of patient).[6]

As these cases demonstrate, the common-law doctrine of informed consent is viewed as generally encompassing the right of a competent individual to refuse medical treatment. Beyond that, these decisions demonstrate both similarity and diversity

5. The *Drabick* court drew support for its analysis from earlier, influential decisions rendered by California courts of appeal. See *Bouvia* v. *Superior Court*, 179 Cal. App. 3d 1127, 225 Cal. Rptr. 297 (1986) (competent 28-year-old quadriplegic had right to removal of nasogastric feeding tube inserted against her will); *Bartling* v. *Superior Court*, 163 Cal. app. 3d 186, 209 Cal. Rptr. 220 (1984) (competent 70-year-old, seriously-ill man had right to the removal of respirator); *Barber* v. *Superior Court*, 147 Cal. App. 3d 1006, 195 Cal. Rptr. 484 (1983) (physicians could not be prosecuted for homicide on account of removing respirator and intravenous feeding tubes of patient in persistent vegetative state).

6. Besides the Missouri Supreme Court in *Cruzan* and the courts in *McConnell, Longeway, Drabick, Bouvia, Barber, O'Connor, Conroy, Jobes,* and *Peter, supra*, appellate courts of at least four other States and one Federal District Court have specifically considered and discussed the issue of withholding or withdrawing artificial nutrition and hydration from incompetent individuals. See *Gray* v. *Romeo*, 697 F. Supp. 580 (RI 1988); *In re Gardner*, 534 A. 2d 947 (Me. 1987); *In re Grant*, 109 Wash. 2d 545, 747 P. 2d 445 (Wash. 1987); *Brophy* v. *New England Sinai Hospital, Inc.*, 398 Mass. 417, 497 N. E. 2d 626 (1986); *Corbett* v. *D'Alessandro*, 487 So. 2d 368 (Fla. App. 1986). All of these courts permitted or would permit the termination of such measures based on rights grounded in the common law, or in the State or Federal Constitution.

in their approach to decision of what all agree is a perplexing question with unusually strong moral and ethical overtones. State courts have available to them for decision a number of sources—state constitutions, statutes, and common law—which are not available to us. In this Court, the question is simply and starkly whether the United States Constitution prohibits Missouri from choosing the rule of decision which it did. This is the first case in which we have been squarely presented with the issue of whether the United States Constitution grants what is in common parlance referred to as a "right to die." We follow the judicious counsel of our decision in *Twin City Bank* v. *Nebeker,* 167 U.S. 196, 202 (1897), where we said that in deciding "a question of such magnitude and importance . . . it is the [better] part of wisdom not to attempt, by any general statement, to cover every possible phase of the subject."

The Fourteenth Amendment provides that no State shall "deprive any person of life, liberty, or property, without due process of law." The principle that a competent person has a constitutionally protected liberty interest in refusing unwanted medical treatment may be inferred from our prior decisions. In *Jacobson* v. *Massachusetts,* 197 U.S. 11, 24–30 (1905), for instance, the Court balanced an individual's liberty interest in declining an unwanted smallpox vaccine against the State's interest in preventing disease. Decisions prior to the incorporation of the Fourth Amendment into the Fourteenth Amendment analyzed searches and seizures involving the body under the Due Process Clause and were thought to implicate substantial liberty interests. See, e.g., *Breithaupt* v. *Abrams,* 352 U.S. 432, 439 (1957) ("As against the right of an individual that his person be held inviolable . . . must be set the interests of society . . .").

Just this Term, in the course of holding that a State's procedures for administering antipsychotic medication to prisoners were sufficient to satisfy due process concerns, we recognized that prisoners possess "a significant liberty interest in avoiding the unwanted administration of antipsychotic drugs under the Due Process Clause of the Fourteenth Amendment." *Washington* v. *Harper,* ——U.S.——,—— (1990) (slip op., at 9); see also *id.,* at ——(slip op., at 17) ("The forcible injection of medication into a nonconsenting person's body represents a substantial interference with that person's liberty"). Still other cases support the recognition of a general liberty interest in refusing medical treatment. *Vitek* v. *Jones,* 445 U.S. 480, 494 (1980) (transfer to mental hospital coupled with mandatory behavior modification treatment implicated liberty interests); *Parham* v. *J. R.,* 442 U.S. 584, 600 (1979) ("a child, in common with adults, has a substantial liberty interest in not being confined unnecessarily for medical treatment").

But determining that a person has a "liberty interest" under the Due Process Clause does not end the inquiry;[7] "whether respondent's constitutional rights have been violated must be determined by balancing his liberty interests against the relevant state interests." *Youngberg* v. *Romeo,* 457 U.S. 307, 321 (1982). See also *Mills* v. *Rogers,* 457 U.S. 291, 299 (1982).

Petitioners insist that under the general holdings of our cases, the forced administration of life-sustaining medical treatment, and even of artificially-delivered food and water essential to life, would implicate a competent person's liberty interest.

---

7. Although many state courts have held that a right to refuse treatment is encompassed by a generalized constitutional right of privacy, we have never so held. We believe this issue is more properly analyzed in terms of a Fourteenth Amendment liberty interest. See *Bowers* v. *Hardwick,* 478 U.S. 186, 194–195 (1986).

Although we think the logic of the cases discussed above would embrace such a liberty interest, the dramatic consequences involved in refusal of such treatment would inform the inquiry as to whether the deprivation of that interest is constitutionally permissible. But for purposes of this case, we assume that the United States Constitution would grant a competent person a constitutionally protected right to refuse lifesaving hydration and nutrition.

Petitioners go on to assert that an incompetent person should possess the same right in this respect as is possessed by a competent person. They rely primarily on our decisions in *Parham* v. *J. R., supra,* and *Youngberg* v. *Romeo,* 457 U.S. 307 (1982). In *Parham,* we held that a mentally disturbed minor child had a liberty interest in "not being confined unnecessarily for medical treatment," 442 U.S., at 600, but we certainly did not intimate that such a minor child, after commitment, would have a liberty interest in refusing treatment. In *Youngberg,* we held that a seriously retarded adult had a liberty interest in safety and freedom from bodily restraint, 457 U.S., at 320. *Youngberg,* however, did not deal with decisions to administer or withhold medical treatment.

The difficulty with petitioners' claim is that in a sense it begs the question: an incompetent person is not able to make an informed and voluntary choice to exercise a hypothetical right to refuse treatment or any other right. Such a "right" must be exercised for her, if at all, by some sort of surrogate. Here, Missouri has in effect recognized that under certain circumstances a surrogate may act for the patient in electing to have hydration and nutrition withdrawn in such a way as to cause death, but it has established a procedural safeguard to assure that the action of the surrogate conforms as best it may to the wishes expressed by the patient while competent. Missouri requires that evidence of the incompetent's wishes as to the withdrawal of treatment be proved by clear and convincing evidence. The question, then, is whether the United States Constitution forbids the establishment of this procedural requirement by the State. We hold that it does not.

Whether or not Missouri's clear and convincing evidence requirement comports with the United States Constitution depends in part on what interests the State may properly seek to protect in this situation. Missouri relies on its interest in the protection and preservation of human life, and there can be no gainsaying this interest. As a general matter, the States—indeed, all civilized nations—demonstrate their commitment to life by treating homicide as serious crime. Moreover, the majority of States in this country have laws imposing criminal penalties on one who assists another to commit suicide.[8] We do not think a State is required to remain neutral in the face of an informed and voluntary decision by a physically-able adult to starve to death.

But in the context presented here, a State has more particular interests at stake. The choice between life and death is a deeply personal decision of obvious and overwhelming finality. We believe Missouri may legitimately seek to safeguard the personal element of this choice through the imposition of heightened evidentiary requirements. It cannot be disputed that the Due Process Clause protects an interest in life as well as an interest in refusing life-sustaining medical treatment. Not all incompetent patients will have loved ones available to serve as surrogate decision-makers. And even where family members are present, "[t]here will, of course, be

---

8. See Smith, All's Well That Ends Well: Toward a Policy of Assisted Rational Suicide or Merely Enlightened Self-Determination?, 22 U. C. Davis L. Rev. 275, 290–291, n. 106 (1989) (compiling statutes).

some unfortunate situations in which family members will not act to protect a patient." *In re Jobes,* 108 N. J. 394, 419, 529 A. 2d 434, 477 (1987). A State is entitled to guard against potential abuses in such situations. Similarly, a State is entitled to consider that a judicial proceeding to make a determination regarding an incompetent's wishes may very well not be an adversarial one, with the added guarantee of accurate factfinding that the adversary process brings with it.[9] See *Ohio* v. *Akron Center for Reproductive Health,*——U.S.——,——(1990) (slip op., at 10–11). Finally, we think a State may properly decline to make judgments about the "quality" of life that a particular individual may enjoy, and simply assert an unqualified interest in the preservation of human life to be weighed against the constitutionally protected interests of the individual.

In our view, Missouri has permissibly sought to advance these interests through the adoption of a "clear and convincing" standard of proof to govern such proceedings. "The function of a standard of proof, as that concept is embodied in the Due Process Clause and in the realm of factfinding, is to 'instruct the factfinder concerning the degree of confidence our society thinks he should have in the correctness of factual conclusions for a particular type of adjudication.'" *Addington* v. *Texas,* 441 U.S. 418, 423 (1979) (quoting *In re Winship,* 397 U.S. 358, 370 (1970) (Harlan, J., concurring)). "This Court has mandated an intermediate standard of proof—'clear and convincing evidence'—when the individual interests at stake in a state proceeding are both 'particularly important' and 'more substantial than mere loss of money.'" *Santosky* v. *Kramer,* 455 U.S. 745, 756 (1982) (quoting *Addington, supra,* at 424). Thus, such a standard has been required in deportation proceedings, *Woodby* v. *INS,* 385 U.S. 276 (1966), in denaturalization proceedings, *Schneiderman* v. *United States,* 320 U.S. 118 (1943), in civil commitment proceedings, *Addington, supra,* and in proceedings for the termination of parental rights. *Santosky, supra.*[10] Further, this level of proof, "or an even higher one, has tradi-

---

9. Since Cruzan was a patient at a state hospital when this litigation commenced, the State has been involved as an adversary from the beginning. However, it can be expected that many of these types of disputes will arise in private institutions, where a guardian *ad litem* or similar party will have been appointed as the sole representative of the incompetent individual in the litigation. In such cases, a guardian may act in entire good faith, and yet not maintain a position truly adversarial to that of the family. Indeed, as noted by the court below, "[t]he guardian *ad litem* [in this case] finds himself in the predicament of believing that it is in Nancy's 'best interest to have the tube feeding discontinued' but 'feeling that an appeal should be made because our responsibility to her as attorneys and guardians *ad litem* was to pursue this matter to the highest court in the state in view of the fact that this is a case of first impression in the State of Missouri.'" 760 S. W. 2d, at 410, n. 1. Cruzan's guardian *ad litem* has also filed a brief in this Court urging reversal of the Missouri Supreme Court's decision. None of this is intended to suggest that the guardian acted the least bit improperly in this proceeding. It is only meant to illustrate the limits which may obtain on the adversarial nature of this type of litigation.

10. We recognize that these cases involved instances where the government sought to take action against an individual. See *Price Waterhouse* v. *Hopkins,* 490 U.S.——,——(1989) (plurality opinion). Here, by contrast, the government seeks to protect the interests of an individual, as well as its own institutional interests, in life. We do not see any reason why important individual interests should be afforded less protection simply because the government finds itself in the position of defending them. "[W]e find it significant that . . . the defendant rather than the plaintiff" seeks the clear and convincing standard of proof—"suggesting that this standard ordinarily serves as a shield rather than . . . a sword." *Id.,* at——. That it is the government that has picked up the shield should be of no moment.

tionally been imposed in cases involving allegations of civil fraud, and in a variety of other kinds of civil cases involving such issues as . . . lost wills, oral contracts to make bequests, and the like." *Woodby, supra,* at 285, n. 18.

We think it self-evident that the interests at stake in the instant proceedings are more substantial, both on an individual and societal level, than those involved in a run-of-the-mine civil dispute. But not only does the standard of proof reflect the importance of a particular adjudication, it also serves as "a societal judgment about how the risk of error should be distributed between the litigants." *Santosky, supra,* 455 U.S. at 755; *Addington, supra,* at 423. The more stringent the burden of proof a party must bear, the more that party bears the risk of an erroneous decision. We believe that Missouri may permissibly place an increased risk of an erroneous decision on those seeking to terminate an incompetent individual's life-sustaining treatment. An erroneous decision not to terminate results in a maintenance of the status quo; the possibility of subsequent developments such as advancements in medical science, the discovery of new evidence regarding the patient's intent, changes in the law, or simply the unexpected death of the patient despite the administration of life-sustaining treatment, at least create the potential that a wrong decision will eventually be corrected or its impact mitigated. An erroneous decision to withdraw life-sustaining treatment, however, is not susceptible of correction. In *Santosky,* one of the factors which led the Court to require proof by clear and convincing evidence in a proceeding to terminate parental rights was that a decision in such a case was final and irrevocable. *Santosky, supra,* at 759. The same must surely be said of the decision to discontinue hydration and nutrition of a patient such as Nancy Cruzan, which all agree will result in her death.

It is also worth noting that most, if not all, States simply forbid oral testimony entirely in determining the wishes of parties in transactions which, while important, simply do not have the consequences that a decision to terminate a person's life does. At common law and by statute in most States, the parole evidence rule prevents the variations of the terms of a written contract by oral testimony. The statute of frauds makes unenforceable oral contracts to leave property by will, and statutes regulating the making of wills universally require that those instruments be in writing. See 2A. Corbin, Contracts § 398, pp. 360–361 (1950); 2 W. Page, Law of Wills §§ 19.3–19.5, pp. 61–71 (1960). There is no doubt that statutes requiring wills to be in writing, and statutes of frauds which require that a contract to make a will be in writing, on occasion frustrate the effectuation of the intent of a particular decedent, just as Missouri's requirement of proof in this case may have frustrated the effectuation of the not-fully-expressed desires of Nancy Cruzan. But the Constitution does not require general rules to work faultlessly; no general rule can.

In sum, we conclude that a State may apply a clear and convincing evidence standard in proceedings where a guardian seeks to discontinue nutrition and hydration of a person diagnosed to be in a persistent vegetative state. We note that many courts which have adopted some sort of substituted judgment procedure in situations like this, whether they limit consideration of evidence to the prior expressed wishes of the incompetent individual, or whether they allow more general proof of what the individual's decision would have been, require a clear and convincing standard of proof for such evidence. See, *e.g., Longeway,* 133 Ill. 2d, at 50–51, 549 N. E. 2d at 300; *McConnell,* 209 Conn., at 707–710, 553 A. 2d at 604–605; *O'Connor,* 72 N. Y., at 529–530, 531 N. E. 2d, at 613; *In re Gardner,* 534 A. 2d 947, 952–953 (Me. 1987); *In re Jobes,* 108 N. J., at 412–413, 529 A. 2d, at 443;

Leach v. *Akron General Medical Center,* 68 Ohio Misc. 1, 11, 426 N. E. 2d 809, 815 (1980).

The Supreme Court of Missouri held that in this case the testimony adduced at trial did not amount to clear and convincing proof of the patient's desire to have hydration and nutrition withdrawn. In so doing it reversed a decision of the Missouri trial court which had found that the evidence "suggest[ed]" Nancy Cruzan would not have desired to continue such measures, App. to Pet. for Cert. A98, but which had not adopted the standard of "clear and convincing evidence" enunciated by the Supreme Court. The testimony adduced at trial consisted primarily of Nancy Cruzan's statements made to a housemate about a year before her accident that she would not want to live should she face life as a "vegetable," and other observations to the same effect. The observations did not deal in term with withdrawal of medical treatment or of hydration and nutrition. We cannot say that the Supreme Court of Missouri committed constitutional error in reaching the conclusion that it did.[11]

Petitioners alternatively contend that Missouri must accept the "substituted judgment" of close family members even in the absence of substantial proof that their views reflect the views of the patient. They rely primarily upon our decisions in *Michael H.* v. *Gerald D.,* 491 U.S.——(1989), and *Parham* v. *J. R.,* 442 U.S. 584 (1979). But we do not think these cases support their claim. In *Michael H.,* we *upheld* the constitutionality of California's favored treatment of traditional family relationships; such a holding may not be turned around into a constitutional requirement that a State *must* recognize the primacy of those relationships in a situation like this. And in *Parham,* where the patient was a minor, we also *upheld* the constitutionality of a state scheme in which parents made certain decisions for mentally ill minors. Here again petitioners would seek to turn a decision which allowed a State to rely on family decisionmaking into a constitutional requirement that the State recognize such decisionmaking. But constitutional law does not work that way.

No doubt is engendered by anything in this record but that Nancy Cruzan's mother and father are loving and caring parents. If the State were required by the United States Constitution to repose a right of "substituted judgment" with anyone, the Cruzans would surely qualify. But we do not think the Due Process Clause requires the State to repose judgment on these matters with anyone but the patient herself. Close family members may have a strong feeling—a feeling not at all ignoble or unworthy, but not entirely disinterested, either—that they do not wish to witness the continuation of the life of a loved one which they regard as hopeless, meaningless, and even degrading. But there is no automatic assurance that the view of close fam-

---

11. The clear and convincing standard of proof has been variously defined in this context as "proof sufficient to persuade the trier of fact that the patient held a firm and settled commitment to the termination of life supports under the circumstances like those presented," *In re Westchester County Medical Center on behalf of O'Connor,* 72 N. Y. 2d 517, 531, N. E. 2d 607, 613 (1988) *(O'Connor),* and as evidence which "produces in the mind of the trier of fact a firm belief or conviction as to the truth of the allegations sought to be established, evidence so clear, direct and weighty and convincing as to enable [the factfinder] to come to a clear conviction, without hesitancy, of the truth of the precise facts in issue." *In re Jobes,* 108 N. J., at 407–408, 529 A. 2d, at 441 (quotation omitted). In both of these cases the evidence of the patient's intent to refuse medical treatment was arguably stronger than that presented here. The New York Court of Appeals and the Supreme Court of New Jersey, respectively, held that the proof failed to meet a clear and convincing threshold. See *O'Connor, supra,* at 526–534, 531 N. E. 2d, at 610–615; *Jobes, supra,* at 442–443.

ily members will necessarily be the same as the patient's would have been had she been confronted with the prospect of her situation while competent. All of the reasons previously discussed for allowing Missouri to require clear and convincing evidence of the patient's wishes lead us to conclude that the State may choose to defer only to those wishes, rather than confide the decision to close family members.[12]

The judgment of the Supreme Court of Missouri is *Affirmed.*

12. We are not faced in this case with the question of whether a State might be required to defer to the decision of a surrogate if competent and probative evidence established that the patient herself had expressed a desire that the decision to terminate life-sustaining treatment be made for her by that individual.

Petitioners also adumbrate in their brief a claim based on the Equal Protection Clause of the Fourteenth Amendment to the effect that Missouri has impermissibly treated incompetent patients differently from competent ones, citing the statement in *Cleburne* v. *Cleburne Living Center, Inc.,* 473, U.S. 432, 439 (1985), that the clause is "essentially a direction that all persons similarly situated should be treated alike." The differences between the choice made *by* a competent person to refuse medical treatment, and the choice made *for* an incompetent person by someone else to refuse medical treatment, are so obviously different that the State is warranted in establishing rigorous procedure for the latter class of cases which do not apply to the former class.

SUPREME COURT OF THE UNITED STATES

No. 88–1503

NANCY BETH CRUZAN, BY HER PARENTS AND CO-GUARDIANS, LESTER L. CRUZAN, ET UX., PETITIONERS *v.* DIRECTOR, MISSOURI DEPARTMENT OF HEALTH, ET AL.

ON WRIT OF CERTIORARI TO THE SUPREME COURT OF MISSOURI

[June 25, 1990]

JUSTICE O'CONNOR, concurring.

I agree that a protected liberty interest in refusing unwanted medical treatment may be inferred from our prior decisions, see *ante* at 13, and that the refusal of artificially delivered food and water is encompassed within that liberty interest. See *ante,* at 15. I write separately to clarify why I believe this to be so.

As the Court notes, the liberty interest in refusing medical treatment flows from decisions involving the State's invasions into the body. See *ante,* at 14. Because our notions of liberty are inextricably entwined with our idea of physical freedom and self-determination, the Court has often deemed state incursions into the body repugnant to the interests protected by the Due Process Clause. See, *e.g., Rochin* v. *California,* 342 U.S. 165, 172 (1952) ("Illegally breaking into the privacy of the petitioner, the struggle to open his mouth and remove what was there, the forcible extraction of his stomach's contents . . . is bound to offend even hardened sensibilities"); *Union Pacific R. Co.* v. *Botsford,* 141 U.S. 250, 251 (1891). Our Fourth Amendment jurisprudence has echoed this same concern. See *Schmerber* v. *California,* 384 U.S. 757, 772 (1966) ("The integrity of an individual's person is a cherished value of our society"); *Winston* v. *Lee,* 470 U.S. 753, 759 (1985) ("A compelled surgical intrusion into an individual's body for evidence . . . implicates expectations of privacy and security of such magnitude that the intrusion may be 'unreasonable' even if likely to produce evidence of a crime"). The State's imposition of medical treatment on an unwilling competent adult necessarily involves some form of restraint and intrusion. A seriously ill or dying patient whose wishes are not honored may feel a captive of the machinery required for life-sustaining measures or other medical interventions. Such forced treatment may burden that individual's liberty interests as much as any state coercion. See, *e.g., Washington* v. *Harper,* 494 U.S.——, —— (1990); *Parham* v. *J. R.,* 442 U.S. 584, 600 (1979) ("It is not disputed that a child, in common with adults, has a substantial liberty interest in not being confined unnecessarily for medical treatment").

The State's artificial provision of nutrition and hydration implicates identical concerns. Artificial feeding cannot readily be distinguished from other forms of medical treatment. See, *e.g.,* Council on Ethical and Judicial Affairs, American Medical Association, AMA Ethical Opinion 2.20, Withholding or Withdrawing Life-Prolonging Medical Treatment, Current Opinions 13 (1989); The Hastings Center, Guidelines on the Termination of Life-Sustaining Treatment and the Care of the Dying 59 (1987).

Whether or not the techniques used to pass food and water into the patient's alimentary tract are termed "medical treatment," it is clear they all involve some degree of intrusion and restraint. Feeding a patient by means of a nasogastric tube requires a physician to pass a long flexible tube through the patient's nose, throat and esophagus and into the stomach. Because of the discomfort such a tube causes, "[m]any patients need to be restrained forcibly and their hands put into large mittens to prevent them from removing the tube." Major, The Medical Procedures for Providing Food and Water: Indications and Effects, in By No Extraordinary Means: The Choice to Forgo Life-Sustaining Food and Water 25 (J. Lynn ed. 1986). A gastronomy tube (as was used to provide food and water to Nancy Cruzan, see *ante,* at 2) or jejunostomy tube must be surgically implanted into the stomach or small intestine. Office of Technology Assessment Task Force, Life-Sustaining Technologies and the Elderly 282 (1988). Requiring a competent adult to endure such procedures against her will burdens the patient's liberty, dignity, and freedom to determine the course of her own treatment. Accordingly, the liberty guaranteed by the Due Process Clause must protect, if it protects anything, an individual's deeply personal decision to reject medical treatment, including the artificial delivery of food and water.

I also write separately to emphasize that the Court does not today decide the issue whether a State must also give effect to the decisions of a surrogate decisionmaker. See *ante,* at 22, n. 13. In my view, such a duty may well be constitutionally required to protect the patient's liberty interest in refusing medical treatment. Few individuals provide explicit oral or written instructions regarding their intent to refuse medical treatment should they become incompetent.[1] States which decline to consider any evidence other than such instructions may frequently fail to honor a patient's intent. Such failures might be avoided if the State considered an equally probative source of evidence: the patient's appointment of a proxy to make health care decisions on her behalf. Delegating the authority to make medical decisions to a family member or friend is becoming a common method of planning for the future. See, *e. g.,* Areen, the Legal Status of Consent Obtained from Families of Adult Patients to Withhold or Withdraw Treatment, 258 JAMA 229, 230 (1987). Several States have recognized the practical wisdom of such a procedure by enacting durable power of attorney statutes that specifically authorize an individual to appoint a surrogate to make medical treatment decisions.[2] Some state courts have sug-

---

1. See 2 President's Commission for the Study of Ethical Problems in Medicine and Biomedical and Behavioral Research, Making Health Care Decisions 241–242 (1982) (36% of those surveyed gave instructions regarding how they would like to be treated if they ever became too sick to make decisions; 23% put those instructions in writing) (Lou Harris Poll, September 1982); American Medical Association Surveys of Physician and Public Opinion on Health Care Issues 29–30 (1988) (56% of those surveyed had told family members their wishes concerning the use of life-sustaining treatment if they entered an irreversible coma; 15% had filled out a living will specifying those wishes).

2. At least 13 states and the District of Columbia have durable power of attorney statutes expressly authorizing the appointment of proxies for making health care decisions. See Alaska Stat. Ann. §§ 13.26.335, 13.26.344(*l*) (Supp. 1989); Cal Civ. Code § 2500 (Supp. 1990); D. C. Code § 21–2205 (1989); Idaho Code § 39–4505 (Supp. 1989); Ill. Rev. Stat., ch. 110 1/2, ¶804–1–804–12 (Supp. 1988); Kan. Stat. Ann. § 58–625 (Supp. 1989); Me. Rev. Stat. Ann., Tit. 18–A, § 5–501 (Supp. 1989); Nev. Rev. Stat. § 449.800 (Supp. 1989); Ohio Rev. Code Ann. § 1337.11 et seq. (Supp. 1989);

gested that an agent appointed pursuant to a general durable power of attorney statute would also be empowered to make health care decisions on behalf of the patient.[3] See, *e.g., In re Peter,* 108 N. J. 365, 378–379, 529 A. 2d 419, 426 (1987); see also 73 Op. Md. Atty. Gen. No. 88–046 (1988) (interpreting Md. Est. & Trusts code Ann. §§ 13–601 to 13–602 (1974), as authorizing a delegatee to make health care decisions). Other States allow an individual to designate a proxy to carry out the intent of a living will.[4] These procedures for surrogate decisionmaking, which appear to be rapidly gaining in acceptance, may be a valuable additional safeguard

---

Ore. Rev. Stat. § 127.510 (1989); Pa. Stat. Ann., Tit. 20, § 5603(h) (Purdon Supp. 1989) R. I. Gen. Laws §§ 23–4.10–1 et seq. (1989); Tex Rev. Civ. Stat. Ann. § 4590h–1 (Vernon Supp. 1990); Vt. Stat. Ann., Tit. 14, § 3451 et seq. (1989).

3. All 50 states and the District of Columbia have general durable power of attorney statutes. See Ala. Code § 26–1–2 (1986); Alaska Stat. Ann. §§ 13–26–350 to 13–26–356 (Supp. 1989); Ariz. Rev. Stat. Ann., § 14–5501 (1975); Ark. code Ann. §§ 28–68–201 to 28–68–203 (1987); Cal. Civ. Code Ann. § 2400 (West Supp. 1990); Colo. Rev. Stat. § 15–14–501 et seq. (1987); Conn. Gen. Stat. § 45–690 (Supp. 1989); Del Code Ann., Tit. 12, §§ 4901–4905 (1987); D. C. Code § 21–2081 et. seq. (1989); Fla. Stat. § 709.08 (1989); Ga. Code Ann. § 10–6–36 (1989); Haw. Rev. Stat. §§ 551D–1 to 551D–7 (Supp. 1989); Idaho Code § 15–5–501 et seq. (Supp. 1989); Ill. Rev. Stat., ch. 110 1\2, ¶ 802–6 (1987); Ind. Code §§ 30–2–11–1 to 30–2–11–7 (1988); Iowa Code § 633.705 (Supp. 1989); Kan. Stat. Ann. § 58–610 (1983); Ky. Rev. Stat. Ann. § 386.093 (Baldwin 1983); La. Civ. Code Ann. § 3027 (West Supp. 1990); Me. Rev. Stat. Ann., Tit. 18–A, § 5–501 et seq. (Supp. 1989); Md. Est. & Trusts Code Ann. §§ 13–601—13 to 602 (1974) (as interpreted by the Attorney General, see 73 Op. Md. Atty. Gen. No. 88–046 (Oct. 17, 1988); Mass. Gen. Laws §§ 201B:1 to 201B:7 (1988); Mich. Comp. Laws §§ 700–495, 700.497 (1980); Minn. Stat. § 523.01 et seq. (1988); Miss. Code Ann. § 87–3–13 (Supp. 1989); Mo. Rev. Stat. § 404.700 (Supp. 1990); Mont. Code Ann. §§ 72–5–501 to 72–5–502 (1989); Neb. Rev. Stat. §§ 30–2664 to 30–2672, 30–2667 (1985); Nev. Rev. Stat. § 111.460 et seq. (1986); N. H. Rev. Stat. Ann. § 506:6 et seq. (Supp. 1989); N. J. Stat. Ann. § 46:2B–8 (1989); N. M. Stat. Ann. §45–5–501 et seq. (1989); N. Y. Gen. Oblig. Law § 5–1602 (McKinney 1989); N. C. Gen. Stat. § 32A–1 et seq. (1987); N. D. Cent. Code §§ 30.1–30 to 01–30.1–30–05 (Supp. 1989); Ohio Rev. Code Ann. § 1337.09 (Supp. 1989); Okla. Stat., Tit. 58, §§ 1071–1077 (Supp. 1989); Ore. Rev. Stat. § 127.005 (1989); Pa. Stat. Ann., Tit. 20, §§ 5601 et seq., 5602(a)(9) (Purdon Supp. 1989); R. I. Gen. Laws § 34–22–6.1 (1984); S. C. Code §§ 62–5–501 to 62–5–502 (1987); S. D. Codified Laws § 59–7–2.1 (1978); Tenn. Code Ann. § 34–6–101 et seq. (1984); Tex Prob. Code Ann. § 36A (Supp. 1990); Utah Code Ann. § 75–5–501 et seq. (1978); Vt. Stat. Ann., Tit. 14, § 3051 et seq. (1989); Va. Code § 11.9.1 et seq. (1989); Wash. Rev. Code § 11.94.020 (1989); W. Va. Code § 39–4–1 et seq. (Supp. 1989); Wis. Stat. § 243.07 (1987–1988) (as interpreted by the Attorney General, see Wis. Op. Atty. Gen. 35–88 (1988); Wyo. Stat. § 3–5–101 et seq. (1985).

4. Thirteen states have living will statutes authorizing the appointment of healthcare proxies. See Ark. Code Ann. § 20–17–202 (Supp. 1989); Del. Code Ann., Tit. 16, § 2502 (1983); Fla. Stat. § 765.05(2) (1989); Idaho Code § 39–4504 (Supp. 1989); Ind. Code § 16–8–11–14(g)(2) (1988); Iowa Code § 144A.7(1)(a) (1989); La. Civ. Code Ann., Art. 40:1299.58.1, 40:1299.58.3(C) (West Supp. 1990); Minn. Stat. § 145B.01 et seq. (Supp. 1989); Texas Health & Safety Code Ann. § 672.003(d) (Supp. 1990); Utah Code Ann. §§ 75–2–1105, 75–2–1106 (Supp. 1989); Va. Code § 54.1–2986 (2) (1988); 1987 Wash. Laws, ch. 162 § 1(1)(b); Wyo. Stat. § 35–22–102 (1988).

of the patient's interest in directing his medical care. Moreover, as patients are likely to select a family member as a surrogate, see 2 President's Commission for the Study of Ethical Problems in Medicine and Biomedical and Behavioral Research, Making Health Care Decisions 240 (1982), giving effect to a proxy's decisions may also protect the "freedom of personal choice in matters of . . . family life." *Cleveland Board of Education* v. *La Fleur*, 414 U.S. 632, 639 (1974).

Today's decision, holding only that the Constitution permits a State to require clear and convincing evidence of Nancy Cruzan's desire to have artificial hydration and nutrition withdrawn, does not preclude a future determination that the Constitution requires the States to implement the decisions of a patient's duly appointed surrogate. Nor does it prevent States from developing other approaches for protecting an incompetent individual's liberty interest in refusing medical treatment. As is evident from the Court's survey of state court decisions, see *ante* at 6–13, no national consensus has yet emerged on the best solution for this difficult and sensitive problem. Today we decide only that one State's practice does not violate the Constitution; the more challenging task of crafting appropriate procedures for safeguarding incompetents' liberty interests is entrusted to the "laboratory" of the States, *New State Ice Co.* v. *Liebmann*, 285 U.S. 262, 311 (1932) (Brandeis, J., dissenting), in the first instance.

SUPREME COURT OF THE UNITED STATES

No. 88–1503

NANCY BETH CRUZAN, BY HER PARENTS AND CO-GUARDIANS, LESTER L. CRUZAN, ET UX., PETITIONERS *v.* DIRECTOR, MISSOURI DEPARTMENT OF HEALTH, ET AL.

ON WRIT OF CERTIORARI TO THE SUPREME COURT OF MISSOURI

[June 25, 1990]

JUSTICE SCALIA, concurring.

The various opinions in this case portray quite clearly the difficult, indeed agonizing, questions that are presented by the constantly increasing power of science to keep the human body alive for longer than any reasonable person would want to inhabit it. The States have begun to grapple with these problems through legislation. I am concerned, from the tenor of today's opinions, that we are poised to confuse that enterprise as successfully as we have confused the enterprise of legislating concerning abortion—requiring it to be conducted against a background of federal constitutional imperatives that are unknown because they are being newly crafted from Term to Term. That would be a great misfortune.

While I agree with the Court's analysis today, and therefore join in its opinion, I would have preferred that we announce, clearly and promptly, that the federal courts have no business in this field; that American law has always accorded the State the power to prevent, by force if necessary, suicide—including suicide by refusing to take appropriate measures necessary to preserve one's life; that the point at which life becomes "worthless," and the point at which the means necessary to preserve it become "extraordinary" or "inappropriate," are neither set forth in the Constitution nor known to the nine Justices of this Court any better than they are known to nine people picked at random from the Kansas City telephone directory; and hence, that even when it *is* demonstrated by clear and convincing evidence that a patient no longer wishes certain measures to be taken to preserve her life, it is up to the citizens of Missouri to decide, through their elected representatives, whether that wish will be honored. It is quite impossible (because the Constitution says nothing about the matter) that those citizens will decide upon a line less lawful than the one we would choose; and it is unlikely (because we know no more about "life-and-death" than they do) that they will decide upon a line less reasonable.

The text of the Due Process Clause does not protect individuals against deprivations of liberty *simpliciter.* It protects them against deprivations of liberty "without due process of law." To determine that such a deprivation would not occur if Nancy Cruzan were forced to take nourishment against her will, it is unnecessary to reopen the historically recurrent debate over whether "due process" includes substantive restrictions. Compare *Murrays' Lessee* v. *Hoboken Land and Improvement Co.,* 18 How. 272 (1856), with *Scott* v. *Sandford,* 19 How. 393, 450 (1857); compare *Tyson & Bro.* v. *United Theatre Ticket Offices, Inc.,* 273 U.S. 418 (1927), with *Olsen* v. *Nebraska ex rel. Western Reference & Bond Assn., Inc.,* 313 U.S. 236, 246–247 (1941); compare *Ferguson* v. *Skrupa,* 372 U.S. 726, 730 (1963), with *Moore* v. *East Cleveland,* 431 U.S. 494, (1977) (plurality opinion); see Easterbrook, Substance and Due Process, 1982 S. Ct. Rev. 85; Monaghan, Our Perfect Constitution, 56 N. Y. U. L. Rev. 353 (1981). It is at least true that no "substantive due process" claim can be maintained unless the claimant demonstrates that the State has deprived him of a right historically and traditionally protected against State interference. *Michael H.* v. *Gerald D.,* 491 U.S. ——, ——(1989) (plurality opinion); *Bowers* v. *Hardwick,* 478 U.S. 186, 192 (1986); *Moore, supra,* at 502–503 (plurality opinion). That cannot possibly be established here.

At common law in England, a suicide—defined as one who "deliberately puts an end to his own existence, or commits any unlawful malicious act, the consequence of which is his own death," 4 W. Blackstone, Commentaries *189—was criminally liable. *Ibid.* Although the States abolished the penalties imposed by the common law (*i.e.,* forfeiture and ignominious burial), they did so to spare the innocent family, and not to legitimize the act. Case law at the time of the Fourteenth Amendment generally held that assisting suicide was a criminal offense. See Marzen, O'Dowd, Crone, & Balch, Suicide: A Constitutional Right?, 24 Duquesne L. Rev. 1, 76 (1985) ("In short, twenty-one of the thirty-seven states, and eighteen of the thirty ratifying states prohibited assisting suicide. Only eight of the states, and seven of the ratifying states, definitely did not"); see also 1 F. Wharton, Criminal Law § 122 (6th rev. ed. 1868). The System of Penal Law presented to the House of Representatives by Representative Livingston in 1828 would have criminalized assisted suicide. E.

Livingston, A System of Penal Law, Penal Code 122 (1828). The Field Penal Code, adopted by the Dakota Territory in 1877, proscribed attempted suicide and assisted suicide. Marzen, O'Dowd, Crone, & Balch, 24 Duquesne L. Rev., at 76–77. And most States that did not explicitly prohibit assisted suicide in 1868 recognized, when the issue arose in the 50 years following the Fourteenth Amendment's ratification, that assisted and (in some cases) attempted suicide were unlawful. *Id.,* at 77–100; 148–242 (surveying development of States' laws). Thus, "there is no significant support for the claim that a right to suicide is so rooted in our tradition that it may be deemed 'fundamental' or 'implicit in the concept of ordered liberty.'" *Id.,* at 100 (quoting *Palko v. Connecticut,* 302 U.S. 319, 325 (1937)).

Petitioners rely on three distinctions to separate Nancy Cruzan's case from ordinary suicide: (1) that she is permanently incapacitated and in pain; (2) that she would bring on her death not by any affirmative act but by merely declining treatment that provides nourishment; and (3) that preventing her from effectuating her presumed wish to die requires violation of her bodily integrity. None of these suffices. Suicide was not excused even when committed "to avoid those ills which [persons] had not the fortitude to endure." 4 Blackstone, *supra,* at *189. "The life of those to whom life has become a burden—of those who are hopelessly diseased or fatally wounded— nay, even the lives of criminals condemned to death, are under the protection of the law, equally as the lives of those who are in the full tide of life's enjoyment, and anxious to continue to live. *Blackburn v. State,* 23 Ohio St. 146, 163 (1873). Thus, a man who prepared a poison, and placed it within reach of his wife, "to put an end to her suffering" from a terminal illness was convicted of murder, *People v. Roberts,* 211 Mich. 187, 198 N. W. 690, 693 (1920); the "incurable suffering of the suicide, as a legal question, could hardly affect the degree of criminality. . . ." Note, 30 Yale L. J. 408, 412 (1921) (discussing *Roberts*). Nor would the imminence of the patient's death have affected liability. "The lives of all are equally under the protection of the law, and under that protection to their last moment. . . . [Assisted suicide] is declared by the law to be murder, irrespective of the wishes or the condition of the party to whom the poison is administered. . . ." *Blackburn, supra,* at 163; see also *Commonwealth v. Bowen,* 13 Mass. 356, 360 (1816).

The second asserted distinction—suggested by the recent cases canvassed by the Court concerning the right to refuse treatment, *ante,* at 5–12—relies on the dichotomy between action and inaction. Suicide, it is said, consists of an affirmative act to end one's life; refusing treatment is not an affirmative act "causing" death, but merely a passive acceptance of the natural process of dying. I readily acknowledge that the distinction between action and inaction has some bearing upon the legislative judgment of what ought to be prevented as suicide—though even there it would seem to me unreasonable to draw the line precisely between action and inaction, rather than between various forms of inaction. It would not make much sense to say that one may not kill oneself by walking into the sea, but may sit on the beach until submerged by the incoming tide; or that one may not intentionally lock oneself into a cold storage locker but may refrain from coming indoors when the temperature drops below freezing. Even as a legislative matter, in other words, the intelligent line does not fall between action and inaction but between those forms of inaction that consist of abstaining from "ordinary" care and those that consist of abstaining from "excessive" or "heroic" measures. Unlike action *vs.* inaction, that is not a line to be discerned by logic or legal analysis, and we should not pretend that it is.

But to return to the principal point for present purposes: the irrelevance of the action-inaction distinction. Starving oneself to death is no different from putting a gun to one's temple as far as the common-law definition of suicide is concerned; the cause of death in both cases is the suicide's conscious decision to "pu[t] an end to his own existence." 4 Blackstone, *supra,* at *189. See *In re Caulk,* 125 N. H. 226, 232, 480 A. 2d 93, 97 (1984); *State ex rel. White* v. *Narick,*——W. Va.——, 292 S. E. 2d 54 (1982); *Von Holden* v. *Chapman,* 87 App. Div. 2d 66, 450 N. Y. S. 2d 623 (1982). Of course the common law rejected the action-inaction distinction in other contexts involving the taking of human life as well. In the prosecution of a parent for the starvation death of her infant, it was no defense that the infant's death was "caused" by no action of the parent but by the natural process of starvation, or by the infant's natural inability to provide for itself. See *Lewis* v. *State,* 72 Ga. 164 (1883); *People* v. *McDonald,* 49 Hun 67, 1 N. Y. S. 703 (1888); *Commonwealth* v. *Hall,* 322 Mass. 523, 528, 78 N. E. 2d 644, 647 (1948) (collecting cases); F. Wharton, Law of Homicide §§ 134–135, 304 (2d ed. 1875); 2 J. Bishop, Commentaries on the Criminal Law § 686 (5th ed. 1872); J. Hawley & M. McGregor, Criminal Law 152 (3d ed. 1899). A physician, moreover, could be criminally liable for failure to provide care that could have extended the patient's life, even if death was immediately caused by the underlying disease that the physician failed to treat. *Barrow* v. *State,* 17 Okla. Cr. 340, 188 P. 351 (1920); *People* v. *Phillips,* 64 Cal. 2d 574, 414 P. 2d 353 (1966).

It is not surprising, therefore, that the early cases considering the claimed right to refuse medical treatment dismissed as specious the nice distinction between "passively submitting to death and actively seeking it. The distinction may be merely verbal, as it would be if an adult sought death by starvation instead of a drug. If the State may interrupt one mode of self-destruction, it may with equal authority interfere with the other." *John F. Kennedy Memorial Hosp.* v. *Heston,* 58 N. J. 576, 581–582, 279 A. 2d 670, 672–673 (1971); see also *Application of President & Directors of Georgetown College, Inc.,* 118 U.S. App. D. C. 80, 88–89, 331 F. 2d 1000, 1008–1009 (Wright, J., in chambers), cert. denied, 377 U.S. 978 (1964).

The third asserted basis of distinction—that frustrating Nancy Cruzan's wish to die in the present case requires interference with her bodily integrity—is likewise inadequate, because such interference is impermissible only if one begs the question whether her refusal to undergo the treatment on her own is suicide. It has always been lawful not only for the State, but even for private citizens, to interfere with bodily integrity to prevent a felony. See *Phillips* v. *Trull,* 11 Johns. 486 (N. Y. 1814); *City Council* v. *Payne,* 2 Nott & McCord 475 (S. C. 1821); *Vandeveer* v. *Mattocks,* 3 Ind. 479 (1852); T. Cooley, Law of Torts 174–175 (1879); Wilgus, Arrest Without a Warrant, 22 Mich. L. Rev. 673 (1924); Restatement of Torts § 119 (1934). That general rule has of course been applied to suicide. At common law, even a private person's use of force to prevent suicide was privileged. *Colby* v. *Jackson,* 12 N. H. 526, 530–531 (1842); *Look* v. *Choate,* 108 Mass. 116, 120 (1871); *Commonwealth* v. *Mink,* 123 Mass. 422, 429 (1877); *In re Doyle,* 16 R. I. 537, 539, 18 A. 159, 159–160 (1889); *Porter* v. *Ritch,* 70 Conn. 235, 255, 39 A. 169, 175 (1898); *Emmerich* v. *Thorley,* 54 N. Y. S. 791, 793–794 (1898); *State* v. *Hembd,* 305 Minn. 120, 130, 232 N. W. 2d 872, 878 (1975); 2 C. Addison, Law of Torts § 819 (1876); Cooley, *supra,* at 179–180. It is not even reasonable, much less required by the Constitution, to maintain that although the State has the right to prevent a person from slashing his wrists it does not have the power, to apply physical force to prevent him from doing so, nor the power should he succeed, to apply, coercively if necessary, medical measures to stop the flow of blood. The state-run hospital, I am certain, is not liable under 42 U.S. C. § 1983 for violation of constitutional rights, nor the private hospital liable under general tort law, if, in a State where suicide is unlawful, it pumps out the stomach of a person who has intentionally taken an overdose of barbiturates, despite that person's wishes to the contrary.

The dissents of JUSTICES BRENNAN and STEVENS make a plausible case for our intervention here only by embracing—the latter explicitly and the former by implication—a political principle that the States are free to adopt, but that is demonstrably not imposed by the Constitution. "The State," says JUSTICE BRENNAN, "has no legitimate general interest in someone's life, completely abstracted from the interest of the person living that life, that could outweigh the person's choice *to avoid medical treatment.*" *Post,* at 14 (emphasis added). The italicized phrase sounds moderate enough, and is all that is needed to cover the present case—but the proposition cannot *logically* be so limited. One who accepts it must also accept, I think, that the State has no such legitimate interest that could outweigh "the person's choice *to put an end to her life.*" Similarly, if one agrees with JUSTICE BRENNAN that "the State's general interest in life must accede to Nancy Cruzan's particularized and intense interest in self-determination *in her choice of medical treatment,*" *ibid.* (emphasis added), he must also believe that the State must accede to her "particularized and intense interest in self-determination *in her choice whether to continue living or to die.*" For insofar as balancing the relative interests of the State and the individual is concerned, there is nothing distinctive about accepting death through the refusal of "medical treatment," as opposed to accepting it through the refusal of food, or through the failure to shut off the engine and get out of the car after parking in one's garage after work. Suppose that Nancy Cruzan were in precisely the condition she is in today, except that she could be fed and digest food and water *without* artificial assistance. How is the State's "interest" in keeping her alive thereby increased, or her interest in deciding whether she wants to continue living reduced? It seems to me, in other words, that JUSTICE BRENNAN's position ultimately rests upon the proposition that it is none of the State's business if a person wants to commit suicide. JUSTICE STEVENS is explicit on the point: "Choices about death touch the core of liberty. . . . [N]ot much may be said with confidence about death unless it is said from faith, and that alone is reason enough to protect the freedom to conform choices about death to individual conscience." *Post,* at 13–14. This is a view that some societies have held, and that our States are free to adopt if they wish. But it is not a view imposed by our constitutional traditions, in which the power of the State to prohibit suicide is unquestionable.

What I have said above is not meant to suggest that I would think it desirable, if we were sure that Nancy Cruzan wanted to die, to keep her alive by the means at issue here. I assert only that the Constitution has nothing to say about the subject. To raise up a constitutional right here we would have to create out of nothing (for it exists neither in text nor tradition) some constitutional principle whereby, although the State may insist that an individual come in out of the cold and eat food, it may not insist that he take medicine; and although it may pump his stomach empty of poison he has ingested, it may not fill his stomach with food he has failed to ingest. Are there, then, no reasonable and humane limits that ought not to be exceeded in requiring an individual to preserve his own life? There obviously are, but they are not set forth in the Due Process Clause. What assures us that those limits will not be exceeded is the same constitutional guarantee that is the source of most of our protection—what protects us, for example, from being assessed a tax of 100% of our income above the subsistence level, from being forbidden to drive cars, or from being required to send our children to school for 10 hours a day, none of which horribles is categorically prohibited by the Constitution. Our salvation is the Equal Protection Clause, which requires the democratic majority to accept for themselves and their loved ones what they impose on you and me. This Court need not, and has no authority to, inject itself into every field of human activity where irrationality and oppression may theoretically occur, and if it tries to do so it will destroy itself.

SUPREME COURT OF THE UNITED STATES

No. 88–1503

NANCY BETH CRUZAN, BY HER PARENTS AND CO-GUARDIANS, LESTER L. CRUZAN, ET UX., PETITIONERS v. DIRECTOR, MISSOURI DEPARTMENT OF HEALTH, ET AL.

ON WRIT OF CERTIORARI TO THE SUPREME COURT OF MISSOURI

[June 25, 1990]

JUSTICE BRENNAN, with whom JUSTICE MARSHALL and JUSTICE BLACKMUN join, dissenting.

> "Medical technology has effectively created a twilight zone of suspended animation where death commences while life, in some form, continues. Some patients, however, want no part of a life sustained only by medical technology. Instead, they prefer a plan of medical treatment that allows nature to take its course and permits them to die with dignity."[1]

Nancy Cruzan has dwelt in that twilight zone for six years. She is oblivious to her surroundings and will remain so. *Cruzan* v. *Harmon,* 760 S. W. 2d 408, 411 (Mo. 1988). Her body twitches only reflexively, without consciousness. *Ibid.* The areas of her brain that once thought, felt, and experienced sensations have degenerated badly and are continuing to do so. The cavities remaining are filling with cerebrospinal fluid. The "'cerebral cortical atrophy is irreversible, permanent, progressive and ongoing.'" *Ibid.* "Nancy will never interact meaningfully with her environment

---

1. *Rasmussen* v. *Fleming,* 154 Ariz. 207, 211, 741 P. 2d 674, 678 (1987) (en banc).

again. She will remain in a persistent vegetative state until her death." *Id.,* at 422.[2] Because she cannot swallow, her nutrition and hydration are delivered through a tube surgically implanted in her stomach.

A grown woman at the time of the accident, Nancy had previously expressed her wish to forgo continuing medical care under circumstances such as these. Her family and her friends are convinced that this is what she would want. See n. 20, *infra.* A guardian ad litem appointed by the trial court is also convinced that this is what Nancy would want. See 760 S. W. 2d, at 444 (Higgins, J., dissenting from denial of rehearing). Yet the Missouri Supreme Court, alone among state courts deciding such a question, has determined that an irreversibly vegetative patient will remain a passive prisoner of medical technology—for Nancy, perhaps for the next 30 years. See *id.,* at 424, 427.

Today the Court, while tentatively accepting that there is some degree of constitutionally protected liberty interest in avoiding unwanted medical treatment, including life-sustaining medical treatment such as artificial nutrition and hydration, affirms the decision of the Missouri Supreme Court. The majority opinion, as I read it, would affirm that decision on the ground that a State may require "clear and convincing" evidence of Nancy Cruzan's prior decision to forgo life-sustaining treatment under circumstances such as hers in order to ensure that her actual wishes are honored. See *ante,* at 17–19, 22. Because I believe that Nancy Cruzan has a fundamental right to be free of unwanted artificial nutrition and hydration, which right is not outweighed by any interests of the State, and because I find that the improperly biased procedural obstacles imposed by the Missouri Supreme Court impermissibly burden that right, I respectfully dissent. Nancy Cruzan is entitled to choose to die with dignity.

I

A

"[T]he timing of death—once a matter of fate—is now a matter of human choice." Office of Technology Assessment Task Force, Life Sustaining Technologies and the Elderly 41 (1988). Of the approximately two million people who die each year, 80% die in hospitals and long-term care institutions,[3] and perhaps 70% of those after a decision to forgo life-sustaining treatment has been made.[4] Nearly every death involves a decision whether to undertake some medical procedure that could prolong the process of dying. Such decisions are difficult and personal. They must be made on the basis of individual values, informed by medical realities, yet within a framework governed by law. The role of the courts is confined to defining that framework, delineating the ways in which government may and may not participate in such decisions.

---

2. Vegetative state patients may *react reflexively* to sounds, movements and normally painful stimuli, but they do not *feel* any pain or *sense* anybody or anything. Vegetative state patients may appear awake but are completely unaware. See Cranford, The Persistent Vegetative State: The Medical Reality, 18 Hastings Ctr. Rep. 27, 28, 31 (1988).

3. See President's Commission for the Study of Ethical Problems in Medicine and Biomedical and Behavioral Research, Deciding to Forego Life Sustaining Treatment 15, n. 1, and 17–18 (1983) (hereafter President's Commission).

4. See Lipton, Do-Not-Resuscitate Decisions in a Community Hospital: Incidence, Implications and Outcomes, 256 JAMA 1164, 1168 (1986).

The question before this Court is a relatively narrow one: whether the Due Process Clause allows Missouri to require a now-incompetent patient in an irreversible persistent vegetative state to remain on life-support absent rigorously clear and convincing evidence that avoiding the treatment represents the patient's prior, express choice. See *ante*, at 13. If a fundamental right is at issue, Missouri's rule of decision must be scrutinized under the standards this court has always applied in such circumstances. As we said in *Zablocki* v. *Redhail*, 434 U.S. 374, 388 (1978), if a requirement imposed by a State "significantly interferes with the exercise of a fundamental right, it cannot be upheld unless it is supported by sufficiently important state interests and is closely tailored to effectuate only those interests." The Constitution imposes on this Court the obligation to "examine carefully . . . the extent to which [the legitimate government interests advanced] are served by the challenged regulation." *Moore* v. *East Cleveland,* 431 U.S. 494, 499 (1977). See also *Carey* v. *Population Services International,* 431 U.S. 678, 690 (1977) (invalidating a requirement that bore "no relation to the State's interest"). An evidentiary rule, just as a substantive prohibition, must meet these standards if it significantly burdens a fundamental liberty interest. Fundamental rights "are protected not only against heavy-handed frontal attack, but also from being stifled by more subtle governmental interference." *Bates* v. *Little Rock,* 361 U.S. 516, 523 (1960).

B

The starting point for our legal analysis must be whether a competent person has a constitutional right to avoid unwanted medical care. Earlier this Term, this Court held that the Due Process Clause of the Fourteenth Amendment confers a significant liberty interest in avoiding unwanted medical treatment. *Washington* v. *Harper,* 494 U.S.——, —— (1990). Today, the court concedes that our prior decisions "support the recognition of a general liberty interest in refusing medical treatment." See *ante*, at 14. The Court, however, avoids discussing either the measure of that liberty interest or its application by assuming, for purposes of this case only, that a competent person has a constitutionally protected liberty interest in being free of unwanted artificial nutrition and hydration. See *ante*, at 15. JUSTICE O'CONNOR's opinion is less parsimonious. She openly affirms that "the Court has often deemed state incursions into the body repugnant to the interests protected by the Due Process Clause," that there is a liberty interest in avoiding unwanted medical treatment and that it encompasses the right to be free of "artificially delivered food and water." See *ante*, at 1.

But if a competent person has a liberty interest to be free of unwanted medical treatment, as both the majority and JUSTICE O'CONNOR concede, it must be fundamental. "We are dealing here with [a decision] which involves one of the basic civil rights of man." *Skinner* v. *Oklahoma ex rel. Williamson,* 316 U.S. 535, 541 (1942) (invalidating a statute authorizing sterilization of certain felons). Whatever other liberties protected by the due Process Clause are fundamental, "those liberties that are 'deeply rooted in this Nation's history and tradition'" are among them. *Bowers* v. *Hardwick,* 478 U.S. 186, 192 (1986) (quoting *Moore* v. *East Cleveland, supra,* at 503 (plurality opinion). "Such a tradition commands respect in part because the Constitution carries the gloss of history." *Richmond Newspapers, Inc.* v. *Virginia,* 448 U.S. 555, 589 (1980) (BRENNAN, J., concurring in judgment).

The right to be free from medical attention without consent, to determine what shall be done with one's own body, *is* deeply rooted in this Nation's traditions, as the majority acknowledges. See *ante,* at 5. This right has long been "firmly entrenched in American tort law" and is securely grounded in the earliest common law. *Ibid.* See also *Mills* v. *Rogers,* 457 U.S. 291, 294, n. 4 (1982) ("the right to refuse any medical treatment emerged from the doctrines of trespass and battery, which were applied to unauthorized touchings by a physician"). "'Anglo-American law starts with the premise of thorough-going self determination. It follows that each man is considered to be master of his own body, and he may, if he be of sound mind, expressly prohibit the performance of lifesaving surgery, or other medical treatment.'" *Natanson* v. *Kline,* 186 Kan. 393, 406–407, 350 P. 2d 1093, 1104 (1960). "The inviolability of the person" has been held as "sacred" and "carefully guarded" as any common law right. *Union Pacific R. Co.* v. *Botsford,* 141 U.S. 250, 251–252 (1891). Thus, freedom from unwanted medical attention is unquestionably among those principles "so rooted in the traditions and conscience of our people as to be ranked as fundamental." *Snyder* v. *Massachusetts,* 291 U.S. 97, 105 (1934).[5]

That there may be serious consequences involved in refusal of the medical treatment at issue here does not vitiate the right under our common law tradition of medical self-determination. It is "a well-established rule of general law . . . that it is the patient, not the physician, who ultimately decides if treatment—any treatment—is to be given at all. . . . The rule has never been qualified in its application by either the nature or purpose of the treatment or the gravity of the consequences of acceding to or foregoing it." *Tune* v. *Walter Reed Army Medical Hospital,* 602 F. Supp. 1452, 1455 (DC 1985). See also *Downer* v. *Veilleux,* 322 A. 2d 82, 91 (Me. 1974) ("The rationale of this rule lies in the fact that every competent adult has the right to forego treatment, or even cure, if it entails what for him are intolerable consequences or risks, however unwise his sense of values may be to others").[6]

No material distinction can be drawn between the treatment to which Nancy Cruzan continues to be subject—artificial nutrition and hydration—and any other

5. See, *e.g., Canterbury* v. *Spence,* 150 U.S. App. D. C. 263, 271, 464 F. 2d 772, 780, cert. denied, 409 U.S. 1064 (1972) ("The root premise" of informed consent "is the concept, fundamental in American jurisprudence, that '[e]very human being of adult years and sound mind has a right to determine what shall be done with his own body'") (quoting *Schloendorff* v. *Society of New York Hospital,* 211 N. Y. 125, 129–130, 105 N. E. 92, 93 (1914) (Cardozo, J.)). See generally *Washington* v. *Harper,* 494 U.S.——, —— (1990) (STEVENS, J., dissenting) (slip op., at 5) ("There is no doubt . . . that a competent individual's right to refuse [psychotropic] medication is a fundamental liberty interest deserving the highest order of protection").

6. Under traditional tort law, exceptions have been found only to protect dependent children. See *Cruzan* v. *Harmon,* 760 S. W. 2d 408, 422, n. 17 (Mo. 1988) (citing cases where Missouri courts have ordered blood transfusions for children over the religious objection of parents); see also *Winthrop University Hospital* v. *Hess,* 128 Misc. 2d 804, 490 N. Y. S. 2d 996 (Sup. Ct. Nassau Co. 1985) (court ordered blood transfusion for religious objector because she was the mother of an infant and had explained that her objection was to the signing of the consent, not the transfusion itself); *Application of President & Directors of Georgetown College, Inc.,* 118 U.S. App. D. C. 80, 88, 331 F. 2d 1000, 1008, cert. denied, 377 U.S. 978 (1964) (blood transfusion ordered for mother of infant). Cf. *In re Estate of Brooks,* 32 Ill. 2d 361, 373, 205 N. E. 2d 435, 441–442 (1965) (finding that lower court erred in ordering a blood transfusion for a woman—whose children were grown–and concluding: "Even though we may consider apellant's beliefs unwise, foolish or ridiculous, in the absence of an overriding danger to society we may not permit interference therewith in the form of a conservatorship established in the waning hours of her life for the sole purpose of compelling her to accept medical treatment forbidden by her religious principles, and previously refused by her with full knowledge of the probable consequences").

medical treatment. See *ante*, at 2 (O'CONNOR, J., concurring). The artificial delivery of nutrition and hydration is undoubtedly medical treatment. The technique to which Nancy Cruzan is subject—artificial feeding through a gastronomy tube—involves a tube implanted surgically into her stomach through incisions in her abdominal wall. It may obstruct the intestinal tract, erode and pierce the stomach wall or cause leakage of the stomach's contents into the abdominal cavity. See Page, Andrassy, & Sandler, Techniques in Delivery of Liquid Diets, in Nutrition in Clinical Surgery 66–67 (M. Deitel 2d ed. 1985). The tube can cause pneumonia from reflux of the stomach's contents into the lung. See Bernard & Forlaw, Complications and Their Prevention, in Enteral and Tube Feeding 553 (J. Rombeau & M. Caldwell eds. 1984). Typically, and in this case (see Tr. 377), commercially prepared formulas are used, rather than fresh food. See Matarese, Enteral Alimentation, in Surgical Nutrition 726 (J. Fischer ed. 1983). The type of formula and method of administration must be experimented with to avoid gastrointestinal problems. *Id.,* at 748. The patient must be monitored daily by medical personnel as to weight, fluid intake and fluid output; blood tests must be done weekly. *Id.,* at 749, 751.

Artificial delivery of food and water is regarded as medical treatment by the medical profession and the Federal Government.[7] According to the American Academy of Neurology, "[t]he artificial provision of nutrition and hydration is a form of medical treatment . . . analogous to other forms of life-sustaining treatment, such as the use of the respirator. When a patient is unconscious, both a respirator and an artificial feeding device serve to support or replace normal bodily functions that are compromised as a result of the patient's illness." Position of the American Academy of Neurology on Certain Aspects of the Care and Management of the Persistent Vegetative State Patient, 39 Neurology 125 (Jan. 1989). See also Council on Ethical and Judicial Affairs of the American Medical Association, Current Opinions, Opinion 2.20 (1989) ("Life-prolonging medical treatment includes medication and artificially or technologically supplied respiration, nutrition or hydration"); President's Commission 88 (life-sustaining treatment includes respirators, kidney dialysis machines, special feeding procedures). The Federal Government permits the cost of the medical devices and formulas used in enteral feeding to be reimbursed under Medicare. See Pub. L. 99–509, § 9340, note following 42 U.S. C. § 1395u, p. 592 (1982 ed., Supp. V). The formulas are regulated by the Federal Drug Administration as "medical foods," see 21 U.S. C. § 360ee, and the feeding tubes are regulated as medical devices, 21 CFR § 876.5980 (1989).

Nor does the fact that Nancy Cruzan is now incompetent deprive her of her fundamental rights. See *Youngberg* v. *Romeo,* 457 U.S. 307, 315–316, 319 (1982) (holding that severely retarded man's liberty interests in safety, freedom from bodily restraint and reasonable training survive involuntary commitment); *Parham* v. *J. R.,* 442 U.S. 584, 600 (1979) (recognizing a child's substantial liberty interest in not being confined unnecessarily for medical treatment); *Jackson* v. *Indiana,* 406 U.S.

---

7. The Missouri court appears to be alone among state courts to suggest otherwise, 760 S. W. 2d, at 419 and 423, although the court did not rely on a distinction between artificial feeding and other forms of medical treatment. *Id.,* at 423. See, *e.g., Delio* v. *Westchester County Medical Center,* 129 App. Div. 2d 1, 19, 516 N. Y. S. 2d 677, 689 (1987) ("review of the decisions in other jurisdictions . . . failed to uncover a single case in which a court confronted with an application to discontinue feeding by artificial means has evaluated medical procedures to provide nutrition and hydration differently from other types of life-sustaining procedures").

715, 730, 738 (1972) (holding that Indiana could not violate the due process and equal protection rights of a mentally retarded deaf mute by committing him for an indefinite amount of time simply because he was incompetent to stand trial on the criminal charges filed against him). As the majority recognizes, *ante*, at 16, the question is not whether an incompetent has constitutional rights, but how such rights may be exercised. As we explained in *Thompson* v. *Oklahoma*, 487 U.S. 815 (1988), "[t]he law must often adjust the manner in which it affords rights to those whose status renders them unable to exercise choice freely and rationally. Children, the insane, and *those who are irreversibly ill with loss of brain function, for instance, all retain 'rights,'* to be sure, but often such rights are only meaningful as they are exercised by agents acting with the best interests of their principals in mind." *Id.*, at 825, n. 23 (emphasis added). "To deny [its] exercise because the patient is unconscious or incompetent would be to deny the right." *Foody* v. *Manchester Memorial Hospital*, 40 Conn. Super. 127, 133, 482 A. 2d 713, 718 (1984).

II

A

The right to be free from unwanted medical attention is a right to evaluate the potential benefit of treatment and its possible consequences according to one's own values and to make a personal decision whether to subject oneself to the intrusion. For a patient like Nancy Cruzan, the sole benefit of medical treatment is being kept metabolically alive. Neither artificial nutrition nor any other form of medical treatment available today can cure or in any way ameliorate her condition.[8] Irreversibly vegetative patients are devoid of thought, emotion and sensation; they are permanently and completely unconscious. See n. 2, *supra*.[9] As the President's

---

8. While brain stem cells can survive 15 to 20 minutes without oxygen, cells in the cerebral hemispheres are destroyed if they are deprived of oxygen for as few as 4 to 6 minutes. See Cranford & Smith, Some Critical Distinctions Between Brain Death and the Persistent Vegetative State, 6 Ethics Sci. & Med. 199, 203 (1979). It is estimated that Nancy's brain was deprived of oxygen from 12 to 14 minutes. See *ante*, at 2. Out of the 100,000 patients who, like Nancy, have fallen into persistant vegetative states in the past 20 years due to loss of oxygen to the brain, there have been only three even partial recoveries documented in the medical literature. Brief for American Medical Association et al. as *Amici Curiae* 11–12. The longest any person has ever been in a persistent vegetative state and recovered was 22 months. See Snyder, Cranford, Rubens, Bundlie, & Rockswold, Delayed Recovery from Postanoxic Persistent Vegetative State, 14 Annals Neurol. 156 (1983). Nancy has been in this state for seven years.

9. The American Academy of Neurology offers three independent bases on which the medical profession rests these neurological conclusions:

"First, direct clinical experience with these patients demonstrates that there is no behavioral indication of any awareness of pain or suffering.

"Second, in all persistent vegetative state patients studied to date, post-mortem examination reveals overwhelming bilateral damage to the cerebral hemispheres to a degree incompatible with consciousness. . . .

"Third, recent data utilizing positron emission tomography indicates that the metabolic rate for glucose in the cerebral cortex is greatly reduced in persistent vegetative state patients, to a degree incompatible with consciousness." Position of the American Academy of Neurology on Certain Aspects of the Care and Management of the Persistent Vegetative State Patient, 39 Neurology 125 (Jan. 1989).

Commission concluded in approving the withdrawal of life support equipment from irreversibly vegetative patients:

> "[T]reatment ordinarily aims to benefit a patient through preserving life, relieving pain and suffering, protecting against disability, and returning maximally effective functioning. If a prognosis of permanent unconsciousness is correct, however, continued treatment cannot confer such benefits. Pain and suffering are absent, as are joy, satisfaction, and pleasure. Disability is total and no return to an even minimal level of social or human functioning is possible." President's Commission 181–182.

There are also affirmative reasons why someone like Nancy might choose to forgo artificial nutrition and hydration under these circumstances. Dying is personal. And it is profound. For many, the thought of an ignoble end, steeped in decay, is abhorrent. A quiet, proud death, bodily integrity intact, is a matter of extreme consequence. "In certain, thankfully rare, circumstances the burden of maintaining the corporeal existence degrades the very humanity it was meant to serve." *Brophy* v. *New England Sinai Hospital, Inc.,* 398 Mass. 417, 434, 497 N. E. 2d 626, 635–636 (1986) (finding the subject of the proceeding "in a condition which [he] has indicated he would consider to be degrading and without human dignity" and holding that "[t]he duty of the State to preserve life must encompass a recognition of an individual's right to avoid circumstances in which the individual himself would feel that efforts to sustain life demean or degrade his humanity"). Another court, hearing a similar case, noted:

> "It is apparent from the testimony that what was on [the patient's] mind was not only the invasiveness of life-sustaining systems, such as the [nasogastric] tube, upon the integrity of his body. It was also the utter helplessness of the permanently comatose person, the wasting of a once strong body, and the submission of the most private bodily functions to the attention of others." *In re Gardner,* 534 A. 2d 947, 953 (Me. 1987).

Such conditions are, for many, humiliating to contemplate,[10] as is visiting a prolonged and anguished vigil on one's parents, spouse, and children. A long, drawn-out death can have a debilitating effect on family members. See Carnwath & Johnson, Psychiatric Morbidity Among Spouses of Patients With Stroke, 294 Brit. Med. J. 409 (1987); Livingston, Families Who Care, 291 Brit. Med. J. 919 (1985). For some, the idea of being remembered in their persistent vegetative states rather than as they were before their illness or accident may be very disturbing.[11]

---

10. Nancy Cruzan, for instance, is totally and permanently disabled. All four of her limbs are severely contracted; her fingernails cut into her wrists. App. to Pet. for Cert. A93. She is incontinent of bowel and bladder. The most intimate aspects of her existence are exposed to and controlled by strangers. Brief for Respondent Guardian Ad Litem 2. Her family is convinced that Nancy would find this state degrading. See n. 20, *infra.*

11. What general information exists about what most people would choose or would prefer to have chosen for them under these circumstance also indicates the importance of ensuring a means for now-incompetent patients to exercise their right to avoid unwanted medical treatment. A 1988 poll conducted by the American Medical Association found that 80% of those

B

Although the right to be free of unwanted medical intervention, like other con-stitutionally protected interests, may not be absolute,[12] no State interest could out-weigh the rights of an individual in Nancy Cruzan's position. Whatever a State's possible interests in mandating life-support treatment under other circumstances, there is no good to be obtained here by Missouri's insistence that Nancy Cruzan remain on life-support systems if it is indeed her wish not to do so. Missouri does not claim, nor could it, that society as a whole will be benefited by Nancy's receiving medical treatment. No third party's situation will be improved and no harm to others will be averted. Cf. nn. 6 and 8, *supra.*[13]

The only state interest asserted here is a general interest in the preservation of life.[14] But the State has no legitimate general interest in someone's life, com-pletely abstracted from the interest of the person living that life, that could outweigh the person's choice to avoid medical treatment. "[T]he regulation of constitutionally

surveyed favored withdrawal of life support systems from hopelessly ill or irreversibly comatose patients if they or their families requested it. New York Times, June 5, 1988, p. 14, col. 4 (cit-ing American Medical News, June 3, 1988, p. 9, col. 1). Another 1988 poll conducted by the Colorado University Graduate School of Public Affairs showed that 85% of those questioned would not want to have their own lives maintained with artificial nutrition and hydration if they became permanently unconscious. The Coloradoan, Sept. 29, 1988, p. 1.

Such attitudes have been translated into considerable political action. Since 1976, 40 States and the District of Columbia have enacted natural death acts, expressly providing for self-determination under some or all of these situations. See Brief for Society for the Right to Die, Inc. as *Amicus Curiae* 8; Wediner, Privacy, Family, and Medical Decision Making for Persistent Vegetative Patients, 11 Cardozo L. Rev. 713, 720 (1990). Thirteen States and the District of Columbia have enacted statutes authorizing the appointment of proxies for making health care decisions. See *ante,* at 4, n. 2 (O'CONNOR, J., concurring).

12. See *Jacobson* v. *Massachusetts,* 197 U.S. 11, 26–27 (1905) (upholding a Massachusetts law imposing fines or imprisonment on those refusing to be vaccinated as "of paramount necessity" to that State's fight against a smallpox epidemic).

13. Were such interests at stake, however, I would find that the Due Process Clause places limits on what invasive medical procedures could be forced on an unwilling comatose patient in pursuit of the interests of a third party. If Missouri were correct that its interests outweigh Nancy's interest in avoiding medical procedures as long as she is free of pain and physical discomfort, see 760 S. W. 2d, at 424, it is not apparent why a State could not choose to remove one of her kid-neys without consent on the ground that society would be better off if the recipient of that kidney were saved from renal poisoning. Nancy cannot feel surgical pain. See n. 2, *supra.* Nor would removal of one kidney be expected to shorten her life expectancy. See the American Medical Association Family Medical Guide 506 (J. Kunz ed. 1982). Patches of her skin could also be removed to provide grafts for burn victims, and scrapings of bone marrow to provide grafts for someone with leukemia. Perhaps the State could lawfully remove more vital organs for trans-planting into others who would then be cured of their ailments, provided the State placed Nancy on some other life-support equipment to replace the lost function. Indeed, why could the State not perform medical experiments on her body, experiments that might save countless lives, and would cause her no greater burden than she already bears by being fed through the gastrostomy tube? This would be too brave a new world for me and, I submit, for our Constitution.

14. The Missouri Supreme Court reviewed the State interests that had been identified by other courts as potentially relevant—prevention of homicide and suicide, protection of inter-ests of innocent third parties, maintenance of the ethical integrity of the medical profession, and preservation of life—and concluded that: "In this case, only the state's interest in the preser-vation of life is implicated." 760 S. W. 2d, at 419.

protected decisions . . . must be predicated on legitimate state concerns *other than* disagreement with the choice the individual has made. . . . Otherwise, the interest in liberty protected by the Due Process Clause would be a nullity." *Hodgson* v. *Minnesota*, __ U.S.__,__ (1990) (Opinion of STEVENS, J.) (slip op., at 14) (emphasis added). Thus, the State's general interest in life must accede to Nancy Cruzan's particularized and intense interest in self-determination in her choice of medical treatment. There is simply nothing legitimately within the State's purview to be gained by superseding her decision.

Moreover, there may be considerable danger that Missouri's rule of decision would impair rather than serve any interest the State does have in sustaining life. Current medical practice recommends use of heroic measures if there is a scintilla of a chance that the patient will recover, on the assumption that the measures will be discontinued should the patient improve. When the President's Commission in 1982 approved the withdrawal of life support equipment from irreversibly vegetative patients, it explained that "[a]n even more troubling wrong occurs when a treatment that might save life or improve health is not started because the health care personnel are afraid that they will find it very difficult to stop the treatment if, as is fairly likely, it proves to be of little benefit and greatly burdens the patient." President's Commission 75. A New Jersey court recognized that families as well as doctors might be discouraged by an inability to stop life-support measures from "even attempting certain types of care [which] could thereby force them into hasty and premature decisions to allow a patient to die." *In re Conroy*, 98 N. J. 321, 370, 486 A. 2d 1209, 1234, (1985). See also Brief or American Academy of Neurology as *Amicus Curiae* 9 (expressing same concern).[15]

---

15. In any event, the State interest identified by the Missouri Supreme Court—a comprehensive and "unqualified" interest in preserving life, *id.*, at 420, 424—is not even well supported by that State's own enactments. In the first place, Missouri has no law requiring every person to procure any needed medical care nor a state health insurance program to underwrite such care. *Id.*, at 429 (Blackmar, J. dissenting). Second, as the state court admitted, Missouri has a living will statute which specifically "allows and encourages the pre-planned termination of life." *Ibid.;* see Mo. Rev. Stat. § 459.015(1) (1986). The fact that Missouri actively provides for its citizens to choose a natural death under certain circumstances suggests that the State's interest in life is not so unqualified as the court below suggests. It is true that this particular statute does not apply to nonterminal patients and does not include artificial nutrition and hydration as one of the measures that may be declined. Nonetheless, Missouri has also not chosen to require court review of every decision to withhold or withdraw life-support made on behalf of an incompetent patient. Such decisions are made every day, without state participation. See 760 S. W. 2d, at 428 (Blackmar, J., dissenting).

In addition, precisely what implication can be drawn from the statute's limitations is unclear given the inclusion of a series of "interpretive" provisions in the Act. The first such provision explains that the Act is to be interpreted consistently with the following: "Each person has the primary right to request or refuse medical treatment subject to the state's interest in protecting innocent third parties, preventing homicide and suicide and preserving good ethical standards in the medical profession." Mo. Rev. Sta. § 459.055(1) (1986). The second of these subsections explains that the Act's provisions are cumulative and not intended to increase or decrease the right of a patient to make decisions or lawfully effect the withholding or withdrawal of medical care. § 459.055(2). The third subsection provides that "no presumption concerning the intention of an individual who has not executed a declaration to consent to the use or withholding of medical procedures" shall be created. § 459.055(3).

Thus, even if it were conceivable that a State could assert an interest sufficiently com-

III

This is not to say that the State has no legitimate interests to assert here. As the majority recognizes, *ante*, at 17, Missouri has a *parents patriae* interest in providing Nancy Cruzan, now incompetent, with as accurate as possible a determination of how she would exercise her rights under these circumstances. Second, if and when it is determined that Nancy Cruzan would want to continue treatment, the State may legitimately assert an interest in providing that treatment. But *until* Nancy's wishes have been determined, the only state interest that may be asserted is an interest in safe-guarding the accuracy of that determination.

Accuracy, therefore, must be our touchstone. Missouri may constitutionally impose only those procedural requirements that serve to enhance the accuracy of a determination of Nancy Cruzan's wishes or are at least consistent with an accurate determination. The Missouri "safeguard" that the Court upholds today does not meet that standard. The determination needed in this context is whether the incompetent person would choose to live in a persistent vegetative state on life-support or to avoid this medical treatment. Missouri's rule of decision imposes a markedly asymmetrical evidentiary burden. Only evidence of specific statements of treatment choice made by the patient when competent is admissible to support a finding that the patient, now in a persistent vegetative state, would wish to avoid further medical treatment. Moreover, this evidence must be clear and convincing. No proof is required to support a finding that the incompetent person would wish to continue treatment.

A

The majority offers several justifications for Missouri's heightened evidentiary standard. First, the majority explains that the State may constitutionally adopt this rule to govern determinations of an incompetent's wishes in order to advance the State's substantive interests, including it unqualified interest in the preservation of human life. See *ante*, at 17–18, and n. 10. Missouri's evidentiary standard, however, cannot rest on the State's own interest in a particular substantive result. To be sure, courts have long erected clear and convincing evidence standards to place the greater risk of erroneous decisions on those bringing disfavored claims.[16] In such cases,

---

pelling to overcome Nancy Cruzan's constitutional right, Missouri law demonstrates a more modest interest at best. See generally *Capital Cities Cable, Inc.* v. *Crisp*, 467 U.S. 691, 715 (1984) (finding that state regulations narrow in scope indicated that State had only a moderate interest in its professed goal).

16. See *Colorado* v. *New Mexico*, 467 U.S. 310 (1984) (requiring clear and convincing evidence before one State is permitted to divert water from another to accommodate society's interests in stabile property rights and efficient use of resources); *New York* v. *New Jersey*, 256 U.S. 296 (1921) (promoting federalism by requiring clear and convincing evidence before using Court's power to control the conduct of one State at the behest of another); *Maxwell Land-Grant Case*, 121 U.S. 325 (1887) (requiring clear, unequivocal, and convincing evidence to set aside, annul or correct a patent or other title to property issued by the Government in order to secure settled expectations concerning property rights); *Marcum* v. *Zaring*, 406 P. 2d 970 (Okla. 1965) (promoting stability of marriage by requiring clear and convincing evidence to prove its invalidity); *Stevenson* v. *Stein*, 412 Pa. 478, 195 A. 2d 268 (1963) (promoting settled expectations concerning property rights by requiring clear and convincing evidence to prove adverse possession).

however, the choice to discourage certain claims was a legitimate, constitutional policy choice. In contrast, Missouri has no such power to disfavor a choice by Nancy Cruzan to avoid medical treatment, because Missouri has no legitimate interest in providing Nancy with treatment until it is established that this represents her choice. See *supra,* at 13–14. Just as a State may not override Nancy's choice directly, it may not do so indirectly through the imposition of a procedural rule.

Second, the majority offers two explanations for why Missouri's clear and convincing evidence standard is a means of enhancing accuracy, but neither is persuasive. The majority initially argues that a clear and convincing evidence standard is necessary to compensate for the possibility that such proceedings will lack the "guarantee of accurate factfinding that the adversary process brings with it," citing *Ohio* v. *Akron Center for Reproductive Health,* —— U.S. ——,—— (1990) (upholding a clear and convincing evidence standard for an *ex parte* proceeding). *Ante,* at 17. Without supporting the Court's decision in that case, I note that the proceeding to determine an incompetent's wishes is quite different from a proceeding to determine whether a minor may bypass notifying her parents before undergoing an abortion on the ground that she is mature enough to make the decision or that the abortion is in her best interests.

An adversarial proceeding is of particular importance when one side has a strong personal interest which needs to be counterbalanced to assure the court that the questions will be fully explored. A minor who has a strong interest in obtaining permission for an abortion without notifying her parents may come forward whether or not society would be satisfied that she has made the decision with the seasoned judgment of an adult. The proceeding here is of a different nature. Barring venal motives, which a trial court has the means of ferreting out, the decision to come forward to request a judicial order to stop treatment represents a slowly and carefully considered resolution by at least one adult and more frequently several adults that discontinuation of treatment is the patient's wish.

In addition, the bypass procedure at issue in *Akron, supra,* is *ex parte* and secret. The court may not notify the minor's parents, siblings or friends. No one may be present to submit evidence unless brought forward by the minor herself. In contrast, the proceeding to determine Nancy Cruzan's wishes was neither *ex parte* nor secret. In a hearing to determine the treatment preferences of an incompetent person, a court is not limited to adjusting burdens of proof as its only means of protecting against a possible imbalance. Indeed, any concern that those who come forward will present a onesided view would be better addressed by appointing a guardian ad litem, who could use the State's powers of discovery to gather and present evidence regarding the patient's wishes. A guardian ad litem's task is to uncover any conflicts of interest and ensure that each party likely to have relevant evidence is consulted and brought forward—for example, other members of the family, friends, clergy, and doctors. See *e.g., In re Colyer,* 99 Wash. 2d 114, 133, 660 P. 2d 738, 748–749 (1983). Missouri's heightened evidentiary standard attempts to achieve balance by discounting evidence; the guardian ad litem technique achieves balance by probing for additional evidence. Where, as here, the family members, friends, doctors and guardian ad litem agree, it is not because the process has failed, as the majority suggests. See *ante,* at 17, n. 9. It is because there is no genuine dispute as to Nancy's preference.

The majority next argues that where, as here, important individual rights are at stake, a clear and convincing evidence standard has long been held to be an appropriate means of enhancing accuracy, citing decisions concerning what process an individual is due before he can be deprived of a liberty interest. See *ante,* at 18–19. In those cases, however, this Court imposed a clear and convincing standard as a constitutional minimum on the basis of its evaluation that one side's interests clearly outweighed the second side's interests and therefore the second side should bear the risk of error. See *Santosky* v. *Kramer,* 455 U.S. 745, 753, 766–767 (1982) (requiring a clear and convincing evidence standard for termination of parental rights because the parent's interest is fundamental but the State has no legitimate interest in termination unless the parent is unfit, and finding that the State's interest in finding the best home for the child does not arise until the parent has been found unfit); *Addington* v. *Texas,* 441 U.S. 418, 426–427 (1979) (requiring clear and convincing evidence in an involuntary commitment hearing because the interest of the individual far outweighs that of a State, which has no legitimate interest in confining individuals who are not mentally ill and do not pose a danger to themselves or others). Moreover, we have always recognized that shifting the risk of error reduces the likelihood of errors in one direction at the cost of increasing the likelihood of errors in the other. See *Addington, supra,* at 423 (contrasting heightened standards of proof to a preponderance standard in which the two sides "share the risk of error in roughly equal fashion" because society does not favor one outcome over the other). In the cases cited by the majority, the imbalance imposed by a heightened evidentiary standard was not only acceptable but required because the standard was deployed to protect an individual's exercise of a fundamental right, as the majority admits, *ante,* at 18, n. 10. In contrast, the Missouri court imposed a clear and convincing standard as an obstacle to the exercise of a fundamental right.

The majority claims that the allocation of the risk of error is justified because it is more important not to terminate lifesupport for someone who would wish it continued than to honor the wishes of someone who would not. An erroneous decision to terminate life-support is irrevocable, says the majority, while an erroneous decision not to terminate "results in a maintenance of the status quo." See *ante,* at 19.[17] But, from the point of view of the patient, an erroneous decision in either direction is irrevocable. An erroneous decision to terminate artificial nutrition and hydration, to be sure, will lead to failure of that last remnant of physiological life, the brain stem, and result in complete brain death. An erroneous decision not to terminate life-support, however, robs a patient of the very qualities protected by the right to avoid unwanted medical treatment. His own degraded existence is perpetuated; his family's suffering is protracted; the memory he leaves a behind becomes more and more distorted.

Even a later decision to grant him his wish cannot undo the intervening harm. But

17. The majority's definition of the "status quo," of course, begs the question. Artificial delivery of nutrition and hydration represents the "status quo" only if the State has chosen to permit doctors and hospitals to keep a patient on life-support systems over the protests of his family or guardian. The "status quo" absent that state interference would be the natural result of his accident or illness (and the family's decision). The majority's definition of status quo, however, is "to a large extent a predictable, yet accidental confluence of technology, psyche, and inertia. The general citizenry . . . never said that it favored the creation of coma wards where permanently unconscious patients would be tended for years and years. Nor did the populace as a whole authorize the preeminence of doctors over families in making treatment decisions for incompetent patients." Rhoden, Litigating Life and Death, 102 Harv. L. Rev. 375, 433–434 (1988).

a later decision is unlikely in any event. "[T]he discovery of new evidence," to which the majority refers, *ibid.*, is more hypothetical than plausible. The majority also misconceives the relevance of the possibility of "advancements in medical science," *ibid.*, by treating it as a reason to force someone to continue medical treatment against his will. The possibility of a medical miracle is indeed part of the calculus, but it is a part of the *patient's* calculus. If current research suggests that some hope for cure or even moderate improvement is possible within the life-span projected, this is a factor that should be and would be accorded significant weight in assessing what the patient himself would choose.[18]

B

Even more than its heightened evidentiary standard, the Missouri court's categorical exclusion of relevant evidence dispenses with any semblance of accurate factfinding. The court adverted to no evidence supporting its decision, but held that no clear and convincing, inherently reliable evidence had been presented to show that Nancy would want to avoid further treatment. In doing so, the court failed to consider statements Nancy had made to family members and a close friend.[19] The

18. For Nancy Cruzan, no such cure or improvement is in view. So much of her brain has deteriorated and been replaced by fluid, see App. to Pet. for Cert. A94, that apparently the only medical advance that could restore consciousness to her body would be a brain transplant. Cf. n. 22, *infra*.

19. The trial court had relied on the testimony of Athena Comer, a long-time friend, co-worker and a housemate for several months, as sufficient to show that Nancy Cruzan would wish to be free of medical treatment under her present circumstances. App. to Pet. for Cert. A94. Ms. Comer described a conversation she and Nancy had while living together, concerning Ms. Comer's sister who had become ill suddenly and died during the night. The Comer family had been told that if she had lived through the night, she would have been in a vegetative state. Nancy had lost a grandmother a few months before. Ms. Comer testified that: "Nancy said she would never want to live [as a vegetative state] because if she couldn't be normal or even, you know, like half way, and do things for yourself, because Nancy always did, that she didn't want to live . . . and we talked about it a lot." Tr. 388–389. She said "several times" that "she wouldn't want to live that way because if she was going to live, she wanted to be able to live, not to just lay in a bed and not be able to move because you can't do anything for yourself." *Id.*, at 390, 396. "[S]he said that she hoped that [all the] people in her family knew that she wouldn't want to live [as a vegetable] because she knew it was usually up to the family whether you lived that way or not." *Id.*, at 399.

The conversation took place approximately a year before Nancy's accident and was described by Ms. Comer as a "very serious" conversation that continued for approximately half an hour without interruption. *Id.*, at 390. The Missouri Supreme Court dismissed Nancy's statement as "unreliable" on the ground that it was an informally expressed reaction to other people's medical conditions. 760 S. W. 2d, at 424.

The Missouri Supreme Court did not refer to other evidence of Nancy's wishes or explain why it was rejected. Nancy's sister Christy, to whom she was very close, testified that she and Nancy had had two very serious conversations about a year and a half before the accident. A day or two after their niece was stillborn (but would have been badly damaged if she had lived), Nancy had said that maybe it was part of a "greater plan" that the baby had been stillborn and did not have to face "the possible life of mere existence." Tr. 537. A month later, after their grandmother had died after a long battle with heart problems, Nancy said that "it was better for my grandmother not to be kind of brought back and forth [by] medical [treatment], brought back from a critical near point of death. . . . *Id.*, at 541.

court also failed to consider testimony from Nancy's mother and sister that they were certain that Nancy would want to discontinue to artificial nutrition and hydration,[20] even after the court found that Nancy's family was loving and without malignant motive. See 760 S. W. 2d, at 412. The court also failed to consider the conclusions of the guardian ad litem, appointed by the trial court, that there was clear and convincing evidence that Nancy would want to discontinue medical treatment and that this was in her best interests. *Id.,* at 444 (Higgins, J., dissenting from denial of rehearing); Brief for Respondent Guardian Ad Litem 2–3. The court did not specifically define what kind of evidence it would consider clear and convincing, but its general discussion suggests that only a living will or equivalently formal directive from the patient when competent would meet this standard. See 760 S. W. 2d, at 424–425.

Too few people execute living wills or equivalently formal directives for such an evidentiary rule to ensure adequately that the wishes of incompetent persons will be honored.[21] While it might be a wise social policy to encourage people to furnish such instructions, no general conclusion about a patient's choice can be drawn from the absence of formalities. The probability of becoming irreversibly vegetative is so low that many people may not feel an urgency to marshal formal evidence of their preferences. Some may not wish to dwell on their own physical deterioration and mortality. Even someone with a resolute determination to avoid life-support under circumstances such as Nancy's would still need to know that such things as living wills exist and how to execute one. Often legal help would be necessary, especially given the majority's apparent willingness to permit States to insist that a person's wishes are not truly known unless the particular medical treatment is specified. See *ante,* at 21.

As a California appellate court observed: "The lack of generalized public awareness of the statutory scheme and the typically human characteristics of procrastination and reluctance to contemplate the need for such arrangements however makes this a tool which will all too often go unused by those who might desire it." *Barber* v. *Superior Court,* 147 Cal. App. 3d 1006, 1015, 194 Cal. Rptr. 484, 489 (1983). When a person tells family or close friends that she does not want her life sustained artificially, she is "express[ing] her wishes in the only terms familiar to her, and . . . as clearly as a lay person should be asked to express them. To require

---

20. Nancy's sister Christy, Nancy's mother, and another of Nancy's friends testified that Nancy would want to discontinue the hydration and nutrition. Christy said that "Nancy would be horrified at the state she is in." *Id.,* at 535. She would also "want to take that burden away from [her family]. *Id.,* at 544. Based on "a lifetime of experience [I know Nancy's wishes] are to discontinue the hydration and the nutrition." *Id.,* at 542. Nancy's mother testified: "Nancy would not want to be like she is now. [I]f it were me up there or Christy or any of us, she would be doing for us what we are trying to do for her. I know she would, . . . as her mother." *Id.,* at 526.

21. Surveys show that the overwhelming majority of Americans have not executed such written instructions. See Emmanuel & Emmanuel, The Medical Directive: A New Comprehensive Advance Care Document, 261 JAMA 3288 (1989) (only 9% of Americans execute advance directives about how they would wish treatment decisions to be handled if they became incompetent); American Medical Association Surveys of Physician and Public Opinion on Health Care Issues 29–30 (1988) (only 15% of those surveyed had executed living wills); 2 President's Commission for the Study of Ethical Problems in Medicine and Biomedical and Behavioral Research, Making Health Care Decisions 241–242 (1982) (23% of those surveyed said that they had put treatment instructions in writing).

more is unrealistic, and for all practical purposes, it precludes the rights of patients to forego life-sustaining treatment." *In re O'Connor,* 72 N. Y. 2d 517, 551, 531 N. E. 2d 607, 626 (1988) (Simons, J., dissenting).[22] When Missouri enacted a living will statute, it specifically provided that the absence of a living will does not warrant a presumption that a patient wishes continued medical treatment. See n. 15, *supra.* Thus, apparently not even Missouri's own legislature believes that a person who does not execute a living will fails to do so because he wishes continuous medical treatment under all circumstances.

The testimony of close friends and family members, on the other hand, may often be the best evidence available of what the patient's choice would be. It is they with whom the patient most likely will have discussed such questions and they who know the patient best. "Family members have a unique knowledge of the patient which is vital to any decision on his or her behalf." Newman, Treatment Refusals for the Critically and Terminally Ill: Proposed Rules for the Family, the Physician, and the State, 3 N. Y. L. S. Human Rights Annual 35, 46 (1985). The Missouri court's decision to ignore this whole category of testimony is also at odds with the practices of other States. See, *e.g., In re Peter,* 108 N. J. 365, 529 A. 2d 419 (1987), *Brophy* v. *New England Sinai Hospital, Inc.,* 398 Mass. 417, 497 N. E. 2d 626 (1986); *In re Severns,* 425 A. 2d 156 (Del. Ch. 1980).

The Missouri court's disdain for Nancy's statements in serious conversations not long before her accident, for the opinions of Nancy's family and friends as to her values, beliefs and certain choice, and even for the opinion of an outside objective factfinder appointed by the State evinces a disdain for Nancy Cruzan's own right to choose. The rules by which an incompetent person's wishes are determined must represent every effort to determine those wishes. The rule that the Missouri court adopted and that this Court upholds, however, skews the result away from a determination that as accurately as possible reflects the individual's own preferences and beliefs. It is a rule that transforms human beings into passive subjects of medical technology.

> "[M]edical care decisions must be guided by the individual patient's interest and values. Allowing persons to determine their own medical treatment is an important way in which society respects persons as individuals. Moreover, the respect due to persons as individuals does not diminish simply because

22. New York is the only State besides Missouri to deny a request to terminate life support on the ground that clear and convincing evidence of prior, expressed intent was absent, although New York did so in the context of very different situations. Mrs. O'Connor, the subject of *In re O'Connor,* had several times expressed her desire not to be placed on life support if she were not going to be able to care for herself. However, both of her daughters testified that they did not know whether their mother would want to decline artificial nutrition and hydration under her present circumstances. Cf. n. 13, *supra,* Moreover, despite damage from several strokes, Mrs. O'Connor was conscious and capable of responding to simple questions and requests and the medical testimony suggested she might improve to some extent. Cf. *supra,* at 1. The New York Court of Appeals also denied permission to terminate blood transfusions for a severely retarded man with terminal cancer because there was no evidence of a treatment choice made by the man when competent, as he had never been competent. See *In re Storar,* 52 N. Y. 2d 363, 420 N. E. 2d 64, cert. denied, 454 U.S. 858 (1981). Again, the court relied on evidence that the man was conscious, functioning in the way he always had, and that the transfusions did not cause him substantial pain (although it was clear he did not like them).

they have become incapable of participating in treatment decisions. . . . [I]t is still possible for others to make a decision that reflects [the patient's] interests more closely than would a purely technological decision to do whatever is possible. Lacking the ability to decide, [a patient] has a right to a decision that takes his interests into account." *In re Drabick,* 200 Cal. app. 3d 185, 208; 245 Cal. Rptr. 840, 854–855 (1988).

C

I do not suggest that States must sit by helplessly if the choices of incompetent patients are in danger of being ignored. See *ante,* at 17. Even if the Court had ruled that Missouri's rule of decision is unconstitutional, as I believe it should have, States would nevertheless remain free to fashion procedural protections to safeguard the interests of incompetents under these circumstances. The Constitution provides merely a framework here: protections must be genuinely aimed at ensuring decisions commensurate with the will of the patient, and must be reliable as instruments to that end. Of the many States which have instituted such protections, Missouri is virtually the only one to have fashioned a rule that lessens the likelihood of accurate determinations. In contrast, nothing in the Constitution prevents States from reviewing the advisability of a family decision, by requiring a court proceeding or by appointing an impartial guardian ad litem.

There are various approaches to determining an incompetent patient's treatment choice in use by the several States today and there may be advantages and disadvantages to each and other approaches not yet envisioned. The choice, in largest part, is and should be left to the States, so long as each State is seeking, in a reliable manner, to discover what the patient would want. But with such momentous interests in the balance, States must avoid procedures that will prejudice the decision. "To err either way—to keep a person alive under circumstances under which he would rather have been allowed to die, or to allow that person to die when he would have chosen to cling to life—would be deeply unfortunate." *In re Conroy,* 98 N. J., at 343, 486 A. 2d, at 1220.

D

Finally, I cannot agree with the majority that where it is not possible to determine what choice an incompetent patient would make, a State's role as *parens patriae* permits the State automatically to make that choice itself. See *ante,* at 22 (explaining that the Due Process Clause does not require a State to confide the decision to "anyone but the patient herself"). Under fair rules of evidence, it is improbable that a court could not determine what the patient's choice would be. Under the rule of decision adopted by Missouri and upheld today by this Court, such occasions might be numerous. But in neither case does it follow that it is constitutionally acceptable for the State invariably to assume the role of deciding for the patient. A State's legitimate interest in safeguarding a patient's choice cannot be furthered by simply appropriating it.

The majority justifies its position by arguing that, while close family members may have a strong feeling about the question, "there is no automatic assurance that the view of close family members will necessarily be the same as the patient's would have been had she been confronted with the prospect of her situation while competent." *Ibid.* I cannot quarrel with this observation. But it leads only to another question: Is there any reason to suppose that a State is *more* likely to make the choice that the patient would have made than someone who knew the patient intimately? To ask this is to answer it. As the New Jersey Supreme Court observed: "Family members are best qualified to make substituted judgments for incompetent patients not only because of their peculiar grasp of the patient's approach to life, but also because of their special bonds with him or her. . . . It is . . . they who treat the patient as a person, rather than a symbol of a cause." *In re Jobes,* 108 N.J. 394, 416, 529 A. 2d 434, 445 (1987). The State, in contrast, is a stranger to the patient.

A State's inability to discern an incompetent patient's choice still need not mean that a State is rendered powerless to protect that choice. But I would find that the Due Process Clause prohibits a State from doing more than that. A State may ensure that the person who makes the decision on the patient's behalf is the one whom the patient himself would have selected to make that choice for him. And a State may exclude from consideration anyone having improper motives. But a State generally must either repose the choice with the person whom the patient himself would most likely have chosen as proxy or leave the decision to the patient's family.[23]

IV

As many as 10,000 patients are being maintained in persistent vegetative states in the United States, and the number is expected to increase significantly in the near future. See Cranford, *supra* n. 2, at 27, 31. Medical technology, developed over the past 20 or so years, is often capable of resuscitating people after they have stopped breathing or their hearts have stopped beating. Some of those people are brought fully back to life. Two decades ago, those who were not and could not swallow and digest food, died. Intravenous solutions could not provide sufficient calories to maintain people for more than a short time. Today, various forms of artificial feeding have been developed that are able to keep people metabolically alive for years, even decades. See Spencer & Palmisano, Specialized Nutritional Support of Patients—A Hospital's Legal Duty?, 11 Quality Rev. Bull. 160, 160–161 (1985). In addition, in this century, chronic or degenerative ailments have replaced communicable diseases as the primary causes of death. See R. Weir, Abating Treatment with Critically Ill Patients 12–13 (1989); President's Commission 15–16. The 80% of Americans who die in hospitals are "likely to meet their end . . . 'in a sedated or comatose state; betubed nasally, abdominally and intravenously; and far more like manipulated objects than like moral subjects.'"[24] A fifth of all adults surviving to age 80 will suffer a progressive dementing disorder prior to death. See Cohen & Eisdorfer, Dementing Disorders, in The Practice of Geriatrics 194 (E. Calkins, P. Davis, & A. Ford eds. 1986).

"[L]aw, equity and justice must not themselves quail and be helpless in the face of modern technological marvels presenting questions hitherto unthought of." *In re*

---

23. Only in the exceedingly rare case where the State cannot find any family member or friend who can be trusted to endeavor genuinely to make the treatment choice the patient would have made does the State become the legitimate surrogate decisionmaker.

24. Fadiman, The Liberation of Lolly and Gronky, Life Magazine, Dec. 1986, p. 72 (quoting medical ethicist Joseph Fletcher).

Quinlan, 70 N. J. 10, 44, 355 A. 2d 647, 665, cert. denied, 429 U.S. 922 (1976). The new medical technology can reclaim those who would have been irretrievably lost a few decades ago and restore them to active lives. For Nancy Cruzan, it failed, and for others with wasting incurable disease it may be doomed to failure. In these unfortunate situations, the bodies and preferences and memories of the victims do not escheat to the State; nor does our Constitution permit the State or any other government to commandeer them. No singularity of feeling exists upon which such a government might confidently rely as *parents patriae.* The President's Commission, after years of research, concluded:

> "In few areas of health care are people's evaluations of their experiences so varied and uniquely personal as in their assessments of the nature and value of the processes associated with dying. For some, every moment of life is of inestimable value; for others, life without some desired level of mental or physical ability is worthless or burdensome. A moderate degree of suffering may be an important means of personal growth and religious experience to one person, but only frightening or despicable to another." President's Commission 276.

Yet Missouri and this Court have displaced Nancy's own assessment of the processes associated with dying. They have discarded evidence of her will, ignored her values, and deprived her of the right to a decision as closely approximating her own choice as humanly possible. They have done so disingenuously in her name, and openly in Missouri's own. That Missouri and this Court may truly be motivated only by concern for incompetent patients makes no matter. As one of our most prominent jurists warned us decades ago: "Experience should teach us to be most on our guard to protect liberty when the government's purposes are beneficent. . . . The greatest dangers to liberty lurk in insidious encroachment by men of zeal, well meaning but without understanding." *Olmstead* v. *United States,* 277 U.S. 438, 479 (1928) (Brandeis, J., dissenting).

I respectfully dissent.

SUPREME COURT OF THE UNITED STATES

No. 88–1503

NANCY BETH CRUZEN, BY HER PARENTS AND CO-GUARDIANS, LESTER L. CRUZAN, ET UX., PETITIONERS v. DIRECTOR, MISSOURI DEPARTMENT OF HEALTH ET AL.

ON WRIT OF CERTIORARI TO THE SUPREME COURT OF MISSOURI

[June 25, 1990]

JUSTICE STEVENS, dissenting.

Our Constitution is born of the proposition that all legitimate governments must secure the equal right of every person to "Life, Liberty, and the pursuit of Happiness."[1] In the ordinary case we quite naturally assume that these three ends are compatible, mutually enhancing, and perhaps even coincident.

The Court would make an exception here. It permits the State's abstract, undifferentiated interest in the preservation of life to overwhelm the best interests of Nancy Beth Cruzan, interests which would, according to an undisputed finding, be served by allowing her guardians to exercise her constitutional right to discontinue medical treatment. Ironically, the Court reaches this conclusion despite endorsing three significant propositions which should save it from any such dilemma. First, a competent individual's decision to refuse life-sustaining medical procedures is an aspect of liberty protected by the Due Process Clause of the Fourteenth Amendment. See *ante,* at 14–15. Second, upon a proper evidentiary showing, a qualified guardian may make that decision on behalf of an incompetent ward. See, e.g., *ante,* at 20. Third, in answering the important question presented by this tragic case, it is wise "not to attempt by any general statement, to cover every possible phase of the subject." See *ante,* at 13 (citation omitted). Together, these considerations suggest that Nancy Cruzan's liberty to be free from medical treatment must be understood in light of the facts and circumstances particular to her.

---

1. It is stated in the Declaration of Independence that:

"We hold these truths to be self-evident, that all men are created equal, that they are endowed by their Creator with certain unalienable Rights, that among these are Life, Liberty and the pursuit of Happiness.—That to secure these rights, Governments are instituted among Men, deriving their just powers from the consent of the governed,—That whenever any Form of Government becomes destructive of these ends, it is the Right of the People to alter or to abolish it, and to institute new Government, laying its foundation on such principles and organizing its powers in such form, as to them shall seem most likely to effect their Safety and Happiness."

I would so hold: in my view, the Constitution requires the State to care for Nancy Cruzan's life in a way that gives appropriate respect to her own best interests.

I

This case is the first in which we consider whether, and how, the Constitution protects the liberty of seriously ill patients to be free from life-sustaining medical treatment. So put, the question is both general and profound. We need not, however, resolve the question in the abstract. Our responsibility as judges both enables and compels us to treat the problem as it is illuminated by the facts of the controversy before us.

The most important of those facts are these: "clear and convincing evidence" established that Nancy Cruzan is "oblivious to her environment except for reflexive responses to sound and perhaps to painful stimuli"; that "she has no cognitive or reflexive ability to swallow food or water"; that "she will never recover" these abilities; and that her "cerebral cortical atrophy is irreversible, permanent, progressive and ongoing." App. to Pet. for Cert. A94–A95. Recovery and consciousness are impossible; the highest cognitive brain function that can be hoped for is a grimace in "recognition of ordinarily painful stimuli" or an "apparent response to sound." *Id.*, at A95.[2]

After thus evaluating Nancy Cruzan's medical condition, the trial judge next examined how the interests of third parties would be affected if Nancy's parents were allowed to withdraw the gastrostomy tube that had been implanted in their daughter. His findings make it clear that the parents' request had no economic motivation,[3] and that granting their request would neither adversely affect any innocent third parties nor breach the ethical standards of the medical profession.[4] He then

---

2. The trial court found as follows on the basis of "clear and convincing evidence:"

"1. That her respiration and circulation are not artificially maintained and within essentially normal limits for a 30 year old female with vital signs recently reported as BP 130/80; pulse 78 and regular; respiration spontaneous at 16 to 18 per minute.

"2. That she is oblivious to her environment except for reflexive responses to sound and perhaps to painful stimuli.

"3. That she has suffered anoxia of the brain resulting in massive enlargement of the ventricle filling with cerebrospinal fluid in the area where the brain has degenerated. This cerebral cortical atrophy is irreversible, permanent, progressive and ongoing.

"4. That her highest cognitive brain function is exhibited by her grimacing perhaps in recognition of ordinarily painful stimuli, indicating the experience of pain and her apparent response to sound.

"5. That she is spastic quadriplegic.

"6. That she has contactures of her four extremities which are slowly progressive with irreversible muscular and tendon damage to all extremities.

"7. That she has no cognitive or reflexive ability to swallow food or water to maintain her daily essential needs. That she will never recover her ability to swallow sufficient to satisfy her needs." App. to Pet. for Cert., at A94–A95.

3. "The only economic considerations in this case rest with Respondent's employer, the State of Missouri, which is bearing the entire cost of care. Our ward is an adult without financial resources other than Social Security whose not inconsiderable medical insurance has been exhausted since January 1986." *Id.*, at A96.

4. "In this case there are no innocent third parties requiring state protection, neither homicide nor suicide will be committed and the consensus of the medical witnesses indicated concerns personal to themselves or the legal consequences of such actions rather than any objec-

considered, and rejected, a religious objection to his decision,[5] and explained why he concluded that the ward's constitutional "right to liberty" outweighed the general public policy on which the State relied:

> "There is a fundamental natural right expressed in our Constitution as the 'right to liberty,' which permits an individual to refuse or direct the withholding or withdrawal of artificial death prolonging procedures when the person has no more cognitive brain function than our Ward and all the physicians agree there is no hope of further recovery while the deterioration of the brain continues with further overall worsening physical contractures. To the extent that the statute or public policy prohibits withholding or withdrawal of nutrition and hydration or euthanasia or mercy killing, if such be the definition, under all circumstances, arbitrarily and with no exceptions, it is in violation of our ward's constitutional rights by depriving her of liberty without due process of law. To decide otherwise that medical treatment once undertaken must be continued irrespective of its lack of success or benefit to the patient in effect gives one's body to medical science without their consent.

"The Co-guardians are required only to exercise their legal authority to act in the best interests of their Ward as they discharge their duty and are free to act or not with this authority as they may determine." *Id.,* at A98–A99 (footnotes omitted).

II

Because he believed he had a duty to do so, the independent guardian ad litem appealed the trial court's order to the Missouri Supreme Court. In that appeal, however, the guardian advised the court that he did not disagree with the trial court's decision. Specifically, he endorsed the critical finding that "it was in Nancy Cruzan's best interests to have the tube feeding discontinued."[6]

That important conclusion thus was not disputed by the litigants. One might reasonably suppose that it would be dispositive: if Nancy Cruzan has no interest in continued treatment, and if she has a liberty interest in being free from unwanted treatment, and if the cessation of treatment would have no adverse impact on third parties, and if no reason exists to doubt the good faith of Nancy's parents, then what possible basis could the State have for insisting upon continued medical treatment? Yet, instead of questioning or endorsing the trial court's conclusions about Nancy Cruzan's interests, the State Supreme Court largely ignored them.

The opinion of that court referred to four different state interests that have been

---

tions that good ethical standards of the profession would be breached if the nutrition and hydration were withdrawn the same as any other artificial death prolonging procedures the statute specifically authorizes." *Id.,* at A98.

5. "Nancy's present unresponsive and hopeless existence is not the will of the Supreme Ruler but of man's will to forcefully feed her when she herself cannot swallow thus fueling respiratory and circulatory pumps to no cognitive purpose for her except sound and perhaps pain." *Id.,* at A97.

6. "Appellant guardian ad litem advised this court:

"'we informed the [trial] court that we felt it was in Nancy Cruzan's best interests to have the tube feeding discontinued. We not find ourselves in the position of appealing from a judgment we basically agree with.'" *Cruzan* v. *Harmon,* 760 S. W. 2d 408, 435 (Mo. 1988) (Higgins, J., dissenting)

identified in other somewhat similar cases, but acknowledged that only the State's general interest in "the preservation of life" was implicated by this case.[7] It defined that interest as follows:

> "The state's interest in life embraces two separate concerns: an interest in the prolongation of the life of the individual patient and an interest in the sanctity of life itself." *Cruzan* v. *Harmon*, 760 S. W. 2d 408, 419 (1988).

Although the court did not characterize this interest as absolute, it repeatedly indicated that it outweighs any countervailing interest that is based on the "quality of life" of any individual patient.[8] In the view of the state-court majority, that general interest is strong enough to foreclose any decision to refuse treatment for an incompetent person unless that person had previously evidenced, in a clear and convincing terms, such a decision for herself. The best interests of the incompetent individual who had never confronted the issue—or perhaps had been incompetent since birth—are entirely irrelevant and unprotected under the reasoning of the State Supreme Court's four-judge majority.

The three dissenting judges found Nancy Cruzan's interests compelling. They agreed with the trial court's evaluation of state policy. In his persuasive dissent, Judge Blackmar explained that decisions about the care of chronically ill patients were traditionally private:

> "My disagreement with the principal opinion lies fundamentally in its emphasis on the interest of and the role of the state, represented by the Attorney General. Decisions about prolongation of life are of recent origin. For most of the world's history, and presently in most parts of the world, such decisions would never arise because the technology would not be available. Decisions about medical treatment have customarily been made by the patient, or by those closest to the

7. "Four state interests have been identified: preservation of life, prevention of homicide and suicide, the protection of interests of innocent third parties and the maintenance of the ethical integrity of the medical profession. *See* Section 459.055(1), RSMo 1986; *Brophy*, 497 N. E. 2d at 634. In this case, only the state's interest in the preservation of life is implicated." *Id.*, at 419.

8. "The state's concern with the sanctity of life rests on the principle that life is precious and worthy of preservation without regard to its quality." *Ibid.*

"It is tempting to equate the state's interest in the preservation of life with some measure of quality of life. As the discussion which follows shows, some courts find quality of life a convenient focus when justifying the termination of treatment. But the state's interest is not in quality of life. The broad policy statements of the legislature make no such distinction; nor shall we. Were quality of life at issue, persons with all manner of handicaps might find the state seeking to terminate their lives. Instead, the state's interest is in life; that interest is unqualified." *Id.*, at 420.

"As we previously stated, however, the state's interest is not in quality of life. The state's interest is an unqualified interest in life." *Id.*, at 422. "The argument made here, that Nancy will not recover, is but a thinly veiled statement that her life in its present form is not worth living. Yet a diminished quality of life does not support a decision to cause death." *Ibid.*

"Given the fact that Nancy is alive and that the burdens of her treatment are not excessive for her, we do not believe her right to refuse treatment, whether that right proceeds from a constitutional right of privacy or a common law right to refuse treatment, outweighs the immense, clear fact of life in which the state maintains a vital interest." *Id.*, at 424.

patient if the patient, because of youth or infirmity, is unable to make the decisions. This is nothing new in substituted decisionmaking. The state is seldom
called upon to be the decisionmaker.

"I would not accept the assumption, inherent in the principal opinion, that,
with our advanced technology, the state must necessarily become involved in a
decision about using extraordinary measures to prolong life. Decisions of this
kind are made daily by the patient or relatives, on the basis of medical advice
and their conclusion as to what is best. Very few cases reach court, and I doubt
whether this case would be before us but for the fact that Nancy lies in a state
hospital. I do not place primary emphasis on the patient's expressions, except
possibly in the very unusual case, of which I find no example in the books, in
which the patient expresses a view that all available life supports should be made
use of. Those closest to the patient are best positioned to make judgments about
the patient's best interest." *Id.*, at 428.

Judge Blackmar then argued that Missouri's policy imposed upon dying individuals and their families a controversial and objectionable view of life's meaning:

"It is unrealistic to say that the preservation of life is an absolute, without regard
to the quality of life. I make this statement only in the context of a case in which
the trial judge has found that there is no chance for amelioration of Nancy's condition. The principal opinion accepts this conclusion. It is appropriate to consider
the quality of life in making decisions about the extraordinary medical treatment.
Those who have made decisions about such matters without resort to the courts
certainly consider the quality of life, and balance this against the unpleasant consequences to the patient. There is evidence that Nancy may react to pain stimuli.
If she has any awareness of her surroundings, her life must be a living hell. She is
unable to express herself or to do anything at all to alter her situation. Her parents, who are her closest relatives, are best able to feel for her and to decide
what is best for her. The state should not substitute its decisions for theirs. Nor
am I impressed with the crypto-philosophers cited in the principal opinion, who
declaim about the sanctity of any life without regard to its quality. They dwell in
ivory towers." *Id.*, at 429.

Finally, Judge Blackmar concluded that the Missouri policy was illegitimate
because it treats life as a theoretical abstraction, severed from, and indeed opposed
to, the person of Nancy Cruzan.

"The Cruzan family appropriately came before the court seeking relief. The circuit
judge properly found the facts and applied the law. His factual findings are supported by the record and his legal conclusions by overwhelming weight of authority. The principal opinion attempts to establish absolutes, but does so at the
expense of human factors. In so doing it unnecessarily subjects Nancy and those
close to her to continuous torture which no family should be forced to endure." *Id.*,
at 429–430.

Although Judge Blackmar did not frame his argument as such, it propounds a
sound constitutional objection to the Missouri majority's reasoning: Missouri's regulation is an unreasonable intrusion upon traditionally private matters encompassed
within the liberty protected by the Due Process Clause.

The portion of this Court's opinion that considers the merits of this case is similarly unsatisfactory. It, too, fails to respect the best interests of the patient.[9] It, too, relies on what is tantamount to a waiver rationale: the dying patient's best interests are put to one side and the entire inquiry is focused on her prior expressions of intent.[10] An innocent person's constitutional right to be free from unwanted medical treatment is thereby categorically limited to those patients who had the foresight to make an unambiguous statement of their wishes while competent. The Court's decision affords no protection to children, to young people who are victims of unexpected accidents or illnesses, or to the countless thousands of elderly persons who either fail to decide, or fail to explain, how they want to be treated if they should experience a similar fate. Because Nancy Beth Cruzan did not have the foresight to preserve her constitutional right in a living will, or some comparable "clear and convincing" alternative, her right is gone forever and her fate is in the hands of the state legislature instead of in those of her family, her independent neutral guardian ad litem, and an impartial judge—all of whom agree on the course of action that is in her best interests. The Court's willingness to find a waiver of this constitutional right reveals a distressing misunderstanding of the importance of individual liberty.

III

It is perhaps predictable that courts might undervalue the liberty at stake here. Because death is so profoundly personal, public reflection upon it is unusual. As this sad case shows, however, such reflection must become more common if we are to deal responsibly with the modern circumstances of death. Medical advances have altered the physiological conditions of death in ways that may be alarming: highly invasive treatment may perpetuate human existence through a merger of body and machine that some might reasonably regard as an insult to life rather than as its continuation. But those same advances, and the reorganization of medical care accompanying the new science and technology, have also transformed the political and social conditions of death: people are less likely to die at home, and more likely to die in relatively public places, such as hospitals or nursing homes.[11]

9. See especially *ante,* at 17 ("we think a State may properly decline to make judgments about the 'quality' of life that a particular individual may enjoy, and simply assert an unqualified interest in the preservation of human life to be weighed against the constitutionally protected interests of the individual"); *ante,* at 18, n. 10 (stating that the government is seeking to protect "its own institutional interests" in life).

10. See, *e.g., ante,* at 19–20.

11. "Until the latter part of this century, medicine had relatively little treatment to offer the dying and the vast majority of persons died at home rather than in the hospital." Brief for American Medical Association et. al. as *Amici Curiae* 6. "In 1985, 83% of deaths [of] Americans age 65 or over occurred in a hospital or nursing home. Sager, Easterling, *et. al., Changes in the Location of Death After Passage of Medicare's Prospective Payment System: A National Study,* 320 New Eng. J. Med. 433, 435 (1989)." *Id.,* at 6, n. 2.

According to the President's Commission for the Study of Ethical Problems in Medicine and Biomedical and Behavioral Research:

"Just as recent years have seen alterations in the underlying causes of death, the places where people die have also changed. For most of recorded history, deaths (of natural causes) usually occurred in the home. "'Everyone knew about death at first hand; there was nothing unfamiliar or even queer about the phenomenon. People seem to have known a lot more about the process itself than is the case today. The "deathbed" was a real place, and the dying person usually knew where he was and when it was time to assemble the family and call for the priest.'

"Even when people did get admitted to a medical care institution, those whose conditions

Ultimate questions that might once have been dealt with in intimacy by a family and its physician[12] have now become the concern of institutions. When the institution is a state hospital, as it is in this case, the government itself becomes involved.[13] Dying nonetheless remains a part of "the life which characteristically has its place in the home," *Poe* v. *Ullman,* 367 U.S. 497, 551 (1961) (Harlan, J., dissenting). The "integrity of that life is something so fundamental that it has been found to draw to its protection the principles of more than one explicitly granted Constitutional right," *id.,* at 551–552, and our decisions have demarcated a "private realm of family life which the state cannot enter." *Prince* v. *Massachusetts,* 321 U.S. 158, 166–167 (1944). The physical boundaries of the home, of course, remain crucial guarantors of the life within it. See, e.g., *Payton* v. *New York,* 445 U.S. 573, 589 (1980); *Stanley* v. *Georgia,* 394 U.S. 557, 565 (1969). Nevertheless, this Court has long recognized that the liberty to make the decisions and choices constitutive of private life is so fundamental to our "concept of ordered liberty," *Palko* v. *Connecticut,* 302 U.S. 319, 325 (1937), that those choices must occasionally be afforded more direct protection. See, *e. g., Meyer* v. *Nebraska,* 262 U.S. 390 (1923); *Griswold* v. *Connecticut,* 381 U.S. 479 (1965); *Roe* v. *Wade,* 410 U.S. 113 (1973); *Thornburgh* v. *American College of Obstetricians and Gynecologists,* 476 U.S. 747, 772–782 (1986) (STEVENS, J., concurring).

Respect for these choices has guided our recognition of rights pertaining to bodily integrity. The constitutional decisions identifying those rights, like the common-law

proved incurable were discharged to the care of their families. This was not only because the health care system could no longer be helpful, but also because alcohol and opiates (the only drugs available to ease pain and suffering) were available without a prescription. Institutional care was reserved for the poor or those without family support; hospitals often aimed more at saving patients' souls than at providing medical care.

"As medicine has been able to do more for dying patients, their care has increasingly been delivered in institutional settings. By 1949, institutions were the sites of 50% of all deaths; by 1958, the figure was 61%; and by 1977, over 70%. Perhaps 80% of all deaths in the United States now occur in hospitals and long-term care institutions, such as nursing homes. The change in where very ill patients are treated permits health care professionals to marshall the instruments of scientific medicine more effectively. But people who are dying may well find such a setting alienating and unsupportive." Deciding to Forego Life-Sustaining Treatment 17–18 (1983) (footnotes omitted), quoting, Thomas, Dying as Failure, 447 Annals Am. Acad. Pol. & Soc. Sci. 1, 3 (1980).¶12. We have recognized that the special relationship between patient and physician will often be encompassed within the domain of private life protected by the Due Process Clause. See, e.g., *Griswold* v. *Connecticut,* 381 U.S. 479, 481 (1965); *Roe* v. *Wade,* 410 U.S. 113, 152–153 (1973); *Thornburgh* v. *American College of Obstetricians and Gynecologists,* 476 U.S. 747, 759 (1986).

13. The Court recognizes that "the State has been involved as an adversary from the beginning" in this case only because Nancy Cruzan "was a patient at a state hospital when this litigation commenced," *ante,* at 17, n. 9. It seems to me, however, that the Court draws precisely the wrong conclusion from this insight. The Court apparently believes that the absence of the State from the litigation would have created a problem, because agreement among the family and the independent guardian ad litem as to Nancy Cruzan's best interests might have prevented her treatment from becoming the focus of a "truly adversarial" proceeding. *Ibid.* It may reasonably be debated whether some judicial process should be required before life-sustaining treatment is discontinued; this issue has divided the state courts. Compare *In re Estate of Longeway,* 133 Ill, 2d 33, 51, 549 N. E. 2d 292, 300 (1989) (requiring judicial approval of guardian's decision) with *In re Hamlin,* 102 Wash. 2d 810, 818–819, 689 P. 2d 1372, 1377–1378 (1984) (discussing circumstances in which judicial approval is unnecessary). Cf. *In*

tradition upon which they built,[14] are mindful that the "makers of our Constitution . . . recognized the significance of man's spiritual nature." *Olmstead* v. *United States,* 277 U.S. 438, 478 (1928) (Brandeis, J., dissenting). It may truly be said that "our notions of liberty are inextricably entwined with our idea of physical freedom and self determination." *Ante,* at 1 (O'CONNOR, J., concurring). Thus we have construed the Due Process Clause to preclude physically invasive recoveries of evidence not only because such procedures are "brutal" but also because they are "offensive to human dignity." *Rochin* v. *California,* 342 U.S. 165, 174 (1952). We have interpreted the Constitution to interpose barriers to a State's efforts to sterilize some criminals not only because the proposed punishment would do "irreparable injury" to bodily integrity, but because "[m]arriage and procreation" concern "the basic civil rights of man." *Skinner* v. *Oklahoma el rel. Williamson,* 316 U.S. 535, 541 (1942). The sanctity, and individual privacy, of the human body is obviously fundamental to liberty. "Every violation of a person's bodily integrity is an invasion of his or her liberty." *Washington* v. *Harper,* 494 U.S. ———, ——— (1990) (STEVENS, J., concurring in part and dissenting in part). Yet, just as the constitutional protection for the "physical curtilage of the home . . . is surely . . . a result of solicitude to protect the privacies of the life within," *Poe* v. *Ullman,* 367 U.S., at 551 (Harlan, J., dissenting), so too the constitutional protection for the human body is surely inseparable from concern for the mind and spirit that dwell therein.

It is against this background of decisional law, and the constitutional tradition which it illuminates, that the right to be free from unwanted life-sustaining medical treatment must be understood. That right presupposes no abandonment of the desire for life. Nor is it reducible to a protection against batteries undertaken in the name of treatment, or to a guarantee against the infliction of bodily discomfort. Choices about death touch the core of liberty. Our duty, and the concomitant freedom, to come to terms with the conditions of our own mortality are undoubtedly "so rooted in the traditions and conscience of our people as to be ranked as fundamental," *Snyder* v. *Massachusetts,* 291 U.S. 97, 105 (1934), and indeed are essential incidents of the unalienable rights to life and liberty endowed us by our Creator. See *Meachum* v. *Fano,* 427 U.S. 215, 230 (1976) (STEVENS, J., dissenting).

The more precise constitutional significance of death is difficult to describe; not much may be said with confidence about death unless it is said from faith, and that alone is reason enough to protect the freedom to conform choices about death to individual conscience. We may also, however, justly assume that death is not life's simple opposite, or its necessary terminus,[15] but rather its completion. Our ethical tradition has long regarded an appreciation of mortality as essential to understanding life's significance. It may, in fact, be impossible to live for anything without being

---

re Torres, 357 N. W. 2d 332, 341, n. 4 (Minn. 1984) ("At oral argument it was disclosed that on an average about 10 life support systems are disconnected weekly in Minnesota"). I tend, however, to agree with Judge Blackmar that the intervention of the State in these proceedings as an *adversary* is not so much a cure as it is part of the disease.

14. See *ante,* at 5; *ante,* at 13. "No right is held more sacred, or is more carefully guarded, by the common law, than the right of every individual to the possession and control of his own person, free from all restraint or interference of others, unless by clear and unquestionable authority of law." *Union Pacific R. Co.* v. *Botsford,* 141 U.S. 250, 251 (1891).

15. Many philosophies and religions have, for example, long venerated the idea that there is a "life after death," and that the human soul endures even after the human body has perished. Surely Missouri would not wish to define its interest in life in a way antithetical to this tradition.

prepared to die for something. Certainly there was no disdain for life in Nathan Hale's most famous declaration or in Patrick Henry's; their words instead bespeak a passion for life that forever preserves their own lives in the memories of their countrymen.[16] From such "honored dead we take increased devotion to that cause for which they gave the last full measure of devotion."[17]

These considerations cast into stark relief the injustice, and unconstitutionality, of Missouri's treatment of Nancy Beth Cruzan. Nancy Cruzan's death, when it comes, cannot be an historic act of heroism; it will inevitably be the consequence of her tragic accident. But Nancy Cruzan's interest in life, no less than that of any other person, includes an interest in how she will be thought of after her death by those whose opinions mattered to her. There can be no doubt that her life made her dear to her family, and to others. How she dies will affect how that life is remembered. The trial court's order authorizing Nancy's parents to cease their daughter's treatment would have permitted the family that cares for Nancy to bring to a close her tragedy and her death. Missouri's objection to that order subordinates Nancy's body, her family, and the lasting significance of her life to the State's own interests. The decision we review thereby interferes with constitutional interests of the highest order.

To be constitutionally permissible, Missouri's intrusion upon these fundamental liberties must, at a minimum, bear a reasonable relationship to a legitimate state end. See, e.g., *Meyer* v. *Nebraska,* 262 U.S., at 400; *Doe* v. *Bolton,* 410 U.S. 179, 194–195, 199 (1973). Missouri asserts that its policy is related to a state interest in the protection of life. In my view, however, it is an effort to define life, rather than to protect it, that is the heart of Missouri's policy. Missouri insists, without regard to Nancy Cruzan's own interests, upon equating her life with the biological persistence of her bodily functions. Nancy Cruzan, it must be remembered, is not now simply incompetent. She is in a persistent vegetative state, and has been so for seven years. The trial court found, and no party contested, that Nancy has no possibility of recovery and no consciousness.

It seems to me that the Court errs insofar as it characterizes this case as involving "judgments about the 'quality' of life that a particular individual may enjoy," *ante,* at 17. Nancy Cruzan is obviously *"alive"* in a physiological sense. But for patients like Nancy Cruzan, who have no consciousness and no chance of recovery, there is a serious question as to whether the mere persistence of their bodies is *"life"* as that word is commonly understood, or as it is used in both the Constitution and the Declaration of Independence.[18] The State's unflagging determination to perpetuate Nancy Cruzan's physical existence is comprehensible only as an effort to define life's meaning, not as an attempt to preserve its sanctity.

16. See, *e.g.,* H. Johnston, Nathan Hale 1776: Biography and Memorials 128–129 (1914); J. Axelrad, Patrick Henry: The Voice of Freedom 110–111 (1947).

17. A. Lincoln, Gettysburg Address, 1 Documents of American History (H. Commager ed.) (9th ed. 1973).

18. The Supreme Judicial Court of Massachusetts observed in this connection: "When we balance the State's interest in prolonging a patient's life against the rights of the patient to reject such prolongation, we must recognize that the State's interest in life encompasses a broader interest than mere corporeal existence. In certain, thankfully rare, circumstances the burden of maintaining the corporeal existence degrades the very humanity it was meant to serve." *Brophy* v. *New England Sinai Hospital, Inc.,* 398 Mass. 417, 433–434, 497 N. E. 2d 626, 635 (1986). The *Brophy* court then stressed that this reflection upon the nature of the State's interest in life was distinguishable from any considerations related to the quality of a particular

This much should be clear from the oddity of Missouri's definition alone. Life, particularly human life, is not commonly thought of as a merely physiological condition or function.[19] Its sanctity is often thought to derive from the impossibility of any such reduction. When people speak of life, they often mean to describe the experiences that comprise a person's history, as when it is said that somebody "led a good life."[20] They may also mean to refer to the practical manifestation of the human spirit, a meaning captured by the familiar observation that somebody "added life" to an assembly. If there is a shared thread among the various opinions on this subject, it may be that life is an activity which is at once the matrix for and an integration of a person's interests. In any event, absent some theological abstraction, the idea of life is not conceived separately from the idea of a living person. Yet, it is by precisely such a separation that Missouri asserts an interest in Nancy Cruzan's life in opposition to Nancy Cruzan's own interests. The resulting definition is uncommon indeed.

The laws punishing homicide, upon which the Court relies, *ante,* at 16, do not support a contrary inference. Obviously, such laws protect both the life *and* interests of those who would otherwise be victims. Even laws against suicide presuppose that those inclined to take their own lives have *some* interest in living, and, indeed, that the depressed people whose lives are preserved may later be thankful for the State's intervention. Likewise, decisions that address the "quality of life" of incompetent, but conscious, patients rest upon the recognition that these patients have *some* interest in continuing their lives, even if that interest pales in some eyes when measured against interests in dignity or comfort. Not so here. Contrary to the Court's suggestion, Missouri's protection of life in a form abstracted from the living is not commonplace; it is aberrant.

---

patient's life, considerations which the court regarded as irrelevant to its inquiry. See also *In re Eichner,* 73 App. Div. 2d 431, 465, 426 N. Y. S. 2d 517, 543 (1980) (A patient in a persistent vegetative state "has *no* health, and, in the true sense, *no* life, for the State to protect"), modified in *In re Storar,* 52 N. Y. 2d 363, 420 N. E. 2d 64 (1981).

19. One learned observer suggests, in the course of discussing persistent vegetative states, that "few of us would accept the preservation of such a reduced level of function as a proper *goal* for medicine, even though we sadly accept it as an unfortunate and unforeseen *result* of treatment that had higher aspirations, and even if we refuse actively to cause such vegetative life to cease." L. Kass, Toward a More Natural Science 203 (1985). This assessment may be controversial. Nevertheless, I again tend to agree with Judge Blackmar, who in his dissent from the Missouri Supreme Court's decision contended that it would be unreasonable for the State to assume that most people *did* in fact hold a view contrary to the one described by Dr. Kass.

My view is further buttressed by the comments of the President's Commission for the Study of Ethical Problems in Medicine and Biomedical and Behavioral Research:

"The primary basis for medical treatment of patients is the prospect that each individual's interests (specifically, the interest in well-being) will be promoted. Thus, treatment ordinarily aims to benefit a patient through preserving life, relieving pain and suffering, protecting against disability, and returning maximally effective functioning. If a prognosis of permanent unconsciousness is correct, however, continued treatment cannot confer such benefits. Pain and suffering are absent, as are joy, satisfaction, and pleasure. Disability is total and no return to an even minimal level of social or human functioning is possible." Deciding to Forego Life-Sustaining Treatment 181–182 (1983).

20. It is this sense of the word that explains its use to describe a biography: for example, Boswell's Life of Johnson or Beveridge's The Life of John Marshall. The reader of a book so titled would be surprised to find that it contained a compilation of biological data.

Nor does Missouri's treatment of Nancy Cruzan find precedent in the various state law cases surveyed by the majority. Despite the Court's assertion that state courts have demonstrated "both similarity and diversity in their approach" to the issue before us, *none* of the decisions surveyed by the Court interposed an absolute bar to the termination of treatment for a patient in a persistent vegetative state. For example, *In re Westchester County Medical Center on behalf of O'Connor*, 72 N.Y. 2d 517, 531 N. E. 2d, at 607 (1988), pertained to an incompetent patient who "was not in a coma or vegetative state. She was conscious, and capable of responding to simple questions or requests sometimes by squeezing the questioner's hand and sometimes verbally." *Id.*, at 524–525, 531 N. E. 2d, at 609–610. Likewise, *In re Storar*, 52 N. Y. 2d 363, 420 N. E. 2d 64 (1981), involved a conscious patient who was incompetent because "profoundly retarded with a mental age of about 18 months." *Id.*, at 373, 420 N. E.. 2d, at 68. When it decided *In re Conroy*, 98 N. J. 321, 486 A. 2d 1209 (1985), the New Jersey Supreme Court noted that "Ms. Conroy was not brain dead, comatose, or in a chronic vegetative state," 98 N. J., at 337, 486 A. 2d, at 1217, and then distinguished *In re Quinlan*, 70 N. J. 10, 355 A. 2d 647 (1976), on the ground that Karen Quinlan had been in a "persistent vegetative or comatose state." 98 N. J., at 358–359, 486 A. 2d, at 1228. By contrast, an unbroken stream of cases has authorized procedures for the cessation of treatment of patients in persistent vegetative states.[21] Considered against

---

21. See, *e.g.*, *In re Estate of Longeway*, 133 Ill. 2d 33, 549 N. E. 2d 292 (1989) (authorizing removal of a gastronomy tube from a permanently unconscious patient after judicial approval is obtained); *McConnell* v. *Beverly Enterprises-Connecticut, Inc.*, 209 Conn. 692, 705, 553 A. 2d 596, 603 (1989) (authorizing, pursuant to statute, removal of a gastronomy tube from patient in a persistent vegetative state, where patient had previously expressed a wish not to have treatment sustained); *Gray* v. *Romeo*, 697 F. Supp. 580 (RI 1988) (authorizing removal of a feeding tube from a patient in a persistent vegetative state); *Rasmussen* v. *Fleming*, 154 Ariz. 207, 741 P. 2d 674 (1987) (en banc) (authorizing procedures for the removal of a feeding tube from a patient in a persistent vegetative state); *In re Gardner*, 534 A. 2d 947 (Me. 1987) (allowing discontinuation of life-sustaining procedures for a patient in a persistent vegetative state); *In re Peter*, 108 N. J. 365, 529 A. 2d 419 (1987) (authorizing procedures for cessation of treatment to elderly nursing home patient in a persistent vegetative state); *In re Jobes*, 108 N. J. 394, 529 A. 2d 434 (1987) (authorizing procedures for cessation of treatment to nonelderly patient determined by "clear and convincing" evidence to be a persistent vegetative state); *Brophy* v. *New England Sinai Hospital, Inc.* 398 Mass. 417, 497 N. E. 2d 626 (1986) (permitting removal of a feeding tube from a patient in a persistent vegetative state); *John F. Kennedy Memorial Hospital, Inc.*, v. *Bludworth*, 452 So. 2d 921 (Fla. 1984) (holding that court approval was not needed to authorize cessation of life-support for patient in a persistent vegetative state who had executed a living will); *In re Torres*, 357 N. W. 2d 332 (Minn. 1984) (authorizing removal of a permanently unconscious patient from life-support systems); *In re L. H. R.*, 253 Ga. 439, 321 S. E. 2d 716 (1984) (allowing parents to terminate life support for infant in a chronic vegetative state); *In re Hamlin*, 102 Wash. 2d 810, 689 P. 2d 1372 (1984) (allowing termination, without judicial intervention, of life support for patient in a vegetative state if doctors and guardian concur; conflicts among doctors and the guardian with respect to cessation of treatment are to be resolved by a trial court); *In re Colyer*, 99 Wash, 2d 114, 660 P. 2d 738 (1983), modified on other grounds, *In re Hamlin*, 102 Wash. 2d 810, 689 P. 2d 1372 (1984) (allowing court-appointed guardian to authorize cessation of treatment of patient in persistent vegetative state); *In re Eichner* (decided with *In re Storar*), 52 N. Y. 2d 363, 420 N. E. 2d 64, cert. denied, 454 U.S. 858 (1981) (authorizing the removal of a patient in a persistent vegetative state from a respirator); *In re Quinlan*, 70 N. J. 10, 355 A. 2d 647, cert. denied, 429 U.S. 922 (1976)

the background of other cases involving patients in persistent vegetative states, instead of against the broader—and inapt—category of cases involving chronically ill incompetent patients, Missouri's decision is anomalous.

In short, there is no reasonable ground fo believing that Nancy Beth Cruzan has any *personal* interest in the perpetuation of what the State has decided is her life. As I have already suggested, it would be possible to hypothesize such an interest on the basis of theological or philosophical conjecture. But even to posit such a basis for the State's action is to condemn it. It is not within the province of secular government to circumscribe the liberties of the people by regulations designed wholly for the purpose of establishing a sectarian definition of life. See *Webster* v. *Reproductive Services,* 492 U.S. ———, ——— (1989) (STEVENS, J., dissenting).

My disagreement with the Court is thus unrelated to its endorsement of the clear and convincing standard of proof for cases of this kind. Indeed, I agree that the controlling facts must be established with unmistakable clarity. The critical question, however, is not how to prove the controlling facts but rather what proven facts should be controlling. In my view, the constitutional answer is clear: the best interests of the individual, especially when buttressed by the interests of all related third parties, must prevail over any general state policy that simply ignores those interests.[22] Indeed, the only apparent *secular* basis for the State's interest in life is the policy's persuasive impact upon people other than Nancy and her family. Yet, "[a]lthough the State may properly perform a teaching function," and although that teaching may foster respect for the sanctity of life, the State may not pursue its project by infringing constitutionally protected interests for "*symbolic* effect." *Carey* v. *Population Services International,* 431 U.S. 678, 715 (1977) (STEVENS, J., concurring in part and concurring in judgment). The failure of Missouri's policy to heed

---

(authorizing, on constitutional grounds, the removal of a patient in a persistent vegetative state from a respirator); *Corbett* v. *D'Alessandro,* 487 So. 2d 368 (Fla. App. 1986) (authorizing removal of nasogastic feeding tube from patient in persistent vegetative state); *In re Drabick,* 200 Cal. App. 3d 185, 218, 245 Cal. Rptr. 840, 861 (1988) ("Life sustaining treatment is not 'necessary' under Probate Code section 2355 if it offers no reasonable possibility of returning the conservatee to cognitive life and if it is not otherwise in the conservatee's best interests, as determined by the conservator in good faith"); *Delioi* v. *Westchester County Medical Center,* 129 App. Div. 2d 1, 516 N. Y. S. 2d 677 (1987) (authorizing discontinuation of artificial feeding for a 33-year-old patient in a persistent vegetative state); *Leach* v. *Akron General Medical Center,* 68 Ohio Misc. 1, 426 N. E. 2d 809 (1980) (authorizing removal of a patient in a persistent vegetative state from a respirator); *In re Severns* 425 A. 2d 156 (Del. Ch. 1980) (authorizing discontinuation of all medical support measures for a patient in a "virtual vegetative state").

These cases are not the only ones which have allowed the cessation of life-sustaining treatment to incompetent patients. See, *e.g., Superintendant of Belchertown State School* v. *Saikewicz,* 373 Mass. 728, 370 N. E. 2d 417 (1977) (holding that treatment could have been withheld from a profoundly mentally retarded patient); *Bouvia* v. *Superior Court of Los Angeles,* 225 Cal. Rptr. 297 (1986) (allowing removal of life-saving nasogastric tube from competent, highly intelligent patient who was in extreme pain).

22. Although my reasoning entails the conclusion that the best interests of the incompetent patient must be respected even when the patient is conscious, rather than in a vegetative state, considerations pertaining to the "quality of life," in addition to considerations about the definition of life, might then be relevant. The State's interest in protecting the life, and thereby the interests, of the incompetent patient would accordingly be more forceful, and the constitutional questions would be correspondingly complicated.

the interests of a dying individual with respect to matters so private is ample evidence of the policy's illegitimacy.

Only because Missouri has arrogated to itself the power to define life, and only because the Court permits this usurpation, are Nancy Cruzan's life and liberty put into disquieting conflict. If Nancy Cruzan's life were defined by reference to her own interests, so that her life expired when her biological existence ceased serving *any* of her own interests, then her constitutionally protected interest in freedom from unwanted treatment would not come into conflict with her constitutionally protected interest in life. Conversely, if there were *any* evidence that Nancy Cruzan herself defined life to encompass every form of biological persistence by a human being, so that the continuation of treatment would serve Nancy's own liberty, then once again there would be no conflict between life and liberty. The opposition of life and liberty in this case are thus not the result of Nancy Cruzan's tragic accident, but are instead the artificial consequence of Missouri's effort, and this Court's willingness, to abstract Nancy Cruzan's life from Nancy Cruzan's person.

IV

Both this Court's majority and the state court's majority express great deference to the policy choice made by the state legislature.[23] That deference is, in my view, based upon a severe error in the Court's constitutional logic. The Court believes that the liberty interest claimed here on behalf of Nancy Cruzan is peculiarly problematic because "an incompetent person is not able to make an informed and voluntary choice to exercise a hypothetical right to refuse treatment or any other right." *Ante,* at 15. The impossibility of such an exercise affords the State, according to the Court, some discretion to interpose "a procedural requirement" that effectively compels the continuation of Nancy Cruzan's treatment.

There is, however, nothing "hypothetical" about Nancy Cruzan's constitutionally protected interest in freedom from unwanted treatment, and the difficulties involved in ascertaining what her interests are do not in any way justify the State's decision to oppose her interests with its own. As this case comes to us, the crucial question—and the question addressed by the Court—is not what Nancy Cruzan's interests are, but whether the State must give effect to them. There is certainly nothing novel about the practice of permitting a next friend to assert constitutional rights on behalf of an incompetent patient who is unable to do so. See, *e. g., Youngberg* v. *Romeo,* 457 U.S. 307, 310 (1982); *Whitmore* v. *Arkansas,* 495 U.S. ———, ——— (1990) (slip op. at 11–13). Thus, if Nancy Cruzan's incapacity to "exercise" her rights is to alter the balance between her interests and the State's, there must be some further explanation of how it does so. The Court offers two possibilities, neither of them satisfactory.

---

23. Thus, the state court wrote:

"This state has expressed a strong policy favoring life. We believe that policy dictates that we err on the side of preserving life. If there is to be a change in that policy, it must come from the people through their elected representatives. Broad policy questions bearing on life and death issues are more properly addressed by representative assemblies. These have vast fact and opinion gathering and synthesizing powers unavailable to courts; the exercise of these powers is particularly appropriate where issues invoke the concerns of medicine, ethics, morality, philosophy, theology and law. Assuming change is appropriate, this issue demands a comprehensive resolution which courts cannot provide." 760 S. W. 2d, at 426.

The first possibility is that the State's policy favoring life is by its nature less intrusive upon the patient's interest than any alternative. The Court suggests that Missouri's policy "results in a maintenance of the status quo," and is subject to reversal, while a decision to terminate treatment "is not susceptible of correction" because death is irreversible. *Ante,* at 19. Yet, this explanation begs the question, for it assumes either that the State's policy is consistent with Nancy Cruzan's own interests, or that no damage is done by ignoring her interests. The first assumption is without basis in the record of this case, and would obviate any need for the State to rely, as it does, upon its own interests rather than upon the patient's. The second assumption is unconscionable. Insofar as Nancy Cruzan has an interest in being remembered for how she lived rather than how she died, the damage done to those memories by the prolongation of her death is irreversible. Insofar as Nancy Cruzan has an interest in the cessation of any pain, the continuation of her pain is irreversible. Insofar as Nancy Cruzan has an interest in a closure to her life consistent with her own beliefs rather than those of the Missouri legislature, the State's imposition of its contrary view is irreversible. To deny the importance of these consequences is in effect to deny that Nancy Cruzan has interests at all, and thereby to deny her personhood in the name of preserving the sanctity of her life.

The second possibility is that the State must be allowed to define the interests of incompetent patients with respect to life-sustaining treatment because there is no procedure capable of determining what those interests are in any particular case. The Court points out various possible "abuses" and inaccuracies that may affect procedures authorizing the termination of treatment. See *ante,* at 17. The Court correctly notes that in some cases there may be a conflict between the interests of an incompetent patient and the interests of members of her family. A State's procedures must guard against the risk that the survivors' interests are not mistaken for the patient's. Yet, the appointment of the neutral guardian ad litem, coupled with the searching inquiry conducted by the trial judge and the imposition of the clear and convincing standard of proof, all effectively avoided that risk in this case. Why such procedural safeguards should not be adequate to avoid a similar risk in other cases is a question the Court simply ignores.

Indeed, to argue that the mere possibility of error in *any* case suffices to allow the State's interests to override the particular interests of incompetent individuals in *every* case, or to argue that the interests of such individuals are unknowable and therefore may be subordinated to the State's concerns, is once again to deny Nancy Cruzan's personhood. The meaning of respect for her personhood, and for that of others who are gravely ill and incapacitated, is, admittedly, not easily defined: choices about life and death are profound ones, not susceptible of resolution by recourse to medical or legal rules. It may be that the best we can do is to ensure that these choices are made by those who will care enough about the patient to investigate her interests with particularity and caution. The Court seems to recognize as much when it cautions against formulating any general or inflexible rule to govern all the cases that might arise in this area of the law. *Ante,* at 13. The Court's deference to the legislature is, however, itself an inflexible rule, one that the Court is willing to apply in this case even though the Court's principal grounds for deferring to Missouri's legislature are hypothetical circumstances not relevant to Nancy Cruzan's interests.

On either explanation, then, the Court's deference seems ultimately to derive from the premise that chronically incompetent persons have no constitutionally cognizable interests at all, and so are not persons within the meaning of the

Constitution. Deference of this sort is patently unconstitutional. It is also dangerous in ways that may not be immediately apparent. Today the State of Missouri has announced its intent to spend several hundred thousand dollars in preserving the life of Nancy Beth Cruzan in order to vindicate its general policy favoring the preservation of human life. Tomorrow, another State equally eager to champion an interest in the "quality of life" might favor a policy designed to ensure quick and comfortable deaths by denying treatment to categories of marginally hopeless cases. If the State in fact has an interest in defining life, and if the State's policy with respect to the termination of life-sustaining treatment commands deference from the judiciary, it is unclear how any resulting conflict between the best interests of the individual and the general policy of the State would be resolved.[24] I believe the Constitution requires that the individual's vital interest in liberty should prevail over the general policy in that case, just as in this.

That a contrary result is readily imaginable under the majority's theory makes manifest that this Court cannot defer to any State policy that drives a theoretical wedge between a person's life, on the one hand, and that person's liberty or happiness, on the other.[25] The consequence of such a theory is to deny the personhood of those whose lives are defined by the State's interests rather than their own. This consequence may be acceptable in theology or in speculative philosophy, see *Meyer*, 262 U.S., at 401–402, but it is radically inconsistent with the foundation of all legitimate government. Our Constitution presupposes a respect for the personhood of every individual, and nowhere is strict adherence to that principle more essential than in the Judicial Branch. See, e.g., *Thornburgh* v. *American College of Obstetricians and Gynecologists*, 476 U.S., at 781–782 (STEVENS, J., concurring).

24. The Supreme Judicial Court of Massachusetts anticipated this possibility in its *Brophy* decision, where it observed that the "duty of the State to preserve life must encompass a recognition of an individual's right to avoid circumstances in which the individual himself would feel that efforts to sustain life demean or degrade his humanity," because otherwise the State's defense of life would be tantamount to an effort by "the State to make decisions regarding the individual's quality of life." 398 Mass., at 434, 497 N. E. 2d, at 635. Accord, *Gray* v. *Romeo*, 697 F. Supp., at 588.

25. Judge Campbell said on behalf of the Florida District Court of Appeal for the Second District:

"we want to acknowledge that we began our deliberations in this matter, as did those who drafted our Declaration of Independence, with the solemnity and the gratefulness of the knowledge 'that all men are . . . endowed by their Creator with . . . Life.' It was not without considerable searching of our hearts, souls, and minds, as well as the jurisprudence of this great Land that we have reached our conclusions. We forcefully affirm that Life having been endowed by our Creator should not be lightly taken nor relinquished. We recognize, however, that we are also endowed with a certain amount of dignity and the right to the 'Pursuit of Happiness.' When, therefore, it may be determined by reason of the advanced scientific and medical technologies of this day that Life has, through causes beyond our control, reached the unconscious and vegetative state where all that remains is the forced function of the body's vital functions, including the artificial sustenance of the body itself, then we recognize the right to allow the natural consequence of the removal of those artificial life sustaining measures." *Corbett* v. *D'Alessandro*, 487 So. 2d, at 371.

V

In this case, as is no doubt true in many others, the predicament confronted by the healthy members of the Cruzan family merely adds emphasis to the best interests finding made by the trial judge. Each of us has an interest in the kind of memories that will survive after death. To that end, individual decisions are often motivated by their impact on others. A member of the kind of family identified in the trial court's findings in this case would likely have not only a normal interest in minimizing the burden that her own illness imposes on others, but also an interest in having their memories of her filled predominantly with thoughts about her past vitality rather than her current condition. The meaning and completion of her life should be controlled by persons who have her best interests at heart—not by a state legislature concerned only with the "preservation of human life."

The Cruzan family's continuing concern provides a concrete reminder that Nancy Cruzan's interests did not disappear with her vitality or her consciousness. However commendable may be the State's interest in human life, it cannot pursue that interest by appropriating Nancy Cruzan's life as a symbol for its own purposes. Lives do not exist in abstraction from persons, and to pretend otherwise is not to honor but to desecrate the State's responsibility for protecting life. A State that seeks to demonstrate its commitment to life may do so by aiding those who are actively struggling for life and health. In this endeavor, unfortunately, no State can lack for opportunities: there can be no need to make an example of tragic cases like that of Nancy Cruzan.

I respectfully dissent.

Appendix 5

A Living Will (Sample)

STATEMENT OF (NAME)

If the time comes when I am incapacitated to the point where I can no longer actively take part in decisions for my own life, and am unable to direct my physician as to my own medical care, I wish this statement to stand as a testament of my wishes. I,_____(name)_____, request that I be allowed to die and not be kept alive through life support systems if my condition is deemed terminal. I do not intend any direct taking of my life, but only that my dying not be unreasonably prolonged. This request is made, after careful reflection, while I am of sound mind.

_____(Name)

_____(Date)

(Witness)_____

(Witness)_____

2. EXAMPLE OF LIVING WILL

To my family, my physician, my lawyer, and all others whom it may concern:

Death is as much a reality as birth, growth, maturity, and old age; it is the one certainty of life. If the time comes when I can no longer take part in decisions for my own future, let this statement stand as an expression of my wishes and directions, while I am still of sound mind.

372

If at such a time the situation should arise in which there is no reasonable expectation of my recovery from extreme physical or mental disability, I direct that I be allowed to die and not be kept alive by medications, artificial means, or "heroic measures." I do, however, ask that medication be mercifully administered to me to alleviate suffering, even though this may shorten my remaining life.

This statement is made after careful consideration and is in accordance with my strong convictions and beliefs. I want the wishes and directions here expressed carried out to the extent permitted by law. Insofar as they are not legally enforceable, I hope that those to whom this Will is addressed will regard themselves as morally bound by these provisions.

Signed_____

Date_____

Witness_____

Witness_____

Copies of this request have been given to_____

_____

_____

3. Declaration

If at any time I should have an incurable injury, disease, or illness certified to be a terminal condition by two (2) physicians who have personally examined me, one (1) of whom shall be my attending physician, and the physicians have determined that my death is imminent and will occur whether or not life-sustaining procedures are utilized and where the application of such procedures would serve only to artificially prolong the dying process, I direct that such procedures be withheld or withdrawn, and that I be permitted to die naturally with only the administration of medication, the administration of food and water, and the performance of any medical procedure that is necessary to provide comfort care or alleviate pain. In the absence of my ability to give directions regarding the use of such lifesustaining procedures, it is my intention that this declaration shall be honored by my family and physician(s) as the final expression of my right to control my medical care and treatment.

Declaration made this _____ day of _____ (*month, year*).

I, _____, being of sound mind, willfully and voluntarily direct that my dying shall not be artificially prolonged under the circumstances set forth in this declaration.

Other instructions:

I am legally competent to make this declaration, and I understand its full import.

Signed:_____

Address:_____

Under penalty of perjury, we state that this declaration was signed by_____in the presence of the undersigned who, at his/her request, in his/her presence, and in the presence of each other, have hereunto signed our names and witnessed this_____day of _____, 19___, and declare: The declarant is personally known to me, and I believe the declarant to be of sound mind. I did not sign the declarant's signature to this declaration. Based upon information and belief, I am not related to the declarant by blood or marriage, a creditor of the declarant, entitled to any portion of the estate of the declarant under any existing testamentary instrument to the declarant, financially or other- wise responsible for the declarant's medical care, or an employee of any such per- son or institution.

_____

Address_____

_____

Appendix 6

The Beginning of Individual Life[1]

Norman L. Geisler

When Did I Begin (Cambridge: Cambridge University, 1988) by Norman Ford is a well-researched and carefully documented prolife book by a noted Catholic scholar who argues, surprisingly, that while genetic human life begins at conception individual human life does not begin until some two weeks later. His thesis deserves careful attention, since many significant issues such as preembryonic experimentation, freezing embryos, genetic engineering, and abortifacients bear on this two-week period after conception.

An Exposition of Ford's View

According to Professor Ford, "it is necessary to distinguish between the concept of genetic and ontological individuality or identity" (117). Genetic identity is established at fertilization. However, Ford does not believe this is to speak "philosophically about the concept of a continuing ontological individual" (117). He thinks the "establishment of the new genetic programme at the completion of fertilization is a necessary, but not a sufficient, condition, for the actualization or coming into being of the new human individual at the embryonic stage of existence" (118).

At the preembryo stage (first fourteen days) "we could legitimately ask whether

---

This appendix originally appeared as "When Did I Begin?: A Review Article," Journal of the Evangelical Theological Society 33 (December 1990): 509–512. Appendix 6 is a slightly edited version of the original article.

the zygote itself would be one or two human individuals" (120). Why? Professor Ford offers several reasons.

First, twinning can occur up to the embryo stage (fourteen days after conception). Thus it seems to him implausible to speak of an individual human being where there is still the possibility of two. We would have to assume, for example, that the original individual (zygote) dies when it becomes the two twins. This means that, say, "Susan, as in the case of the zygote, would cease to exist in giving origin to her identical twin offsprings, Margaret and Sally. In this case these would be the grandchildren of their unsuspecting mother and father" (136). But, adds Ford, "there is no evidence to suggest an individual person ever ceases to exist when twinning occurs" (136).

Second, Ford argues that experiments on sheep and mice, which like humans have intrauterine pregnancies, show that there is not one individual being before the completion of implantation into the uterus (fourteen days after conception in humans). For "the early blastomeres of sheep and mouse embryos could easily be disaggregated and be variously combined by techniques of micromanipulation" (139). That is to say, by taking cells from one embryo and combining them with those from another, scientists have been able to produce wholly new individual beings. For example, by this method "chimeric" animals have been produced that are part sheep and part goat. But if different embryos can be "taken apart" and "reassembled" during the period before implantation, it is obvious that there is not necessarily one continuing individual human being from the point of conception.

Ford concludes: "Though these experimental manipulations have not been performed on human embryos, they do shed light on the character of the developmental and regulatory potential of the human embryo as well." He adds: "This is because of the acknowledged similarity existing in the early stages of embryonic development of all eutherian mammals." For example, "the mouse and sheep embryo in particular very closely resemble, but are not identical to, the human embryos . . . both before and after the implantation stage" (144).

In view of this evidence, Ford believes "it is very difficult to sustain that the human embryo could be a human individual prior to the blastocyst stage when it differentiates into that which will develop into the embryo, fetus and adult human . . ." (156). This "collection of cells, though loosely strung together, is hardly yet one thing, nor is it several. It is not yet determined to be either one or several" (178). Only "from the fourteenth or fifteenth day onwards, there is no doubt that it is Tom or Dick or Harry that is developing, or all three of them, but as three individuals" (178).

What, then, is it before the end of the second week, if not an individual human being? According to Ford, it is a "potential" human person (122–23). It is genetically human but not actually an individual human. It has all the human characteristics necessary for individual life, but it is not yet an individual human person.

Borrowing from Aristotle and Aquinas, who distinguished between form and matter and claimed that the soul is the form of the body, Ford believes an individual human soul could inhabit a body that is not yet formed. And since the individual body does not appear until the "primitive streak" stage (about two weeks after conception), it is at this point that Ford believes the zygote becomes an actual, individual human person. Quoting Anne McLaren with approval, Ford writes:

If we are talking not about the origin of life . . . but about the origin of an individual life, one can trace back directly from the newborn baby to the foetus, and back further to the origin of the individual embryo at the primitive streak stage in the embryonic plate at sixteen or seventeen days [after conception]. If one tries to trace back further than that there is no longer a coherent entity. Instead there is a larger collection of cells, some of which are going to take part in the subsequent development of the embryo and some of which are not (174–75).

So, according to Ford, it is at this "primitive streak" stage when an individual, indivisible (except by death) human life begins. And it is here that he places the origin of the human soul, which serves as the form of that body until death separates the two. Here the ontological individual begins, as opposed to the genetic individual (179). After this point, no more twinning is possible. There is one individual who is in continuity as an embryo, fetus, child, and adult.

An Evaluation of Ford's View

There are many commendable things about Ford's presentation. First of all, he is a prolifer who respects the absolute value of human life from its very inception. Second, as a Catholic theologian he takes seriously the teachings of the church on the sanctity of life. Third, as a philosopher he thinks clearly and deeply about the implications of the issue. Fourth, he takes into consideration not only the scientific evidence but also all the biblical data and theological pronouncements about when human life begins. Fifth, he stands in the venerable tradition of Thomas Aquinas, updating his view as the scientific evidence seems to indicate. Sixth, his approach is not simply a priori; he does not begin with a theological pronouncement about the origin of individual life and then makes all the evidence fit it. Finally, Ford is not dogmatic about his conclusion but confesses, "Though I believe my arguments show that the human individual begins with the appearance of the primitive streak, and not before, it would be presumptuous to declare that my claim was definitely right and opposing opinions were definitely wrong" (182).

Notwithstanding these many positive features, there are several serious shortcomings of his conclusions worthy of note.

First, at best Ford's conclusions show only that *individual* human life begins two weeks after conception, not that *actual* human life begins there. Indeed, he admits that there is a living human nature from the very moment of conception (115). This being the case, the next point follows.

Second, if human life begins from conception, it is moot to debate when a continuous individual (person) begins. Human life has sanctity whether or not it is yet individuated. Hence, even if Ford were correct about when a continuous individual life begins, nonetheless, protectable human life admittedly begins at conception.

Third, Ford confesses that his argument is ultimately philosophical, not purely factual. When dealing with life-and-death matters this is precarious, for the decision to terminate life cannot be left to philosophers. Some philosophers (or theologians) argue that it begins at implantation, some at animation, some at birth, and some later at self-consciousness. In short, unless a scientific (factual) basis is used to determine when human life begins over which there is no debate, then there is no practical way to reach an agreement on which to formulate laws that protect human life.

Fourth, as Ford admits, his opinion on this matter is not the only possible one. In spite of his arguments, it is still possible that individual human life begins at conception. Several points are relevant here.

1. The later splitting into twins could be a nonsexual form of "parenting" akin to cloning. Ford even acknowledges this is a possibility.
2. Every zygote before twinning is still a genetically unique individual who is distinct from the parent. That is to say, simply because identical twins result from a zygote split, it does not logically follow that a zygote prior to twinning is not fully human. To draw this conclusion is to beg the question. In other words, twinning seems to be neither a necessary nor a sufficient condition to reject the full humanness of the zygote. Professor Robert Wennberg provides a parable which is helpful on this point:

Imagine that we lived in a world in which a certain small percentage of teenagers replicated themselves by some mysterious natural means, splitting in two upon reaching their sixteenth birthday. We would not in the least be inclined to conclude that no human being could therefore be considered a person prior to becoming sixteen years of age; nor would we conclude that life could be taken with greater impunity prior to replication than afterward. The real oddity—to press the parallel would be two teenagers becoming one. However, in all of this we still would not judge the individual's claim to life to be undermined in any way. We might puzzle over questions of personal identity . . . but we would not allow these strange replications and fusions to influence our thinking about an individual's right to life. Nor therefore does it seem that such considerations are relevant in determining the point at which an individual might assume a right to life in utero.[1]

3. Ford's argument is based on the unproven assumption that human generation is the same as that of mice and sheep. He even admits there is no experimental proof for this assumption.
4. Also, the argument assumes the Aristotelian premise that humans can generate a genetically distinct but nonhuman offspring, that only later becomes human.
5. He overlooks the fact that a new, unique, genetically human being is produced at the moment of conception (fertilization). This is not a potential human individual but an actual one. Ford even calls it an individual (102) and admits that it is alive and possesses all its genetic characteristics for life at fertilization. Ford admits that "at fertilization there begins a new, genetically unique, living *individual,* when the sperm and the ovum lose their separate individualities to form a single living cell, a zygote" (102, emphasis added).
6. In this regard, Ford falls into the same trap as many proabortionists who argue that the zygote (or even later embryo for many) is like an acorn, only a potential life (124). But this is not true. An acorn, like a human zygote, is a tiny, living oak tree in a dormant state. Planting the acorn

---

1. Robert Wennberg, Life in the Balance: Exploring the Abortion Controversy (Grand Rapids: Eerdmans, 1985), p. 71.

does not begin the life of an oak tree, but only its growth. Likewise, a living human zygote being implanted in its mother's womb, does not begin its unique, individual life; it simply facilitates its further growth.

7. As Ford seems to imply, if human life is protected not from conception but only from implantation, then a number of serious moral and legal implications follow. Noncontraceptive birth control (e.g., IUD, RU-486) even experimentation on human zygotes are not ruled out absolutely. In brief, the "unalienable" right to life is thereby alienated from an admittedly individual human being for the first two weeks of its life.

Conclusion

Philosophers and theologians will continue to argue over the precise point at which God allegedly implants a human soul in the body. Meanwhile, let human beings and human governments protect what we know to be human life from the very moment that a distinct, unique human nature begins—the point of fertilization. As professor Jerome LeJeune noted, "a human nature . . . is entirely constant from fecundation [fertilization] to normal death" (127). Ford's citation of a report by the New Zealand Royal Commission of Inquiry into Contraception, Sterilization and Abortion, 1977, says it well:

From a biological point of view there is no argument as to when life begins. evidence was given to us by eminent scientists from all over the world. None of them suggested that human life begins at any time other than at conception (115).

Bibliography

Books

Abelson, Raziel, and Marie-Louise Friquegnon. eds., *Ethics for Modern Life*. New York: St. Martin's Press, 1987.

Archer, Gleason. *Encyclopedia of Bible Difficulties*. Grand Rapids: Zondervan Publishing House, 1982.

Beachump, Tom, and James Childress. *Principles of Biomedical Ethics*. 3rd edition. New York: Oxford University Press, 1989.

Beck, F., D. B. Moffat, and D. P. Davies. *Human Embryology*. Oxford: Blackwell, 1985.

Brennan, William. *The Abortion Holocaust: Today's Final Solution*. St. Louis: Landmark Press, 1983.

Brody, Baruch. *Abortion and the Sanctity of Human Life*. Cambridge: M.I.T. Press, 1975.

Brown, Harold O. J. *Death Before Birth*. Nashville, Tenn.: Thomas Nelson, 1977.

Burtchaell, James Tunstead. *Rachel Weeping: The Case Against Abortion*. San Francisco: Harper & Row, 1984.

Callahan, Daniel. *Abortion: Law, Choice and Morality*. New York: Macmillan, 1970.

Cameron, Nigel M., and Pamela F. Sims. *Abortion: The Crisis in Morals and Medicine*. Leicester, England: InterVarsity Press, 1986.

Campbell, Robert, and Diane Collinson. *Ending Lives*. New York: Basil Blackwell, 1988.

Clayman, Charles B. ed., *American Medical Association Encyclopedia of Medicine*. New York: Random House, 1989.

David, John Jefferson. *Abortion and the Christian*. Phillipsburg, N.J.: Presbyterian and Reformed, 1984.

———. *Evangelical Ethics*. Phillipsburg, N.J.: Presbyterian and Reformed, 1985.

Day, Beth, and Albert W. Liley. *Modern Motherhood*. New York: Random House, 1968.

Feinberg, Joel, ed. 2nd ed. *The Problem of Abortion*. Belmont, Calif.: Wadsworth, 1984.

381

Fletcher, Joseph. "Ethics and Euthanasia." *Ethical Issues in Death and Dying*. Robert F. Weir, ed. New York: Columbia, 1977.

------. *Humanhood: Essays in Biomedical Ethics* (chapters 12–13). Buffalo: Prometheus, 1979.

------. "Sanctity of Life Versus Quality of Life." *Euthanasia: The Moral Issues.* Robert M. Baird and Stuart E. Rosenbaum, eds. Buffalo: Prometheus, 1989.

Frame, John. *Medical Ethics.* Phillipsburg, N.J.: Presbyterian and Reformed, 1988.

Gardner, R. F. R. *Abortion: The Personal Dilemma.* Grand Rapids: Eerdmans Publishing Co., 1972.

Geisler, Norman L., *Christian Ethics: Options and Issues.* Grand Rapids: Baker Book House, 1989.

------. *Options in Contemporary Christian Ethics.* Grand Rapids: Baker Book House, 1981.

Goldberg, David Theo., ed. *Ethical Theory and Social Issues: Historical Texts and Contemporary Readings.* New York: Holt, Rinehart and Winston, 1989.

Gorman, Michael J. *Abortion and the Early Church.* Downers Grove, Ill.: InterVarsity Press, 1982.

Grisez, Germain. *Abortion: The Myths, the Realities, and the Arguments.* New York: Corpus Books, 1970.

Hamilton, Edith, and Huntington Cairns. eds. *The Collected Dialogues of Plato, Including the Letters.* Princeton, N.J.: Princeton University Press, 1961.

Hauerwas, Stanley. *Suffering Presence.* Notre Dame, Ind.: University of Notre Dame Press, 1987.

Henry, Carl R. H., ed. *Baker Dictionary of Christian Ethics.* Grand Rapids: Baker Book House, 1973.

Hensley, Jeff Lane, ed. *The Zero People.* Ann Arbor: Servant Books, 1983.

Hilgers, Thomas, Dennis J. Horan, and David Mall, eds. *New Perspectives on Human Abortion.* Frederick, Md.: University Publications of America, 1981.

Horan, Dennis, Edward R. Grant, and Paige C. Cunninghan, eds. *Abortion and the Constitution: Reversing* Roe v. Wade *Through the Courts.* Washington, D.C.: Georgetown University Press, 1987.

Hume, David. "Of Suicide," in *Dialogues Concerning Natural Religion and the Posthumous Essays.* Richard Popkin, ed. Indianapolis: Hackett, 1980.

Johnson, Oliver A., ed. *Ethics: Selections from Classical and Contemporary Writers.* 6th edition. New York: Holt, Rinehart Winston, 1989.

Koop, C. Everett. *The Right to Live: The Right to Die.* Wheaton, Ill.: Tyndale House, 1976.

Krason, Stephen M. *Abortion: Politics, Morality, and the Constitution.* Lanham, Md.: University Press of America, 1984.

Kreeft, Peter. *The Unaborted Socrates.* Downers Grove, Ill.: InterVarsity Press, 1984.

Kuback, Michael M., and Carlo Valenti, ed. *Intrauterine Fetal Visualization.* Oxford: Excerptat Medica; New York: American Elseview Publishing, 1976.

Laetsch, Watson M. *Plants: Basic Concepts of Botany.* Boston: Little, Brown and Company, 1979.

Mall, David, and Walter F. Watts, eds. *The Psychological Aspects of Abortion.* Washington, D. C.: University Publications of America, 1979.

Mappes, Thomas A., and Janes S. Zembaty, eds. *Biomedical Ethics.* New York: McGraw-Hill, 1981.

Martin, Walter R. *Abortion: Is is Always Murder?* Santa Ana, Calif.: Vision House, 1977.

McCormick, Richard A. *How Brave a New World?* Garden City, N.Y.: Doubleday, 1981.

Montgomery, John Warwick. *Slaughter of the Innocents: Abortion, Birth Control, Divorce in Light of Science, Law and Theology.* Westchester, Ill.: Crossway Books, 1981.

Moore, Keith. *The Developing Human: Clinically Oriented Embryology.* Philadelphia: W. B. Saunders, 1977.

Moreland, J. P., and Norman Geisler, *The Life and Death Debate.* Westport, Conn.: Praeger Books, 1990.

Nathanson, Bernard. *Aborting America.* New York: Doubleday, 1979.

Noonan, John T., ed. *The Morality of Abortion.* Cambridge: Harvard University Press, 1970.

President's Commission for the Study of Ethical Problems in Medicine and Biomedical and Behavioral Research, Deciding to Forego Life-Sustaining Treatment: A Report on the Ethical, Medical, and Legal Issues in Treatment Decisions. Washington, D. C.: U.S. Government Printing Office, 1983.

Pretzel, Paul W. "Philosophical and Ethical Considerations of Suicide Prevention." *Ethical Issues in Death and Dying.* Robert F. Weir, ed. New York: Columbia, 1977.

Putka, John S. "The Supreme Court and Abortion: The Socio-Political Impact of Judicial Activism." Ph.D. dissertation. University of Cincinnati, 1979.

Rachels, James, ed. *The Right Thing to Do.* New York: Random House, 1989.

Radl, Shirley. *Over Our Live Bodies: Preserving Choice in America.* Dallas: Steve Davis Publishing, 1990.

Ramsey, Paul. *The Patient as Person* (chapter 1). New Haven: Yale, 1970.

Reardon, David C. *Aborted Women: Silent No More.* Westchester, Ill.: Crossway Books, 1987.

Sanger, Margaret. *Woman and the New Race.* New York: Truth Publishing, 1920.

Schaeffer, Francis A., and C. Everett Koop. *Whatever Happened to the Human Race?* Old Tappan, N.J.: Fleming H. Revell, 1979.

Schmitt, B. D., and C. H. Kempe. *Child Abuse: Management and Prevention of the Battered Child Syndrome.* Basel: Ciba-Geigy, 1975.

Sider, Ron. *Completely Pro-Life: Building a Consistent Stance.* Downers Grove, Ill.: InterVarsity Press, 1987.

Spring, Beth, and Ed Larson. *Euthanasia.* Portland: Multnomah Press, 1988.

Thomas, Kenneth R. *The Right to Die: Fundamental Life Decisions After Cruzan v. Director, Missouri Department of Health.* A CRS Report for Congress. The Library of Congress. August 3, 1990.

Tooley Michael. *Abortion and Infanticide.* Oxford: Clarendon, 1986.

Tribe, Laurence H. *Abortion: the Clash of Absolutes.* New York: W. W. Norton, 1990.

Varga, Andrew. rev. ed. *The Main Issues in Bioethics.* New York: Paulist Press, 1984.

Wardle, Lynn, and Mary Anne Q. Wood. *A Lawyer Looks at Abortion.* Provo, Utah: Brigham Young University Press, 1982.

Wennberg, Robert. *Critical Choices: Euthanasia, Suicide, and the Right to Die?* Grand Rapids: Eerdmans Publishing Co., 1989.

————. *Life in the Balance: Exploring the Abortion Controversy.* Grand Rapids: Eerdmans' Publishing Co., 1985.

Willke, J. C., and Barbara Willke. *Abortion: Questions and Answers.* Cincinnati: Hayes Publishing Company, 1985, also rev. ed. 1988.

Journals and Magazines

"Alternative to Abortion." *Pentecostal Evangel* (Feb. 11, 1990).

American College of Surgeons Bulletin (Aug. 1988).

American Journal of Obstetrics and Gynecology 118 (1 Jan 1974).

Beckwith, Francis J. "Abortion and Argument: A Response to Mollenkott." *Journal of Biblical Ethics in Medicine* 3 (Summer 1989).

————. "Abortion and Public Policy: A Response to Some Arguments." *Journal of the Evangelical Theological Society* 32 (December 1989).

————. "Brave New Bible: Responding to the 'Moderate' Evangelical Position on Abortion." *Journal of the Evangelical Theological Society* 33 (December 1990).

————. "Rights, Filial Obligations, and Medical Risks." *APA Newsletter on Philosophy and Medicine* 89:3 (Winter 1990).

————. "The Problem of Hypocrisy." *Christian's Research Journal* 10 (Summer 1987).

————. "Utilitarian Arguments, Abortion Rights, and Justice Blackmun's Dissent in Webster: Some Philosophical Observations." *Simon Greenleaf Law Review*, forthcoming.

Boykin, John. "Whose Choice? Which Life?" *The Stanford Magazine* (December 1989).

British Medical News (2 April 1973).

Byrn, Robert. "Compulsory Lifesaving Treatment of Competent Adults." *Fordham Law Review* 44 (1975).

Calderone, Mary. "Illegal Abortion as a Public Health Problem." *American Journal of Public Health* 50 (July 1960).

Clark, David K. "An Evaluation of the Quality of Life Argument for Infanticide." *Simon Greenleaf Law Review* 5 (1985–86).

Destro, Robert A. "Abortion and the Constitution: The Need for a Life-Perspective Amendment." *California Law Review* 63 (1975).

Ely, John Hart. "The Wages of Crying Wolf: A Comment on *Roe* v. *Wade*." *Yale Law Journal* 82 (1973).

Fost, N. "Passive Euthanasia of Patients with Down's Syndrome" *Archives of Internal Medicine* 13 (December 1982).

Gourevitch, Danielle. "Suicide Among the Sick in Classical Antiquity." *Bulletin of the History of Medicine* 43 (1969).

Haag, Ernest Van Den. "Is There A Middle Ground." *National Review* (December 22, 1979).

Haley, Jacqueline Nolan. "Haunting Shadows from the Rubble of Roe's Right to Privacy." *Suffolk University Law Review* 9 (1974).

Harrison, Stanley M. "The Supreme Court and Abortional Reform: Means to an End." *New York Law Forum* 19 (1974).

Hopkin, William R. "*Roe* v. *Wade* and the Traditional Legal Standards Concerning Pregnancy." *Temple Law Quarterly* 47 (1974).

Humber, John M. "Abortion: The Avoidable Moral Dilemma." *Journal of Value Inquiry* 9 (1975).

Kline, Meredith G. "Lex Talionis & the Human Fetus." *Simon Greenleaf Law Review* 5 (1985–86).

Koop, C. Everett. "The Right to Die (II)." *Human Life Review* 2:2 (Spring 1976).

Kreeft, Peter. "Personhood Begins at Conception." *Journal of Biblical Ethics in Medicine* 4 (Winter 1990).

LaRue, Janet. "Abortion: Justice Harry A. Blackmun and the *Roe* v. *Wade Decision.*" *Simon Greenleaf Law Review* 2 (1982) 830.

Marquis, Don. "Why Abortion Is Immoral." *Journal of Philosophy* 68 (April 1989).

Mavrodes, George I. "Abortion and Imagination: Reflections on Mollenkott's 'Reproductive Choice.'" *Christian Scholar's Review* 18 (December 1988).

Means, Cyril. "The Phoenix of Abortional Freedom: Is a Prenumbral or Ninth-Amendment Right About to Arise from the Nineteenth-Century Legislative Ashes of a Fourteenth-Century Common-Law Liberty?" *New York Law Forum* 17 (1971).

Medical World News (June 1973)

Methvin, Eugene H. "Hitler & Stalin: Twentieth Century Super Killers." *National Review* (May 31, 1985).

Mollenkott, Virginia Ray. "Reproductive Choice: Basic to Justice for Women." *Christian Scholar's Review* 17 (March 1988).

Montgomery, John Warwick. "The Rights of Unborn Children." *Simon Greenleaf Law Review* 5 (1985–86).

O'Meara, Thomas. "Abortion: The Court Decides a Non-Case." *The Supreme Court Review* (1974).

Quill, Timothy E., M.D., "Death and Dignity: A Case of Individualized Decision Making." *New England Journal of Medicine* (March 7, 1991).

Rice, Charles E. "Overruling *Roe* v. *Wade*" An Analysis of the Proposed Constitutional Amendments." *Boston College Industrial and Commercial Law Review* 15 (December 1973).

Rosemblum, Victor G., and Clarke D. Forsythe. "The Right to Assisted Suicide: Protection of Autonomy or an Open Door to Social Killing?" *Issues in Law & Medicine* 6 (Summer 1990).

Rosen, Mortimer. "The Secret Brain: Learning Before Birth." *Harper's* (April 1978).

Singer, Peter. "Sanctity of Life or Quality of Life?" *Pediatrics* 73 (July 1973).

Spaulding, J., and J. Cavernar. "Psychosis Following Therapeutic Abortion." *American Journal of Psychiatry* 135 (March 1978).

Spero, Rabbi Aryeh. "Therefore Choose Life." *Policy Review* (Spring 1989).

Waltke, Bruce. "Reflections from the Old Testament on Abortion." *Journal of the Evangelical Theological Society* 19 (1976).

Webster v. Reproductive Health Services (1989). *The United States Law Week* 57 (July 27, 1989).

Wesley, Patricia A., M.D., "Dying Safely: An Analysis of 'A Case of Individualized Decision-Making' by Timothy E. Quill, M.D." Paper presented at the First Annual Meeting of University Faculty for Life. Kennedy Institute of Ethics. Georgetown University, Washington, D. C., June 8–10, 1991.

Witherspoon, Joseph. "Reexamining *Roe:* Nineteenth-Century Abortion Statutes and the Fourteenth Amendment." *St. Mary's Law Journal* 17 (1985).

Newspapers

Blakeslee, Sandra. "Fetus Returned to Womb Following Surgery." *New York Times,* (7 October 1986). Sec. C, p. 1, 3.

Bronner, Ethan. "Most in US Favor Ban on Majority of Abortions Poll Finds." *The Boston Globe* 235, (31 March 1989): 1, 12.

The News & Daily Advance, Lynchburg, Va., Friday (June 8, 1990): C-2.

Roanoke Times & World News, (30 June 1983): A4.

Index

Abargi, Martin, 60–61
Abortion, and infanticide, 133–35;
    death from, 69, 71–72. 98–100;
    education concerning, 67;
    elimination of, 67; ethics of, 84–95;
    future of, 67–72; funding of, 63,
    65–66; laws, 55; legal aspects,
    history of, 46–48; laws forbidding,
    115–16; methods of, 31–37; on
    demand, 49, 52, 116; philosophy of,
    84–95; safety of, 99; social benefits
    of, 112–117
Abortion, illegal, consequences of,
    72–75
Adams, Peter A. J., 139
Adoption, 104
Alzheimer's disease, 117, 150
Amendments, first, 66; fifth, 40, 46,
    67–68; fourteenth, 40–42, 46, 54,
    58, 67–68, 86
American Civil Liberties Union, 100,
    185
American Medical Association, 37–38,
    48, 99, 160
Amniocentesis, 117
Anencephalic, 30
Anti-abortion, 108; prochoice, 92–93
Antipromulgation, 167, 173, 176
Aquinas, Thomas, 48, 174
Aristotle, 157
Atheism, 120
Augustine, 48, 174

"Back alley butchers," 69, 71, 112
Balch, Thomas J., 59

Balche, Burke, 92
Ballot language, 122–26
Baptism, 101
Bauman, Michael, 82
Bernadin, Cardinal, 106
Bias and political process, 119–127
Bill of Rights, 40. *See also* Amendments;
    Constitution
Birth certificate, 116
Birth control, 31, 35–37
Birth control pill, 36
Black market, 69
Blackmun, Harry, 42–43, 47, 54, 57, 59,
    60, 61, 63, 64, 66, 94
Bork, Robert, 59
Brain waves. *See* Fetus
Brody, Baruch, 124
Brogan, Patricia, 118
Bryan, Richard, 92
Burger, Warren, 52
Burtchael, James T., 105
Bush, George, 68, 73

Calderone, Mary, 71
Callahan, Sidney, 107
Callahan, Daniel, 107, 122
Callihan's Exec'r v. *Johnson*, 45
Calvin, John, 48
Capital punishment, 106–107
Child abuse, 74, 79, 101–102
Child pornography, 69
Childbirth, safety, 99
Chorionic villus sampling, 117, 119
City of Akron v. *Akron Center for
    Reproductive Health*, 61

Civil disobedience, 165–85; biblical
    basis for, 170–73, 175–78
Civil rights. *See* Equal rights
Clark, David K., 137
Coat hanger, 69, 70, 72
Code of Hammurabi, 47
Collins, Vincent J., 22
Coma, 86–88
Common law, 40, 44, 47, 55–56, 58,
    159–60
Conception, 16–21, 44, 85
Condom, 36
Constitution, 42–45, 47, 56–57, 78
Contraception, 31, 35–37, 54, 113, 115;
    artificial, 31–37; prolifers, 36–37
Court rulings, 148. *See also* Supreme
    Court rulings
Cruzen, Nancy Beth, 148–149
Cuomo, Mario, 92
Cyronics, 150

Declaration of Independence, 39–40,
    44, 167
Del Papa, Frankie Sue, 121–22
Destro, Robert A., 51
Diaphragm, 36
Dilation & curettage, 31–32
Dilation & evacuation, 31, 33–34
Doe v. *Bolton*, 48–50, 52, 64, 82, 88, 97,
    120
Donne, John, 62
Douglas, Willim, 53
Down Syndrome, 103–104, 131–32,
    135–37
Dred Scott, 44–45
Drunk driving, 62, 74, 79

Ely, John Hart, 51-52, 59
Embryo, 16, 20–21
English, Jane, 25
English common law. *See* Common law
Equal Rights, 78, 81, 97; Amendment,
    68
Erickson, Nancy, 94
Euthanasia, abortion and, 147; active,
    141–42, 145, 147, 149–52; ethics of,
    153–55, 161–62; in America,
    146–47; infanticide and, 147;

martyrdom and, 156; medical
    aspects of, 160–63; practice of,
    146–47, 149–50; passive, 141–42,
    145, 147, 151–52, 156; practice of,
    146–47, 149–50; starvation and, 149;
    suicide and, 155–57; western history
    of, 157–60
Evans, Mark, 117

Fathers, absence of, 115; rights of,
    90–91
Feminism, abortion rights, 93–95
Fetology, 27
Fetus, abuse, 102; blood type, 23, 27;
    bodily systems, 23; brain waves,
    22–23, 27; crying, 24; dreaming, 24;
    experimentation, 138–39; health,
    103–104; hearing, 24; nervous
    system, 22; organ procurement,
    117, 139; pain, 22, 33–34; swimming
    of, 23; thumb sucking, 23–24;
    viability of, 24–25, 26, 27, 51–52,
    64–65, 85
Finnis, John, 74
Fletcher, John C., 110, 119
Fletcher, Joseph, 103, 134, 147
Florian, Hans, 150
Food, artifical means of providing,
    142–44; withholding of, 162–63
Forsythe, Clarke, 159
Fraim, Richard, 110

Genetic blueprint, 17
Genetic deformities. *See* Handicapped
Genocide, 75, 93, 111, 115
Gilbert, Rosell, 149–150
Golbus, Mitchell, 117
Goodlin, Robert c., 138
Griswold v. *Connecticut*, 54

Haley, Jacqueline N., 51
Handicapped, 25–31, 102–103, 137–38,
    139, 146; opposition to abortion,
    28–30
Harris v. *McRae*, 66
Harrison, Everly, 135
Harrison, Stanley M., 51
Hastings Center Report, 110, 119

Heard, Franklin, 37
Hentoff, Nat, 120
Hippocrates, 47
Hippocratic oath, 48, 157–58
Hitler, Adolf, 78, 104, 178
Homicide, 55
Hopkin, William R., Jr., 52
Horan, Dennis J., 59, 92
Human clones, 19
Human consciousness, 133
Human life, development of, 21;
    potential of, 20
Human rights. *See* Equal rights
Humber, James, 37
Humphrey, Derek, 147
Hyde Amendment, 66
Hysterotomy, 31, 32, 102

Incest, 74
Infanticide, 85–86, 131–39, 141
Informed consent laws, 67
IUD, 31, 36

Jackson, Laird, 119
Jefferson, Thomas, 167
Jehovah's Witnesses v. *King County Hospital Unit,* 148
Judeo-Christian tradition, 58

Kekomaki, Martti, 139
Kennedy, Anthony, 63, 66
Kent, Dora, 150
Kevorkian, Jack, 144
King, Martin Luther, Jr., 174, 182
Koop, C. Everett, 28–29, 31
Krason, Stephen, 83, 134
Kuhse, Helga, 17

Lang, Robert E., 51
Langstone, Esther, 134
Lederberg, Joshua, 133
LeJeune, Jerome, 16, 103
Lethal injections, 162
Levin, Michael, 90
Liley, Albert, 27
Lincoln, Abraham, 61
Living wills, 145, 149

MADD, 62
Marquis, Don, 37
Marshall, Thurgood, 64, 66, 68
Marzen, Thomas, 50
Maternal health, 49, 50, 51, 52, 53, 57, 64, 98–99
Maternal stress, 49, 115
Mavrodes, George, 111
McCorvey, Norma, 53–54
McKay, Brian, 121
Means, Cyril, 43, 159
Medical treatments, accepting, 144;
    withholding of, 135, 143, 156
Michelman, Ket, 94
Midwives, 48
Miranda, 185
Mollenkott, Virginia R., 80
Montgomery, John W., 37, 44, 53
Moreland, J. P., 153
Mother Teresa, 78

Nathanson, Bernard, 37, 71, 72, 74, 124
National Abortion Rights Action League, 43, 71, 94
News media, 109–111
Nineteenth-century statutes. *See* Amendments; Constitution
Nix v. *State,* 45
Noonan, John T., 52

O'Connor, Sandra Day, 60, 63, 66
Ohio v. *Akron,* 61
O'Meara, Thomas, 50
Operation Rescue, 166, 167, 174–75, 186–87
Organ procurement, fetal. *See* Fetus
Ovid, 47
Ovum, 15, 16, 17, 31; death of 31

Pain, fetal. *See* Fetus
Parental consent, 62, 67; notification, 62
Parthenogenesis, 18
Persistent vegetative state, 148, 161–62
Planned Parenthood of Central Missouri v. *Danford,* 61, 90, 111
Plato, 157
Pollings, 115

Population growth, 113–114
Poverty, 114–115, 139, 146
Pratt, Lawrence, 118
Prematurity, 137–38
Prenatal testing, 117, 119
Proabortion, 116, 134–35
Prochoice, 17, 69–71, 79, 80
Prolife, 17, 36–38, 79–80, 104–112, 116,
    119–27, 165–66; biblical basis of,
    1170–71; medical groups, 38
Prostaglandin, 31, 33, 34, 35, 72
Pythagoras, 157
Pythagoreans, 60, 157

Quickening, 43–44, 58, 85
Quinlan, Karen Ann, 147–148

Rachels, James, 151–153
Radford, Barbara, 118
Ramsey, Paul, 134
Rape, 53–54, 74, 81–84; pregnancy,
    82–83; psychological problems of,
    83;
Ray, A. Chadwick, 85, 87
Reagan, Ronald, 63
Reardon, David C., 74, 99
Recombination, 18, 19
Refus, 47
Rehnquist, William, 63, 66
Religion, 75, 80–81, 120, 158–59
Religious burial, 100–101
Resch, Bela A., 139
Reyes, 139
Rice, Charles E., 52
Right of privacy, 56
Right to life, 41, 45, 73, 78
Right-to-life amendment, 67–68
Roe, Jane, 53, 57
Roe v. Wade, 25, 42–43, 45–49, 51, 52,
    53, 54, 57, 62–64, 67, 68–69, 71, 82,
    85, 88–89, 94, 97, 102, 112, 117,
    120, 122
Roman Catholics, 36–37
Rosemblum, Victor, G., 50, 159
Roth, Michael A., 118
RU-486, 31, 35, 36
Rust v. Sullivan, 64, 65–66
Rutherford, Samuel, 167

SADD, 62
Salem Witch trials, 78
Saline abortion, 31, 32, 34, 102
Sanger, Margaret, 134
Santa Clara v. Sanford, 46, 86
Scalia, Atonio, 63, 66, 68
Schaeffer, Francis, 167–68
Schwarz, Stephen, 33, 87, 88
Self-induced abortion, 72
Senate Judiciary Committee, 49
Seneca, 47, 158
Sex-selection, 17; abortions, 115,
    117–119
Sider, Ron, 106
Singer, Peter, 17, 134
Slavery, 44–45, 60, 61, 75, 116
Souter, David, 63, 66, 68
Sperm, 15
Spermicides, 36
Stalin, Joseph, 78, 178
Starvation, 142–43, 149
Steinburg v Ohio, 42
Sterilization, 36
Stevens, 66
Stoicism, 47, 60, 82, 158
Storer, Horatio, 37
Suction curettage, 31, 32, 72, 102
Suicide, 144–45, 155–57, 158–59
Suicide machine, 144–45
Supreme Court rulings, 61, 62–66
Sustenance, removal of, 162–63

Tarkanian, Danny, 109
ten Boom, Corrie, 179
Teratomas, 30
Terry, Randall, 175, 186
Test-tube babies, 21
Thalidomide, 29–30
Therapeutic abortion, 66
Thomas, Clarence, 64, 68
Thomson, Judith Jarvis, 88–92
Tiglath-Pileser I, 47
Tooley, Michael, 133, 135
Tribe, Laurence H., 35, 54, 59, 81, 89,
    94
Twinning, 17, 18, 19

U.S. Judiciary Committee, 50

Valladares, Armando, 185
Van Den Haag, Ernest, 124
Varga, Andrew, 18
Vauz, Kenneth, 151

Wardle, Lynn, 52
Warren, Mary Anne, 70
Watson, James, 132
Webster, 62–64, 67, 68, 94, 181

Weenberg, Robert, 19, 159
Wertheimer, Roger, 53
Wetz, Dorothy C., 110, 119
White, Byron, 63, 66
Whitehead, John, 174
Will, George, 136
Willke, John, 108
Witherspoon, 44
Wood, Mary Anne Q., 52